The Making of
INDIA

The Making of
INDIA

THE UNTOLD STORY OF BRITISH ENTERPRISE

KARTAR LALVANI

B L O O M S B U R Y
LONDON · OXFORD · NEW YORK · NEW DELHI · SYDNEY

Bloomsbury Continuum

An imprint of Bloomsbury Publishing Plc

50 Bedford Square   1385 Broadway
London   New York
WC1B 3DP   NY 10018
UK   USA

www.bloomsbury.com

Bloomsbury, Continuum and the Diana logo are trademarks of Bloomsbury Publishing Plc

First published 2016

British Library Cataloguing-in-Publication Data
A catalogue record for this book is available from the British Library.

ISBN: HB: 9781472924827
       ePDF: 9781472924841
       ePub: 9781472924834

4 6 8 10 9 7 5 3

Printed and bound in Great Britain by CPI Group (UK) Ltd, Croydon CR0 4YY

To find out more about our authors and books visit www.bloomsbury.com. Here you will find extracts, author interviews, details of forthcoming events and the option to sign up for our newsletters.

*I dedicate this book to the spirit of everlasting friendship
and prosperity between two great countries
– India and Great Britain.*

*In this spirit, all author proceeds from the sale of the books are to
be donated to support a new Indo-British foundation, to continue
research into the shared history of Britain and India, and to ensure a
legacy based on fact and mutual understanding for future generations
of students, both in Britain and in India.*

*It is my enduring wish that future generations are empowered with
the facts, so the young of these two great nations can live hand in
hand, free of resentment or shame of their shared history, and
with all the opportunity and possibility made available to them by those
devoted, and often unsung, pioneers who helped to shape the future of
two great nations and change the course of destiny for so many.*

*I have dedicated my life to realising the blessings and opportunities
afforded to me by the unique Anglo-Indian connection.
For me, one question endures above all others:
What would India be like today if the British had
simply chosen to stay at home?*

India's great poet and Nobel laureate (1913) RABINDRANATH TAGORE wrote the following in his great work *Gitanjali*. Tagore's words were recalled by former Prime Minister Dr. Manmohan Singh in his acceptance speech for his Honorary Degree from Oxford University on 8 July 2005:

> The West has today opened its door.
> There are treasures for us to take.
> We will take and we will also give,
> From the open shores of India's immense humanity.

As far as VICEROY RIPON saw, the question for him was clear-cut: '[Was India] to be ruled for the benefit of the Indian people of all races, classes and creeds, or in the sole interest of a small body of Europeans in India?' (Viceroy Lord Ripon: 1882, Calcutta.) He opted for the former and indeed set the trend for more liberalism in the governance of India, paving the way for the preparation of the emerging great nation's journey towards self-rule 55 years later in 1947.

In 1931 MAHATMA GANDHI spoke to Prof. A.D. Lindsay, the master of Balliol College, Oxford, who questioned Gandhi: 'How far would you cut India off from the Empire?' His reply was precise: 'From the Empire, completely; from the British nation not at all, if I want India to gain and not to grieve.'

Contents

List of Illustrations

Map from Lady Isabel Burton's travel log, published in 1879; her husband was the explorer and geographer, Sir Richard Francis Burton, who had been employed by the East India Company. The text is just discernible in the background.

Author's note: For the reader's ease, places retain their historical names in the context of historical events, though particularly antiquated spellings have been avoided. The integrity of excerpts from original writings has been maintained. I drew on many accounts imparted to us for posterity. There was much to be uncovered in the detail of these very many logs, reports and often impassioned petitions for progress.

Excerpt from the Address by Prime Minister Dr Manmohan Singh in acceptance of his Honorary Degree from Oxford University, 8 July 2005

What impelled the Mahatma [Gandhi] to take such a positive view of Britain and the British people even as he challenged the Empire and colonial rule? I believe it was, undoubtedly, his recognition of the elements of fair play that characterised so much of the ways of the British in India.

...[E]ven at the height of our campaign for freedom from colonial rule, we did not entirely reject the British claim to good governance. We merely asserted our natural right to self-governance.

Today, with the balance and perspective offered by the passage of time and the benefit of hindsight, it is possible for an Indian Prime Minister to assert that India's experience with Britain had its beneficial consequences too. Our notions of the rule of law, of a Constitutional government, of a free press, of a professional civil service, of modern universities and research laboratories have all been fashioned in the crucible where an age-old civilization of India met the dominant Empire of the day. These are all elements that we still value and cherish. Our judiciary, our legal system, our bureaucracy and our police are all great institutions, derived from British–Indian administration and they have served our country exceedingly well.

...Our Constitution remains a testimony to the enduring interplay between what is essentially Indian and what is very British in our intellectual heritage.

... The success of our experiment of building a democracy within the framework of a multi-cultural, multi-ethnic, multi-lingual, and multi-religious society will encourage all societies to walk the path we have trodden. In this journey, and this is an exciting journey, both Britain and India have learnt from each other and have much to teach the world. This is perhaps the most enduring aspect of the Indo-British encounter.

Foreword
by Professor Ram Jethmalani

MP and Advocate in the Supreme Court of India
Former Cabinet Minister of Law

Many Indian patriots may not like to hear or read that an Indian, though today domiciled in the UK, should publicly confess that Indians should be grateful for some of the valuable, almost colossal, benefits that British rule bestowed on India. The fear is genuine and I am almost sure that such patriots exist in very large numbers.

False conceit often trumps unpleasant truth. A highly educated author belonging to the brave Sikh community should without the slightest hesitation publish and declare the truth, the whole truth and nothing but the truth. Loyalty to history cannot be diluted by an irrational fear. The author's impeccable reputation as a renowned inventor, research scientist and humble philanthropist guarantees that no sensible person will suspect any fly in the ointment. Dr Lalvani is no sycophant nor buyable with material reward. Besides I fully concur with him that Indians should be grateful for some of the permanent blessings of colonial rule, which only the unique attributes of the British could have conferred on us.

India and Pakistan are the heirs of the Indus Civilization (also known as the Harappan Civilization), which flourished in our part of the world more than 5000 years before the birth of Christ. Europe had long and fondly believed history had started with the Greeks and that India was a dark continent inhabited by barbarians until their civilized cousins, the Aryans, brought to them the light of civilization. This insolence was shattered in 1924 by the breathtaking discoveries of the Harappa and Mohenjo-Daro cities. The excavations headed by the British archaeologist Sir John Marshall indisputably established that during the third and fourth millennia BC there existed in India very highly developed cities, housed with wells and bathrooms, elaborate drainage systems, and a general condition of citizens superior to that prevailing in contemporary Babylonia and Egypt. There was much more to make India proud but I must skip the temptation to beat my own drum.

As civilizations mature and ebb, humans become weak and sometimes indifferent to the external affairs of this world. These brave ancestors of ours met Alexander, the Macedonian Emperor, on the banks of the Indus.

So the story goes that they laughed hysterically when he told them about his plans of world conquest. By ridicule and strength, they persuaded him to abandon his foolish plan and return to his native place. But they did give him a glimpse of their spiritual life. Even so, India continued its decline into debilitating indifference to the world around it. Foreign invaders and plunderers took advantage and continued to pour into India: Mohammed bin Kasim in the 8th century, followed later by Mahmud Ghaznavi, Mohammed Ghori of Afghanistan (who defeated mighty Delhi), the Lodhis, the Mughals, and the later Persian and Afghan invasions of the 18th century which entirely emptied Delhi.

By the 16th century, India was part of the Mughal Empire, a dynasty that gave us the magnificent early emperors Akbar the Great and Shah Jahan the Magnificent. They became respectable Indians and ruled justly, earning the respect of their subjects. Unfortunately their descendants turned out to be religious fanatics and forfeited the respect and loyalty of their subjects. But the dynasty left remarkable architecture including the famous Taj Mahal, local industry and exports.

The British had ventured into India during the regime of Emperor Akbar, initially, of course, as traders. By the early 18th century, we were so helpless, emaciated and corrupt that a British mercantile company called the East India Company was almost a sovereign power. These men had strong physiques, the benefit of scientific discoveries and the dawn of the industrial revolution, and superior education and weapons of war.

Yes, like all colonial powers, even Britain practised economic exploitation, but in the process conferred large benefits on us. The British ruled us, but surely they rescued the majority of Indians from the hated *jizya* tax, which was payable by all non-Muslims, converting them into degraded and inferior serfs of sort. Let us not also forget that it was the British and an East India Company man that abolished sati. They also resurrected our heritage, restoring the wastelands of Agra and its neglected Taj Mahal, and much more, to their former glory.

History of this crazy world is a long story of changes in every aspect of human life: the rise and fall of ruling dynasties, ever-changing ethical and religious beliefs, periods of peace and growth, new discoveries of science, and war, famine and destruction – vast changes between prosperity and penury.

The Europeans had developed a new outlook of respect for India within a few decades. India was making a strong claim to self-rule and political independence. Dr Lalvani has good cause to be appreciative of the great good the British connection has brought to us. They prepared us for self-rule and finally made a graceful exit.

Even in the period of British parliamentary rule, when democracy and a secular Constitution for free India was still a distant dream, the education of leaders such as Gandhiji and Jawaharlal Nehru in British universities had created a longing for democracy, rule of law, an independent judiciary to make the weak prevail against the strong, the elimination of religious fanaticism and hatred, and a life guided wholly by reason and logic but inspired by love and compassion. Our new Constitution of free India anxiously copied the British model of governance. Debates in our Constituent Assembly testify to this finest gift for which we do owe to the British a great deal of appreciation and gratitude.

Even before the discovery of the ancient Harappa Civilization, the West had discovered in Swami Vivekananda an amazing Indian philosopher, with very few to rival him in his intellectual attainments. He attempted to combine Indian spirituality with Western materialism and became the main force behind the Vedanta movement in the West. The West has not forgotten his speech at the World Parliament of Religions in Chicago, Illinois, in September 1893. Years before the amazing Harappa discoveries, and right in their own country, he attacked the American attitude of contempt for the Blacks and their praise for the Whites. The Americans learnt a lot from what this great Indian said to them. India rose in the esteem of our rulers, too, and I am almost sure that after the first quarter of the 20th century was over the British had decided that their rule was to end soon and a new era of mutual respect and cooperation would begin. The heirs of Harappa can't remain slaves. The peaceful transformation of the next quarter of the century is proof of British grace and goodwill.

While I write this, it is impossible to ignore the great British theosophist Dr Annie Besant who was a scholar of the Hindu Shastras and accepted as an axiom for life the shastric principle *Vasudhaiva Kutumbakam,* meaning 'the whole world is my family'. Besant wrote and lectured on Hinduism. She was a poet, an excellent orator and a versatile tornado of power and passion. She loved India, became a political leader, and in her speech in South India at the first student conference of the Home Rule League in June 1916 she advised the students to get ready to be the leaders of India by mastering history, logic and political economy. Besant obviously had a strong intuition that British Rule was coming to an end and India deserved its freedom. It is equally impossible to ignore the contribution of the architect of the Indian National Congress, the retired Indian Civil Service officer Allan Octavian Hume.

While coming to the end of writing this foreword, I remind myself that I am the country's oldest practising lawyer and teacher of law. I can't resist citing judicial precedents to support my views. When our Constituent Assembly was drafting the new Constitution of free India we doubtless had decided to copy a Westminster model of democracy. We created a Council of Ministers to aid and advise the President but we forgot to provide in express terms that the President of India will normally be bound by it. This lacuna, somewhat serious in a written and detailed constitution, was noticed only after about a quarter of a century after the Constitution came into force in 1950. The void was later filled by a judgement of the Supreme Court of India. One of our finest judges, Justice Krishna Iyer, in his inimitable style wrote: 'Not the Potomac but the Thames fertilizes the flow of the Yamuna, if we may adopt a riverine imagery. In this thesis we are fortified by the precedent of this Court, strengthened by the Constituent Assembly proceedings and reinforced by the actual working of the organ involved for about a "silver jubilee span of time".' Thus was laid the rule that the President of India is as much bound by ministerial advice as the British monarch.

Dr Lalvani is on the right track.

Ram Jethmalani

Professor Ram Jethmalani is a Member of the Indian Parliament; Former Cabinet Minister of Law, Justice and Company Affairs; Former Chairman of the Bar Council of India; and Professor Emeritus of Law. He is a senior advocate in the Supreme Court of India and, at 93 years of age, is thought to be the world's oldest full-time practising barrister and university lecturer in law.

Preface

TIME TO RECOGNISE THE POSITIVE SIDE OF THE IMPERIAL COIN: SETTING THE RECORD STRAIGHT

Had I been old enough to have been an adult during the last decades of British rule, I, too, would have joined the struggle for independence; the impulse towards freedom is a logical and appropriate response to external rule. However, well over half a century after Independence, with the benefit of hindsight, are we not obliged to look back dispassionately and objectively in an attempt to recognise the lasting legacy we inherited and to give credit where credit is due?

Of course, the British also benefited in innumerable ways and, yes, some undoubtedly took unfair advantage of their unique position of power, more so during the period of the East India Company rule. **All of that and more has been amply described in several books on colonial history, most of which were written by the British themselves, and none of it is contested here.**

There were, however, two sides to British rule: one was commercial and at times exploitative, particularly under the early rule of the East India Company, a private trading monopoly; the other was liberal and that liberalism was high minded and enduring in its benefaction, with a legacy and feats of public works that remain unparalleled today. Such liberalism meshed with the deep roots of Indian culture that is peaceful and harmonious.

I am a product of that Indo-British culture which developed during the long years of British rule in India and has continued to evolve thereafter in Britain and India in recent decades. I came to England in 1956 for my postgraduate studies in pharmacy in London, followed by a doctorate in medicinal chemistry at the University of Bonn. I have imbibed and inherited values that people of both nations have cherished. I feel equally at home in both countries and love them both equally and passionately – a patriotic Brit while also very much Indian – and hence the reason for my taking on this challenge of writing about a subject which has been my passion for the past several decades.

In my view – now belonging to the generation after Independence – it is time that we put the once-necessary rhetoric politicians used to build a new nation to one side and, on the grounds of fairness and historical accuracy, acknowledge the positive aspects of the colonial period. By doing so, we can incorporate a balanced portrayal of both sides of the imperial coin and bring perspective to the shared history of these two great nations not only in our thinking but also in school curricula. This new clarity would help to build better understanding, lasting harmony and mutual respect in a troubled world, and rebuild an important international and mutually beneficial relationship between Britain and India for generations to come.

In 2007 the eminent writer and businessman Jaithirth Rao wrote: 'The British gave us a sense of our past ... they mapped our country, analysed and described it in memorable prose.' Yet, my fear is that we are slipping into a collective amnesia of our history, leading older generations to lament whether or not things were better under the British and the younger generations to view the British as plunderers who brought India to its knees. A middle ground is needed to avoid falling into a despondency when it comes to the urgency of the colossal social and economic problems India faces today of widespread inequality and poverty. There is a danger that some of our modern-day leaders and opinion-makers are leaning too much on this political expediency to avoid the uncomfortable question of why there remains in India so much widespread poverty and inequality. One of the things Britain did not introduce to India was corruption, even though the East India Company did indeed benefit from the widely prevailing corrupt practices already rampant in the subcontinent.

I would like to state simply that although there were wrongs committed by the British against India, as widely recognised by the British themselves, there is much more that was and remains fair and positive. My overarching aim in writing the book is not only to set the record straight but also to help foster good modern-day relations based on partnership, equality and friendship without the baggage of a purely negative and wasteful interpretation of history but instead with a recognition that the historical record does actually contain the seeds of a harmonious future Indo-British cooperation. We should have a relationship not based on suspicion and the weight of inaccurate opinion, but rather based on the realities of the relationship: with the over-arching goodwill, dedication and commitment, which were the mark of the pioneers of the Raj.

It continues to sadden me that even when I speak to my British compatriots there is an uncomfortable reluctance to speak of British rule in India or to acknowledge the many positive aspects of the shared history. This reticence, shame and misunderstanding of our past is something I dearly

EDUCATION AND A HARMONIOUS INDO-BRITISH LEGACY FOR FUTURE GENERATIONS

OVER THE LAST FIVE DECADES of my stay in Britain, it is remarkable that I have not encountered a single native Brit who has stated any form of belief that the British benefited India. In fact quite the opposite; sadly most appear to have no idea that without what the British laid down for India, it would most likely have remained a conglomeration of 20 disparate states and as many languages.

Therefore, if I have one special message, it is this: I believe it is vital that future generations of students, both in Britain and in India, should be empowered with the facts to understand the truth about what the British achieved over 100 years ago, and how it directly created the India of today.

The British especially should learn and remember, with some deserved pride, what their forefathers built and created: an Indian nation that has no parallel in history. These next generations of British children belong to this great tradition, and should take pride in remembering and emulating their great-grandfathers' skills, enterprise and endeavours. Future generations of British Indian children should understand the British contribution with balance and perspective.

In India, opening students' eyes to the legacy of the British contribution will do India the world of good. In an article in *Asian Age* published in 2014, the writer Mohan Guruswamy raised the problem of historic bias in the curricula of India:

> As a young student ... in recently independent India, the first history lessons ... [were] about the British. We were taught that the rule was a most benign and beneficial period for Indians... reforms like the abolition of sati and the building of great canal systems and railways happened during this period. The unification of India into one great political entity also happened in this period...
>
> Quite clearly if Indian society has to be inclusive, all its various peoples must share a common perspective of the past. This is not so at present, to my mind at least the history textbooks need to be rewritten.

I wholly agree and feel most strongly that the textbooks are in need of revision; the untold truth is a betrayal to the young in India and to future generations.

The British introduced the modern education system to India, and by 1856 had established three major universities in Calcutta, Bombay and

Madras. Alongside these great institutions, a new culture of public libraries and museums was also firmly established.

To help achieve better education, it is my wish to establish further
research on the vast and unique Indo-British legacy at a seat of academic
excellence, perhaps at Oxford or Cambridge, as it was these very same great
institutions that provided and sent the best of Britain's talent to India.

Therefore, my entire author proceeds from the sale of this book will be
donated to support a new Indo-British foundation, with a remit to continue
further detailed and unbiased research into this subject, including the
revisiting of school curricula in India and the UK, to bring new areas
to light and expand on the themes dealt with in this book and impress
upon the departments of education in India and the UK the dire need for
updating the respective curricula.

Through this continuous education, I hope that we can ultimately help
the young of these two great nations live in hand in hand, with better
understanding for generations to come. My hope is that this book will
seed more work, to help ensure that the previously untold truth about the
British contribution is still understood and spoken about 1000 years from
now, when the worldwide Indian diaspora created by the British legacy
will continue to lead in positions across the globe.

wish to move beyond so we can forge honest and open relations and mutual
opportunity. In 55 years, I have not heard of one single Briton speak about
the positive legacy of British rule in India; so, it was a long-awaited relief
to hear of one courageous man who spoke honestly in the face of criticism.
When the British Prime Minister David Cameron was posed the question of
whether he was proud of Britain's colonial history, he answered truthfully:
'[T]here is an enormous amount to be proud of in what the British Empire
did ... there were bad events as well as good events and the bad events we
should learn from and the good events we should celebrate.'

It is my deepest hope that in the coming years the power of India's cherished democracy will be harnessed to lift the country's poorest 40% out
of abject poverty and illiteracy into a state of health, dignity and freedom
from hunger. Having speculated on how the fragmented, deeply divided
and weak subcontinent might have developed were it not for the unifying
effect of the Raj, or had the British been supplanted by other colonial powers
such as those already with a base in India – the Portuguese or French – one
can appreciate more deeply the benefits conferred on India by the unique

200-year-long relationship with Britain. Both France and Portugal had mixed reputations where their colonial administration was concerned, with their handing back of power most often acrimonious and bloody affairs.

The attitude of the British towards Indians with their deeply rooted liberal tradition was in fact much better and as is often said to have been *fair* though it may not have been always *welcome*. No one can be in a better position to compare or appreciate this than Indians themselves, having experienced many barbarous invasions in the pre-British era. Of these the most devastating being the Persian (which robbed Delhi of the world's finest collection of jewels, including the famous Koh-i-noor diamond – later retrieved by the Sikh kingdom of the Punjab) and then the successive Afghan invasions, which saw the looting, pillaging and the entire emptying of the most prosperous Delhi and its neighbouring north-western regions of the then Punjab and Kashmir, with the cities of Lahore and Agra also devastated and emptied by the raiding armies while the British were still confined to Bengal about 1000 miles away.

During the long innings of British rule in India, only one period was particularly imperialistic and I tend to believe that it had something to do with the rise of militant nationalism. Commentators have referred to the reforming British influence on 18- and 19th-century Indian society. The suggestion being that the British showed, by their own example, reasonable 'limits' in their governance, which in turn set the dos and don'ts in society. It was given to the British to explain that personal liberty comes with social responsibility. Restraint, moderation, temperance, discretion and such other values, to me at least, are direct influences of the British.

The wealth of archived information on the development of the huge infrastructure in a country with a quarter of the world's population in the 19th and 20th centuries is extraordinary and a testimony to the painstaking and systematic documentation carried out by the Raj's officers and archivists for posterity. Dormant and accumulated files filled with documents and photographs, covered in 200 years of archive dust, in Britain's libraries and engineering institutions – especially the revered Institution of Civil Engineers (ICE) in London – provide many fascinating yet little-known stories of the many challenging individual projects of enterprise, audacity and adventure. The object of this book is to distil the essence of this unparalleled episode of transglobal nation-building and capture the spirit of Britain's unsung, yet heroic, pioneers in India, rather than to give a detailed account of every aspect of Britain's legacy in India.

Given the wealth of valuable original information that I found waiting to be uncovered during my research, it is surprising that the many positive aspects of colonial rule have remained hitherto untold. As a British Indian, it gives me great pride to give due recognition to the positive side of the imperial coin, which I discovered to be so much stronger and greater than widely acknowledged, compressed in a single volume of 432 pages. The book I envisaged and planned with the help of my friend and contributor, a retired British railway engineer, the late Peter English, who died in 2007, was to detail how this great British enterprise and its contributions in the 19th and 20th centuries helped to create a unified India, out of multi-cultural multi-linguistic and divided regions of the vast Indian subcontinent.

This book is a long-overdue recognition of the effort and ingenuity of those courageous pioneers who have so often, and so wrongly, been derided as no more than corrupt plunderers bent on pillaging the wealth of the people and the land they conquered. The practicalities of publishing a single volume meant vast amounts of valuable material sadly had to be left out of this book which, despite its length, is just a glimpse of the awe-inspiring endeavour of those early British pioneers. It is my hope that someone else will be able to take up the challenge of producing an exhaustive work, inevitably running into many volumes.

Although I am a scientist, the subject of Indian history has always fascinated me; should any paragraph appear to be dogmatic or contentious, it is purely a result of my attempt, as a scientist, to condense a large amount of facts and information and over 200 years of history into a succinct overview, and in this regard I respectfully request the reader's forgiveness. I would humbly request the reader to read with an open mind and form their own considered opinion. The detail in the following 22 succinct chapters is the culmination of my devotion and over a decade's research, and I hope provides ample evidence to bring to light the under-appreciated reality that, in almost every walk of life, Great Britain has made a significant contribution to *The Making of India*.

Kartar Lalvani OBE
PhD DSc FRPharmS

*Empires have often ended in fire, destruction, blood
and carnage as befell those of Rome, Spain, Portugal,
Ottoman and France. The British Empire, which
covered approximately two-fifths of the world and held
commercial influence over three-quarters of the globe,
lowered the flag and withdrew from their far-flung
territories in a generally stately manner
with tea, pomp, ceremony and cricket.*
KARTAR LALVANI

Chapter 1

THE ARGUMENT:
BALANCE AND PERSPECTIVE

Besides security from foreign invaders and internal plunderers, let us ask
ourselves whether we could have rescued ourselves from the stigma of female
murder (burning of widows) but for the English? Whether we could have other-
wise obtained the power of equalizing ourselves with the rulers of the country in
regard not only to civil but to criminal jurisprudence?
RAM MOHAN ROY[†]

This story began in the 17th century, when a small sea-faring island, one-tenth the size of the Indian subcontinent, dispatched fragile sailing ships laden with iron, tools and workers over a distance of 12 000 miles on a six-month voyage via the Cape of Good Hope, in search of new opportunities. Over the next three centuries, the girders for every bridge, the track for every mile of railway, the locomotives and the vast array of machinery required at the outset to build every piece of infrastructure in India were all made in Britain and loaded onto countless craft and transported on a hazardous journey to the subcontinent, where they were assembled according to plans laid by the finest engineers of the time, who arrived by the same route. In the end they helped build a new nation. The sheer audacity and scale of such an endeavour, the courage and enterprise, have no parallel in world history. This book is the first to assess in a single volume all aspects of Britain's remarkable contribution in providing India with its lasting institutional and physical infrastructure, which continues to underpin the world's largest democracy in the 21st century.

[†] Ram Mohan Roy (1772–1833), founder of the progressive spiritual and reformist movement, Brahmo Samaj. In the words of Rabindranath Tagore: 'Raja Ram Mohan Roy inaugurated the modern age in India. He was the father of Indian Renaissance and the prophet of Indian nationalism.' Gandhi and Nehru, too, praised his legacy: 'Roy was undoubtedly the Father of advanced liberal thought in Hinduism.' (Mahatma Gandhi) 'He was more than a scholar and investigator. He was a reformer above all.' (Jawaharlal Nehru) (See also page 49 for the opening lines to Roy's quote.)

The indisputable fact is that India as a nation, as it stands today, was originally created by a small, distant island nation. India has endured as a democracy and a unified nation thanks to the all-important and fully functional infrastructure of an independent civil service and judiciary, a disciplined and apolitical army and a well-drilled and efficient police force, all developed by the imperial power. Of course, the labour was local, indeed skilful, and the indigenous cultures were ancient and sophisticated, but it is worth pausing to consider what India would be like today if the British had chosen to stay at home.

The East India Company: from trade to exploitation; from conquest to hegemony

The English East India Company (EIC), which has been the focus of much criticism over the years, established itself at Surat on the west coast of India in 1613, to exploit the lucrative spice trade. The Company's initial voyages from Surat were exceedingly profitable. But competition from the Dutch East India Company soon undermined the Company's profits. Under the Anglo-Dutch merger of these companies in 1688, a deal was struck which, as historian Niall Ferguson explains, 'effectively gave Indonesia and the spice trade to the Dutch, leaving the English to develop the newer Indian textiles trade'. It was deemed prudent that, rather than operate as competitors, Asia could be sliced up for the two companies' mutual benefit and thus allowing hostilities in India between the Dutch and the British to be brought to an end. The result proved crucial for the English as the demand for textiles soon 'outgrew the market for spices'. The merger also introduced the English to a number of key financial institutions that the Dutch had pioneered. One result was that the Bank of England was founded in 1694 using the Dutch model to manage the government's borrowings and the national currency. A system of national public debt was funded by the stock exchange, and the apparatus for low-interest borrowing became a reality for the British government. The shift from spices to cloth also resulted in the relocation of the EIC's Asian base from Surat to the three newly created cities – or 'Presidencies' – of Calcutta, Madras and Bombay, each built by the English. Such was the output of these centres that, '[I]n the seventeenth century ... there was only one outlet the discerning English shopper would buy her clothes from. For sheer quality, Indian fabrics, designs, workmanship and technology were in a league of their own'.

In 1700 France had an economy twice the size of England's and a population almost three times as large. And, like England, France had reached out across the seas to the world beyond Europe. In 1664 the French had set up their own East India Company, the Compagnie des Indes Orientales, with its base at Pondicherry, not far south of the English settlement at Madras. The danger of the French winning the struggle for global mastery over Britain, and thereby controlling India, was very real until 1757, when Robert Clive achieved his spectacular victory gaining further political influence in India and stemming French influence by defeating France's local allies in the famous battle of Plassey. The alternative to Clive's victory was not Indian sovereignty – for India did not exist then except as a large number of disparate, independently governed princely states – but conquest and domination by the French. Just 16 years prior to the Company's triumph at Plassey in Bengal, which gave it a firm grip on the fortunes and markets of the three major Eastern Provinces of Bengal, Bihar and Orissa, India had already suffered four waves of devastating and humiliating invasions from Persia and Afghanistan, which conquered and looted vast areas of northwest India, including the immensely prosperous capital, Delhi, the Punjab, Kashmir and Agra, reducing the 300-year-old Mughal dynasty to penury.

Divide and rule – or simply exploit endemic corruption and divisions?

By the time of Clive's second decisive victory against the combined forces of the nawabs of Bengal and Oudh and the Mughal Emperor Shah Alam II at Buxar in 1764, ended French influence in India, he was already convinced about the EIC's future domination of India. Instead of boasting of his own courage and bravery, Robert Clive effectively handed credit for his most spectacular victories at Plassey and Buxar to the betrayal of Indians by Indians in key positions, deceiving their own people, as explained in his letter to the EIC's directors in London which detailed how appalled he was at the extent of the corruption he witnessed: 'I can assert with some degree of confidence that this rich and flourishing kingdom may be totally subdued by so small a force as two thousand Europeans.' His justifications to his own mind and to his superiors are clear, characterising most of the ruling elite and their entourage as 'indolent, luxurious, ignorant and cowardly beyond all conception ... [They] attempt everything by treachery rather than force ... What is it, then, can enable us to secure our present acquisitions or improve upon them but such a force as leaves nothing to the power of treachery or ingratitude?'

Clive's letter also gives lie to the myth that the British introduced corruption and bribery to India. Corruption has always been the biggest single enemy of India from within and was larger than all its external enemies put together. It was the prevailing corruption and its unscrupulous exploitation by the EIC that repeatedly ensured the Company's endless successes and victories in most of the dozen-odd important campaigns in which the Company's forces engaged in the conquest of India. Ubiquitous corruption and greed helped to breed brokers and traitors within the individual feudal Indian states, and many battles were lost against the often less formidable forces of the Company because of the treachery of informers and touts; indeed, the Company was often inundated with more collaborators than it could cope with. The long-standing prevalence of endemic deceit and corruption in Indian politics and public life have betrayed and compromised India's enormous potential before, during and after the British Raj.

The evidence from Clive's correspondence echoed an 800-year history of treachery, such as that of Raja Jaichand, from the 12th century, who was responsible for mighty Delhi's defeat inflicted at the hands of Muhammad Ghori of Afghanistan. The Afghan invasion of India in 1761 in the battle of Panipat (near Jaipur) scored victory against India's most powerful Maratha Army due to the deceit of the Maharaja Madho Singh of Jaipur who was in correspondence with the Afghan King Abdali, inviting him to invade India.

The outcome of the Afghan invasions, facilitated by the princely rivalries and a lack of a united Indian identity, left the Marathas irrevocably weakened. Likewise, Clive's victory in the historic battle of Plassey in Bengal in 1757 against the combined French and the Nawab's forces was facilitated by the two traitors Mir Jafar and Jagat Seth – the head of Bengal's principal bank who was described by the mid-18th century French traveller and representative Jean Law as the '*chief cause* of all the *revolutions in Bengal*'. Their complicity was instrumental in Clive's victory at Plassey against the more formidable Indian side. Clive's observations in the mid-18th century remained valid and useful to the Company during the next 100 years of its spectacular expansion, benefiting from the frequent opportunities provided by the corruption and divisions that often prevailed among the native factions.

So, who *really* looted India?

It is often said that the British callously looted India of its riches. There can be no doubt that there were many examples of extensive exploitation, particularly during the hegemony of the EIC rule, which was particularly extreme in the eastern states. Certainly the British benefited economically from Indian raw materials, labour and products, and few more so than the much-criticised 'nabobs' who amassed huge personal fortunes in the early days of rule in India. It is also true that the crucial role and great sacrifice of many Indians and the deployment of the Indian Army in both world wars and other British campaigns continues to be under-recognised. However, the following important, but not so well-known, facts should help to put the economic legacy of the Raj in its true perspective.

India was said to have been the world's richest economy before the advent of the EIC, but by the time the prosperous regions of Bengal and Bihar came under the Company's control in 1757, the richest parts and heartland of the Mughal Empire – the fabulous city of Delhi and its environs, and the north-western regions including the wealthy provinces of Punjab and Uttar Pradesh and the great cities of Agra and Lahore – had already been entirely ransacked and looted in the devastating Afghan and Persian invasions, and the local economies crippled. The EIC's early exploitation and draining of the economy in Bengal and the eastern states of India cannot be denied or defended, but very little is said about Britain's role in generating India's recovery, and the regeneration of its economy and self esteem after the repeated invasions from Persia and Afghanistan.

Only two decades before the major EIC successes in east India, at Plassey and Buxar, India's most fabulous and world-renowned capital, Delhi, and its rich surrounding regions of north-west India, including the Punjab and Agra, already had been ravaged and emptied by the Persians and Afghans.

King Nadir Shah of Persia's invasion of Delhi and the north-west regions of India in 1739 – 18 years before Clive's victory at Plassey in Bengal – was the most savage and devastating India had ever known. In the fighting, which lasted a mere two hours, 20 000 Indian soldiers were slaughtered and a far greater number enslaved. The statistics are astounding and little mentioned in military history annals.

India's capital, Delhi, by far the richest and most prosperous city in the world, was entirely ransacked and emptied of all riches and the great historic treasures, including the ancient Peacock Throne and the famous Koh-i-noor and Darya-i-noor diamonds. The Persian looting and butchery in India went on in full fury for over a month. The Imperial Palace of the Red Fort in Delhi was left in ruins, emptied of all the most valuable jewels, gold, silver, ancient crowns and precious stones. Looting extended to the houses of all nobles and ministers of the Mughal court. The returning caravans included thousands of young women and slaves, with elephants and camels loaded with Delhi's treasure.

Within a decade of this trauma which had left over 100 000 dead, there followed three further devastating invasions by the Afghan king, Abdali, emptying Delhi of every conceivable treasure and valuable asset which had escaped the previous purges by the Persian invaders. The pattern of each invasion was similar to the previous looting: always with the forcible abduction of young women and slaves, along with horses. The Afghans outdid the Persians by taking away even the kitchen utensils, beds, furniture and clothing of the well-to-do. Every trader's shop was cleared of its merchandise, crippling all trade and economic activity. The demolished 300-year-old Mughal dynasty and empire, with its capital, Delhi, once the world's richest and proudest city, was described by the contemporary administrator and historian Ghulam Husain Tabatabai after the series of merciless invasions from Persia and Afghanistan about 40 years before the British entry into Delhi:

> ... India has gone to ruin and every one of its discouraged inhabitants have broken their hearts: Life itself has become disgustful to most ... the earth is totally overwhelmed with an everlasting darkness.

This was an India that had fallen to its lowest depth – financially, economically, morally, and militarily. India had also been crushed by its own masters – emperors, king-makers, nobles, subhedars, jagirdars and mansabdars. 'I have travelled from Bengal to Delhi,' the mid-18th-century French representative Jean Law told Tabatabai in April 1759, 'but nowhere have I found anything from anyone except oppression of the poor and plundering of the wayfarers... This anarchy has arisen from the perfidy of the nobles who exist solely for ruining a world of people'.

The succinct argument as to the question of who really looted the prosperous North-West region of India, along with its magnificent capital, Delhi, is that quite simply the British did not enter Delhi until the beginning of the 19th century. The arrival of the British in 1803 in the desperate and desolate remains of a crushed, bankrupted, savaged and demoralised capital city of Delhi brought an end to anarchy and misrule. Delhi breathed again and the new era of social and civic reform, stability and reconstruction revived the city and its economy and gave a new lease of life and confidence to its citizens. A further collateral benefit was the absence of any more humiliating and barbarian invasions over the next two centuries; and indeed to the present day.

As for the history of the Koh-i-noor, the diamond was mined in the year 1646 in Golconda (South India) and came into the possession of the Mughal King in Delhi. It was plundered from Delhi as war booty – representing a fraction of the massive loot – by the Persian King Nadir Shah in 1739. The Koh-i-noor was retrieved 74 years later in 1813 by the formidable Sikh kingdom under the Maharaja Ranjit Singh, who had inflicted the crushing defeat of the Afghans, and brought to its capital city of Lahore. The diamond formally came into the new ownership of the EIC after the defeat of the Sikhs, betrayed by their Dogra ministers in the Second Anglo-Sikh war in 1848. The Company rewarded the Dogra brothers for their treachery, giving them the entire province of Kashmir out of the conquered territory of the Sikh Empire. The Company had retained the Koh-i-noor and its Court of Directors in London gifted it to Queen Victoria in a ceremonial presentation to the Queen from the young Sikh Maharaja Daleep Singh residing in England.

Anarchy – divided and weakened native rule

The following decades saw the decline of the Mughal Empire. Abdali's raids had left in their wake a power vacuum in Delhi, with the Mughal emperor Shah Alam II (r. 1759–1806) – about whom went the saying 'Padishah Shah Alam, az Dilli ta Palam' ('He is called the Ruler of the World, though his rule may be limited from Delhi to Palam'), a distance of about 15 km – forced to flee the city. Shah Alam himself lamented:

> … through the perfidiousness of the nobility and vassals this anarchy has arisen, and every one proclaims himself a sovereign in his own place, and they are at variance with one another, the strong prevailing over the weak.

By then the Maratha Empire was the largest and most powerful kingdom in India, and Delhi came under its control.

The EIC is reined in and British Parliament takes over

As a divided Indian elite allowed foreign interests to establish a firm foothold in India, with the French, Portuguese and British all wresting for control with their makeshift and expedient allegiances with the Indian nobles, increasingly the British government was turning its attention to the interests of the Indian nation and people.

It is truly remarkable that throughout the 300 years of British presence in India there is not a single incidence on record of any of the British soldiers and staff having betrayed their country while on duty in India, a distance of 12 000 sailing miles away from their home.

Whilst it is remarkable how rare are the examples of EIC employees or Raj officers betraying their Company or country to the advantage of their Indian opponents, the enormous wealth amassed by a few was enough to spark widespread publicity and debate back on British shores – a debate whose legacy continues today – as concerns heightened over the 'looting' of India, without regard for its future prosperity. It was an acknowledged fact that many EIC employees were free – simply because of the distance from their employer – to operate outside of Company interests, and profit as a result of their own independent enterprise.

As a handful of these 'interlopers' amassed huge personal fortunes, back in Britain there was a growing discontent with the EIC and the morality of its practices. It is extraordinary that, well over two centuries ago, the British Parliament, in 1788, felt it its moral obligation to hold Company employees to account, even though their misdemeanours occurred in the corporate rather than public sector and in foreign lands over six months' sailing away.

The EIC had effectively turned a blind eye to the 'interlopers' in their midst who amassed fortunes and influence from their own endeavours. EIC headquarters in Leadenhall Street, London allowed the expediency of these pioneering Company men and adventurers as they understood their useful-ness and utilised their connections. For some, it would seem Lord Acton's insight that 'all power corrupts and absolute power corrupts absolutely' rings true. The near six-month lapse in communications with London al-lowed the concentration of almost unbridled power in the hands of a few young ambitious (and modestly paid) Company employees and traders.

Over two to three decades, strategic territorial and monetary gains were made following the battles of Plassey and Buxar, fired by personal greed, pride and opportunity. The corruption and accumulation of private fortunes by some Company executives became contentious topics back home in the British Parliament, with the increasing notoriety of a few men including Robert Clive, Paul Benfield, a property developer and moneylender, and the first Governor-General of India (initially titled Governor-General of Bengal), Warren Hastings. Hastings' seven-year gruelling impeachment trial was the longest in British legal history, and the focus of intense public interest. An incensed British public queued to attend the trial that was to hold the former Governor-General accountable for his negligence in allowing the zamindars to brutalise the Indian farmers 12 000 miles away.

An example of the fair and scrupulous application of English law cannot be more evident than with the proceedings against Hastings in favour of Indian interests. It was attended by the monarch, the royal family, 170 lords and the 200 members of the House of Commons who had voted to impeach the Company's Governor-General in the national interest. This unprecedented trial, spearheaded by Edmund Burke and the playwright and Whig MP Richard Sheridan, may have set a lasting example, as there were few further instances of such misdemeanours during the subsequent 150 years of British rule. Such men as Burke became determined critics of the EIC's practices in India and considered it their duty to implement regulation and British standards of legality in India.

Edmund Burke himself was only too aware of the interconnectedness of the success of the EIC and the strength of the British economy. As he put it 'to say the Company was in a state of distress was neither more nor less than to say the country was in a state of distress'. Yet, despite the Company's key role in helping Britain's foreign trade and expanding economy back home in the 18th and 19th centuries, it was not spared from the critical probing eye of the British Parliament.

Horace Walpole, MP (1717–1797) wrote: 'The Groans of India have mounted to heaven, where the heaven-born general Lord Clive will certainly be disallowed.' Walpole, the man of letters and son of the Liberal British Prime Minister, Sir Robert Walpole, was not the only one to criticise Clive and other EIC men as freebooters, plunderers and usurpers. There were many others in England who held similar views. The proceedings against the Company-appointed Governor-General Warren Hastings for his misconduct in India were a notably moral British intervention to curb the greed and deceit that was disfiguring the Company's rule in India. The critics within the British government understood that the practices were ultimately unsustainable for both India and British prosperity.

The EIC had largely failed to deliver its financial promise after the conquest of Bengal. Moreover, the famine of 1769–70, when an estimated third of the rural population of Bengal starved to death, highlighted to Parliament the need for regulation. Adam Smith and other critics accused the EIC of price-fixing rice and other complaints of stock hoarding could no longer be ignored. Pragmatists in the British Parliament understood that EIC abuses linked to the Company's commercial interests were short-sighted and could not be tolerated. Yet, famine was not in EIC interests. The famines caused a substantial decline in the Company's earnings and share price in London, resulting in mounting debts, necessitating government bailouts that would ultimately draw the EIC firmly under parliamentary control. The EIC was still a mercantile operation and less interested in the administration of land and governance policies preferring to utilise the indigenous apparatus for tax collection and administration.

Possibly the worst action was the punitive burden of taxation levied on impoverished farmers in the states of Bengal-Bihar and Orissa (now Odisha), soon after 1765, when the EIC won the right of revenue collection – known as the diwani – from the Mughal Emperor, the titular sovereign of the country. The Company's short-sighted greed led to a horrendous blunder concerning the role of revenue collection. In order to tax such a vast land, the EIC collectors relied on native intermediaries, zamindars (native landlords), to collect taxes. Complaints arose of zamindars ruthlessly collecting from the peasantry whilst at the same time reneging on their commitments, with failure to make full or timely payments, and amassing huge fortunes at the expense of responsible land management. Bribery of EIC collectors by the native collectors was also a concern. Moreover, the punitive tax burdens put in place by the EIC encouraged the use of the land for the farming of cash crops, such as poppies for the opium trade. When drought-conditions resulted in widespread famine and starvation for millions of poor farmers and their families, lessons were learnt form the severe and haphazard methods of tax collection.

In 1773, under the Regulating Act, Hastings had been endowed with the responsibility of cleaning up EIC affairs. He had significant experience in Indian affairs and made some inroads to reforming the tax system by appointing British tax-collectors, who were ordered not to take bribes, and dismissing native collectors. Though Hastings was a keen and respectful student of Indian administration and culture, and his rule was characterised by a period of better Anglo-Indian integration among EIC employees, he was loath to grant the zamindars the status of proprietors of their land, fearing widespread corruption and believing such an entitlement would bolster zamindars' interests at the further expense of the peasantry's.

However, pressure from all sides was mounting on Hastings. Reluctant to limit tax revenue and needing to address the failure of payments by those zamindars protesting unfair and unrealistic levies, Hastings, in 1777, stipulated that taxes would be assessed and adjusted yearly. The measure appeased neither the EIC – who faced an uncertain revenue stream – nor the zamindars who complained bitterly at the lack of consistency and security this arbitrary measure afforded them. Hastings' adversaries were mounting. By 1781, the zamindars were in revolt and, by 1784, the EIC was in dire financial straits. With a debt of £8.4 million – equivalent to more than £10 billion in today's value – on its books, EIC directors were forced to turn to the British government for help. Back at home, politicians wanted the EIC reined in further and the arbitrary taxation system in India addressed. Parliament reacted with the India Act of 1784. A year later, Hastings had resigned as governor-general and his impeachment was secured.

William Pitt's India Act of 1784, passed 'to clean up the East India Company' brought the Company under the control of the Crown. It also stipulated that 'permanent rules' were to be established in order to enshrine the 'principles of moderation and justice' in the rule of India. Gradually, a survey of every acre of land was attempted and its carrying capacity (productivity) assessed, so that a fairer levy could be made. The main theme was consistency of tax revenue, so that the big and small landowning farmers knew that taxes and levies would not be changed each year. The intention was to allow proper planning of long-term land use and thus increased productivity to become possible for farmers. This issue is well documented by B.H. Baden-Powell in his *Land-Systems of British India*, published in 1892.

The first appointed governor-general under the new Act was Charles Cornwallis. Under Cornwallis, the zamindars' status was overhauled from that of a mere revenue official into the absolute proprietor of his district, with full property rights on the sole condition that he paid over a fixed sum yearly to the EIC collector. This was a momentous mistake. Cornwallis feared charges of corruption if he were to allow EIC men to collect revenue based on unfixed rates. Though well-meaning perhaps the outcome was hugely detrimental to the millions of Indians who worked the land. The administration for tax collection introduced a system that created a native landed gentry and reduced the peasantry to tenants, creating 'feudalism at the top and serfdom at the bottom' and a hated system of rack-renting. Rural society was divided into the land-owning zamindars and the tenants at their mercy. Even more mistaken was the resolution of Cornwallis to make the tax settlement permanent, thus rendering it impossible for the EIC to increase revenue, and allowing the 'unearned increment' of the land to go directly to this factitious class of landowners. However, the settlement was also put forward at a time when the political landscape and sensibilities of Parliament and the British public were changing. By the 1780s, as the EIC was gradually reined in, the previous hostilities harboured by the British public towards the EIC, with its excesses and exploitation of India's resources, moderated somewhat and shifted to view India as an opportunity for a new landscape of rule where British principles might find their 'highest expression' in the service of India and its people.

The death knell finally sounded for the EIC in the aftermath of the Great Indian Mutiny in 1857. Amid further reports of malpractices and reprisals after the Mutiny there was no longer a sound financial or political case to uphold the Company. The 'fighting company' that had established the 'far-flung empire' had outlived its purpose, as a new political age of accountability and free trade emerged and Parliament turned its attention to India.

It is important to recognise that there is a substantial list on the credit side for infrastructural progress and reform in many sectors under the EIC's hegemony. The great cities of Bombay, Calcutta and Madras were founded and the era saw the establishment of the first universities and museums in India, including colleges of law, medicine and engineering. Railways, roads and canals were mapped and constructed, sewerage and water systems put in place, and postal and telegraph systems implemented – all connecting India as a unified nation and to the outside world. Industrialisation was taking hold, with mining, shipbuilding and the textile industries proliferating, providing employment to millions of Indians. There were investments in mines, tea and coffee plantations, irrigation, forestry and mapping – which saw the first definitive *Atlas of India* with a vast compendium of geological and geographical information on a scale of four miles to an inch.

James Rennell (1742–1830) arrived in India in 1760 commissioned to map southern India and Ceylon. Under EIC patronage – reluctantly granted by the Court of Directors in London due to the expense – his surveys later extended to Bengal-Bihar and Orissa, and to the foothills of the Himalayas. Whilst it is popular to explain such endeavours with the cynical view that mapping was carried out primarily to gain strategic military advantage in the subcontinent, such one-sided arguments do a great disservice to the personal motivations and sacrifices – Rennell's health suffered enormously from his efforts in India – of devoted men such as Rennell, whose patronage was taken over by the apolitical Royal Society who recognised his enormous contribution to science. From the second half of the 1760s until 1800 the Court of Directors of the EIC, were largely against further military expansion, unable to see an economic justification for further expansion.

Whilst the EIC's abuses are well documented, attention must also be given to its introduction of major social reforms in India, including the eradication of thuggee (violent highway robbery), ensuring safe travel, the prohibition of female infanticide, and the banning of sati (suttee), the burning of widows on the husband's funeral pyre. On 4 December 1829, the newly appointed Governor-General Lord William Bentinck, with the backing of the EIC Court of Directors, took the bold move of illegalising the barbaric practice of widow immolation. The EIC had not been deaf to the teachings of the great reformer Ram Mohan Roy. Aware of the backlash they would face, they put forward as support for the move Roy's justifications to his countrymen for the abolition of sati. At great personal risk, Roy had appealed to his own countrymen for the abolition of sati. Roy, conscious of maintaining peace in India, did not go so far as to petition the EIC to legislate to end the practice; in fact he warned the EIC that such a move could incite an uprising. There was no commercial gain to be had; the risk of revolt was real. This was a matter of compassion and an injustice that Bentinck could not ignore. After more than 2000 years, not one Indian ruler had intervened. It took a foreigner and a commercial venture with a huge amount to lose to make punishable by law a centuries-old abuse.

Perhaps most enduring of all was the uniting of several dozen different independent states into one centrally governed, unified India underpinned by the English language and the emergence of a codified English legal system. All helped to progress the transformation of a modern India after the British left in 1947. For a private company, with a responsibility to its shareholders' interests, to introduce social, humanitarian reforms is an exception that is unheard of since.

In the years following the failed Indian Army Mutiny of 1857 and the Company's disproportionate and cruel reprisals, the British Parliament dismantled the anomaly whereby a private corporation had governed a vast subcontinent and hundreds of millions of people for over 100 years. The EIC's administrative role was replaced by the increasingly direct involvement of the British government in the governance of India, which brought significant investment and many reforms to an administrative system designed specifically for the subcontinent: the Indian Civil Service (ICS). The new ICS, 'celebrated for its sea-green incorruptibility', set the tone for a new era of British rule free from interference by a private monopoly. The ICS was to become an enduring model of transparent, impartial and highly effective governance, staffed by many of Britain's most talented and highly educated young men, and as time went on by Indians who passed the demanding entry examination. The once-accepted irregularities of the EIC became history.

Emergence of a unified system of governance

Among the many valuable legacies left behind by the British, three of the several vital and great institutions were those of: (i) the all-important Indian Civil Service (ICS); (ii) the English legal system with its impeccable nationwide judicial network; and (iii) the formation of the well-drilled, highly disciplined, unified and loyal Indian Army – all descended from the parliament-driven reform to the EIC administration and critical in the uniting of the subcontinent and the legacy of a secular democracy.

The Indian Civil Service (ICS)

The most valuable, extraordinary and enormous role of the British administrative innovation in the ICS, and its unselfish and ceaseless toil in the service of India, alone would take volumes to describe, so here I will confine myself to touching on only two aspects.

On average, in each province upon the leadership of one or two British ICS officers was built an administration employing thousands of Indians ranking from senior managers and clerks down to peons and servants. The scholarly and highly trained British civil servants, sent to India throughout the Raj period, most deservingly earned the reputation for being minutely just, scrupulously honest and inflexibly upright, introducing the culture and tradition of impartial and good governance without corruption. How did fewer than 1000 British civil servants in the ICS manage to govern effectively and judiciously a vast subcontinent of 500 million people of diverse caste, culture, language and religion spread over 1.27 million square miles, with distances of about 2000 miles from Burma in the east to Baluchistan in the west, with similar distances between Kashmir in the north to Kerala in the south? This has set the singular example of the most widely stretched, superbly efficient and dynamic bureaucracy for delivering sound and transparent secular governance in human history. A single and dynamic dedicated British district-head effectively managed the lives of over half a million Indians. The ICS was soon being referred to as 'the steel frame' of the British Raj.

By 1922 15% of the civil servants were Indian. Recruitment to the ICS was determined by an open examination held in London, which was of course prohibitive to many Indians due to sheer distance and cost. However, the Government of India Act in 1919 overturned this situation and the first recruitment exam in India for the ICS was held in Allahabad. By 1941 Indians outnumbered the British in the ICS. The consequence of this should not be overlooked. When the French and Spanish withdrew from their colonies they left in their wake power vacuums in the native administrative structures, which they had controlled and filled entirely by Europeans who then left, resulting in power struggles and instability. When the British handed over power, they did so to highly qualified civil servants in a fully functional democracy.

Judiciary and imperial conduct – a liberal critique

From the very early days of colonial rule a system of parliamentary inquiries, committees, discussions and debates was constituted to oversee the working of the Indian administration and intervene in its affairs when it was felt necessary. It is true that Indians were less involved in the policy- and decision-making during those years, but there was always a strong body of liberal opinion in England and in the British Parliament, usually by the members of the Liberal Party, known then as the Whigs, that often championed Indian causes. Within a couple of decades after the institution of direct rule from Westminster in 1858, Indians felt quite free to organise themselves in discussion groups, debating societies, associations and the gymkhana clubs that helped introduce the culture of team sport and team spirit.

The judiciary was one of the most valuable institutions and legacies inherited under colonial rule, replacing the outdated Sharia and Hindu laws with English law, providing rights of contract, rights of private property, rights of personal liberty, rights against inequality and abuses of tyranny, crime and corruption. The year 2015 marked the 800th anniversary of Magna Carta, one of the most important documents in British and world history that is a cornerstone of individual liberties and codifies a challenge to arbitrary rule. The great writ of habeas corpus, the most powerful bulwark of British liberty, became available to every inhabitant of India. The British established a codification of law. The Code of Criminal Procedure laid down in clear, precise and exact terms, the law applicable for the first time to all citizens, of high and low breed, irrespective of caste, creed and religion. This written code of law was in itself an amazing achievement. The British also set up a gradation of courts, civil and criminal, for the trial of petty and heinous crimes with the right of appeal in the High Courts and even to the Privy Council in London.

Gladstone's Liberal government in London appointed the liberal Marquis of Ripon as the Viceroy of India in 1880. Lord Ripon did not approve of the prevailing practice of not allowing Indian judges, qualified in Britain, to conduct trials of white defendants in criminal cases. Soon after taking up his post, Ripon advised the Law Member of his Council, C.P. Ilbert, also a liberal, to draft a bill to revoke this indefensible anomaly. The reaction by the white community to the Ilbert Bill was fierce; some called it a White Munity. Both Ripon and Ilbert stood resolute. As far as Viceroy Ripon was concerned, the question for him was clear-cut: '[was India] to be ruled for the benefit of the Indian people of all races, classes and creeds, or in the sole interest of a small body of Europeans?' He opted for the former and indeed set the trend for more liberalism in governance by future viceroys.

It was men like Ripon in India and the periodic liberal voice in Britain that helped maintain the peaceful equilibrium between the governed and the governors for over two centuries. It was most remarkable that an Englishman, Lord Ripon, who perhaps sowed the first seed of India's path towards its freedom, was hailed in Bombay as Lord Buddha by a leading nationalist figure, Pherozeshah Mehta, in 1884, followed by other Indians in Calcutta and elsewhere, giving Lord Ripon the title of Mahatma (meaning Saint) Ripon about 40 years before Mr Gandhi – who eventually led India to its freedom 29 years after arriving from South Africa in 1918 – came to be called Mahatma Gandhi. The untimely death in 1920 of Lokmanya Tilak, the frontrunner and pioneering freedom leader – known as the father of Indian unrest – provided the political vacuum and the platform of opportunity for the leadership to be taken up by M.K. Gandhi, who had returned to India only a couple of years earlier from South Africa.

A unified and professional Indian Army

It was the spirit of loyalty and integrity within the ranks of the British Army that set the example for the new, professional Indian Army raised by the British. From the early days of the EIC, soldiers were recruited from different castes, cultures and religions. Many were divided further by the different languages of the vast subcontinent. Yet they were transformed under their conquerors into a unified, secular, courageous and disciplined Indian Army. Indian soldiers subsequently under imperial rule earned a good number

19th Lancers, officers and men, c.1860s (Courtesy of the British Library)

of Victoria Crosses and many other gallantry medals for their valour and unflinching loyalty in the two world wars and other campaigns. Throughout the British rule of 250 years in India they lost only one war in 1799, defeated by the brave and powerful Marathas who deployed history's first military rockets with a substantial range of nearly one kilometre – a specimen remains on display at the British Science Museum – as well as their most innovative, lightweight and agile cannons, with firepower, accuracy and mobility significantly superior to those of the British.

The British made the Indian soldier conscious and proud of his military heritage. There was great pride in living up to the legend. Handbooks on all communities active in the army were written by British officers (often quite junior) who had done an immense amount of research and investigation. The handbooks were updated from time to time and all were published by the Government of India. Examples of these handbooks include *The Sikhs 1896, The Sikhs 1899, The Rajputs 1898, The Marathas 1898, The Brahmans 1899, The Dogras 1899, The Dekhani Mussalmans 1902, The Dekhani Mussalmans 1908, The Hindustani Mussalmans 1914, The Jats, The Gujars,* and *The Ahirs 1914*, and there were a number of such handbooks on the Gurkhas. This reflects the extensive research by the British and the deep understanding and appreciation of the distinct characteristics, skills and spirits of India's various ethnic groups which tended to bring the best out of each group, helped by the founding principles of secularism in the British Indian Army which remain proudly intact today. The high standards of training and discipline painstakingly introduced in army ranks remain thanks to the ethos and culture inculcated by great military academies, the like of Sandhurst, established in India over 100 years ago, along with the wider range of elaborate infrastructure, including that of arms and ammunition

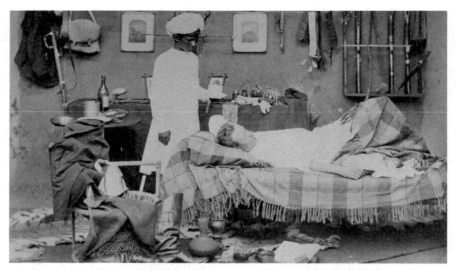

Madras Army Officer with his bearer. Living conditions were basic and the Madras climate often took its toll, c.1880s (Courtesy of the British Library)

production factories. The secular, loyal and apolitical Indian Army is one of the most valuable institutions inherited from the colonial period and one which India remains proud of to this day. The year 2009 marked the Indian celebrations of the 250th anniversary of the founding of the Madras Regimental Centre, raised by Robert Clive on 4 December 1758. Just a few decades later, the Madras Native Infantry, under the command of Major-General Arthur Wellesley (later the Duke of Wellington), spearheaded the defeat of Tipu Sultan, the ruler of Mysore and long-time foe of the EIC. (Tipu Sultan forged alliances with the French to the alarm of the EIC and at a time when the French were expanding their empire and looking to over-take the British in India.) The year 2014 witnessed the 250th anniversary celebration of the founding of the Army Medical Services in 1764.

Just how strong the bond was between the soldiers of the Indian Army, irrespective of religion, caste or background, was poignantly described by General S.K. Sinha – the former Vice-Chief of Army Staff who later served as Governor of Assam and Kashmir – in an article for the *Asian Age* published on 29 January 2015:

> The undivided Indian Army was a unique institution set up by the British in India… [A]ll combat units, except the Gorkhas and Garhwalis, had a mixed composition of Muslims and non-Muslims. They fought wars together and lived as friendly comrades in peace, owing loyalty to their

Maharajah of Patiala inspecting a guard of honour at the opening of the Indian gate, Brighton, 1921 (Courtesy of Royal Pavilion & Museums, Brighton & Hove)

regiments. Political developments with the emergence of the Congress and the Muslim League did not affect them. The Indian Army was totally apolitical till June 3, 1947, when the British government announced the Partition of India. In fact, during the Partition holocaust and till that date, both Muslim and non-Muslim soldiers remained totally impartial in dealing with communal violence.

...I recall that I had served with a Punjabi Muslim company of 6 Jat Regiment before Partition, during the war in Burma. When Muslim troops from my regimental centre at Bareilly were being sent to 8 Punjab Regiment in Pakistan I had gone to the centre to wish them goodbye. This was a sentimental moment for both, those going to Pakistan and others remaining in India... When officers of the Indian Army were departing for Pakistan, the Indian officers organised a function at Delhi Gymkhana Club to bid them farewell. Brigadier K.M. Cariappa was the chief host. We presented a silver trophy to them. The trophy showed two soldiers, one Muslim and the other non-Muslim, wearing their different turbans, in kneeling position, ready to fire against a common enemy.

The enduring positive influence of Christianity

Secularism defined British rule. It is true that Christian missionaries operated freely in India, but at no time was there any conspicuous or determined drive to convert Indians to any branch of Christianity. Imperial power was never used for this purpose. After 200 long years of British rule, apart from the Anglo-Indians, until Independence in 1947, a mere 1% of the population had been converted to Christianity. By contrast, in Portuguese-held Goa conversions to Christianity reached over 25% and the figure in Pondicherry under French rule was significantly higher. The national average of those practising Christianity in India today remains at around 2% – with about an equal proportion of Protestants and Catholics.

Christian missionaries' pioneering and charitable initiative was for the most part directed to the opening of effective hospitals, homes for lepers and the founding of abidingly egalitarian educational institutions. They introduced the culture of charity in healthcare and education, and helped to set higher standards of learning in India, introducing modern education and discipline in schools and colleges. These social and charitable Christian initiatives in India indeed helped to bring about a better understanding among Indians about performance of their social duties towards fellow Indians. As a result, some non-Christians turned their efforts to the creation of public charities and schemes of social betterment. Christian organisations in India still observe the long tradition of working with poor and marginalised communities through income generation and sustainable livelihood programmes and encouraging small saving schemes. Their efforts in providing education to the slum-based communities and and running adult literacy classes are exemplary.

Unification and opportunity

'Secularism' and 'democracy' are essentially British contributions to the evolution of Indian thought, culture and politics. Freedom to profess and practise one's faith and respect for the faith of others was a British precept. Leaders of the Indian freedom movement learnt the blessings of democracy from the liberal education made possible by British scholars and teachers. Indians who could afford it went to England, received their education in British schools and colleges, and imbibed the values and morals in which the British themselves were grounded. Civil and political rights did not depend on the manner in which one worshipped god and gods. Whether one paid obeisance or not did not affect anyone's civil or political rights and there was an understanding that secularism and democracy go together as key partners. The British introduced uniform education systems and enforced uniform law.

India's first secular revolution began with the British Indian Army recruitment in the mid-18th century, which as already explored, was open to men of all castes, creeds, cultures and religions, enabling them to work together for the first time. The culture of this secular comradeship introduced by the British amongst the natives lent itself to the private sector and gained further momentum with the vast employment opportunities that arose a century later in 1850, with the start of the national network of post and telegraph systems, and soon to be augmented with the massive opportunities provided by the introduction of the great Indian railways. The Indian Army, the post and telegraph, and the railways were the three largest employers of men of all religions, castes, creeds and languages under the British and continue to be so today, almost 70 years after Independence. In fact the railway system as it is today – and was, under British rule – is the world's largest employer, with over 1.6 million employees on its payroll.

India: beneficiary of history's greatest transnational infrastructure programme

The physical infrastructure fashioned by the British not only comprised the founding of great cities such as Madras, Calcutta and Bombay, but also included the extension and modernisation of many existing towns and the nationwide establishment of universities, libraries and museums, as well as specialist engineering, medical and law colleges to develop the vocational professions. These urban centres were eventually connected by the vast national railway network and an efficient post and telegraph system, as well as an extensive development of canals, dams, irrigation, sanitation, roads and dockyards.

The railway played a pivotal role in unifying India into a modern nation. It was the railways that made it possible for the leaders of reform such as Keshab Chandra Sen, Bhau Daji and Surendranath Bannerjee to travel around the country to establish first-hand contact with the freedom-seeking leaders of the regions. From its inception in the early 1850s, a staggering 10 000 miles of track had already been constructed within the first 25 years of railway construction in India; and, by 1947, 45 000 miles, including 136 000 bridges linked the remotest parts of the subcontinent to one another. While the monumental task of developing the vast railway network in India enabled the British to secure their colonial hold with more effective governance, the railways were also a great boon for moving commodities and people from the interior to the ports, and connecting almost all cities and regions in India. By 1930, it was estimated that every town of importance had a railway station and that less than 1% of all villages were further than 50 miles from a railhead.

This unprecedented connectivity through the world's largest railway network transformed and revolutionised the attitudes, habits and social outlook of the entire Indian people, forming a platform for the development of India's emerging collective identity as a unified nation. As the historian of post-Independence India S.R. Mehrotra observed, 'The railway compartment in which people of all castes, creeds and provinces were huddled together, became the symbol of a new and united India in the making.'

The connectivity that the railways brought about resulted in a broadening of outlook – in the physical and philosophical sense – and a widening of understanding between peoples of diverse cultures, castes, languages, religions and regions. The railway in India established itself as a world within a world, bringing with it immense opportunities for a mobile, connected populace. The British built more railways in India alone than America, France, Spain, Belgium, the Netherlands and other European colonists built together in all their colonies. While the railway was introduced to India soon after its development in Europe and the US, London was connected telegraphically to India in 1852, a year before it was connected to New York, and soon had a national telegraphic and postal network. These modern forms of transport and communication, together with the all-important English language and freedom of the press, brought about the Indian communication revolution in the 19th century.

The importance of the simultaneous introduction of the English language and its dissemination through a new education system cannot be overestimated, enabling as it did effective communication between linguistically disparate regions. The inheritance of English has played a very important role in post-Independence India. The importance of protecting regional languages is recognised in the Constitution but the fact remains that they are 'regional'. To those pushing for the adoption of Hindi as the national language, the lawyer and writer C. Rajagopalachari replied succinctly: 'Let them remember that the people in South India can shout with more strength and vigour.' High standards of English have facilitated India's modern-day pre-eminence in several spheres, including information technology, business process and outsourcing besides the recognition in the literary world, with several of the world's great English language writers being Indians.

Did Indians have freedom of enterprise?

It is often heard in India that during the Raj Indians were deprived of business opportunities and freedom to operate. This is far from the truth. There is ample evidence that native enterprise had economic opportunities almost equal to those of the British in business and industry. Indeed, there are glowing examples of indigenous enterprise, initiative and business skills among the Parsi community, who often proved to be significantly ahead of British entrepreneurs in their achievements.

Lovji Nusserwanji Wadia built the first dry-dock facility in Bombay in 1755. The Wadias earned an enviable reputation as builders of some of the finest and sturdiest world-class sailing ships in the 18th and 19th centuries. They built 170 ships for the EIC alone between 1735 and 1836, and the Wadias' reputation led to general orders from the British Navy.

Ardaseer Cursetjee (1808–1877) began his career with Wadia. Under EIC patronage he visited England on a one-year study trip to learn about steam technology. As chief engineer of the Bombay Steam Factory he had over 100 British engineers under his supervision. The *Bombay Courier* reported that Cursetjee recognised 'the great advantage which might be derived from the introduction of steam as a means of irrigating garden land and improving agricultural resources of the country'. Such was his eminence in London he was appointed a non-resident member of the Royal Society and an associate of the renowned Institution of Civil Engineers (ICE).

Dwarkanath Tagore (1794–1846) – grandfather to Rabindranath Tagore and a close friend of the reformer Ram Mohan Roy – was a leading Bengali entrepreneur in the steamship and coal industries, founding Anglo-Indian joint ventures and hugely active in Calcutta's mercantile and social circles.

India's first cotton mill – The Bombay Spinning Mill – was founded in 1854 by a Parsi entrepreneur, Cowasji Davar, followed by the Tatas opening steam-powered cotton mills in 1874, thus encouraging other Indian business and trading families to invest in the industrial enterprises. By 1896, Indian mills supplied about 8% of India's cloth consumption, reaching 80% of domestic consumption by 1945. The Tatas were the most creative of the first-generation Indian industrialists. They were the first Indians to invest substantially in heavy engineering, chemicals and power generation. Soon, more Indian entrepreneurs entered the textile industry in a big way between 1870 and 1940, and many more small-scale industries emerged in engineering and the production of consumer goods nationwide. India's first major steel plant, built in 1902, was built not by a British corporation but by the Tatas; and India's first five-star hotel, the Taj Mahal in Bombay, too, was a Tata enterprise, opening its doors in 1903. The Tatas were also the first Indians to enter into the business of tea plantations and hydroelectric power. India's first postal air-service was introduced by Tata and its first commercial airline was a Tata initiative launched in 1935 – allowed by the British, but later curbed and taken over by the Indian government soon after Independence.

The emergence of Parsis as great entrepreneurs over the 100 years before Independence helped to create the awareness for a culture of free enterprise among other indigenous business communities, who were greatly encouraged by the opportunities that appeared with the increased freedom, reforms and liberalism that followed the demise of the EIC and its replacement by direct rule from British Parliament. This change opened the door to Indian entrepreneurship and meaningful participation in key aspects of colonial administration and governance. Interestingly, several diverse communities actually flourished in different professional niches, each of which was fundamental to the development of the Raj and the making of India. The erudite scholars of Bengal, south India and Bombay State were soon passing the formidable ICS examinations in open competition with Britain's brightest graduates – and then excelling in senior posts in the service. They were also among the earliest learned Indians to make names for themselves internationally in science and academia, and this culture spread steadily to other regions of India. India's first silent feature film was produced by an enterprising Marathi genius, Dadasaheb Phalke, in 1913 and Moti Gidwani was credited with India's first colour film in 1937.

Dadabhai Naoroji was the first Indian elected in 1892 as a Liberal MP to the House of Commons, followed by Sir Mancherjee in 1895 and Shapoorji Saklatvala in 1922 – all three were Parsis. The fourth parliamentarian was Lord Sinha of Raipur, raised to the peerage in 1919. He was the first and only Indian to be awarded a hereditary peerage, and also the first Indian appointed as a minister of the British Government. Other Parsis followed their lead. In 1929 Sam Pirosha Khambatta from Bombay was called to the Bar in Middle Temple. In 1949 Khambatta made history as the first Indian to be appointed QC.

Another key arena in which indigenous communities made major lasting contributions was the British Indian Army, excelling in the two world wars and many other campaigns where the Sikhs and the Gurkhas, along with other Indian regiments, provided outstanding military service. The Sikhs did exceptionally well during the arduous British campaigns in Afghanistan and Waziristan. Having also excelled in the Indian Police Force, they were frequently seconded by the British for policing duties in Singapore, Hong Kong, Malaya, Shanghai and other outposts of empire. The British engineer Joseph Harrison noted the Sikhs' aptitude for executing and managing major engineering works, including bridge building and railway construction. When the Calcutta to Delhi railway was extended into the Punjab in 1863, Harrison commended the punctuality of the resulting Lahore–Amritsar train link, writing:

> We Europeans were all but declared redundant due to the tall and sturdy Sikhs in funny hats. They have replaced most of the British expatriate drivers and firemen and virtually all our maintenance workmen.

The Sikhs' success in agriculture and public works became widely recognised. James Bell, the supervisor of the enormous construction project of the Empress Bridge over the River Sutlej in Punjab, commented: 'for sheer quality and quantity of work where little supervision, if any, is required, we look to the hard-working Sikhs.' The extraordinary feat of building the Kalka–Simla Mountain Railway, which included 103 tunnels and 869 bridges, was accomplished in a little over three years, despite traversing the most difficult terrain ever encountered in the building of Indian railways. On its completion in 1903 the *Railway Gazette* observed that only one manager and one consultant engaged from Britain were required, with the entire line being managed directly by Sikh engineers and staff.

The manifold talents of various indigenous communities including Hindus and Muslims across the subcontinent were increasingly harnessed and developed by the British to build the country's infrastructure and to administer its civil service: ranging from the systematic expansion of large-scale irrigated agriculture to the maintenance of law and order; and the staffing of hospitals and universities to the defence of its borders – even to fight on behalf of Britain and its empire. Thus, although British rule in India began somewhat ignominiously tied with the commercial exploitations of the EIC, there is a case that it evolved into a system of relatively enlightened and fair governance that brought out the best in many Indians across the subcontinent, with each of the different communities, including Parsis, Bengalis, south Indians, Marathas, Sikhs, Gurkhas, Punjabis and frontier Muslims, and several other communities, playing essential and unique roles alongside the British in the making of India.

An Indian heritage: the gift of 'a sense of our past'

The eminent writer and businessman Jaithirth Rao presented his views on the British contribution to the Indian subcontinent in the *Indian Express* on 15 August 2007:

> The British gave us a sense of our past, they gave us our feel for the land in real material terms ... between the Survey of India, the Botanical Survey of India, the Archaeological Survey of India, the Geological Survey of India, the Census of India and the numerous District Gazetteers they mapped our country, analysed and described it in memorable prose.

India was shaped and modernised by the valuable legacy of institutions of British democracy, with fair and sound governance, well-administered law and order, social justice and a modern and progressive education system. A new culture of museums, universities, colleges and libraries was also established. Many embarrassing and incriminating historical documents from the colonial period, which could have been easily destroyed before the transfer of power in 1947, were carefully classified and preserved in State as well as National Archives. Many historians who have been critical of imperial policies have often themselves greatly benefited from this British sense of fairness and value for history.

The British showed great sensitivity and refinement of taste in their appreciation of Indian art, architecture and heritage nationwide, regardless of whether the origins were Hindu, Muslim, Sikh, Jain or Buddhist. The preservation, restoration and conservation of long-neglected monuments across the subcontinent received tremendous impetus during Lord Nathaniel Curzon's tenure as viceroy. The preservation of India's heritage to this day is owed largely to his far-sighted stewardship. Even Jawaharlal Nehru acknowledged this legacy and reminds us that Curzon 'restored all that was beautiful in India'. Curzon introduced the Ancient Monuments Preservation Act of 1904 to prevent the misuse and neglect of historic monuments. He issued orders for the restoration and beautification of the great heritage sites scattered across the continent. Agra became the scene of one of the first and certainly the best known of the great works of conservation and extensive restoration: the Taj Mahal regained its lost glamour and seduction, and the dusty wastes in Agra were converted into verdant parks and gardens; neglected and half-tumbled-down ruins were restored to their original design.

This colonial contribution greatly helped India to establish a new culture of appreciation for the priceless heritage of ancient art and architecture dating back millennia. It also resulted in many discoveries including that of the Ajanta-Ellora cave temples, the ancient university towns of Nalanda and Texella and the five-millennium-old civilization of Mohenjo-Daro. Sir John Marshall (1876–1958) in 1921-22 was the first European to discover this so-called Indus Valley civilisation. 'The Indus Valley civilisation is quite unlike any other civilisation for its time; well ahead in planning and prosperity that must be classed as unique in world history', according to Marshall.

Also very worthy of mention is ancient Hampi, the site of the ancient capital of the Vijayanagar kings, who dominated south India from 1336 to 1565. It was a 'beautiful city, being 24 metres round and enclosed by many hills', according to the Italian visitor Caesar Frederick in 1567. Hampi was the earliest seat of the dynasty and in the 1920s attracted much attention from the archaeologist and author R. Sewell. Sewell documented the city and its surrounding civilisation and published his research in his book *The Forgotten Empire*. The rich history of this South Indian civilisation is too often overlooked in studies of Indian history.

Even in the early days of EIC rule in India, devoted Company men began to uncover India's past. Men such as Sir William Jones (1749–1795), appointed by the EIC to the position of judge in the newly established Supreme Court in Bengal but remembered principally as the great polymath, Indologist and founder of the Asiatic Society, and James Prinsep (1799–1840), the gifted engineer who deciphered the Brahmi script, which led to the unearthing of the great history of Ashoka (r. 269–233 BC), dedicated every minute of their spare time to the rich Indian cultures, languages and histories that had fallen into historical oblivion. The book *Ashoka: The Search for India's Lost Emperor* by Charles Allen, published in 2012, reveals the painstaking efforts of these devoted men and those that followed them in bringing to light Ashoka's great empire.

The British also took the initiative in preserving India's wildlife. In 1905 Kaziranga Forest in Assam became India's first national park where an endangered species, rhinoceros, could live free from molestation by humans and under government protection. The British fascination with Indian wildlife is also exemplified by the fact that all the books on the birds and mammals of India were originally written by the British, often by amateur naturalists. The British-founded Bombay Natural History Society remains a world-class organisation. Likewise, the first books on Indian flora and botany were also pioneered by the British. Eminent botanist Sir Joseph Hooker's book *Flora of British India* was published in 1872.

Thanks to the spirit of enquiry and scholarship among the many meticulous and dedicated British officials from the time of the EIC onwards, India has been left with an enduring canon of ancient literary works including medicine, mathematics, astronomy – and all are available today in English, fuelling the international interest in Indian studies and history. Many of those enthusiastic amateur scholars, who toiled away in their time off-duty, produced seminal contributions to their respective subjects, which in many cases opened the world's eyes for the first time to the sophistication of ancient Indian civilizations.

The British interest in India's past extended beyond art and architectural heritage. The physical landscape was surveyed and mapped, with its geography, ethnography, geology and more besides studied. One of the most extraordinary aspects of colonial history is the 'classification' of the many different ethnic groups. Many members of the British civil establishment spent much of their time delving into the different tribal customs, traditions, histories and ways of life of indigenous communities. Most people in India do accept these scholarly works as perhaps the only authoritative accounts of their origins, cultures, customs and languages. The 200-year window of British governance was perhaps the only period in a thousand years of Indian history to date, when the minorities and the people of different religions and regions felt more secure and less discriminated against, with a notable absence of conflicts, killings and persecutions related to caste, culture, language and religious distinctions.

Financial consequences of empire: benefit and burden

It is often said that Britain's riches and economy between the 18th and 20th century were mostly due to its exploitation of its colonies. This proposition becomes somewhat debatable when one thinks rationally. How was it that Spain and Portugal, which owned and fully exploited some of the largest colonies in history, remained poor in spite of not having been affected by two world wars? Conversely, how would one explain the rich economies of the industrious and enterprising nations of Sweden and Switzerland without any colonial history? Furthermore, Europe's modern-day economic powerhouse, Germany, had only a few meagre colonies for a short time span in Africa, and yet twice emerged as the most powerful nation in the world – once at the very beginning of the 20th century and again in the late 1930s – and yet again experienced an 'economic miracle' within ten years of its total decimation in 1945. Europe's economic and military history of 19th and 20th centuries thus suggests that the real legacy of imperial rule is probably little more than colonial baggage. Indeed 'Imperial Preference' may have weakened the British economy by making British manufacturing inefficient and non-competitive.

The argument provides some credibility to several authors and lobbyists since the days of the world-renowned Liberal free-market British economist Adam Smith, whose book *The Wealth of Nations* was published in 1776. The Indian Nobel laureate economist Amartya Sen has hailed Smith as the founder of modern economics and the workings of the market economy. Smith is also renowned as the father of concepts such as 'free market', 'supply and demand' and 'division of labour'. Smith set a precedent and provided a respectability and pedigree to the *laissez-faire* and liberalist argument. His economic principles and criticisms of the EIC heavily influenced Burke and such British classical liberal-thinkers as the campaigner Richard Cobden and politician John Bright – the indefatigable reformers who brought about the repeal of the Corn Laws in England in 1846 in a landmark victory for the rising and industrial middle classes against the old order of landowners. Cobden and Bright, like Smith, questioned whether the building of an empire was financially worthwhile for Britain. To them, free economic integration with the rest of world economy mattered more than the coercive integration of imperialism. Investments in the domestic industry – rather than in far-flung colonies – would increase home employment and productivity, helping greater export output. Cobden envisaged that laissez-faire international trade would bring peoples and governments together, moving nations into an era of peace as a result of closer relationships and interdependence – that 'Free Trade would have the tendency to unite mankind in the bonds of peace' in Cobden's own words.

Sharing Smith's criticisms of the monopolistic practices and abuses of the EIC, reformers such as Cobden and Bright were at the forefront in the refocusing of policy in India – 'from plunder to public works'. In correspondence between Bright and Cobden, Bright provides his argument for maintaining British colonial rule in India. His belief being that of a moral obligation: that the answer to the problems that the British faced in the wake of the Mutiny in 1857 was to confer 'on the Indian people whatever good it is in our power to give them', and as such that this good could 'only come from the most just government which we [the British] are able to confer upon countless of millions [of Indians]'. This paternalist view of colonial rule may have its critics but there is the question of how India would be today if, in 1857, the British had left India.

Colonies also caused an unaffordable long-term brain drain, particularly after the Mutiny, with the emigration from Britain to India of many of the finest engineers, architects, academics and the dedicated ICS administrators. In 1856 Cobden went to the extent of saying that it would 'be a happy day when England has not an acre of territory in Continental Asia'.

Historian Niall Ferguson quotes an interesting point from his research:

> One historian, writing in the new *Oxford History of the British Empire*, has gone so far as to speculate that if Britain had got rid of the Empire in the mid 1840s she could have reaped a "decolonisation dividend" in the form of a 25 per cent tax cut.

The result of which would have been increased consumer spending at home and domestic industrial growth. The common thread in the above debate is the notion that the benefits of international exchange could have been reaped by Britain without the cost and burden of maintaining the empire.

Colonial power relinquished and the foundations for liberty

Indians know of the desolate and ravaged Delhi that was inherited by the British in 1803, and today's New Delhi, which was inherited by independent India in 1947. Emperor King George V and Queen Mary arrived in Bombay on 2 December 1911. On the 12th, the emperor and empress rode in state to the spectacular, grand domed tent of the special Durbar (court) outside Delhi. It was here that the king announced the news that Delhi would replace Calcutta as India's capital. When King George V laid the foundation stone of New Delhi on 15 December 1911, he said:

> It is my desire that the planning and designing of the public buildings in Delhi to be erected will be considered with greatest deliberation and care so that the new creation may be in every way worthy of this ancient and beautiful city.

Such was the level of concern and care for this dream project conceived for India by distant little Britain. King George's dream indeed came true, manifesting as a marvel of British genius and created by two of the greatest British architects: Edwin Lutyens and Herbert Baker. What these men created in less than two decades was, and is, an astounding achievement. An architectural

Maharajahs at the 1903 Delhi Durbar for Edward VII's coronation (Courtesy of the British Library)

masterpiece, New Delhi was clearly built to last a thousand years. Standing before the magnificent President's Palace (Rashtrapati Bhavan) and Parliament, buildings of breathtaking proportions and classical elegance, one is inspired with awe and confidence in this seat of power from which the vast subcontinent was to have been ruled by future generations of viceroys. When the time came to renounce the imperial dream of Britain's everlasting empire – with India as the jewel in its crown – power was relinquished with, for the most part, good grace and mutual respect. No doubt the British themselves had appreciably matured and improved as rulers since EIC rule and the Indian Mutiny in 1857. This spirit of handing over power to a people that had, after nearly two centuries of colonial rule, come to be seen as respected allies and friends is nowhere better encapsulated than in this inscription left by the British on the Indian Parliament building:

Parliament House, New Delhi, 1920s (Courtesy of the British Library)

Liberty does not descend to a people. A people must raise themselves to liberty. It is a blessing that must be earned before it can be enjoyed.

To the modern reader such a statement may seem shockingly conde-scending but if we reflect more dispassionately at a bygone age, there is a sentiment that the British recognised in India a responsibility to unite and instil democratic ideals rather than abandoning the country to a fractious anarchy, which may well have been the case had the British left India in 1857. We must look back with some perspective and consider the creation of a unified and democratic spirit in India that did not exist before British rule. A hundred years after King George V laid the foundation stone for New Delhi – on 15 December 1911 – the following comment was made by a sen-ior Indian journalist and the spokesperson for the BJP, Swapan Dasgupta, in the *Asian Age* on 12 December 2011:

> It [the Durbar] was also a moment in India's history that will live on de-spite the contrived derision of the "post-colonial" mind. The Raj's Delhi is as much a show of India as is *Shahjehanabad*, the creation of rulers who came from Central Asia. The latter is celebrated; the former isn't even commemorated. That's why India has no sense of history, only an overdose of hateful politics.

This is what the eminent Oxford historian, Niall Ferguson had to say in his book *Empire: How Britain Made the Modern World:*

> [O]n the other side of the balance sheet were the immense British invest-ments in Indian infrastructure, irrigation and industry. By the 1880s the British had invested £270 million in India, not much less than one-fifth of their entire investment overseas. By 1914 the figure had reached £400 mil-lion. The British increased the area of irrigated land by a factor of eight, so that by the end of the Raj a quarter of all land was irrigated, compared with just 5 per cent of it under the Mughals. They created an Indian coal industry from scratch which by 1914 produced nearly 16 million tons a year. They increased the number of jute spindles by a factor of ten. There were also marked improvements in public health, which increased Indian average life expectancy by eleven years.* [* From 21 years to 32…]. It was the British who introduced quinine as an anti-malarial prophylactic, carried out public programmes of vaccination against smallpox – often in the face of local resistance – and laboured to improve the urban water supplies that were so often the bearers of cholera and other diseases. And, although it is simply impossible to quantify, it is hard to believe that there were not some advantages in being governed by as incorruptible a bureau-cracy as the Indian Civil Service.

The democratic spirit – liberal press laws and free press

The foremost institution that served to nurture and nourish the democratic spirit in India was the free press. India was bound to attain independence sooner or later, but it could not have emerged as a democratic nation without having experienced a free press during the Raj. Although the first attempt to launch a newspaper in India was crushed by the officials of the EIC by deporting the English publisher William Bolts, within a few years of Bolts' failed venture the *Bengal Gazette* appeared in Calcutta in 1780, under the editorship of James Augustus Hickey, now commonly recognised as the father of a free press in India. Hickey suffered a martyr's fate for libelling the disgraced Governor-General Warren Hastings, but he was successful in setting an example of a strong free press in India, an example that was soon emulated by many others: first the British residents and soon by Indians. By 1800 there were about 40 English newspapers. Within a few decades, India had a vigorous free press with newspapers and magazines of a diverse nature coming out in different languages from almost every nook and corner of the country: Madras in 1794, Calcutta around 1820, Bombay in 1822, Ahmedabad in 1849 and Orissa in 1872.

It was the catalyst provided by this free press that inspired and encouraged Indians of different classes, cultures and religions to create free, voluntary organisations to represent their interests. A vast network of interest groups was built in the country over the years with government patronage. Industrialists, businessmen and merchants created numerous trade organisations. The Calcutta Chamber of Commerce was founded as early as 1834, followed by the Bombay and Madras Chambers in 1836, the Punjab Chamber in 1905, the Industrial Association of Western India in 1880, the Bombay Stock Exchange Association in 1875, the Calcutta Stock Exchange in 1908 and the Madras Stock Exchange in 1937. India's premier body today, the Confederation of Indian Industry (CII), was founded in 1895 in Calcutta and moved to Delhi in 1975. In addition, a large number of similar associations were formed by activists of different individual trades such as iron and steel merchants, food grain wholesalers and cloth merchants. These served as a fertile seedbed for nurturing and organising interest groups on democratic lines, and settling issues through discussion and debate.

It was this native free press permitted by the ruling EIC that, in later years, became the vehicle of Indian agitation for economic and political reforms and finally of Indian independence. The British-Indian editors by and large conformed to their professional values, which were guided by the proprietor's brief and the editor's inclination, experience and reason. The British-Indian or Anglo-Indian editors took positions either pro- or anti-British rule. The *Bombay Gazette*, which published Bhaskar Pandurang Tarkhadkar's open letters of protest, and the removal of Dr George Buist from the editorial chair of the *Bombay Times* for taking an anti-Indian position are glaring examples. Samuel Digby, brother of William Digby, was an outspoken critic of the British government's India policy and did not hesitate to make it known to others. He remained close to Indian progressives even after returning to London in 1886.

Unknown to many, this freedom of expression during the Raj period was underpinned by the remarkably relaxed and liberal press laws enacted by the British in their colonies. The 148-year-old liberal colonial Press and Registration of Books (PRB) Act of 1867 still remains intact and unaltered nearly 70 years after India's independence. In contrast, other equally long-standing laws enacted by the British, which opposed freedom of expression against British rule, are still around including the law of 1870, which was used to convict Mahatma Gandhi in 1922 for promoting disaffection, and which was used recently – in 2010 – by the Indian judiciary to sentence the human rights activist and medical doctor, Binayak Sen, to life imprisonment.

Hume's Congress

The Indian National Congress was founded in 1885 by Allan Octavian Hume (1829–1912), a liberal ICS officer from Britain. Hume was the founder and moving spirit behind the organisation of India's first national-level political party, which subsequently led India to independence. Hume had already distinguished himself in his career with the ICS. He was a strong advocator of education, introducing scholarships for higher education and lobbying for women's education. He was typical in many ways of the British ICS officer who devoted himself in service to India. Bold and outspoken, he was never one to shy away from openly criticising British policy if he thought it was not in the interests of India.

Having retired from the ICS in 1882 he wrote to the students of Calcutta University calling on them to organise and form a national political party. Within a decade of its formation, Hume's Congress attracted a large body of highly accomplished, motivated and dedicated nationalists, including Lokmanya Tilak, M.G. Ranade, Dadabhai Naoroji, Sorabjee Shapurjee, Subash Bose, V.D. Savarkar, Subramaniam Bharati, W.C. Bannerjee, K.T.

Telang, Acharya Kripalani, Lala Lajpat Rai, Kharak Singh, Tara Singh, Raj Gopal Acharya, Badruddin Tayabji, Dinsha Wacha, R.L. Mitra, G.K. Gokale, Vallabhbhai Patel, J.L. Nehru, M.A. Jinnah, L.M. Ghosh, Bankim C. Chatterjee, Abdul Kalam Azad, R.G. Bhandarkar and Aruna Asaf Ali and several other distinguished leaders. After his return to Britain in 1894 Hume continued to take a keen interest in the progress of the Indian National Congress.

The secret of success of the post-Independence Congress Party lay in the firm and long experience that the Indians had gained under the British from working in numerous well-organised democratic institutions, centres of knowledge, learning and research, and voluntary organisations that had been built under colonial patronage. The nationwide spread of the printing press, newspapers and relatively free public debate gave voice and wide-spread appeal to its politics and message. Here, I feel compelled to cite the words of Niall Ferguson, the distinguished Scottish academic and historian, who eloquently highlighted the virtuous and fateful British trait which permeated the Raj, as well as the whole empire:

> I do not mean to claim that all British imperialists were liberals; some were very far from it. But what is very striking about the history of the Empire is that whenever the British were behaving despotically, there was almost always a liberal critique of that behaviour from within British society. Indeed, so powerful and consistent was this tendency to judge Britain's imperial conduct by the yardstick of liberty that it gave the British Empire something of a self-liquidating character. Once a colonized society had sufficiently adopted the other institutions the British brought with them, it became very hard for the British to prohibit that political liberty to which they attached so much significance themselves.

Why then is it, that even in modern times, some Indian politicians, including those at the highest level, remain bent on attacking Britain, wrongly and adversely influencing and affecting the generations after Independence in 1947?

Partition, Independence and the aftermath

While, for the most part, after 1947 the ICS needed only a few years for its drift into the new post-Independence culture of corruption, the judiciary managed to resist for longer. This is what the former director of the Central Bureau of Investigation, Mr Joginder Singh, had to say in a national daily, *Asian Age*, on 25 August 2007:

20 years ago in 1988, Rajiv Gandhi said: out of every Rupee sent by Delhi, only 15% reached the intended destination … most government schemes have built-in margin for corruption. No scheme ever stipulates the possible action that could follow the malpractice… Indian bureaucracy has let the country down… According to National Commission (NCEUS) report 2007, public servants received over Rupees 4,000 crores (1 billion dollars) in corruption last year, besides the cuts from several government schemes. 65% of India's working population live on half a dollar per day… Agriculture is fertile ground for poverty … 84% of farmers spent more than they earned and are often in debt trap… Legal system is overloaded with 33,635 cases pending in Supreme Court, 3,341,040 in High Courts and over 25 million cases in subordinate courts.

Within just five months of Indian independence, in January 1948, a few days before his assassination, Mahatma Gandhi wrote to the Home Minister Vallabhbhai Patel enclosing a letter from a fellow Congress friend Mr Kentatappaya of Hyderabad. The letter is summarised as follows:

Freedom was the only absorbing factor that guided us to follow Gandhi's leadership. Now that the goal has been reached all moral restrictions have been lost… People have begun to say that British governance was much better … the condition of our people has unquestionably deteriorated… The British denied us political freedom, protecting their vested interests but we have destroyed every shred of freedom even that of human soul … morality upheld by Gandhi is far from Congress's motive … they are corrupt … indulge openly in bribery, nepotism sanctioned by their corrupt members in power… Even the district collectors and Revenue officials do not feel free… A strict and honest officer cannot hold his position because false reports are carried to his ministers…

Demise of the mighty Maharajas: usurped by the British; robbed of wealth by the post-Independence State

Whilst the hypocrisy of and exploitation by the EIC and imperial rule are widely recognised, the fact that these same qualities have so often characterised the imperious rule of iconic post-Independence leaders is barely discussed. The fate of the Maharajas is a case in point. The EIC had entered into treaties with 560 independent states, setting out their relationship with the sovereign power. Geographically these states occupied nearly half of India, being ruled and managed by as many Rajas, Maharajas and Nawabs. In 1848 the EIC had arbitrarily introduced a *doctrine of lapse*, by which, if any princely ruler were to die without an heir, then his state would be annexed to British India. Adoption of a child was disallowed by the doctrine. The EIC managed to annex six out of the total of 560 states and principalities during the nine years prior to the Indian Army Mutiny of 1857. The EIC's deceit and greed, even though it was for the benefit of its shareholders, have been justly criticised and condemned by historians as treachery and a violation of its earlier treaties with the Maharajas.

During India's Independence negotiations, all Maharajas in their spirit of patriotism, renouncing all their riches and entitlements, jointly agreed to surrender the ownership of their states to the new sovereign Government of India for an agreed token sum of money, sanctioned by the government to be paid annually to each Maharaja. This paltry amount was guaranteed against any future reduction or confiscation, as the agreed amount which served as the livelihood for the sustenance and upkeep of the henceforth stateless Maharajas and their families. They were allowed to retain their title of Maharaja, which served as little more than a hollow reminder of their ostentatious past. The agreement was ratified by the Indian Parliament and solemnly incorporated into the Indian Constitution. It was a sacred document, and the promises it made were sacred, too, so at least the Maharajas believed.

But only 24 years later, in 1971, there came the thunderbolt of an arbitrary decision by the Government, going back on its solemn word given by the founding fathers of the new India on the eve of Independence. Distraught and shattered by the news of the impending dishonouring of these solemn agreements, the Maharajas collectively challenged the Government's decision in the Supreme Court, which upheld the Maharajas' challenge, rejecting Prime Minister Indira Gandhi's argument that the President of India, which in substance meant the Government of India, had inherited the primacy of the British Crown. The court ruled that the President and the Government had no constitutional power to nullify the covenants made to the princes, which had been solemnly incorporated into the text of the basic law of the nation.

Instead of honouring the Supreme Court's decision and upholding the sanctity of the Constitution, the all-powerful Indira Gandhi undermined the Constitution by exercising her brute majority in the subservient Parliament. The decision of the nation's highest court and the sacrosanct name of its founding fathers were violated and drowned in the mud of political expediency. It is not my aim to defend the feudal rule historically practised by many maharajas, but robbing all of the 560 princes – who had already surrendered all their territories, collectively comprising almost half of the newly emerging India – of their paltry annual amount of Privy Purse, emoluments worth in total less than £150 million per year in today's money, was an unparalleled act of public misconduct by the leader of the world's largest democracy. This was a democratic Indian government governed by rule of law and the Constitution, recognising *sanctity of contract*. This misappropriation of property through a breach of contract far surpassed the EIC's sin of having taken back only about 6 of the 560 states, by the much-criticised EIC, which was a 17th-century private trading organisation operating in a distant land and not bound by the conventional rules of law.

The uncomfortable truth – lost opportunity

Why is it that despite starting with the best legacy of all former colonies, with a fully functional civil and physical infrastructure at the outset of independence, India still has about 400 million living in abject poverty and illiteracy? At the centre of all discussions about India during the last three centuries, the poverty of its masses has been most conspicuous. Until India became independent this extreme poverty was blamed on British colonial rule. It is now almost 70 years since the British left India and the country became independent and the situation has not changed.

At the end of World War II, India was a well-functioning economy for that time, with a trade surplus and a fair amount of sterling and dollar reserves, and was better off than most of the countries between Turkey and Japan, including China, Hong Kong, Singapore, Taiwan and Korea, and even ended as creditors of Britain. With half the world reeling from the horrors of war, India had emerged intact and in good shape, with all essential infrastructure in place for take-off by 1947, the year of Independence. The post-war boom offered the opportunity to build upon the great legacies left behind by the British – an opportunity which was sadly missed due to India's close proximity to the Soviet Bloc in preference to the prosperous US and Western democracies. The money India provided to Britain for its war efforts against Japan and Germany was promptly repaid with interest.

In its first prime minister, Jawaharlal Nehru, India had a figurehead of towering authority and incorruptibility, who espoused and exemplified the high principles of public life. However, his inspirational vision for the nation's future could not be matched by his Soviet-backed socialist economic strategy and foreign policy, while the country lacked the means of raising adequate capital to realise Nehru's declared promise to the people of India. He betrayed his nation by keeping a misplaced distance from the economically successful and friendly western democracies of the free world and their capital markets, thereby blocking much-needed foreign direct investments for the crucial post-Independence decades of his newly freed India, the world's largest democracy.

Instead, Nehru astonished the free world by developing close affinity with the dictatorial and totalitarian regime of Stalin's USSR, a war-torn, devastated, poor and isolated economy. The USSR was a conglomerate of (around) 12 ruthlessly controlled colonised states, besides the ten newly acquired and occupied East European countries in 1945. This was a far more iniquitous regime than the British rule in India, which Nehru had personally fought, along with other freedom seeking leaders, for over four decades. He focused on and personally relished in raising India's 'non-aligned' profile in third-world politics throughout the 17 years of his rule, besides also proudly leading an international club of autocrats and dictators, such as Nasser (Egypt), Sukarno (Indonesia), Tito (the former Yugoslavia), Nkrumah (Ghana) and Zhou Enlai (China), while sadly failing to deliver practical solutions for the most pressing domestic issues: poverty, health, primary literacy, social justice, the domestic economy and welfare. As a result, India's pace of industrial growth was seriously stunted, depriving the country of precious financial development funds from the US and European nations, due to Nehru's very personal choice of adopting rigid socialist policies, with a lack of regard for the urgent tasks at hand of uplifting India's most deprived and desperately poor population. Even after 12 unproductive post-Independence years down the path of socialism, Nehru, when speaking in 1959 on the 11th anniversary of Mahatma Gandhi's death, publicly announced that: 'any going back on my declared pledge to establish socialism in India would be a betrayal of the nation', criticising national and world leaders who were advising better routes for India's economic development.

At the most critical time of the Chinese invasion of India in 1962, none of Nehru's cultivated non-aligned comrades offered any moral or material support. Only Britain, Israel and the US came forward with total and unconditional help, even though Nehru had refused full diplomatic representation to the State of Israel and often spited the mighty and rich US in favour of his close association with the isolated and struggling economies of the USSR and China. The new state of Israel promptly delivered two ship-loads of arms free of charge and the prime minister, Ben-Gurion, announced he was waiting to hear from India about whatever further help was required. Immediate and most valuable US support by word and deed came with squadrons of bombers, and other large quantities of essential munitions to help India ward off further Chinese intrusions. Britain's RAF cargo planes soon arrived in India carrying self-loading rifles and other necessary munitions, replacing India's desperately outdated 303 rifles.

Despite these exceptionally generous and positive gestures from its hitherto-ignored natural allies, there were still no signs of change in Nehru's less-than-friendly attitude towards the US, the richest and most powerful democracy in the world. Forty-five painfully long years of inward-looking closed-door socialist economic policies imposed by Nehru cost India most dearly, resulting in over 400 million illiterate citizens left in poverty and hunger, deprived of all dignity and hope and resigned to their fate and karma – a tragedy amounting to an abuse of their fundamental human rights.

In sharp contrast to the first four-and-a-half stagnant decades of Nehru's era of shutting doors on itself, India today – only 20 years after opening its gates to the world economy, free trade and liberal thinking – has found a position on the global economic ladder and rapidly made very significant gains. These extraordinary advances achieved in a short space of time, warrant in-depth investigation by economic historians to quantify the extent of the lost opportunities for economic productivity and wealth creation during the Nehru era of the first four decades after Independence. Such parochial and narrow-minded resistance to economic and social change drove India to the verge of bankruptcy in the early 1990s, before the government was compelled to make a U-turn two decades ago.

India's average annual economic (GDP) growth rate for the 30 years from 1950 to 1980 was 3.5%, no better than the rate of population growth. After the economic reform – which began in 1991 under the leadership of a non-political and determined finance minister Dr Manmohan Singh – the decade up until 2000 saw the average annual growth rate rise to 5.9% pa. And, in the decade to 2010, annual growth has risen further to 7.3%. In Forbes' list of World Billionaires 2011, 50 Indians are included. As reported in the *Times of India*, by 2015 Forbes listed 14 Indian families in the inaugural list of Forbes' 50 richest families in Asia. The barrier to entry was US$2.9 billion and a minimum of three generations 'actively involved in building their … fortunes'. Indians hold 14 of the 50 spots, the most from any jurisdiction. Worldwide, Forbes' list included 100 Indians in 2015, the number having doubled in four years. With such rapid progress since the mid-1990s, how much more could have been achieved for the Indian people if this approach had been endorsed from the outset of Independence? Those four lost decades have meant that poverty in India will take far longer to alleviate.

Partition and separation – the closed-door era

The strong-headed Nehru has often been blamed by some historians for causing, or at best for not preventing, the partition of the subcontinent into the separate countries of India and Pakistan which resulted in the historic massacre of at least two million innocent people as a result of the boundary changes involved in Independence. In his book *Jinnah: India – Partition – Independence*, published in 2009, Jaswant Singh MP, a senior leader in the Bharatiya Janata Party (BJP) and former Minister for External Affairs, mentions Jinnah's secular and nationalist credentials and terms him as 'a champion of Hindu–Muslim unity'. He blames the Congress, controlled by Nehru and Gandhi, for the partition and specifically underlines the fact that Jinnah never attacked Hindus or Hinduism, nor did Islam ever come into his thinking. Jinnah's opposition, according to the author, was focused on the Congress and its leadership. He also feels that Nehru's incomprehensible tactlessness, more so his inability to restrain himself from promulgating his views to the press on almost every occasion, not only generated huge contention and multiple controversies, but also developed Jinnah's animus into almost hatred towards the Congress and Nehru and Gandhi.

Former RSS (Rashtriya Swayamsevak Sangh – a Hindu nationalist organisation) Chief, K.S. Sudarshan, too, in a recent interview expressed the view that Jinnah was a true nationalist and a promoter of Hindu–Muslim unity until pushed into a corner by the Congress which, by the beginning of 1947, Nehru had persuaded to his own thinking. According to Sudarshan, Gandhi's soft spot for Nehru resulted in the partition of India. Jinnah's assertion that 'Muslims are a separate nation' was the later-date argument of a lawyer. He had nursed a feeling that as a secular national leader he also stood a fair chance at representing both communities. The only hurdle to the idea of his becoming the first prime minister was the Congress leadership. If Nehru had shown some grace, knowing well of Jinnah's terminal illness, and had allowed Jinnah to lead the new nation for the first term as prime minister, the cruel partition, with the resulting post-Independence genocide and the painful migration of many millions of refugees, as well as the continuing boundary disputes and ill will between the two countries, might have been avoided.

Many people in India have argued whether things were not better in many spheres of life during the British days. It is a common refrain among the older generations that governance was then not so decrepit, bribery was not so rampant, favouritism not so common, corruption and plunder of public funds not so pervasive, injustice not so blatant, and bureaucracy not so partisan as today. All these upsetting features of contemporary life in India begin to look even more ghastly when one looks at the continuing poverty of a large mass of the nation's population, the battered state of primary education and medical facilities, an inadequate power supply, and a lack of clean drinking water in the cities. Worse still is the lack of any water in many villages and the highly unsatisfactory condition of roads, ports and airports.

The contrasting conditions in the care and responsibility involved in the development of many towns and cities during and after the British rule is nowhere better illustrated than in the 2009 illustrated book *Bombay Then, Mumbai Now*, which catalogues and contrasts the urban development of Mumbai, pre- and post-Independence. Unfortunately, even the soaring success of today's newly liberalised Indian economy has not, as yet, filtered down to benefit the nation's poorest sections, and one-third of Indian children remain undernourished to this day.

The Washington-based advocacy group Global Financial Integrity (GFI) calculated in August 2010 that during the period corresponding to India's highest GDP growth, income inequality actually increased. Similar comments voiced earlier, in February 2010, by Anthony Barnett, editor of openDemocracy (oD) – *OpenDemocracy.net* – said: 'But India's absolute poverty condemns a now wealthy, modern society. It has to be willed not just regretted or blamed on 'neo-liberalism' to have lasted so extensively.' Nor has the liberalised economy extinguished large-scale corruption, given the unedifying fact that the country with the largest amounts of private numbered bank deposits in Switzerland is India. Moreover, an astounding US$125 billion of public money was siphoned out of India by the nexus of corrupt politicians, officials and big business from 2000 to 2008, according to GFI. A well-known example of such irregularities in public finances was the grossly substandard, massively over-budget and embarrassingly delayed construction for the 2010 Commonwealth Games, which consumed over £5 billion of public funds. Given the seven years' advance notice for the project, the low labour rates in India and the fact that the army, too, had to be called in to help finish the job, one can only imagine the level of mismanagement and the financial scale of the corruption in this national 'show-case' project, which has proved to be the most expensive Commonwealth Games in history. Fortunately for India, the sportsmen and athletes, rising to the occasion with dedication and professionalism, salvaged and restored the nation's pride with 101 medals, taking India to second place.

Dr Manmohan Singh's pioneering chain of reforms during his tenure as Finance Minister (1995–1999) rapidly opened up India's four-decades-long suffocated economy in the 1990s. This was later followed by another very bold landmark initiative by the senior BJP Cabinet minister in the coalition National Democratic Alliance (NDA) government, Professor Ram Jethmalani's most courageous repeal of Nehru's four-decades-old pernicious Land Ceiling Act, which liberated the construction industries, resulting in an unprecedented nationwide rapid growth in the building and housing sectors, which created vast employment opportunities for over one million labourers and a large number of civil engineers and architects. Despite these important advances, there still persisted the culture of an inward-looking, misguided pride combined with a long-standing suspicion of the outside world in many quarters and at high levels. This attitude, akin to a siege mentality, had deprived India of enormous early opportunities for foreign direct investment and technology for the vital first 40 years post-Independence.

This closed-door mentality also prevented the arrival of free foreign aid and highly skilled relief workers to India's natural disaster zones on several occasions, including the devastating Latur earthquake of 1993, the unprecedented ferocious cyclone and floods in coastal Orissa in 1999 and the Asian tsunami of 2004 which savaged coastal areas of Tamil Nadu. Earlier, too, the many thousands who died and the 500 000 poor rural populace rendered homeless by the major cyclones that struck Orissa in 1971 and Andhra Pradesh in 1977, were similarly deprived of outside international assistance.

Despite their awesome scale none of these natural tragedies was officially declared National Calamities, a designation which would have automatically triggered inflows of foreign relief, aid and expert assistance. The government has thus repeatedly deprived the poorest Indians of their right to receive emergency international relief which would have helped to mitigate the effects of the devastation on hundreds of thousands of poor peasants who had lost their lives, homes and livelihoods.

The callous and negligent stance of government officials towards India's poorest classes also contributed to the scandal that followed the worst industrial accident in history, which killed 20 000 people in Bhopal. Compensation for victims remains derisory and the toxic site, which has never been cleaned up, has continued to contaminate water supplies causing serious health problems and birth defects. An explanation for why the tragedy continues more than 30 years on was offered by Indra Sinha in his careful analysis published in *The Guardian* on 4 December 2009 – 25 years after the disaster:

> When people ask, "Why is the disaster continuing? Why has the factory not been cleaned? Why have Union Carbide and Dow not faced justice?", the answer is this: Union Carbide's victims are still dying in Bhopal because India itself is dying under the corrupt and self-serving rule of rotten leaders.

'Walking on two legs' – economic growth, social justice and a colossal task

Rajiv Gandhi was the first Indian prime minister to show signs of fresh and open thinking, attempting to break out of the 40-year-old tightly knit, suffocating socialist web that had shut out India's natural allies among the prosperous Western democracies. He started with the all-important liberalisation of the fledgling information technology sector, making him the founding father of India's globally prominent position in IT and software technology today. Sadly, before he could make a major impact, the compassionate and trusting Prime Minister Rajiv and his dream were betrayed by some of his close associates in the cabinet and an inward-looking and corrupt civil service, still obsessed with the closed and constrictive relationship with the Soviet Union and a socialist doctrine. They did not appreciate Rajiv's bold, honest and innocent admission that only 15% of the money sanctioned by New Delhi reaches the intended welfare projects in the provinces.

By a remarkable turn of destiny in Indian politics, Rajiv's unfinished mission was taken up by his widow Sonia Gandhi, Chairman of the National Advisory Committee of the Congress Party. Sonia was unanimously supported by her victorious Congress Party for the post of prime minister. Instead, she declared her choice and decision for a world-class economist and a leader of high integrity in Dr Manmohan Singh for prime minister. With a history of sound administrative expertise at the World Bank and also as the governor of the Reserve Bank of India, Singh's appointment attracted nationwide applause for Sonia's excellent choice. Dr Singh had already established himself as India's most successful and popular Finance Minister, having decisively turned around the nation's economy during his five-year term from 1991 to 1996. He is renowned for having introduced innovative economic reforms while courageously slashing the 45-year-long stifling government controls. Each of his five progressive and carefully planned budget presentations were enthusiastically received and drew nationwide applause from the business and industry communities and economists. Simultaneously he courageously initiated his pioneering process of the privatisation of public sector companies, which allowed the dismantling of the State's control on India's economy and removed the obstacles that stood in the way of foreign direct investment. Singh had joined the Cabinet as Finance Minister in the most critical year of 1991, when India was facing a serious economic crisis, with foreign reserves well under US$1 billion, enough to pay for only a few weeks' import bills. His pioneering initiatives for a liberal market economy were reflected in the resulting early signs of economic recovery.

Recovery received further impetus a decade later when Sonia Gandhi invited him for the prime minister's post in 2004, an appointment which resulted in the country's foreign reserves increasing to almost $300 billion, while the annual GDP levels were maintained between 5% and 9%. The humble and compassionate Dr Singh was the first prime minister to admit the existence of widespread illiteracy and malnutrition, describing the continued hunger of India's hundreds of millions of abject poor as 'a matter of national shame'. It is notable that this courageous confession, the first of its kind from an Indian prime minister in 60 years, came from the first national leader to attempt to tackle, head-on, this chronic and long-neglected human rights violation, while simultaneously attempting to breathe life into the economy.

Unfortunately the lack of unity amongst ministers belonging to the coalition's minority partners hampered his attempts. Singh's candid admission of the dire condition of millions of Indian citizens did, however, lend further credibility to his unaccomplished promise: to simultaneously prioritise the parallel goals of economic growth and social justice, which he had eloquently described as 'walking on two legs'.

It was 62 years after Independence, in August 2009, when the determined Dr Singh with the support of Sonia Gandhi made history by passing through Parliament the long-awaited bill, The Right of Children to Free and Compulsory Education. It is a sad reflection on post-Independence India that it took more than half a century to have this fundamental human right enshrined in Indian law. Sonia Gandhi and Manmohan Singh will be remembered for their passionate efforts in scoring the landmark victory in March 2010 of getting the Women's Reservation Bill cleared through Parliament, despite 14 years of acrimony and political obstacles deployed against the revolutionary bill.

Yet another remarkable achievement in the same era by the determined duo was that of the giant legislative leap forward in clearing the Right to Information (RTI) Act of 2005, which was passed after many years of campaigning by NGOs, despite stiff opposition from political power-brokers, many quarters of the government and the opposition. So profound has been its impact in the empowerment of the underprivileged and uneducated that it has been described as a second gaining of independence. This was followed by two more landmark bills: the National Rural Employment Guarantee Act 2005 – a social security measure that aims to guarantee the 'right to work' and ensure livelihood; and, a year later, the Tribal Land Act 2006, concerning the rights of forest-dwelling communities to land and other resources denied to them for many decades. The above landmark bills rolled out in 2005, 2006, 2009 and 2010 were followed by yet another major triumph by Singh and Sonia Gandhi, with the innovative Food Security Bill 2013 for the poor, which passed through Parliament despite fierce resistance from the main opposition party.

India's five-yearly national elections in mid-2014 resulted in a resounding victory for the main opposition party, the BJP, providing the second opportunity for forming the government after a gap of ten years. Mr Narendra Modi, the popular and charismatic leader of the BJP, was responsible for their landslide victory and for Congress's debacle, while the other major political parties faltered in disarray. Modi's spectacular and meteoric rise from the Chief Ministership of one state to the prime ministership of a whole country astonished everyone. The rapid ascent of this great orator received further impetus with the help of the unprecedented media support for Mr Modi, and all of that has immensely benefited his party overnight, after its 50-year-long struggle in the political arena. The electorate, too, placed its faith in Modi's three main election promises: economic development, elimination of corruption, and – to use his innovative slogan – 'less government, more governance'. All three tenets are inextricably linked. The conversion of these campaign promises into practice is going to be a colossal task. If he should succeed, Narendra Modi could well become India's strongest prime minister since Independence, leading India to firmly establish itself as a global economic power.

The former central Cabinet Minister, Mr Jagmohan, wrote the following in the national daily the *Asian Age* on India's Independence Day anniversary on 15 August 2008:

> 61 years after independence India has today the largest number of poor, the largest number of illiterate and malnourished people in the world with ever widening income gap... Post 1947 India has been badly let down by its leadership in almost all walks of life... It is a culture of callousness, corruption and conceit that dominates Indian Public life ... 6 out of 7 women are illiterate.

It is also very distressing to learn about the prevalence of slavery in today's modern-day democratic India despite having inherited a powerful and first-class judiciary, a well-regulated and codified law and order system, and the vast, organised institution of the Indian police force, which was, painstakingly trained by and introduced to India by the British before Independence.

This is what we now read in the Global Slavery Index (GSI) 2014 published by the Walk Free Foundation in Perth, Australia (17 November 2014): that, in terms of absolute numbers of people in modern slavery, India remains top of the GSI, with an estimated 14.29 million people, including children, trapped in modern-day slavery in India, and 2.09 million in Pakistan. India accounts for approximately 40% of the world total of 35.8 million people under bondage. The report states that in India all forms of modern slavery exist through human trafficking, forced labour, debt bondage, forced marriage and commercial sexual exploitation. Bonded labour which sees families enslaved for generations, trafficking and forced sexual exploitation are particularly prevalent, with the lower castes and migrant workers disproportionately affected.

Yet in the midst of this discreditable reality, India's political classes take great pride in India being the largest democracy in the world. Although the maintenance of democracy in a country the size of India is undoubtedly a worthy achievement, it is important to recognise that the foundations of today's lasting democracy, and the all-important culture of fair, effective and innovative central and provincial governance in a country of over 20 languages, many castes and religions, were laid during the long years of stable British rule and sustained by the egalitarian institutions and infrastructure inherited in 1947.

Perhaps therefore the more pertinent question is not how democracy in India has been sustained, but rather what tangible benefit has it brought to the 400 million Indian citizens who continue to live below the poverty line?

Philanthropy in India

In addition to the British contributions to industry and administration, a culture of philanthropy and social responsibility was absorbed into Indian society and industry. The spirit of British philanthropy was responsible for the founding of many higher education institutions during the Raj including Hindu College (today the Presidency University, Kolkata) in 1816 and the Elphinstone College, Mumbai, in 1827. Many dedicated missionaries and nurses also arrived from Britain to 'serve the Empire and the poor'. During the 200 years of British rule, the Parsis, more than any other community, observed and absorbed this culture and the value of social philanthropy for the common good. There can be no better example of Parsi philanthropy than that of the prodigious Tatas. A formidable 66% block-shareholding in Tata's flagship promoter company, Tata Sons – which in turn holds 22 key companies, including Tata Steel, Tata Motors and Tata Power – belong to Tata-registered charities making a huge contribution to the health and social welfare of many millions of Indians.

For many others, however, philanthropy often amounted to no more than the building of temples, and even today half of all donations by non-profit organisations go to religious activities. Almost 70 years after Independence, there has been little change in the charitable attitude of rich Indians. Reuters' report from Mumbai on the First Indian Philanthropy Forum of 24 March 2010 highlighted this fact by stating: 'in fact the wealthiest social class has the lowest level of giving.' Only 10% of charitable giving in India comes from individuals and the corporate sector, compared to 75% in the US. The report further identified that the proportion of personal wealth donated to non-religious causes is extremely low compared to other countries; if this is considered in the context of the huge need – with about 40% of Indians still living below the poverty line – this presents a significant obstacle on the path to national development. It is likely that more charitable funds reach the needy in India from foreign individual donors, including the huge endowments of the Bill & Melinda Gates Foundation and Warren Buffet, than from wealthy Indians, even though several of the world's richest billionaires are Indians. Gates and Buffet have begun successfully to spread their ethos of charitable giving in the US, enlisting many billionaires alongside them. Not only have most of India's new 100-odd billionaires failed to be inspired by the examples of Gates and Buffet, but even the latter's visit to India to harness a modest fraction of personal wealth towards improved healthcare and poverty alleviation met with little enthusiasm.

Although many of India's billionaires are unmoved to act on the inhumane deprivations suffered daily by their hundreds of millions of impoverished compatriots, a single visit by H.R.H. Prince Charles was enough to initiate an innovative new programme to improve the housing of slum-dwellers in Kolkata and Bengaluru (Bangalore). The notable and laudable exception – besides the long-standing tradition of Tata's philanthropy – has been the emergence of several leading philanthropic billionaires during the last decade, including Azim Premji of Wipro Ltd and Narayana Murthy of Infosys; their shining example is encouraging and has received richly deserved national attention, which has encouraged several more billionaires and other affluent business houses to follow their lead.

Reconciliation – 'balance and perspective'

The great Indian thinker, reformer and philosopher Raja Ram Mohan Roy (1772–1833) put forward an interesting view of British rule – and one that was remarkably balanced for the time:

> [T]hough it is impossible for a thinking man not to feel the evils of political subjection and dependence on a foreign people, yet when we reflect on the advantages which we have derived and may hope to derive from our connection with Great Britain, we may be reconciled to the present state of things which promises permanent benefits to our posterity.

Speaking at the Raja's first death centenary in the year 1933, the Nobel laureate Rabindranath Tagore described Roy as a man of dynamic power of personality, with a prophetic purity of vision and unconquerable heroism of soul, shedding radiance all over the land. As the founder of the popular and progressive spiritual and reformist movement known as Brahmo Samaj, Roy's views on how British rule modernised and improved Indian society were not held in isolation but were shared by many.

At about the same time, in his articles on India published in the *New York Daily Tribune* from 1853 to 1857, another major historical figure, Karl Marx, whilst denouncing the injustice of colonial exploitation, also recognised that British rule was nonetheless performing a painful but necessary task in terms of 'historical progress'. British administration and modernisation were replacing the hierarchical and taboo-laden social order of ancient India with a new, secular and progressive society. This in turn prepared the ground for India to enter the world stage in the 20th century, not only with its long-awaited independence but also with contemporary administrative, legal and social systems that were fit for purpose and, moreover, gave India a head start over other former colonies.

Never during these colonial years did relations between the ruling British and the subject Indians ever become as inimical, belligerent or violent as of that between the Dutch and Indonesians, the French and the Algerians, or the French and the Vietnamese, or as happened in the Spanish and Portuguese colonies. On the 60th anniversary of Independence, Jaithirth Rao founder of the IT software company Mphasis wrote in *The Indian Express*:

> The best minds among Indians of that era appreciated the contributions of the Raj. This was true of Dadabhoy Naoroji and R.C. Dutt, who were critics of British fiscal policy in India. It was true of great reformer Ram Mohan Roy, who told the Frenchman Victor Jacquemont that he wanted British rule to "continue for many years". It was true of Vivekananda, who admired the Kshatriya spirit of the Anglo-Saxon peoples. It was true of Syed Ahmed Khan, who felt that British rule made possible an evenly balanced Indian polity. It was true of Gandhi, whose opposition to British rule never deprived him of his admiration for the country of his youth. He was most upset with the prospect of Hitler bombing the "beautiful country" of Britain. It was true of Nehru, who acknowledged the debt he owed to the ideas developed by the British parliamentary system. It was true of Ambedkar, who saw British rule as the liberator of India's depressed classes. It was true of Ramaswami Naicker, who saw British rule as the catalyst that made possible a revolt against the entrenched homo hierarchicus.

Indian leaders that were harnessing the nationalist movement and organising it into a major political force for change had virtually all shared the experience of being educated overseas, principally in British universities, which were breeding grounds for the exchange of ideas concerning freedoms, universal suffrage and democracy. Most, too, had experienced racial prejudice, yet many also formed lifelong friendships with British reformers who were equally influenced by their Indian friends' philosophies and their desire for freedom from colonial rule.

By and large, most of the leaders of both the Indian freedom struggle and the British – in India and Britain – were able to maintain their equilibrium throughout: the British as colonial rulers of what most of them recognised and cherished as a highly civilized nation; and the Indians as the suffering subjects of a colonial administration which they were determined to end, but without completely breaking with its past. Despite their long-fought and hard-won freedom struggle, Indians continued to cherish their respect for and faith in the unique British sense of justice and fair play. Without this reciprocity of sentiments and respect for the values of an ultimately just and fair system of governance between the rulers and the ruled, the transition from colonial rule to independence would not have been so peaceful and orderly, nor would relations between the two nations have remained close well over half a century after parting company in 1947. This cordial and mutually respectful relationship was candidly recognised by the former Indian Prime Minister Manmohan Singh in a recent speech:

> What is significant about the Indo-British relationship is the fact that despite the economic impact of colonial rule, the relationship between individual Indians and Britons, even at the time of our Independence, was relaxed and, I may even say, benign...

Singh advised historians to revisit the historic Indo–British encounter with 'balance and perspective'. The above recognition and appreciation of the generally fair and mature nature of British society and the sound colonial governance that stemmed from it, is perhaps best exemplified by the fact that before World War II there were only five members in the Commonwealth. In 1947 India became the 6th. Today there are 55 members, and almost all former colonies of imperial Britain, with the exception of the two that did not qualify, Aden (now Yemen) and Burma (now Myanmar), gladly and voluntarily opted to join the British Commonwealth after gaining their independence.

My hope in the long-lasting relationship between India and Britain is pinned on my faith in India's ancient and valuable heritage of philosophical past and Britain's traditionally gentle manner of dealing with the political irritants and provocations, often with patience and reticence. London's diplomacy in ignoring the Indian Prime Minister Inder Kumar Gujral's rude and undiplomatic outburst calling Britain a third-rate power in the middle of a state visit by Queen Elizabeth, astonishing and embarrassing over a million of the Indian diaspora in Britain, is an example from 1997, although unfortunately no Indian parliamentarian or politician from Britain showed any concern.

Fortunately, however, India is moving forward in this regard. Just eight years after Gujral's ill-judged statement, the subsequent Prime Minister Dr Manmohan Singh, signalled the arrival of a more mature and balanced perspective in his acceptance address for the honorary Doctorate of Civil Law by the University of Oxford in 2005:

> Our notions of the rule of law, of a Constitutional government, of a free press, of a professional civil service, of modern universities and research laboratories have all been fashioned in the crucible where an age-old civilization of India met the dominant Empire of the day. These are all elements which we still value and cherish. Our judiciary, our legal system, our bureaucracy and our police are all great institutions, derived from British-Indian administration and they have served our country exceedingly well.
>
> .... even at the height of our campaign for freedom from colonial rule, we did not entirely reject the British claim to good governance. We merely asserted our natural right to self-governance.

Even though Dr Singh's carefully worded statement attracted fire from sections of the Indian media and political classes at the time, today, with the perspective offered by the passage of time and the benefit of hindsight, it is possible for an Indian prime minister to assert that India's experience with Britain also had its beneficial consequences.

It is encouraging that there is the beginning of a return to balance. A recently published book *Beyond the Call of Duty* by Veena Prasad and V. Raghunathan celebrates the prolific achievements of a dozen British gentlemen who devoted their lives to the greater good of India. There were many more.

As a scientist, I graciously request the reader to survey the meticulously researched evidence in the following 21 chapters for themselves. It is my wish that future generations are empowered with fact and both Britain and India are lifted above historical amnesia and political expediency.

To provide a country with an enduring civil and physical infrastructure required grand plans. From the first boats making the 12 000-mile journey via the Cape of Good and carrying the girders for more than 100 000 bridges, track for 45 000 miles of railway and countless pieces of machinery to the creation of colleges, hospitals, museums and libraries, the following

21 chapters chart a course through the unparalleled feats that established India as the world's largest democracy, culminating with a globally powerful Indian diaspora that has its roots in the immense early globalisation of the EIC and the opportunity that followed in its wake. It also stands as a testament to the spectacular talent and audacious vision of the finest British civil engineers and civil servants of the 19th century tasked with laying the foundations for a new, unified India, often under arduous conditions and sometimes at great personal sacrifice.

There is much that remains positive and a legacy to those first easterly-bound sailing ships, carrying the materials, manpower and ingenuity that began *The Making of India.*

Chapter 2

THE EAST INDIA COMPANY: AMBITIONS TO RULE THE WAVES

Before the EIC there was no Calcutta.
After a century of development the swamps became the
Eastern capital of the world's greatest empire bar none.
WINSTON CHURCHILL

Love it or loathe it, the East India Company (EIC) stamped its presence on India bringing with it triumphs and disasters. For 250 years, from the first intrepid voyages in small ships heading for a land thousands of miles away to its eventual dissolution in 1858, the Company ruthlessly pursued its ambitions. The irony is that such was the strength of the foundations that the much-reviled EIC built in its all-conquering drive, that India in the 21st century is now playing a leading role in enterprises around the world. So our story about the Making of India begins with the EIC: not to examine its motives or morals, but to study the origins of the infrastructure, at all levels, which has enabled India to grow into the nation it is today.

Queen Elizabeth I sanctioned two great trading companies before the founding of the EIC. The first was the Muscovy Company, for Russian trade, in 1555, with the second concession going to the Turkey Company in 1581. The latter had been approved with the express purpose of trading over-land, in 1593 as far as the East Indies, and it was later renamed the Levant Company. The Levant Company experienced great difficulties with its trade route and little good came of it, but all was not lost. Two prominent members had sailed to Sumatra and Bantam via the Cape in 1596, prompting a number of other merchants to raise money for a voyage to India. On 24 September 1599 they put together £30,133 3s. 8d. and applied to Elizabeth for a charter. However, political wrangles were under way as Britain sought an honourable peace with Spain – eventually achieved in 1604 by King

James I – and the document put forward to Elizabeth by the merchants was amended so that it would not include trading 'where the Spaniards and Portuguese have any castle, fort, blockhouse or commandant'. Finally, on the last day of the year 1600, the EIC was incorporated as 'the Governor and Company of Merchants of London trading into the East Indies'. The number of subscribers was 217.

The EIC's first voyage began on 16 February 1601. Individual shareholders themselves undertook the early trading expeditions, known as 'separate' voyages. This must have demanded some courage, as there was only one rudimentary map available – the Mercator projection, which is still used today. England was still at war with Spain and Portugal, and probably because the Portuguese were strong along the coasts of India, the first two voyages were not directed there. When a richly laden Portuguese carrack that had left a 'factory' – trading house – at Bantam was captured, the queen was secretly pleased, although she had to show a different face to the Portuguese ambassador.

The ships of the third voyage were the *Red Dragon* of 700 tons and the *Hector* of 500 tons, with a pinnace, the *Consent*, a mere 150 tons, and a company of 280 merchants and mariners all told. The general of this fleet of 'cockle shells' was William Keeling, who took passage in the *Hector*. The outward voyage was not successful to begin with and after 13 months the vessels docked at Aden.

On a later attempt from Aden, Captain Hawkins dropped anchor at the entrance to the River Tapti on 24 August 1608 in the *Hector* – the first ship to fly the English flag off the coast of India. He disembarked at Surat and visited the court of the Mughal Emperor Jahangir (1569–1627) at Agra. The emperor received Hawkins favourably and subsequently granted the English permission to settle in Surat. However, the Portuguese were strong enough in India to get the decree revoked, and Hawkins waited in vain for two years at Agra, marrying an Armenian wife at Jahangir's suggestion. In the end, Hawkins gave up and he and his wife embarked on an England-bound ship in January 1612.

The EIC did, however, establish its first trading factory in 1611 at Machilipatnam. In the first 12 years of settlement, only two factories appeared to have been built on Indian soil, with the second in the charge of one Thomas Aldworth in Surat. Meanwhile, the political map of the world was being redrawn and, in 1615, English naval squadrons were driving Portuguese vessels from Indian Ocean waters.

The factory at Surat was now permanent. Aldworth, who had adapted well to his host country, pronounced India to be 'the only key to open all the rich and best trade in the Indies'. He was astute in his assessment: the nutmeg from Indonesia – recognised as part of the East Indies and held tenaciously in the hands of the Dutch – he declared to be 'more than worth its weight in gold'.

The era of great trading companies had grown from Queen Elizabeth's steadfast determination to keep all predators at cannon range. In part she looked to the EIC to check foreign aggression, making sure the Company possessed the tools and funds to complete her wishes – thus the 'fighting company' operated as both a mercantile operation and a military presence. The growth of England into a great maritime nation and trading empire, with the EIC at the forefront, was established.

When Elizabeth died in 1603, the new monarch – King James I of England, James VI of Scotland (1566–1625) – was equally ready for the task of building up England's navy, which went hand in hand with construct-ing vessels for the EIC. The shipyards at Chatham, Woolwich and Deptford were considerably expanded. Deptford – formed by the EIC itself – also built two fine Indiamen, the *Trades Increase* and the *Peppercorn*, in 1609. These vessels were possibly the first constructed under contract for the EIC.

The first great city of the British Empire, established by the EIC, was Madras. When earlier EIC trading posts 'north of the sliver of no man's land that was to be called Madras' came under pressure from the Dutch and Portuguese, Francis Day, 'an Honourable John Company factor' as well as its broker, sailed south to look for a better settlement. He stumbled across a sandy spit of surf-wracked beach some three miles long and one mile across, protected on two sides by rivers and on the third by an angry sea. But of greater importance was an encounter with a local governor of the waning Vijayanaga Empire who was willing to sell 'that useless strip of land'. It was on that land grant of July 1639 that Day and his superi-or, Andrew Cogan, and their dubashes, or agents, built a fortified factory, christening it on St George's Day, 23 April 1640, as Fort St George. This fort was the first major construction of the British Empire – courtesy of the EIC – and remains today a tourist attraction.

Fully settled into Madras, the small settlement grew over the next hun-dred years into a thriving metropolis with garden houses, hard-core roads and major improvements to the rivers so that the local people could wash clothes. Food grown there benefited both communities and the 'factory' became the first factory of the colonial powers in the real sense, as some manufacturing – or packaging of goods – took place there from around 1660.

EIC merchants also settled on the west coast of India, especially between Mangalore and Bombay. In 1534 the Portuguese had captured the islands of Bombay (*Bom Baía* – literally the 'Good Bay') and established a factory there. The territories passed to the English Crown in 1662 as part of the dowry in the marriage of Charles II and the Portuguese Catherine of Braganza. In 1668 the EIC leased Bombay from the Crown.

At Karwar, an English factory was established from 1638 until 1752 to advance the pepper trade. The Company was beginning to realise, in the same way as its Dutch East India Company rival, that countries east of Arabia were rich in spices, and that huge profits were likely to accrue for those with the will and cannon to augment their cause. However, the threat from the Dutch East India Company was eliminated under the terms of the Anglo-Dutch merger in 1688. The resulting shift in English trade from spices to cloth also resulted in the relocation of EIC bases to the three newly created and British-built cities of Calcutta, Madras and Bombay.

In 1690 the Nawab of Bengal granted the EIC the rights to establish a trading post in the territories that would become Calcutta, located on the eastern banks of the Hooghly River. The original EIC Fort William was built in 1694. By the 1720s, Calcutta had overtaken Madras as the principal port of trade and was expanding rapidly, with the population increasing from 10 000 to 400 000 by 1756. By the 1750s the disease-ridden swamplands of the territory were beginning to undergo the transformation into a thriving trade centre. The relative safety of its fortifications and the boon to trade development through the EIC attracted an influx of local Indian merchants and artisans. The newly created 'Company' town was 'fast becoming the centre of Bengali enterprise and culture'.

However, relations with the local Nawabs and the EIC had been deteriorating. Power struggles within the Mughal Empire and rivalry between the French and English in India heightened tensions as all parties vied for an increased stake in trade and territories. Setback to the EIC's hegemony in Calcutta came in June 1756 when the Nawab of Bengal Siraj ud-Daulah's forces captured Fort William. The capture has gone down in history as the infamous and much-retold 'Black Hole of Calcutta' controversy.

EIC retribution was swift and opportunistic. In January 1757 Robert Clive's forces retook Calcutta with little resistance from the Nawab's troops.

Though a treaty forged in February of that year between the English and Siraj ud-Daulah saw the EIC regain its trading rights, neither side believed this to be a permanent settlement. Siraj ud-Daulah was negotiating with the French – then at war with the English – while the English were colluding with the Seths – the banking dynasty – and Mir Jafar who held ambitions to be the next Nawab of Bengal. On 23 June 1757 the armies of Clive and Siraj ud-Daulah confronted each other at 'the mango grove of' Plassey. While a small minority bravely fought the English, the vast majority did not enter the battle as they were under the command of the traitor Mir Jafar who headed Siraj ud-Daulah's army. The 'skirmish' led to the remark 'that Clive won the battle of Plassey in spite of himself'. Mir Jafar, heavily in debt to the EIC, became little more than a 'puppet nawab' and within a decade the civil and revenue administration of Bengal – the diwani – was granted to the EIC. The outcome of the battle of Plassey allowed the English to consolidate its claim in India and push the French out of southern India. In 1772 Calcutta was declared the capital of Bengal and became the headquarters of the EIC.

Trade expansion

At the outset, EIC shareholders assessed Indian trade to be all but confined to goods of quality exported from London, for which India would exchange spices and fine muslin cloth. English trade on a large scale began with Bengal in about 1633, before the acquisition of the province and when the economy of the rich India was ahead of that of Britain. By 1700, some 20 vessels carried an estimated 2000 tons of goods. In 1759 30 vessels with an aggregate burden of 4000 tons sailed from Calcutta. The chief Indian exports were opium from western India, Bihar and Rangpur, silk manufactured goods and raw silk from Murshidabad and Rajshahi, plus cotton cloth from Patna. Apart from a few textiles, the principal import was bullion.

The Company plied the south India routes with dozens of ships, creating a thriving trade in cotton and silk piece goods, indigo, saltpetre and spices, before installing the first steam engine in Calcutta. 'Ships were virtually laden up to the gunwales' according to one observer. Most EIC vessels would return after a year at sea to sell their Indian spices and wares in England, making a handsome profit for those investors prepared to wait for a high return on capital. However, the EIC faced stern opposition to its monopoly from another group of English investors; the two entities merged in 1708 as the United Company of Merchants of England Trading to the East Indies, or the United Company. The United Company was organised into a court of 24 directors, elected annually, that worked through committees. The United Company carried on in its laissez-faire approach to trading, retaining the name EIC.

After the EIC acquired control of Bengal in 1757, Indian policy was influenced, until 1773 – when the British Parliament passed the Regulating Act – by shareholders' meetings, where shareholders' votes could be bought by the purchase of shares. The organisation still provided thousands of regular jobs back in London. Cash in hand spoke volumes against 'more bread tomorrow', while the Company's interest in land politics, other than to expand trade, was virtually nil, relying on the local zamindars and officials to collect revenue in an unregulated system open to abuses.

Internationally, however, the EIC was probably the most liberal, generous and public-spirited concern that ever held a trading charter. Its treatment of both officers and petty officers was truly royal in its munificence. Gifts of valuable plate and thousands of pounds of money were invariably awarded to captains who successfully defended their ships against the foe, and the EIC was constantly helping the Admiralty with both money and ships.

In 1779 it offered a bounty for the raising of 6000 seamen and, not content with this, built three ships, the *Ganges*, the *Carnatic* and the *Bombay Castle*, at its own expense, according to Basil Lubbock in his book *The Blackwall Frigates* (1927). When those three ships were built, Iberia could not challenge Britain on the oceans or in the iron workshops: Britain's forge-masters were strengthening and arming most ocean-going vessels with the latest technological advances in cannons.

During the EIC rule, opportunities for participation in commerce and industry remained wide open. Before the arrival of the railways, shipbuilding was a viable industry in Bombay and was mostly in the hands of the Parsis. The first East Indiamen constructed in India conformed to the same tonnage rules as other merchant ships of the day built in England throughout the early to middle 18th century. When voyaging to England they sailed in convoy at least until clear of the Bay of Biscay. Spain still retained grandiose ideas of expanding her empire in the East, while the Portuguese and French endeavoured to increase their meagre possessions on Indian territory; rival Holland, then secure in Indonesia, was perhaps casting covetous eyes over Britain's hegemony in India. To ward off this threat, cannon was hauled aboard East Indiamen from Britain or transferred from ships held in abeyance in Indian waters onto vessels constructed in Bombay and Calcutta for their maiden voyages to either London or Canton. Britain's unassailable lead in shipbuilding sustained her advantage over Continental Europe's rival powers.

Industrial and social progress seemed to go hand in hand with world trade, especially when stimulated by EIC commerce. Virtually from its inception the EIC had the Midas touch, and it secured much employment in Britain for all classes, especially artisans within the shipbuilding industries. An early piece of industry that accompanied EIC officials to Calcutta was in the form of horology: a freestanding clock crafted by the Lancashire clockmaker Ainsworth Thwaites. Ornate and beautifully detailed, the clock was manufactured around 1740. Yet, within decades the cargo of EIC ships changed considerably as they were loaded with heavy manufactured goods to be used for the building of a physical infrastructure in India.

Opportunity under the EIC was not just confined to British markets. In India, too, trading operations and opportunity were expanding rapidly, as historian Tirthankar Roy explains:

> The rise of Indo-European trade did not happen at the expense of Indian traders. It was quite the opposite in fact. The parts where the Europeans had their stations were located too far away from the other. [EIC's] shipping lines were insufficient to create necessary links between these ports, and between them and the smaller coastal markets where useful goods were available. This sphere of subsidiary or feeder supplies, called country trade, engaged a large number of Indians as well as Europeans. When the Company reduced its trading operations towards the end of the eighteenth century, the country traders moved into India–China trade.

Shipbuilding in India for the EIC
Surat and Bombay

Some form of shipbuilding began on the coast at Bombay in 1717, but little of this enterprise has been documented for posterity. However, the Parsis were well-established merchants in the 18th century and shipbuilding was a Parsi monopoly for as long as one could recall. Trading vessels were built in many Bombay shipyards using the finest teak and other available timbers, mainly from the Konkan, Karwar and Malabar forests, before India witnessed the huge ocean-going vessels from the EIC. The Parsis knew teak better than Europeans and, with rising oak prices, this fine wood that did not split or warp was in demand. Soon, shipbuilding along modern

European lines was undertaken at Bombay as well as at Surat and the once Portuguese-controlled town of Daman.

At Surat in 1720 the Parsis built a dock with EIC design and assistance. They also designed the five shipyards that followed, and were responsible for virtually every ship constructed by indigenous hands. The origins of this enterprise go back to Lovji Nusserwanji Wadia, a renowned Parsi entrepreneur from Surat. In 1735 the EIC determined to move its shipbuilding operations to Bombay and enlisted Wadia to select a site for the dockyard. Wadia built the first dry-dock facilities at Bombay between 1748 and 1766 to EIC designs. In reality, the dockyard was created to receive His Majesty's squadrons to protect English interests in Bombay.

It was not until nearly 50 years later when the EIC took a keen interest in the port. Wadia died in 1774; his business was extended from 1803 by members of his family. Hugh McIntosh (1768–1840) received a contract from the EIC to construct the first import–export docks in Bombay in 1803. The Company knew full well the benefit of docking facilities, the more so when the Dutch East India Company's warships were threatening to gain the ascendancy in eastern waters. In 1807 the new docks had earned the EIC a reported £65,634. In addition, a Captain R.B. Crosier began work on a new dry dock in 1805 – believed to be similar to the East India Docks in London – but the military engineer Captain William Cowper (1774–1825) soon took over. Cowper had served as an ensign with the Bombay Engineers at Cannanore in 1795. Like many other military engineers at the time, he was seconded to civil works following the defeat of the French by British forces in the fourth Mysore War of 1799. Cowper was confronted by problems of hard rock, difficulties with tides and a lack of skilled workmen. There were then no steam engines to make light of the arduous work in India. However, in 1808 Cowper had completed the first new dry dock, with the inaugural vessel built there being named *Minden*. A second, known as the Duncan Docks after Jonathan Duncan (1756–1811), Governor of Bombay, followed and both docks served for the better part of 50 years.

At the beginning of the 19th century there were eight firms of Parsi shipbuilders, two in Surat and six in Bombay, all monopolising the docks, with the EIC constructing its own workshops and launching slipways. The energy for increasing trade of both the Parsis and the EIC knew no limitations when new opportunities appeared.

The opium trade was one line of business about which neither possessed any qualms. The EIC and the huge trading house of Jardine, Matheson &

Company were, from about 1820, 'up to their neck in this vile trade', according to some ships' masters who refused the temptation. Most of the East Indiamen engaged in the trade from the 1820s onwards were constructed in British, Bombay and Kidderpore dockyards. The first of the large British opium clippers was the *Red Rover*, launched into the Hooghly by the Hooghly Dock Company in December 1829. It was owned by a Captain Clifton, formerly of the Royal Navy and the EIC, who no doubt saw profit in the opium trade until a perhaps more lucrative offer arrived in the form of a sale of the vessel to Jardine, Matheson who would continue to carry the drug. The *Red Rover* was lost at sea in the 1870s.

By the beginning of the 19th century, about 10 000 Parsis resided in Bombay. Their activities were at the cutting edge of commercial success, especially in shipbuilding. When the EIC lost its last monopoly rights in 1833, opening up the trade to China, a number of large EIC sailing ships were 'sold to the Parsis at a discount price', adding further impetus to local trading. The ships were renowned for their longevity. By around 1835 to 1840, Parsis owned the largest indigenous block of shipping tonnage in India, most of it constructed in Bombay; in addition, smaller vessels were built at Surat. With this kind of head start, the entry of the Parsis into early textile, cotton and jute manufacture was almost inevitable.

The 36-gun frigate *Pitt*, built in Bombay in 1805, was not only the first EIC ship to be constructed of teak, it also incorporated the latest techniques in iron substitutes for timber. The EIC had by this time acquired a monopoly and could construct docks and harbours at the whim of its representatives and with impunity. The time had arrived when local commerce could rival shipyards on the Thames and Medway. It was only a matter of time before Indian labour adopted skills that had taken years to nurture throughout Britain. From around that time, the Indian artisan was established and soon placed into a position of trust when undertaking a craft job. Under British supervision he was quick to master his trade and the apprenticeship system was thus established in India.

The building of ships continued in a feverish manner in Bombay, and to a lesser degree in Calcutta. Bombay had established new engineering works based upon metal, although it was Calcutta which then possessed Burn's Howrah Iron Works, the largest single engineering workshop in India. One ship launched in 1813 was the *Cornwallis*, at 74 tons, which was converted to screw propulsion in 1855. The *Cornwallis* was medium-sized for an ocean-going vessel.

The *Earl of Balcarres* was one of the best-known ships of her day. Constructed entirely of teak in the Company's expanded Bombay Dockyard in 1815, she was 1417 tons and carried two tiers of guns. She was unusually fast for her day, making a passage from London to Bombay in 79 days. After 19 years of faithful service, and when by no means past her prime, she was sold for £10,700. Her new owner sailed the vessel for another 35 years and she eventually ended her career as a hulk on the west coast of Africa.

So successful were innovations applied to both *Cornwallis* and the *Earl of Balcarres* that HMS *Trincomalee* was built using Malabar teak, and was launched in Bombay in 1817. The *Trincomalee* was acclaimed as the largest vessel constructed east of the Bosphorus, housing 46 guns and displacing 1500 tons. This fine tribute to British design and Indian craftsmanship is preserved in all her glory as a floating museum in Hartlepool.

The EIC controlled the Mazagon Dockyard – completed in 1774 – in Bombay and began building medium-sized vessels that were soon diverted from trading with England to hauling opium to China. In 1839 the *Mary Gordon*, of 250 tons, was launched at the dockyard – one of only two ships in a lean year – and became a regular opium clipper.

The heyday of Bombay's shipbuilding – and indeed that of the rest of Britain's Indian Empire – was between 1830 and 1841, but regrettably it was channelled to serve the highly lucrative opium trade that broke out in the war with China from the 1840s. Twenty-six vessels dedicated to this commerce were launched, of which seven were constructed in Bombay, twelve in Calcutta – including Howrah – five in Moulmein, Burma, and two in Chittagong. They ranged in sizes from the *Caroline* at 85 tons (Bombay, 1842), to the *Cowasjee Family* at 431 tons (Howrah, 1835) – named after the entrepreneurial Cowasji (Cowasjee) family who were shipwrights and merchants of Bombay and Calcutta.

From 1736 to 1857, 267 ships and small boats varying from 23 tons to 2298 tons were built in Bombay, with four at more than 2000 tons each and 30 in excess of 1000 tons each. Wadia Industry alone constructed 170 ships for the EIC between 1735 and 1836, and this success led to general orders from the British Navy.

Calcutta–Howrah

From the middle of the 18th century, the absence of docking facilities in Calcutta became a major concern to the EIC, as ships had to be taken over

Banks of the Hooghly River, Calcutta, c.1870s (Courtesy of the British Library)

2000 miles to Bombay for repair. A dock was first built in 1790 near Bankashall Ghat. In 1781 the EIC had apportioned a plot of land to a Colonel Watson, an engineer with the EIC, for the construction of wet docks at the southern end of the port. Earlier, Watson had built a marine yard at Kidderpore and in 1783 he started working on the construction of the wet dock, until a legal dispute compelled him to abandon the whole project and he returned to shipbuilding. In 1803 the EIC 'master builder' W. Waddell set up the EIC Kidderpore Docks. In 1807, upon Waddell's retirement, the resident Anglo-Indian shipbuilders James and Robert Kyd bought the docks.

The name Kyd surfaces from time to time in Calcutta's early imperial history, with some claiming that Kidderpore was named after the enterprising family – though most sources agree that this is an inaccuracy. Their father was Colonel Robert Kyd who had served in the Bengal Engineers before rising to Military Secretary to the Government of Bengal. He is remembered chiefly as a distinguished botanist and for founding the EIC Botanic Garden (see Chapter 21) at Calcutta – a response inspired chiefly by his shock at the 1770 famine, which led to his study of drought-resistant crops. The Botanic Gardens also helped supply the EIC with a supply of teak for its shipbuilding interests. By the late 1820s, over 200 ships had been built on the Hooghly, with most of them built at the Kidderpore docks.

Possibly the first sailing ship of any significance to be built in Calcutta was the *William Money*. She was constructed at Kidderpore in 1820 of teak, saul and oak. With a width of 142 ft and breadth of 37 ft, she comprised three decks – including the poop – and with her three masts weighed 835 tons. The *William Money* must have been robustly constructed for her day, for she regularly sailed between Australia and Calcutta, and was sold to a Liverpool shipping firm in 1856. She fell out of register in 1859 and nothing further was heard of her.

Bombay had stolen a swift march on Calcutta as a result of better harbours and a shorter sea route to London. However, that did not deter the EIC, which was the only shipbuilder of consequence in Calcutta, including Kidderpore and Howrah. To a considerably lesser degree than in Bombay, the Parsis were active in Calcutta's maritime industry. In 1821 they built the especially fine *Charles Forbes* at a cost of Rs.300,000 that was to distinguish her as a tea clipper.

One of the first truly large sailing vessels built in Calcutta was the *Java*, in about 1830, which was fully equipped and presented to a British captain by a grateful father for saving the life of his daughter from bandits. The figurehead of the *Java* represented a naked woman with her hands clasped as if in prayer for deliverance. The vessel, of around 1000 tons, was built of teak and mounted 30 guns. In 1856 she was sold to John Hall, the engineers of Deptford, and in 1865 she sailed to Gibraltar to end her days as a coal hulk. A seaman noted the *Java* still at Gibraltar in the 1890s, providing the same coal hulk service.

Of all the vessels built at Calcutta (Kidderpore) the barque *Waterwitch* was assessed by mariners as 'perhaps the most beautiful clipper we have seen'. She was launched in 1831 and registered as 363 tons. She made two round trips to Canton, hauling opium out and tea on the return. Her phenomenal speed enabled the vessel to outpace all others in arriving with this cargo and collecting cash for its sale. In 1836 she took only a fortnight to reach Singapore from Calcutta. Under a new skipper, Captain Reynell, she made so much money that he 'bought the Steam Ferry Bridges at Calcutta'. In 1838 the *Waterwitch* arrived in Canton from Calcutta five days ahead of her rivals. In 1839 her record speeds were becoming revered throughout the maritime industry. The vessel was chartered that year for Rs.8,000 to carry Calcutta mail to England. She returned to the opium trade in 1844 while carrying mail to Canton. The last passage made by this renowned vessel was from Calcutta to Hong Kong in 1853, taking merely 31 days. The following

March she was moored in the Min River, China. Nothing further was heard of this ship.

Not all vessels were as lucky as the *Waterwitch*. Two Kidderpore clippers suffered immediate fates. Launched on 25 September 1838, the *Syren*, 191 tons, was loaded for China and never heard of again. The *Nymph*, launched two months later, suffered the same fate. Built in the incredibly short time of three months, she went missing on her maiden voyage to Canton.

Five days before the 1839 launch of the *Mary Gordon* in Bombay, 'the finest country craft ever built in India under British superintendence' slipped into the Hooghly from Kidderpore Dock. This was the *Rustomjee Cowasjee*, of 764 tons, that, like the *Sylph* before her in 1831, had been specially built for her owner by the EIC's Sir Robert Seppings. The vessel occasionally carried opium but was usually a hired transport in the opium war that flared in Chinese waters.

The Indian share of the total tonnage of sailing ships over 80 tons registered at the Port of Calcutta was small in 1805, at about 5.2%; it fell to 4% in 1817, increasing to 8% in 1826. In the period 1801 to 1805, the average tonnage of vessels built in Calcutta, for which statistics are available, was 5571 tons, plummeting to 2313 tons over the next five years. Despite a slight increase between 1811 and 1815 to 6508 tons, the overall trend was a steady decline. However, ships were growing in size. Over the next decade, 57% were registered in the port as being constructed in either Howrah or Calcutta itself and 29% in other Bay of Bengal shipyards, with Chittagong enjoying a healthy trade in shipbuilding mainly because of the cheap and freely available good timber. Most river craft constructed in Calcutta were between 30 and 50 tons, although some vessels of up to 180 tons were in use.

Calcutta's eminence as a port during Queen Victoria's reign was recognised globally to be directly due to Imperial Britain. When Job Charnock settled in 'the Kalicut swamp' in 1690, nothing existed. British imperialism cleared the swamp without one piece of mechanised machinery, and within 150 years Kalicut – or Calcutta – was recognised as 'the city of palaces and foundry excellence'. British rule was the greatest factor in Bengal's history. At the end of World War II, Calcutta renewed its status as a thriving port and centre for engineering excellence, but Independence brought immediate decline from which she has never returned to her former glory.

At the times of their greatness, the various East India companies built some of the finest ships the world has ever seen. In the Dutch shipyards of Rotterdam and Amsterdam, the French Biscay port of Lorient – specially constructed and named for this eastern trade – and the English dockyard at Deptford, a succession of magnificent ships slid down the slipways – ships that were larger and finer than any others in the world.

Throughout all this pioneering work, there was one undermining factor – the dilapidated financial condition of EIC coffers. The EIC was barely solvent in 1835, despite an all but total monopoly on trade – trade that stretched to Singapore, Australia and China.

EIC – fighting to the bitter end

After gaining a good deal of territorial and political control of early 18th-century Bengal, the 'fighting Company' soon took an opportunistic turn. Its commercial and territorial greed, fuelled by its obligations to the demanding board of directors and shareholders in Britain, led to its engaging in rampant, unorthodox and unethical business and monetary practices. By the late 18th century Britain was the richest and mightiest nation in the world and its economic dependence on Indian commerce was significantly reduced. The EIC put exports from India to Britain in 1790 as amounting to 27 000 tons, although no value or type of goods was mentioned. By 1817 the situation had changed radically, with imports from the east to Britain amounting to 80 700 tons, and exports from Britain to India and Ceylon topping 'an insignificant 109 400 tons'. It was only a matter of a few years before Britain was running a huge trade deficit which, surprisingly, continued right up until Independence in 1947.

Yet, the phenomenal increase of English trade with both Europe and India reflected the boost given to the changing times by embryonic steam engine power. During the first quarter of the 19th century, imperial ties with India were still of paramount importance. The EIC rigidly controlled most commerce inside and outside India, demonstrating India's great value, which usually won the day and the political argument.

Dissolution of the EIC came about after the Indian Mutiny in 1857. Its monopoly in India had been officially removed by legislation in 1813. However, the expansion of trade and improved transportation as a result of the steam locomotive – with the East India Railway virtually set up and financed from EIC funds – make a mockery of the suggestion that the EIC's monopoly was over. Prior to the EIC 'losing total control' in India from 1834, the Company operated much as before, conducting trade between India, Britain and China. Additionally, divergence into the opium trade after the supposed end of its monopoly in India saw the EIC earning fortunes from the Chinese. It failed, however, to achieve the monopoly on opium as 'just about everybody and his uncle who possessed a seaworthy vessel was flogging the stuff through Canton'.

A good example of the increase in trade that benefited all parts of India and especially the Port of Calcutta can be assessed from early photographs taken when steam and sail worked in harmony. The EIC continued to make many final decisions for the next decade irrespective of Parliament. The simple fact was that Parliament had no reliable alternative but to dispatch communication around the Cape in EIC vessels between 1834 and about 1845, until the partial overland route through Egypt began to gain outright favour for mail and luggage.

However, the EIC's monopoly over both routes was short-lived. Other rival shipping and trading concerns appeared determined to undermine the secure interests of the EIC. Before an answer from Calcutta to a dispatch from London was forthcoming – taking at least eight months in 1840, although this was much quicker than two decades earlier – the Company had made decisions on the spot that affected India, and these were quickly implemented without London's approval. Right up until 1857 there was proof of its influence in the decisions taken to build railways, with the East India Railway and its juxtaposed Bengal coal mines virtually a monopoly of the EIC or controlled through its subsidiary companies. With competition from rival shipping companies, its necessity was waning. Amid continued reports of EIC malpractices and reprisals after the Mutiny and with the EIC burdened by debts, there was no longer a sound financial or political case to uphold the Company. The 'fighting company' had outlived its purpose.

Colonial India remained of great importance to Britain politically, strategically and above all for its everlasting reservoir of low-cost manpower and soldiers who helped the empire expand and who sustained the British colonial territories in the Far East, Middle East, Africa and the West Indies, not to mention later playing a significant and sacrificial role in two world wars. Moreover, the political landscape of Britain by 1857 was dramatically altered to that of a century ago in the heyday of the EIC's monopoly. In the second half of the 19th century a new counter ideology of laissez-faire trade was gaining popularity amongst policy-makers in Britain. A growing agitation with the practices of the EIC had developed among the British public. Change was being demanded in India, with a shift towards increased accountability and social improvement.

British expatriate individuals and businesses were also well established and innovating in India. By the turn of the century, and particularly after the EIC lost its official monopoly in 1813, it became more difficult to demarcate the formal operations of the EIC from the enterprise of private individuals, civil engineers and 'new money' in an unrestricted market. After 1815, as discussed in Chapters 3 and 4, it would be free enterprise demanding faster routes to India.

The EIC had applied a 'divine right' policy to its operations, subsequently attempting to stifle concerted and damaging dissent. Yet, it had also built a huge and profitable trading empire that ultimately benefited the general public of Britain and India alike. It revolutionised British and Indian life-styles and established modern-day global trading systems. With its early approach to genuine infrastructure, it was responsible for creating millions of jobs that, today, India – and to a certain degree, the UK – would other-wise be without.

Chapter 3

ROUTES TO INDIA

The making of the Panama and Suez Canals appear to us to be the greatest works of the future; they will increase and strengthen the happy bonds by which people of every clime, of every race, and of every faith, are united to England, and will for ever connect the general welfare of nations to the prosperity of our country, their safety to our power, and their independence to our liberty.
ARTICLE IN THE BRITISH PRESS, 1852

For the first century of its existence – 1601 to 1700 – the EIC gave no thought to reaching India by any route other than via the Cape. On many of the early voyages the Cape was not touched at all, as the more dependable westerly winds were found far to the south, near latitude 45 degrees. From this region a course was shaped through the Mozambique Channel, with stops in Madagascar, or on the East Africa coast, before touching in at Ceylon. However, with ships increasing in size and sturdiness many vessels kept well to the east of Madagascar, where good winds were found that helped the EIC's galleons continue directly on to Madras or Bengal without embracing any African port.

Before the advent of steam propulsion the East Indiamen, as well as vessels from Holland and France, sailed courses that were rarely identical. They sailed down the English Channel for the open Atlantic and on into the Bay of Biscay. From there, any one of three or four routes would be taken depending upon the character of the vessel and the skill of the skipper, the season of the year and the presumed location of enemies. However, this was all about to change.

In 1795, amid the political turmoil of the Napoleonic Wars, the British captured Cape Town in response to petition from the EIC. With France's invasion of the Netherlands the previous year, the Company was quick to recognise the potential threat of losing access to the Cape – which had been under the control of the Dutch East India Company – should it fall into

French control. After a brief departure under the terms of a general truce in Europe, the British recaptured the Cape again in 1806. British control of Cape Town, along with changes in sailing techniques, led to the shaping of more direct courses from Cape Verde to the tip of Africa. With Cape Town safely in British hands and heavily defended, the South African city became a regular and assured halfway station. The South Atlantic island of St Helena retained much of its importance as a fresh-watering point, but vessels in tip-top condition found this call unnecessary.

The return voyages from Calcutta and Madras differed little once ships were in European waters and not greatly even in the Indian Ocean. Voyages were calculated to take full advantage of the trade winds, which at this point had reversed their directions. Even so, despite radical improvements in maritime technology, ships sailing the Cape route subjected their passengers to long, difficult and tiresome voyages. Such irritations became more profound when the trade winds abated and long calms ensued. Despite this, the comfort of vessels plying the routes to 'the Indies' radically improved, with some vessels being much like 'floating hotels', providing comforts, luxuries and 'a table fit for a king' that was unheard of when the first ships sailed around the Cape in the early 1600s.

One such example, *The Hope,* represented the highest form of sailing vessel ever developed. It was in many ways unsurpassed for opulence and comfort, with an excellent dinner table, in an era when the Cape route could not be challenged. Sailing vessels well into the 1840s could out-speed the embryonic steamships that P&O commissioned for the India route from London. Sail was also free from fuel costs and the time wasted coaling in ports, but this was only an advantage if sufficient wind was at hand.

After 1815, businesses began to demand faster routes when ships plying the Cape voyage were loaded with manufactured goods. An iron bridge from the Butterley Company, in Ripley, Derbyshire, established in 1790, was the first heavy cargo ever documented to be exported to India. Increasing numbers of expatriate Englishmen – clerks, tradesmen, civil engineers and soldiers – expressed a frustration that embarrassed the Indian government, although the potentiality of steam navigation tempered these frustrations. While most expatriates were resigned to the fact that Africa had to be circumnavigated, others began considering an overland route through Egypt, with the minimum of sea travel.

By 1820, cartographers from many European countries had mapped out much of the world – especially around Africa via India to Burma, and

Europe via the Middle East to India through Persia. Those merchants who had much to gain from better and faster communications with Britain's Indian Empire began to look seriously at alternative routes. They considered whether it would be better to sail through the Mediterranean to Alexandria now 'the French menace was eradicated', or to take a completely overland route via Turkey and Mesopotamia, perhaps using the Mediterranean as far as Constantinople, then horse and boat via the Euphrates. The advent of steamboat technology partially convinced many that the Cape route was still the best option, once coaling stations were established. The immediate benefit was that steam-powered vessels could chug the seas when sailing ships were becalmed in the absence of trade winds.

While alternative routes were being surveyed, sailing ships grew rapidly in size. This increase in dimensions, when augmented by technical improvements to seaworthiness, was of paramount importance. In 1815 Butterley had exported a three-span cast-iron bridge to the Nawab of Oudh in Lucknow, containing some 2750 individual castings, of which fewer than 20 pieces were found to be broken on arrival. At around 1300 tons, a large East Indiaman had a size and capacity that surpassed what was only dreamt of 50 years earlier. Furthermore, such a vessel was capable of carrying a complete iron bridge – something no other craft had then achieved.

In the same decade, an 8-hp engine was sent by steamship to the same Nawab of Oudh in disassembled manageable parts. Watt beam engines were sold to both the Calcutta and the Bombay mints (see also p. 257), and steam engines from London were finding markets to pump water in a thirsty subcontinent. Carrying also the supporting machinery – all cast in iron – each vessel had no alternative but to go round Africa powered by wind.

Meanwhile, the EIC was building up its fleet of steamships, placing further orders with Thames shipyards. In 1839 the *Cleopatra,* of 814 tons, was launched at the Northfleet Dockyard of William and Henry Pitcher. The same firm later constructed the *Sesostris* of 876 tons and the *Queen* of 766 tons. However, each vessel was forced to sail around the Cape.

Sailing ships continued to ply the Cape route well into the late 19th century; only when the Suez Canal passage was taken over in 1875 'for a song to the tune of £4 million' by an astute Prime Minister, Benjamin Disraeli (1804–1881) had sailing vessels outlived their usefulness. With the canal in British hands and under Royal Navy control, all attempts at finding alternative routes to India, such as through Turkey and Mesopotamia, were also scuppered.

Fast passages of large sailing ships

Until the advent of steamships, the fast passages and the relative comfort for first-class officials on East Indiamen around the Cape were still eagerly sought after. Although speed was not sought at the expense of comfort in the building of these vessels, and with sail always reduced at night, they were still often able to compete with early paddle steamers once a good wind gripped the ship.

In 1819 the newly launched *Thames,* of 1425 tons, was one of the finest ships of her age. In 1831 she made a record voyage from China to Portland in 115 days and regularly completed a London-to-Bombay trip in less than 83 days. As far back as 1820, the *Lord Wellington* went from London to Calcutta in 82 days without ever travelling more than 200 miles a day. In the same year, the *Castle Huntly* left Torbay on 1 April and arrived in Bombay after 77 days. The *Thomas Coutts* was also a fast vessel. She arrived in Bombay from London after 82 days, then proceeded to China and, sailing for home via St Helena, made the fastest voyage to the east on record. The whole journey had taken just over a year. The *Earl of Balcarres,* built entirely of teak in Bombay and weighing 1417 tons, was unusually fast for her type, in 1836 completing a passage to Bombay in 79 days. By 1835, it was possible on a few occasions for a letter dispatched from the EIC's headquarters in London to be answered in slightly less than six months – an unprecedented achievement at the time. The growth in the size of sailing ships, combined with a corresponding reduction in the time taken to reach India, began to convince many that the embryonic paddle steamers – capable of only 180 miles per day – could not challenge sail for a swift passage.

Despite all these improvements and the further development of larger and stronger vessels, from early in the 18th century one of the greatest menaces to East Indiamen arose from the number of French pirates that haunted the usual courses to and from India. As East Indiamen were primarily cargo vessels, the French not infrequently captured them during the pioneering days when a safe route to India was being established. Although the pirates were armed as heavily as possible, EIC vessels never surrendered without giving a good account of themselves. Many of the engagements were extremely bloody, and when such encounters made headlines in London-based newspapers such as *The Times* or the *Morning Chronicle* they initially deterred newcomers to the EIC from establishing careers in India. However, the opportunity to 'sail around the Cape to India' attracted strong interest once the bad news was confined to history. The early cannon aboard East Indiamen were often not sufficient against these marauders, whose chosen method of attack was to surround their quarry with numbers of small boats packed with pirates who swarmed on board and massacred crew and passengers alike. However, after the British capture of Cape Town such attacks became less frequent when suitably armed ships could give chase and deal out retribution. There was no quarter given on either side. The subsequent building on the Thames and Medway of small, fast and heavily gunned frigates signalled the decline of piracy with the odds gradually favouring Britain. Later, steamships and the breech-loaded gun blasted the enemy into Davy Jones' Locker at the height of imperial British power.

The Red Sea and Egyptian overland route

When Warren Hastings was appointed Governor of Bengal in 1774, after serving an apprenticeship as a junior clerk with the EIC from the age of 17, some consideration was given to alternative routes to India either overland through Turkey and Mesopotamia or via Suez. A few journeys had been undertaken via Alexandria and Suez when a vessel was plying the Indian Ocean to Persia or Egypt, but for all practical purposes the Cape route was still an automatic choice. At least the long and hazardous journey had been made relatively safe to convey officials and urgent dispatches to India.

In 1698 Henry Tistew, who had formerly been English Consul at Tripoli, Syria, passed through Egypt making his way down the Red Sea and on to Surat with the idea of a trade route to India. Strictly speaking, Christians were then forbidden to enter the Red Sea beyond the coffee-port of Mocha. However, trade with Jeddah was tolerated by the local chiefs who considered an increase in their coffers and prestige to be more important than any inflexible religious dictates from Mecca.

Definite projects for using Egypt for trade and communication began with the arrival at Alexandria on June 1768 of James Bruce, lately British Consul in Algiers. On his way to Asia via the Red Sea, he scrutinised Egypt with a critical eye. He was astonished to find that none of his countrymen was established in Egypt at that time. In the 1770s, English trade with Egypt was in the ascendancy. At the close of 1775, Ambassador John Murray in Constantinople, a strong advocate of getting to India through Egypt, returned to London and presented his findings to the EIC. A treaty was set up with both Egypt and Turkey to allow messages and trade through Egypt. In the following four years, sailing vessels arrived at Alexandria from England and at Suez from India at about the same time. Mail took some 25 days from Cairo to London; all-important correspondence was marked 'received overland' and had priority for the next vessel. The realisation of this service prompted English civil servants and merchants alike to establish possibly the first direct through mail service via Egypt from Calcutta to London. Sadly, shortly after the sailing of two vessels from Calcutta early in 1774, Hastings wrote to his home authorities that 'soon after the departure of both vessels, they were overtaken by a violent gale in the bay in which the [trading] ship received great damage ... and the schooner has not since been heard of'. However, from 1777 the sloop-of-war *Swallow* was making record journeys to Suez with dispatches from Hastings, despite initial frustrations from the Sublime Porte – the Ottoman court in Constantinople. The Turks were becoming increasingly concerned about British supremacy in all waters that they travelled through, yet had nothing with which to challenge the might of EIC warships. Within a year the Turks relented, perhaps from a showing of English strength in the form of 13 men-of-war at Suez.

The year 1778 was perhaps the start of the era of great dispatch routes to India. English vessels were 'all but queuing up at Egyptian ports either side to pass mails and parcels to overland couriers'. With the capture of Pondicherry, and most French activities in India temporarily paralysed, one further obstacle had been removed, ensuring that India was indeed England's 'Jewel in the Crown'. George Baldwin, merchant and political agent in Egypt, was pleased to note that a letter from England to Madras via Alexandria, river boat to Cairo, camel to Suez and fast gunship around Ceylon to Calcutta, 'took a mere 68 days'. It was, indeed, a great achievement.

The British victory over the French at the battle of Aboukir Bay (1798) ushered in a new era in the route to India. Additionally, political insurrection in Cairo and upheavals in Turkey played directly into London's hands. In 1801 a combined strength of English and Indian forces landed in Egypt, co-operating with troops in the Mediterranean to take control of Cairo and Alexandria. Captain Sterling commented most favourably upon his loyal Indian troops as being 'steadfast in battle and humane in victory'. It was a calculated move in the quest to strengthen links with India. These victories convinced the Bombay government to establish bases in the Red Sea, to obstruct any lingering French wallowing in the wake of Aboukir Bay. One such base was prepared for the receipt of communications on the island of Perim, but the very unhealthy environment proved to be a death trap for EIC troops.

Within a few months the survivors – who included many brave Sikhs – were transferred to Aden, then a British colony. The government considered Aden as merely a temporary measure, and it was soon closed down.

The first definitive scheme for a line of steam vessels between England and India using the overland route through Egypt was the product of an English naval officer – James Henry Johnson (1787–1851). Having entered the Royal Navy in 1803, he found himself at the end of the naval wars with Napoleon on half pay and meagre rations. Steadfastly determined to push his ideals for a more direct route to India than that around the Cape, he was cold-shouldered by the General Steam Navigation Company (which had been newly incorporated by an Act of Parliament). However, he found a considerable degree of support from a number of influential businessmen in England and India on the subject of steam communication. In 1822 he attempted to form a company with the immediate object of establishing a steam service from Calcutta to Suez. Johnson did, however, captain the *Enterprise* (see Chapter 4) built with private English investment and spurred on by the offer of a prize funded by the Calcutta Steam Committee and the Nawab of Oudh. The *Enterprise* was the first steamship from England to India via the Cape. Though it did not attain its 70-day target, it did prove that steamship navigation via the Cape was possible.

In 1832 the British Admiralty had three armed steam packets in regular service between Gibraltar and Malta, which had replaced five conventional sailing vessels used on that section. These warships were ideal to guard vessels of the EIC sailing to Alexandria, giving rise to further consideration of Egypt as a viable alternative to the Cape route. The selection of the overland route through Egypt in preference to the Cape route was made when steam locomotives took over. Britain's railway builders felt confident that a line through Egypt would entirely replace sail around Africa for both passengers and goods, then comprising heavy foundry products. As early as 1845, an order was placed for iron rails, ties and other railway equipment, and Rowland Macdonald Stephenson was eventually contracted to construct and equip – with carriages from Ashbury, of Manchester – the first railway in Egypt.

To cater for the gradual leaning away from Cape travel to Egypt, the EIC added three steamships to its fleet: the 606-ton *Atlanta,* constructed by Blackwall Shipyard, the Clyde-built 670-ton *Berenice* – both launched in 1838 – and also the *Semiramis* of 700 tons. Later, a host of vessels, including the impressive 946-ton *Auckland*, were built in the dockyard at Bombay. Initial problems with the paddle wheels in monsoon rains were overcome when newly designed paddles of greater strength were dispatched from Fawcett, Preston's Liverpool foundry. A further week was thus trimmed off the overall journey time from Bombay to London.

The Peninsular & Oriental Steamship Company (P&O) and the Nile route

From the start, P&O had grandiose plans and they were not long in coming to fruition. The company started a steamship service in 1837, with Falmouth as its main UK port. 'Navigation through canals and along the River Nile and the Mahmoudieh Canal, gave rise to the great Peninsular & Orient Steamship Company,' stated Charles Manby, agent for the EIC, when the steamship company set its eyes on pioneering a route to India through Egypt. Granted privileges by the Pasha in 1841, P&O's passenger services were in big demand. The firm increasingly encouraged the overland route to be adopted and at its behest the passage through Egypt underwent a series of mild improvements. The Nile River saw four P&O steamers make regular journeys. Indeed, the trusty and reliable camel service was increased from 50 animals in 1843 to 2563 in 1846, to convey passengers and mail from Cairo to Suez. Meanwhile, the tiny *Lotus* paddle steamer was supplemented by the *Cairo*, an iron paddle steamer, in 1841, described by a P&O official as 'a remarkable vessel, similar in appearance to the steamer called the *Watermen*, running between London and Woolwich'. The *Cairo* accommodated 100 passengers. The Nile route was indeed popular even before the final arrival of the railway, and a new steamer, the *Delta*, was shipped out in 1844 to replace one of its vintage vessels. P&O placed much faith in the Nile route to India. The company had spent large sums in Egypt on the docks, warehouses, lighters and coal dumps at Alexandria and Suez; hotels at Suez and Cairo; a large share of the railway that it had financed for the pasha; fruit, vegetable and sheep farms to feed the passengers; steamers on the Nile; plus roads, vehicles, camels and ships' stores, which were said to stock everything from needles to anchors. Even the lighthouse down the Red Sea, which everyone used, had been sited, built and manned by P&O.

The completion of a railway through Egypt, even under the auspices of the Pasha, must surely have given a great impetus to finalising measures for regular monthly steam transit on the Suez line. Only the completion of the Suez Canal under the Frenchman Ferdinand de Lesseps (1805–1894) in 1869 further reduced the time it took to travel to India.

Chapter 4

SHIPS AND SHIPBUILDING:
THE AGE OF STEAM

*On approaching Calcutta, the smoking chimneys of steam-engines are
now seen in every direction, on either side of the river, presenting the
gratifying appearance of a seat of numerous extensive manufactories
vying with many British cities.*
JOACHIM HAYWARD STOCQUELER, JOURNALIST, 1844

In 1818 the world's first all-iron ship, *Vulcan*, was launched. A year later a
paddle-wheeled steam vessel had crossed the Atlantic. Shortly afterwards,
steam maritime technology chugged up the River Gumti in Lucknow under
the aegis of the industrious Vizier – Nawab – of Oudh. Not unnaturally, the
powerful personal interests that drove trade throughout the EIC's monopoly
were increasingly concerned as to why England and India were not yet
connected by this 'novel means of propulsion'. The EIC's principal rival,
the Dutch East India Company, was not found wanting when it came to
purchasing steam engines and, ironically, these initially came from English
foundries. With Britain master of the seas and with 'a God-given right to
check any challenge to this hegemony', according to *The Times* in London,
Parliament and commerce were united in getting mail to India as fast as
possible. Steam navigation around the Cape of Good Hope seemed to be the
answer. Yet the feasibility of an overland route was also gaining credence.

Directors of the EIC were fully aware of the rapid technological changes
in the maritime industry. Even so, they did not show unrestrained enthusiasm
for this new means of propulsion. Sailing vessels had proved themselves
in design – it was size then that mattered. In a mere 25 years, the tonnage
of ocean-going vessels had virtually doubled. EIC directors had focused on
opium trading, an activity that resulted in the Chinese Opium War from
1839 to 1842. The firm had tied up the majority of its sailing vessels in this
commerce and made huge profits. The steam engine had yet to prove itself

as being totally reliable but its superiority in waters where wind was absent for days on end could not be questioned or ignored. Other companies, such as P&O, grasped the new technology in its early stages and waited for the rewards to tumble into their coffers. The way was then clear for the likes of P&O, British India Steam Navigation Company (BISNC) and their rivals to steal a quick march on the EIC, from which the monopoly could never recover. Lucrative mail contracts awarded to others in preference to the EIC sealed its fate in ocean communication.

Private enterprise flourished throughout India as never before. Indigenous and English merchants, maritime traders and the rising industrialist classes set up shop in a virtually unrestricted market. Steamboats were still in their infancy but the technology was sweeping India. Even though the building of steamships was rapidly overtaking that of sailing vessels, reliance on wind power was not totally obsolete. From the shipyards of Bombay, Calcutta, Chittagong and Moulmein, sailing vessels were launched on a regular basis. Possibly one of the last large sailing ships to be built in Britain for an East India trader was the second of two vessels from John Reid & Company, shipbuilders of Port Glasgow. The ship owner, John Kerr, who had earlier contracted two vessels, each of 1200 tons, from the same shipbuilder, envisaged sail to be the key to financial success, and new vessels of 1500 tons were delivered in the winter of 1871. When John Reid delivered the last of those large sailing ships, Clyde shipbuilders reported for the first quarter of 1871 the launch of 36 ships with an aggregate tonnage of 42 500 tons – 28% up on 1868. All were steamships. The days of sailing vessels were all but confined to history.

Early steamships in India

There is much speculation as to which steam vessel was the first in the employ of the EIC. However, what is now thought to be the first engine to drive a set of paddle wheels on behalf of the Company was used to remove silted earth from the Hooghly River bed. An 8-hp engine, which arrived from Birmingham in 1817 or 1818, presumably of James Watt & Co (later Boulton & Watt) manufacture, had done nothing except gather dust in a Calcutta godown (warehouse) until purchased by the EIC for use on a dredger. Coupled to a double set of revolving buckets mounted on a barge, the engine performed the humble duty of scooping mud from the river bottom to clear a pathway for Calcutta-bound sailing ships. The Blackwall

Shipyard on the Thames built its first paddle steamer in 1821. In the following year, it constructed a wooden paddle steamer, *Indiaman*, for the EIC, but little is known of this vessel.

The first vessel in India to be propelled by steam was one assembled in Lucknow for the Nawab of Oudh. Little is known of this pioneering steam vessel, which is believed to have been solely for the use of the Nawab's son. However, it can be safely assumed that such a means of mechanical propulsion must have caught the eye of locals and British officials alike. Her dimensions were length 50 ft, breadth 9 ft and depth 4 ft. The Derbyshire-based Butterley Company cast the engine in 1819; it consisted of a single cylinder that drove the pleasure yacht's side paddles at 7 to 8 mph. Presumably wood was the fuel for the boiler as there is no evidence that coal was then used.

Shortly afterwards, the government was directed to the subject of steam navigation and in this respect, as in most enterprises to benefit mankind, private adventurers took the lead. In all, Butterley shipped about 150 engines to India before 1830, and was the firm with the greatest number of units installed in India at that time.

The first wholly Indian-built paddle steamer took to the rivers one year after the Nawab's pioneering role. A small vessel, the *Snake* was designed and constructed by a Parsi in Bombay and was plying the Indus River in 1820. She is recorded as the first steamer on the Indus 'or any river in India'

THE NAWAB OF OUDH – AN EARLY PROPONENT OF BRITISH STEAM TECHNOLOGY

A LITTLE-KNOWN WATT ENGINE was supplied to the Nawab of Oudh in 1814. It was installed in a grand building reflecting the combination of the Islamic and Raj styles of the day. Containing two boilers and using wood as the primary fuel, the engine was used to pump water to the Nawab's palace.

The first steam vessel that sailed on Indian waters had been ordered for his son. The Nawab also purchased the first cast-iron bridge installed in India and exported from Butterley in 1815. In that same year, the Nawab ordered from Henry Jessop, then in Butterley's employ, a small steam engine that was also built at Butterley's foundry in Ripley, Derbyshire, to work the *punkas* or large fans in the Nawab's palace in Lucknow. The cost is known to have been £250.

and was an unqualified success in that, having being twice wrecked in 1837 and 1854, she survived until 1880. The *Snake* provided a service for both passengers and freight until larger and more powerful screw-driven ships relegated her to the status of a museum attraction.

The first steamboat to carry fare-paying passengers in India appeared on the scene more by accident than design. It happened that the health of one of the EIC's merchants in China broke down before he could launch a steam-engined vessel on the Canton River, and he put up the parts for sale in Calcutta. The government – in other words the EIC – declined his tender, but a group of merchants took up the venture and distributed shares among the principal agency houses. The contract for a wooden hull to receive the engines went to Calcutta's premier builder of European-designed ships, Kyd & Company.

Between 1781 and 1821, many sailing ships capable of undertaking ocean voyages were made from the abundance of teak wood in both India and Burma. James Kyd – 'the master shipbuilder of Calcutta' – had contributed much to the development of the sailing ship in India. In 1823 he diversified and constructed his first steamship, the pioneering *Diana*, at his Kidderpore Docks. Local press reports relate that Bengalis once crowded both riverbanks to witness her surprising manoeuvres 'and marvel at yet another triumph from the repository of science and invention', according to an EIC official. One inherent defect in her design was the inadequate capacity of her engines – believed to have been cast at Maudslay, Sons & Field – which were not powerful enough to tow the massive East Indiamen sailing ships of up to 1000 tons that still hauled the bulk of India's trade.

The following year, Maudslay, Sons & Field launched the *Lord William Bentinck*. After successfully completing her trials, the vessel was taken to pieces and, along with a second tug, the *Thames*, stowed aboard an outward-bound East Indiaman, the *Larkins*. Weighing anchor in March 1833 with two crated steamers below decks, she also carried several engineers, engine drivers and boilermakers among the ship's company. When the *Larkins* reached Calcutta five months later, it took several weeks to set up shop for the final assembly but both the tug and the principal vessel were ready for steam in April 1834. The *Lord William Bentinck* glistened under her shining double-coats of paint and lavish decorations and, flying three large ensigns, was launched with unprecedented ceremony into the Hooghly.

Shipping in the Hooghly, 1890s (Courtesy of the British Library)

Calcutta and Bombay Steam Committees

It is difficult to draw a line of demarcation between vessels that were directly owned and operated by the EIC and those in private hands. Anglo-Indian joint stock companies and managing agencies proliferated in the early 19th century. Indian 'artisan-mechanics' were quick to learn from men such as William Jones (not to be confused with Sir William Jones, the great Indologist). After arriving in India in 1800, Jones worked as a private mechanic for ten years before being able to found a paper factory. The EIC Court of Directors viewed such private enterprise as unwelcome competition. Jones went on to discover coal at Burdwan in 1815. Enterprising to the end, he worked as an architect of Bishop's College before his death in 1821.

Dissatisfaction at the way communications were progressing had been expressed on numerous occasions by the business and merchant class of India, and not only the British. A rising Indian middle class joined forces to demand from the government better communications all round. Governor-General Lord William Cavendish-Bentinck (known as Lord Bentinck) was not deaf to reality, and with various private well-heeled organisations setting up steamboat services to rival that of the government, there appears to have been no opposition to competition. In respect of the maritime industry, there appears to have been a quiet period from when the EIC officially lost its monopoly in 1813 until the entry into Calcutta of P&O's *Hindostan,* 2018 tons, in 1842. Along with her sister ship the *Hindostan,* P&O's *Bentinck* was backed with 'new' money. The vessels were technically well advanced, with watertight bulkheads and luxury cabins.

Two firms, the Bengal Committee and the Calcutta Steam Committee, both elected to construct their own vessels. Consortiums of businessmen and merchants, such committees were active in petitioning Lord Bentinck to promote steamship service between Britain and India. They were also eager to develop a reliable and readily available tugging service on the Hooghly, a dangerous stretch of water that took sailing ships 15 days to tow ships from Calcutta to the mouth of the Hooghly; the steam tug took only two days.

The Calcutta Steam Tug Association was formed in 1836 by leading Bengali entrepreneur Dwarkanath Tagore – grandfather to Rabindranath Tagore and a close friend of the reformer Ram Mohan Roy – following his purchase at auction of the steamer *Forbes,* which was to be used essentially for Hooghly River service. It was a shrewd move as the enterprising Tagore had just bought a coal mine at Raniganj (see also Chapter 13). The 302-ton towboat had been launched on 29 January 1829, from the New Howrah Dockyard, Kidderpore. Her previous owners, Mackintosh & Company – well connected with the EIC, who chipped in with costs – had proposed to use her in a novel way. She was to tow a sailing ship out to China against the monsoon, the sailing ship providing coal from her hold. Such an expensive proposition could only have been considered from the opium trade. The *Forbes* was built of teak, with two engines from Boulton & Watt, the company that also provided her copper boiler. Boulton & Watt had become one of the most important engineering firms in Britain with its innovative steam engine. The *Forbes* was of such a considerable size that she had the stability and power to sail as far as Suez. Such acquisitions of formerly EIC-funded steamboats by private Anglo–Indian joint-stock ventures fuelled a burgeoning and unrestricted market.

In 1838, persuaded by the esteemed engineer Ardaseer Cursetjee Wadia (1808–1877), the Indian Steam Committee voted that all vessels for Indian service should be built in India. In the discussions, the Howrah-built *Forbes* was compared to the English-built *Enterprise.* Though the latter was found wanting by the group, the pioneering vessel had earned its place in steamship history and the Calcutta Steam Committee played a significant role in its inception as they vied for a steamship service between Britain and India.

PS *Enterprise* – the first steamship
from England to India

In 1823 the Calcutta Steam Committee and the Nawab of Oudh offered a prize of Rs.80,000 to the owners of the first steamer to reach Calcutta from Europe, with a target of 70 days. On 22 February 1825, the PS *Enterprise* was launched from the dockyard of Messrs Gordon and Company, of Deptford, with engines cast in 1824 from Maudslay, Sons & Field, of Lambeth – then London's largest engineering foundry. This steamship was the sole known vessel from Gordon's yard, which is surprising as the innovative ship was to achieve fame as the first steam-powered vessel to make the voyage from England to India (Calcutta).

The *Enterprise* was believed to have been 464 tons gross with sufficient space to carry 380 tons of coal to feed both engines, although this coal quantity is subject to doubt. Her copper boilers were steamed on seawater. Much of the coal was stacked over the boilers, where it nearly ignited. At the start of her voyage from Falmouth she drew 17 ft, and carried 17 mainly EIC officials, despite being a ship privately built with no corporate connection to the EIC. She took 102½ days to reach Bengal – at least three weeks longer than an East Indiaman. The normal speed of the vessel was 6 or 7 knots. She did not fulfil the conditions for the prize, which required a ship to reach Calcutta in not more than 70 days, but she did receive half the prize.

The log recalls that 62 days were under steam, 40 days under sail and 10.5 days in harbour coaling – for example, at Cape Town and Colombo. The tiny engine was obviously far from ideal for such a voyage – a fact the captain confirmed with significant criticism. Irrespective of sentiment, the excellence of the shipbuilder, and of the engine- and boilermaker, cannot be denied. Also, the seamanship of the captain and crew deserves special merit for that pioneering voyage. Captain James Henry Johnson was a determined advocate of establishing a Calcutta–Suez route and had considerable backing from private businessmen in both England and India. A Thomas Waghorn of the Bengal Pilot Service piloted the *Enterprise* up the Hooghly to Calcutta. Waghorn and Johnson no doubt must have shared their enthusiasm for an overland route to India via the Red Sea. In 1827 the Calcutta Steam Committee approached Waghorn with funding to assess the logistics of an overland route.

The *Enterprise* was promptly sold to the Government of Bengal. The adherence to steam propulsion was justified when the vessel was called on for dispatch service between Calcutta and Burma at the time of the Anglo-Burmese War (1824–6), and then went into service as a tug on the Hooghly. In 1829 she was sold to the Government of Bombay and carried Indian mail to Suez when the overland service to Alexandria began. In 1834 she was dismantled. Her two 60-hp engines were installed in a new vessel of the same name built in Calcutta especially to receive them.

The *Hugh Lindsay* – Bombay to Suez

Sir John Malcolm (1769–1833), the Governor of Bombay, was determined to establish a permanent steamer service between Bombay and Suez. Talk of an overland route was then hot news and various travellers had made the idea feasible. Under Malcolm's instructions to the EIC, an order for a steam vessel was placed with the fourth-generation master shipbuilder Nowroji Jamsetji Wadia (1774–1860) in Bombay.

The vessel, built of teak with boilers and engines from Maudslay, Sons & Field was the first steamship constructed for and owned by the EIC. Named *Hugh Lindsay*, the 411-ton vessel with two 80-ihp engines, was ready for commissioning in 1829. To test the use of this vessel on regular services to Suez, coal depots had to be established and navigation charts of the Red Sea prepared.

The *Hugh Lindsay* made four voyages to the Red Sea, clearly demonstrating the feasibility of the line. However, she was inefficient and had to be supplemented by the aforementioned impressive tugboat, the *Forbes*. After the completion of trials, the paddle steamer left Bombay for Suez on an unheralded voyage on 20 March 1830, arriving one month later.

Of the 33 days taken, 12 had been required for coaling, as her capacity was only for five-and-a-half days' sailing – not enough for the 1710 miles between Bombay and Aden. She carried mail that eventually reached England in 59 days – extremely quick for the time, although EIC directors felt 'this fact did not counterbalance the cost of the vessel, equipment and expenses'.

However, Thomas Waghorn was persuaded. Encouraged by the *Hugh Lindsay*'s passage he devoted his efforts to the realisation of an overland travel service facilitating the passage of travellers and mail across the 84 miles of desert between Alexandria and the port of Suez. He soon faced fierce competition.

The EIC loses steam

By the 1830s, the number of EIC steamships in Indian waters – that is, between Suez and Calcutta – was growing at a phenomenal rate. To the *Atlantis* and *Berenice*, sent out from England in 1836 and in early 1837, was added the *Semiramis*, at 1031 tons and 250 ihp (indicated horsepower) with six guns, in April 1838. This vessel proved not to be the equal of its rivals during the monsoons. She was added to the EIC's Bombay-based fleet at a time when other vessels were being constructed in its dockyard with engines brought out from England. Originally fuelled by wood, she was converted to coal and stationed in Aden from 1842. Steam service throughout the Indian Ocean was fully established with 'fairly regular sailings to Suez'. In 1839 the Court of Directors bought an English coastal service vessel from the packet service. The *Kilkenny*, which once carried pigs from Waterford to Bristol, weighed 684 tons. Renamed *Zenobia*, she was dispatched around the Cape to Bombay.

In 1839 the largest steamship to be built in Bombay was the *Victoria*, a splendid vessel of 705 tons with engines rated at 230 ihp. She was captained by Commander Henry Ormsby, who had taken part in one of the earliest surveys of the Euphrates Valley through Mesopotamia. *Victoria* was then the fastest vessel in the EIC's fleet and the pride of Bombay. One year later, the *Auckland*, 946 tons, was launched from the same dockyard.

The Company by then had practically become a ward of the British government, and it was partly for this reason that the time was already passing when the Company's monopoly was seen as prohibiting any competition in its domains beyond the Mediterranean. EIC's competitors loomed aggressively on the horizon and were already stealing a march on the firm. Further technological developments in steam propulsion were now out of the EIC's hands.

The Peninsular & Oriental Steamship Company (P&O)

Navigation through canals and along the Nile gave rise to the great Peninsular & Orient Steamship Company (P&O), established in 1837 but incorporated in 1840. P&O's standing had increased rapidly and Lord Bentinck suggested the company start a service to the subcontinent. P&O successfully tendered for effectively half the route in the form of an extension of its Gibraltar service to Alexandria in 1839. The growth of revenue into P&O's coffers convinced the directors that reliance on sail was obsolete and that steam-vessel and engine sizes must rise phenomenally.

While purchasing new, medium-sized ships for internal Egyptian waters, the firm placed an order for the *Hindostan* to complement its eastern fleet. Of 2017 tons with engines from Fawcett, Preston, she made her maiden voyage to Calcutta in 87 days around the Cape in autumn 1842. On that epic journey, she carried 150 passengers of which 60 occupied first-class cabins; the fare was £40. Shortly afterwards a sister ship, the *Bentinck*, also with Fawcett, Preston engines, was dispatched from Southampton to Calcutta, making the Cape voyage in about the same number of days. This unprecedented feat was achieved from running the first 4000 miles under steam without taking on additional coal, which had to be sent ahead of both vessels in conventional sailing ships. For many years the *Bentinck* was to hold the record for the fastest journey between Suez and Calcutta.

P&O had the future of the empire in mind. A series of monthly services began between Calcutta, Madras, Ceylon, Aden and Suez, which proved to be highly practical from the start. The first mail destined for Calcutta was carried from London in 1843. In that same year the *Hindostan* logged 25 days 3 hours from Calcutta to Suez, a distance of 4787 miles, against a stiff monsoon all the way.

During the first decade of P&O's regular London-to-Calcutta service, reliability was the keyword. Almost invariably on time, the contrast with vessels of the Admiralty and the EIC, which were seldom punctual, was well noted by EIC officials and passengers alike. In 1854 P&O could boast 25 vessels in regular service. That same year witnessed an achievement that convinced all fledgling maritime nations that Great Britain ruled the seas. A leviathan for its day, the screw ship *Himalaya*, of 3500 tons, was the largest ship afloat. In 1854 the average speed of a paddle steamer was 8 or 9 knots. The *Himalaya* could sustain 12 knots for most of its voyage, with 14 knots over shorter passages.

As a regular route, the Cape could not compete with Suez, principally because the London to Bombay voyage was some 8000 miles longer. P&O could take mail and passengers from England to India by the short route. Two new ships, *Great Liverpool*, and *Oriental*, plied the Mediterranean from England to Egypt, while the *Hindostan* or the *Bentinck* operated from Egypt to Calcutta.

The Southampton iron steamship firm of Summers & Day was contracted in 1858 to construct the largest vessel ever built in the south of England.

P&O had a canny insight into the future and especially that of India. The Indian Civil Service, after the Mutiny and the demise of the EIC, was being built up. Railway expansion warranted a huge amount of cargo space and, despite the growth in competitive shipping lines, such as William Mackinnon's BISNC, P&O viewed the economic future with unbridled optimism. This new vessel from Summers & Day, the *Northam*, contained square sails as well as engines from the builder's own foundry. Weighing 1667 tons and measuring 274 ft in length, she was soon hauling railway equipment and machinery.

P&O also had the shrewdness to name its vessels with an Indian or Ceylonese connection. In 1853 the *Colombo* was launched at Robert Napier's Glasgow yard, with beam engines from the builder himself. In 1862 the *Poonah,* an iron-screw steamer, was purchased from the Thames Ironworks & Shipbuilding Company. Engined by Humphrys & Tennant, this 2152-ton vessel served the ship operator until 1889. The following year saw the launch of the *Golconda,* also constructed by Thames Ironworks & Shipbuilding with its own engines.

In 1869 the clippers, which had just about reached their perfection as regards design and passenger comforts, received a severe blow when the Suez Canal was opened, shortening the route to India by several thousand miles. Sailing ships were barred from the canal, allowing steamships to dominate the lucrative Indian trade. P&O took full advantage of this, and with most British-built vessels equipped with compound engines and improved efficiency and a shorter route, coal consumption was cut by as much as 40%. In addition, coal mines throughout India were being opened up on a massive scale (see Chapter 15). The huge ports of Bombay, Madras and Calcutta were, by 1870, well stocked with coal yards to fuel hungry vessels then approaching displacements exceeding 4000 tons.

The era had quickly arrived when fast, sturdy, comfortable propeller-driven vessels were regularly launched from the newly established ship and engine builders on the Clyde. P&O had stolen a march on its rivals, although not for long. However, the shipping company deserves full credit for innovation and progress. Bombay and London were being reached within one month, and as vessels increased in size the south-west monsoon lost most of its power to terrify navigators.

In 1870, the year after the Suez Canal was opened, P&O's fleet stood at 44 ships of an average 1857 tons per vessel. By 1884, it had grown to 50 ships of about twice that size. The canal had been dredged and widened to take a new generation of large steamers, including the *Peshawur*, of 3900 tons, that also contained three masts of sail. One of the most handsome ships built by P&O, in 1876, combining both engines and sail, was the *Nepaul*. Of 3536 tons, she was then the second-largest vessel in the company's fleet.

The weight of the huge horizontal steam engines (mostly from Lancashire) needed to power the growing number of mills in Bombay, along with the mammoth Beyer-Garratt-type locomotives introduced from Manchester (and first designed in 1907 with the inaugural order for Darjeeling in 1910), simply could not be hauled in the earlier vessels that P&O ordered for India service. P&O anticipated the demand for larger vessels with additional cargo space and extra berths for passengers to serve the empire and especially India. In 1896 an order was placed with Caird & Company's Greenock yard for three vessels, the first named *India*. It was the 50th vessel the yard had built for the firm. In addition, the Palmer Company, of Jarrow, had on hand a cargo-carrying steamship of a similar size to the *India* but especially notable for having twin screws in place of a single screw. She was capable of carrying the heaviest locomotives that British foundries produced, as well as the largest stationary steam engines then exported to the cotton and jute mills of Bombay and Bengal. The 8000-ton *India* was 500 ft long and was capable of accommodating 320 first-class and 160 second-class passengers. The ship was designed to serve the needs of empire, with its luxurious cabins that favoured government officials travelling to the Raj. On her maiden voyage 'she maintained for a considerable time a speed of 18.33 knots'. P&O had indeed come a long way from its first steam vessel of only 206 tons, the *William Fawcett*, built by Fawcett, of Liverpool.

The two world wars of the 20th century proved perilous for P&O's route to India. The 7920-ton steamship *Persia*, which was launched in 1900, was torpedoed in December 1915 with the loss of 330 passengers and crew, including the master, with only two children surviving. She had been a popular vessel on the London to Bombay run, having undertaken a total of 70 round trips. On that fateful run, the vessel was carrying an estimated £3 million in gold to the Government of India to pay for war material.

One of the most beautiful and elegant of all P&O vessels seen regularly in Indian waters was the *Rawalpindi,* launched in 1925. Of 16700 gross tons, she was one of four sister ships requisitioned by the Admiralty in 1939 for war service. She was never to grace an Indian shoreline again. She was kitted out as an armed merchant cruiser with eight 6-inch main guns, but was no match for two German battleships when sighted off south-east Iceland.

The British India Steam Navigation Company (BISNC)

When the firm of Mackinnon, Mackenzie & Company was formed by Robert Mackenzie (1813–1853) and William (later Sir William) Mackinnon (1823–1893) in December 1847, there must have been a sly 'P&O are not going to rule the roost' thought to their venture. Both men came from Campbeltown, Argyll, Scotland. Mackinnon's first exposure to trade in the tropics was when he served in the Glasgow office of a Portuguese East India merchant. Mackenzie was already settled in India by 1836, and well known in Bengal as a 'free merchant' – not in the service of the EIC. By 1846, Mackenzie had prospered into the position of General Agent in Bengal for the new river steamship service, the India General Steam Navigation Company (IGSNC). Mackenzie was aware that ships from Britain arrived in Calcutta with merely wool as ballast or carrying immigrants – including the last dwindling retinue of EIC officials – plus home-produced goods such as Scotch whisky, the usual brands of beers and quality French brandy.

It was due to the EIC, still the *de facto* rulers in Burma, that this partnership was presented with its first great opportunity. Tenders were invited to haul mail between Rangoon and Calcutta. The bid of Mackinnon, Mackenzie was accepted, ironically over a similarly attractive offer from P&O. The partnership then needed to purchase fast, flexible vessels that could operate in all waters – and quickly. Mackinnon returned to Glasgow to raise all necessary funds and, once acquired, formed the Calcutta & Burmah Steam Navigation Company (CBSNC) in September 1856. The first steamer purchased was the *Baltic*, built by the Dunbarton shipbuilder Denny in 1852 and originally engaged in the Baltic trade with Russia, and the *Cape of Good Hope*, built by C.J. Mare, bridge-builder, of Blackwall, London, in 1856. It must be assumed that no regular mail service then existed between Rangoon and Calcutta, or at most a meagre one. Initial good fortune quickly turned to disaster when the *Cape of Good Hope* collided with P&O's *Nemesis* and sank in the Hooghly in March 1859; mercifully, all 145 passengers and crew were saved.

The CBSNC's name was changed in 1862 to British India Steam Navigation Company (BISNC) – to reflect the widening trade undertaken. Six vessels ranging from 359 tons to 1132 tons were then under construction in Britain; all had sails to support their engines. The shipping company's initial routes under its new name were confined to services between the Persian Gulf, India, Burma and Singapore. In 1864 it owned 21 vessels

Bishop's College, Calcutta, c.1870. The college stands on the banks of the Hoogh-ly next to the Botanic Gardens. It was acquired in 1880 by the Civil Engineering College (Courtesy of the British Library)

valued at £427,127 9s 3d. The opening of the Suez Canal in the following year saw the firm in fierce competition with P&O over its share of carrying troops from the UK to Bombay. BISNC's prospects took off exponentially. In 1876 a regular UK–Suez–Colombo–Madras–Calcutta service was established. According to Duncan Haw's book *British India S.N. Co.*, when the BISNC merged with P&O and its name all but ceased to be recognised in the mid 1980s, it owned, managed or operated some 526 ships, with only a handful exceeding 20 000 tons.

Inland waterways

Under successive governors, the waterways of the Punjab were deemed ripe for commercial exploitation from the 1820s. When India's new Governor-General, Lord Bentinck, had settled into his new Calcutta abode, the *Hooghly* and the *Berhampooter* were engaged in a sporting trial of speed between the Bishop's College and Diamond Harbour. The *Hooghly* proved to be the faster of the two and was subsequently selected for an exploratory voyage, starting on 8 September 1828, to Allahabad. The voyage took up to 23 days, of which two were spent in Patna and Benares. The little vessel had moved under its own steam for a total of 240 hours at an average speed of 3.5 mph. The return voyage was not without mishap, including 'touching the river bottom' but they were 'fortunately soon extricated'. When the *Hooghly* arrived triumphantly at Calcutta's Chandpal Ghat, the first steamboat trip on 800 miles of the Ganges had been successfully completed – although not quite as far as Allahabad. Only 14 days were required for the return trip, which included two days at Benares to refit and repair. It was not only a triumph for British engineering and tenacity against the odds, but also an equal accolade for the Indian workmanship that assembled the vessel.

In early October 1830, the year after the tugboat *Forbes* attempted to tow a sailing ship to China, Kyd's shipyard launched a light wooden-hulled tugging vessel at 112 ft long and 18 ft wide. When empty, her draught was only 10 inches, and when loaded with 50 tons she drew no more than 2 ft. Named the *Soonamooky*, this 80-ton vessel hauled Lord Bentinck's suite 720 miles up the Ganges to Benares in 24 days, including a total of 20 days in steam. Bentinck was so impressed with the diminutive vessel that he gave the go-ahead to expand steamboat exploration within India.

In 1831 the EIC put forward a proposal to open up a trade route down the Indus River. The following year, a commercial treaty was signed by Lord Bentinck and Ranjit Singh (1780–1839), the Sikh ruler of Punjab, in Lahore, with 'the two contracting parties binding themselves never to look with the eye of covetousness upon the possession of each other'. The area, prosperous with agriculture, was relatively stable and developing rapidly with the expansion of canals. Above all it was navigable. Steam propulsion was regarded as the sole viable means of transport as sailing vessels were useless upstream. The abolition of transit duties in 1835 prompted the establishment of steam river transport throughout the Punjab as well as the beginnings of tea cultivation in the Assam (see Chapter 17). The Punjab's huge, wide and swiftly flowing rivers were fertile waterways as a testing ground for paddle-steamer engines and auxiliary equipment.

An added asset throughout the Punjab was the indigenous Sikh. According to the governor of the Punjab, and endorsed by Lord Cranbourne (1830–1903) in the *Madras Athenaeum*: 'The turbaned Punjabi is equally at home driving steam-boats as he is at servicing the vessels. They [the Sikhs] are reliable after the minimum of instruction, fully capable of replacing the Welsh captain and Scottish steam engineer.'

Native Punjabi dhow-type riverboats or medium-sized steamers hauled most of the area's export trade downstream into the Indian Ocean. The ports of Bombay and Karachi were rapidly expanded to cater for the amount of goods, not only imported from Britain but also exported to 'the mother country and other colonies'. Many marine engine foundries employed a Sikh engineer in Multan or Karachi to service their companies' products.

EIC river steamers

It appears that the first flotilla of river steamers established by the EIC was inaugurated in 1832 up the Ganges. The paddle steamers were named, in order of building: *Lord William Bentinck, Thames, Brahmapootra, Megna, Jumna, Indus, Hurringutta, Damooda* and the *Mahanuddy*. Their principal dimensions were 140 ft long and 25 ft wide, with a draught of 8 ft.

In 1842, Sir Charles Napier raised the issue of the Indus with Queen Victoria's government, and in 1843, following Napier's conquest of the Sind, a regular service of steamships was established by the EIC. The EIC, now grudgingly seeing the advantages of steam propulsion for inland waters, built two small steamers of light draught, possibly in Bombay. Each was 80 ft long with an 18 ft beam and a laden draught of 4 ft. While innovative for their day – at least in India – these vessels could carry only a few passengers and the barest of stores.

While railways for India were still on the drawing board, the era was propitious for steam navigation. In 1851 Laird of Birkenhead constructed a fleet of steamers drawing 24 in. to 31 in. and sometimes, loaded, to 39 in. These nifty little vessels ran the 600 miles from the Indian Ocean to Multan, and occasionally another 200 miles to Jhelum or Ferozepur. However, navigating the inland rivers was a costly endeavour for the EIC. The Sukkur, situated on the west bank of the Indus River in the Sind province, was well known for its meandering river and treacherous currents. Although Karachi to Multan was just 800 miles, voyages upriver took some five weeks, with progress limited to the hours of daylight. The downward passage was usually achieved in seven to ten days, stopping at night to take on wood fuel and to allow the passengers to sleep.

Although there was some qualified success later, the EIC's operations as a state company were costly. The chief difficulty to overcome in India was the shallowness of the rivers and their swift currents in parts. Plying both the Indus and the Ganges sapped a great deal of strength from the EIC. It was quite literally an uphill task – in the direction of the Himalayas – requiring great energy and feats of determination, careful judgement and navigation. It must have come as a great relief to the Company when the Indus Flotilla Company considered taking over its routes and vessels. The next move for navigating the Indus was a combination of steamers and railways. For all practical purposes, the EIC was out of marine ventures and no doubt relieved at the thought of others being saddled with those problems.

The Indus River trade and Indus Flotilla Company (IFC)

The Indus Flotilla Company (IFC), established in 1858 by the Scinde (Sind), Punjab & Delhi Railway (SPDR), which had been set up three years earlier, was incorporated to supplement its own railway company. It took over the EIC (which was now dissolved) routes and vessels. Reports from India complained that most rivers were not navigable north of Attock; but as far as Attock, Punjabi pilots, who knew their territory and rivers intimately, provided invaluable service to the IFC.

The Scottish Shipbuilders Association was in no doubt that all-year-round working could not be achieved when the river depth was 8 ft to 9 ft in some weeks, while in others there would not be as many inches. Fully aware of the potential for trade on the Indus and other rivers, and keen to capitalise before rivals gained the initiative, the IFC invited shipbuilders to tender with designs for vessels of around 200 ft length. The result was the acceptance of John Scott Russell's tender for the construction of the *Stanley* with a draught of less than 2 ft.

The IFC contracted six more vessels built upon the same principle as the *Stanley*, but with extra hull stiffening. These vessels were built by Richardson & Duck, of Stockton, with engines from Kitson & Hewitson of Leeds, established in 1835, which was later more renowned for locomotives and delivered more than 50 to four Indian railway companies between 1855 and 1856. The IFC reported that over the next decade its seven steamers were capable of hauling 200 tons of cargo with a draught of 3 ft 6 in., 'and were highly successful', according to the builder.

In 1861 India was still on edge in the wake of the Mutiny. Britain was determined that nothing would upset the status quo of her empire and quickly arranged for an increase in troops and troopships to carry men and logistics at short notice to any potential trouble spots. The IFC was involved in an unnamed troopship built by M. Pearce & Company, of Stockton-on-Tees. At that point, it was the largest vessel to sail on the Lower Indus River. At 377 ft long with a beam of 46 ft over the paddle boxes and a draught of a mere 2 ft, her weight was recorded at 739 tons. Her engines were of the horizontal design from James Watt.

The vessel made nearly 12 mph over the measured mile in trials. She incorporated berth frames of galvanised steel that could accommodate 800 troops and their officers. Special speaking tubes were installed from the captain to this engine room – an innovation for its day. Fortunately the ship was never called into military service and was taken over by the IFC for freight and passenger duties only. The vessel served for over 20 years before being scrapped.

By 1862, the IFC had increased its fleet to 15 steamers and some 30 barges, with later versions having corrugated-iron hulls built on the Thames. The vessels were shipped out in sections and assembled in Karachi. One of these Indus steamers, appropriately named the *Indus*, of 218 ft length, 19 ft 6 in. beam and 4 ft draught, was designed by T. A. Yarrow, with an engine by John Scott Russell. The *Indus* had a displacement of 400 tons and a length of 200 ft, with two barges loaded with 500 tons of cargo lashed one on each side. Other IFC purchases included a steamer with a 3 ft draught that could displace 432 tons. This allowed for 137 tons of cargo and 37 tons of fuel – ample for her longest run between stations. Her barges when hauling 150 tons would have a 3 ft draught. When fully loaded, steamers and both barges could haul 400 tons, costing the customer a mere penny per ton per mile upriver and half that cost on the return journey to Karachi.

The IFC maintained that after covering operating expenses 'the return was good for their investors'. It was assessed at the time that the expense of running the better class of vessels amounted to £450 per annum, which covered fuel, wages and stores.

The demand for vessels to ply Indus waters was increasing yearly. It was still a British market for building paddle steamers and building all engines for the larger vessels, despite the rising eminence of Calcutta-based Garden Reach Shipyard and Kidderpore to challenge British supremacy. Both shipyards imported engines from Smethwick, the Clyde and London. However, the IFC maintained its preference for its larger ships to be launched on the Clyde or the Tyne. In 1864 it placed an order with J. Wigham Richardson & Company, of Walker-on-the-Tyne, for the *Sir Herbert Maddock*. The vessel was exclusively adapted for towing, with barges lashed alongside during her performance trials.

Meanwhile, competition was hotting up, with the Punjab now viewed as 'India's breadbasket and an area where labour was plentiful with much of it eager and adaptable to learn new skills'. A rival firm, the Oriental Inland Steam Navigation Company (OISNC), also established in 1858, had purchased some old steamers from the EIC, and then contracted for a new Clyde-built vessel. The OISNC sought to exploit Bourne's 'patent train'. Bourne's system of 'floating steam trains' was a novel approach to solving the problem of hauling huge amounts of cargo in the shallow channels of the Indian rivers in the dry season, when there was insufficient water to float in. The vessels from the 1850s were designed with paddle wheels that were only 6 inches below the keel, and that could be used as a crawler for the Bourne steam train. Most vessels contained a supplementary engine fitted with wheel gearing to reduce speed when crawling. The general concept was to close-couple a steamer with a string of barges so that the bow resistance of the train would amount to no more than that of a single vessel.

The OISNC experimental Clyde-built 'steam train', the *Jumna*, was built by J. Reid & Company, of Glasgow, with a draught of 4 ft 6 in. and a Penn & Napier engine. The 'train', consisting of a steamer and five barges, was 930 ft in overall length, with a 30 ft beam and 8 ft depth of hold. The engines came from Fawcett, Preston. Trials were successful on the Clyde. After successful acceptance by engineer John Penn, an engine builder of London, the vessel and barges were dismantled and crated for use on the Ganges.

On arrival and assembly, further trials were undertaken in Karachi Harbour over a measured distance of 3850 yards. Without a train the 200 ft steamer, with her beam of 20 ft when loaded to a mean draught of 3 ft, attained a speed of 9.4 mph. On adding the barges, the speed fell to 7.19 mph, and further reduced to 4.33 mph when fully loaded. After trials, one train loaded with barges and a crew of 32 Europeans and 42 Punjabis took 23 days to achieve 420 miles. But the idea proved unwieldy. In swirling currents and river zigzags, two attempts failed when the train foundered on the riverbanks. The whole project came to an ignominious end in Karachi Harbour. The drawbar between the steamer and the first barge broke. The barges doubled around the steamer, which had almost stopped, stove in the stern and the steamer sank in 24 ft of water. Fortunately, there was no loss of life, but that disaster was the inglorious end of Mr Bourne's 'patent train' and no efforts were made to salvage the steamer.

In 1862 the OISNC broadened its horizons. It enjoyed a commercial operation with the Burma Steam Company in sharing the steamer *Rifle* to carry mail from Burma to Karachi. Once her cargo was discharged in Karachi, it was transferred onto the new company-owned steamer *Indus* for the 23-day trip to Multan hauling two heavily laden barges. However, all was not progressing smoothly with OISNC's operations. It was feared that the river trains plying Indus waters would not be a success. Modifications were incorporated to allow the steamer to take a barge on each side and this system 'worked tolerably well but with a much reduced speed'. Reluctantly accepting the disappointment of its new steamer, perhaps labouring with loads for which it was not designed, the company all but collapsed when the *Indus* was eventually grounded amidships and broke her back in late 1863. In essence, other OISNC's vessels – and especially the earlier steamers – were no good for all-year service throughout any inland waterway compared with those of its main rival, the IFC.

To compound OISNC's problems, the SPDR had extended its lines to Kotri from Karachi, a distance of 130 miles, spreading its tentacles even further. However, the route could then only be used for about seven months of the year. Between April and September, the north-west monsoons caused heavy surf along the coast that all but shut down rail traffic. The next move was for the SPDR and the IFC to combine their operations fully while still trading separately.

The IFC continued to function until 1878, when the Indus Valley State Railway was inaugurated; it had provided a regular service between Kotri and Multan, a distance of 570 miles, for the SPDR. The new railway was the last link to be forged in the chain of railways providing through connections across India from Karachi and Lahore to Calcutta. At the time the company ceased trading, passenger traffic was mainly Indian. Cabin accommodation was all but discontinued as most locals slept on deck; even the few Europeans preferred to sleep on the first-class decks. With more space, therefore, for cargo, the principal up-freight was general merchandise, piece goods, beer and metals, while the down-freight was wheat, cotton, raw and manufactured silks, wool, indigo and various kinds of oil seeds. The Punjab, then the fastest growing area in India, was stable and the 'Sikhs were adaptable and good at just about anything they put their mechanically trained hands to', commented Captain Johnson, who ran IFC's office in Karachi.

Steamers on the Ganges and Brahmaputra

The EIC had also played a significant part in opening up the Ganges and Brahmaputra rivers to steam navigation from 1832. In the year of the Mutiny, 1857, the *Koel* and the *Kolydyne* were added, and were much larger than earlier vessels crated from Britain. Napier & Company of Glasgow constructed the hulls, engines and boilers. Two years later, with commerce expanding inland, the flotilla was augmented with the *Sir Robert Peel* and the *Jabuna*, each fitted with a James Watt oscillating engine.

Local shipbuilding in Calcutta, notably from the Garden Reach Shipyard, was responsible for the *Ganges,* with engines imported from

England. Three large paddle steamers designed to ply East Bengal waters were shipped out from Laird & Company of Birkenhead. The *Spey, Teviot* and *Tweed* were each 240 ft long and were suitable in every respect for heavy freight and troop movements, with all vessels under government control. By 1860 many rivers had been dredged and in some instances widened to allow the larger and more powerful paddle steamers to make the 1250-mile journey from Calcutta to Allahabad.

In February 1844, the India General Steam-Navigation Company (IGSNC) was founded with a capital of Rs.18 lacks. It was the tea industry in Assam and Cachar that gave the greatest impetus to inland waterway transport in the east of the country, and the IGSNC was one pioneering firm that established a regular service in those waters. The first steamers imported in crates from mainly Clyde shipbuilders were the *Sir Frederick Currie, Charles Allen, Lady Thackwell, James Hulme, Calcutta, Bombay, Madras, Colgong, Rajmahal, Agra, Lahore* and *Simla*. These paddle steamers were built as required between 1844 and 1861, generally following government guidelines in respect of construction and accommodation details.

Each vessel was advanced in power output, with higher boiler pressures and larger engines. The use of greater horsepower was a shrewd judgement, as additional barges were required to haul tea and other produce from Assam and the northern regions to Bengal and UK markets. 'Steamers were piling up in Calcutta and jockeying for berths to export the best of India [tea] to the Mother Country' proudly – if not pompously – stated *The Times* in 1863.

The last four in that list of steamers were larger vessels overall, at 225 ft long, with a 28 ft beam and a depth of only 9 ft. These were principally used for Brahmaputra River service, competing against vessels of the East India Railway (EIR), which was criticised for poor river transport service. It does appear that the shipping line took over all EIR's services from 1861 as 'the EIR does not find the inauguration of riverboat services remunerative', according to its spokesman. Business was good. Locals saw the benefit of calling on barge captains for transport and 'no reasonable request was turned down', according to a company official. A dozen new ships were crated and shipped out from the Clyde in the late 1860s but even that increase in shipping failed to satisfy the needs of locals and merchants engaged in tea trading. By 1889, a fleet of 61 steamers and 73 flat barges was available for service, some of which were chartered from the East Bengal State Railway (EBSR).

Another rival firm was established in about 1850. The Calcutta Steam-Navigation Company was set up with mainly local capital and served the needs of indigenous Bengalis in and around Calcutta. Raniganj coal was the fuel used. Both rival firms enjoyed brisk business hauling coal from Dinapore and Raniganj, tapping all collieries alongside the river where it was reported that 'coal for our steamers can be had at good rates', as one captain logged in a memo to his superiors.

The outright success of 'steam trains', earning a very good reputation on the Indus, prompted capitalists and merchants alike to consider a similar service on the Ganges. Steam vessels had plied this river from the early days of controlled navigation but not to the extent that had developed in the Punjab. In 1861 J. Reid Shipbuilders, Port Glasgow, constructed a huge steamship and five barges on the Clyde to the principles of Bourne's patent river 'steam train. The ship, named *Jumna*, after the river, when under test in the Firth of Forth, was 930 ft long overall with a 30 ft beam and 8 ft depth of hold, fitted with huge engines with surface condensers from Fawcett, Preston. The train, constructed of iron, was very light, with a small draught. It was designed for carrying 3000 tons of cargo or capable of hauling 2000 troops complete with their weapons. On test, a speed of 7 knots was sustained, with a maximum of 9.5 knots attained at its peak. After acceptance, the ship and barges were dismantled and conveyed in two vessels around the Cape to Calcutta. It was to be the largest 'vessel train' seen on Ganges waters.

Although the OISNC was experiencing difficulties in Indus waters, the firm was farsighted in its plans to profit from freight and passenger services on the Ganges and Brahmaputra rivers. It was fully aware of the long lead time required in building flat-bottomed steamers in – mainly – the Glasgow area, proving the vessel, and then dismantling for crating and transport around the Cape to Calcutta, so the firm established its own shipyard at Garden Reach in 1861. The new complex was created initially to assemble steamers that arrived crated from British shipbuilders, before a foundry was built to cast certain parts and it began purchasing material to construct the hulls.

The company by then had begun a service to Assam for the expanding tea-plantation communities that were 'coming out from Britain in droves and with marked success. It is also expected that cotton shall be grown', according to the *Calcutta Englishman* in August 1861. The newspaper sang the praises of the OISNC and its new fleet of steamers that penetrated further inland towards the Himalayas, with vessels operating on the Ganges, Brahmaputra and Indus rivers. The Garden Reach Shipyard exists today, with two paddle steamers preserved.

Towing one or two cargo flats with a carrying capacity of between 600 tons and 1000 tons from Calcutta to Dibrugarh on the Hooghly through monsoon rains was a slow and onerous task. The Assam government was far from satisfied with the service in the early 1880s. It approached an alternative flotilla company, Macneill & Company, for faster vessels, with all specifications telegraphed to Britain. The arrival of the new vessels greatly accelerated the service and days were knocked off the Assam to Calcutta service with the use of lighter-draught vessels incorporating larger engines.

To keep pace with fast-moving times on the Ganges and Brahmaputra rivers, the IGSNC established a dockyard in Calcutta for the construction of its own vessels, with most parts imported from Glasgow. Operated in conjunction with the EBSR, it proved a viable service when run between Goalunda and Dibrugarh, as there was then only one service that took nine hours.

By 1885, the service to and from Assam had radically improved, but the IGSNC was not allowing this triumph to overshadow its own operations. In 1886 the Assam government entered into an agreement with the company for larger vessels that could steam at over 11 mph. The shipping line then placed orders with Bow, McLachlan of Paisley for eight 160 ft vessels. When commissioned, the vessels steamed at 11.6 mph. So successful were these ships that some were transferred to Sunderbunds service through newly hacked-out channels of both rivers to haul jute, rice and other commodities from Narayanganj and Seraganj to Calcutta.

Indian shipbuilding, British engine manufacturers and advanced marine technology

The Horseley Iron Works, established in 1792, was the major foundry and engine manufacturer in the north Birmingham area of Tipton and looked towards the EIC for marine engine orders. In 1825 the Horseley Iron Works cast four engines for Wm Evans at Rotherhithe 'for the India trade'. They were named by the works *Emulous*, *Gunga Saugor*, *King of Oude* and *Courier*, supposedly after the steamships' names. A Mr J. W. Taylor, who went bankrupt after the *Emulous* arrived in Calcutta, purchased the engines. Although no more is heard of them, they launched the Tipton firm as a major competitor to James Watt (Boulton & Watt) and Maudslay, Sons & Field in this innovative field of engineering.

Another firm that had served EIC interests was the renowned Liverpool Phoenix Foundry of Fawcett, Preston & Company. Established in 1758 by George Perry, it grew to become, by 1820, one of the largest and most diverse foundries in Britain, if not the world. The company's logbooks have not survived, but it cast many beam engines for the EIC, including a 50-ihp unit for a Calcutta steam tug in 1840. Later, for P&O, it designed and manufactured the 2000-ihp engine for the *Himalaya*, which became the fastest vessel afloat, knocking many days off the time required for a sailing vessel to travel from London to Calcutta. In 1841 Fawcett, Preston – known locally as 'Fossetts' – had built some 31 steam vessels and twice as many marine engines. In that same year, 779 steam-propelled ships were registered in the British Isles alone.

One of the most famous engineering firms, with a finger in virtually every steam-engine pie, was the renowned shipbuilder Sir William Fairbairn & Company. A mechanical engineer who pioneered the advancement of iron-bridge design, Fairbairn's (1789–1874) career began as a millwright in Manchester. Having mastered his trade, he acquired sufficient capital to establish a shipyard in London's Millwall in 1835, with the blessing and backing of EIC maritime officials in the newly named East India Dock. One of his first major orders was, naturally, from the EIC. Although his workmanship had yet to be empirically proven, his client possessed sufficient faith in his charisma to place orders from 1836 for 12 iron paddle steamers, each of around 240 tons, to navigate the River Ganges. Fairbairn followed that immediate success by being contracted by the fledgling P&O for the 1700-ton *Pottinger*, which was in direct competition with EIC vessels. Later, having advanced iron-casting technology, the firm produced Lancashire-type boilers with two flues, ships' hulls with wrought iron, and more robust structural beams for railway bridges. Fairbairn & Company's products, which ultimately benefited the EIC during its declining years, were to be widely used throughout the whole of India during and long after Sir William's death.

Maudslay, Sons & Field was faced with some fierce competition for engines, boilers and machinery following the firm's success in powering the pioneering PS *Enterprise*. One such rival was J. & G. Rennie, of Blackfriars, which, in 1859, built a series of shallow-draught river steamers for the

Indian government – believed to be the first major order placed by the new authority. These were among the very earliest successful designs for twin-screw ships. In 1874 six more river steamers for the same client enabled it to bring famine relief: of only 85 tons each, these sturdy vessels were capable of carrying 27 tons of grain with a 3 ft draught.

River paddle steamers increased in size, and in a very short time these vessels led to triple-expansion engines driving twin-screw ships. Foundries based on the Clyde and Tyne had taken over most of the work that once went to Birmingham and London. More and more vessels were fitted with Napier engines from Glasgow. Hard on Napier's heels was the Dumbarton shipbuilder Denny – founded by William Denny (1779–1838) – which built its own engines for a host of shallow-draught vessels that later dominated both Indian and, especially, Burmese waters.

Denny also built most of the BISNC's vessels – being stretched to capacity also to supply the Irrawaddy Flotilla Company (IFC) as well as British interests in Africa. BISNC at one time had a contract with Denny that the shipyard would not build any vessels for its competitors. This did not, however, preclude BISNC from contracting Burn, in Calcutta, or C. Brown, in Bombay, to build the 'odd few Dinky toys of up to 300 tons for tramping', according to one post-1918 skipper, possibly from the P&O. It would be fair to state that no British yard then would be interested in such a small order. What the BISNC required was local shipbuilding and service facilities. Bombay was a natural choice, with Calcutta a runner-up.

Calcutta's shipbuilding industry was capable of rivalling Britain for smaller vessels, although the city did not possess the expertise to design and manufacture reliable modern engines, preferring to import mainly from Denny. Calcutta-based shipyards also received many orders for vessels that could not be manufactured in time from Glasgow.

A consultant engineer, Alexander Joseph Bolton MICE (Member of the Institution of Civil Engineers) supplied drawings and specifications to Burn & Company of Howrah (see p. 267) for three new ships for the India General Steam-Navigation Company (IGSNC) – *Varuna*, *Indra* and *Rama* – which were in service by 1889. Records from Denny indicate that in 1888 the firm supplied engines for all three ships – all paddle steamers – and were the first deliveries from the Scottish shipbuilder to be installed at the local yards of Garden Reach and the Howrah Iron Works. They cost about £19,000 each and the hulls were built of steel from the Steel Company of Scotland. At 216 ft long, each vessel displaced some 840 tons. Boilers and machinery from Denny, of Dumbarton weighed 297 tons. The cargo capacity of the ships was nearly 100 tons, and on trials each ship attained a speed of 15.4 mph. Around 60 more Denny engines were contracted from the various shipping companies that owned yards in Calcutta, with the last unit assembled at Garden Reach in 1954 for the IGSNC.

In 1895, despite all innovations incorporated into marine technology, paddle steamers still held sway with ship operators' owners. Screw vessels had only made limited progress into India's inland waterways. A new generation of vessels still retained the trusty locomotive-type boilers driving 10 ft diameter paddles, to haul huge tea cargoes the 600 miles from Assam to Calcutta to connect up with BISNC and P&O screw ships destined for Europe. Many of these new vessels were launched from the Garden Reach Shipyard or Burns' own ironworks. Displacing 445 tons, each vessel could steam at 15 mph. The weight-carrying capacity was assessed at 25 tons of passengers, 60 tons of coal, 20 tons of boiler water and around 100 tons of general freight, including tea. Worthington pumps from Newark were fitted along with a steam-driven dynamo for a powerful searchlight.

The firm of J. Reid & Company, of Port Glasgow, established in 1852, saw future profit from establishing its presence in ship construction at Garden Reach. The firm was connected with the Rivers Steam Navigation Company (RSNC) and appears to have built its first 'receiving flat', capable of hauling 14 tons, in 1861. An unusual feature of this ship from a listing of all RSNC's vessels was an electric searchlight installed on this, and a subsequent flats constructed in the same year. Dynamo technology had somehow infiltrated India in its most embryonic stage of development. By 1916, the shipping company at its Garden Reach Shipyard had constructed 417 vessels, including 70 paddle steamers, 22 twin-screw ships, 26 stern wheelers, 20 tugs and launches, 190 running and receiving flats and 50 steam-powered cargo boats. Its first motor vessel, *Gondola,* with a 27 bhp motor, was launched in 1909. By 1926 the company's fleet had grown by an additional 100 vessels of all descriptions.

Tugboats in Calcutta, Madras, Bombay and Karachi were very much in vogue for dealing with the emergent high-tonnage steamers of P&O. In 1840 Dwarkanath Tagore's Steam Tug Association brought out from England a tug, which was fitted with a wooden hull at Kidderpore. The increasing size of sailing vessels using the Hooghly necessitated the building of larger tugs. The Clive Steam Tug Company, owned by R. Stewart and J. H. Mudie, of Calcutta, in 1894 ordered the largest tug ever seen in the port's waters.

Denny agreed to finance the firm and wait for payment in instalments for the vessel. Including the voyage to Calcutta, the tug, 740 tons and with a coal capacity of 172 tons, cost £30,000. The Thames shipyard of John Stewart & Sons constructed engines, boilers and paddles for a small tug believed to be one of the first vessels built in Calcutta's Garden Reach Shipyard. The tug is known to have been in service in 1876.

The India government's Bengal Pilot Service was another key stakeholder in the steamship market in India. This long-established service dating back to the early days of EIC activity on the Hooghly put in an order for the *Celerity,* a combined sail-steamer auxiliary barque vessel, to convey pilots to and from the Sandheads off the mouth of the Hooghly River. There were three competitors for the contract, placed on 5 January 1859. Palmers placed a bid of £20,000, while Smiths – also from Newcastle – offered £21,625. Denny also submitted a bid of £20,000 that included £5,656 for machinery, with a 15% profit built in, but trimmed the offer to £18,750 to win the order. By then, Denny had supplied some 80 vessels for service in Burma and India 'and knew the market well'. The vessel was completed shortly after machinery was installed in August of that year. She cost the company money, though. Budgeted at £870 for the voyage to Calcutta, transport costs came to £2,005. Overall, the firm lost £1,762 on this prestigious contract. The ship served well into the 20th century.

While Britain was constructing huge steamships capable of hauling a complete train and bridge parts in one vessel to India, native Indians – having learnt their trades from British marine engineers – were not found wanting in developing their own maritime and shipbuilding industries. The Indus General Steam-Navigation Company, established around 1875, had established its own shipyard at Garden Reach, Calcutta. Labour was plentiful and the British-inaugurated indentured apprenticeship system, then a permanent feature of Indian industry, was eagerly sought. In 1877 the Indus General Steam-Navigation Company laid down the keel of the paddle steamer *Tezpore* in its shipyard. Constructed of iron and with eight bulkheads, she was as near watertight as any vessel plying Indian waters could be. Her draught when empty was 3 ft and a mere 5 ft when fully laden. Four boilers constructed on the patented plans of Captain G. Scott, the company's secretary, enabled *Tezpore* to achieve 13 mph on first-grade coal.

By 1900, there was not a river that British and Calcutta shipbuilding had not opened up for commerce. The industry which was a major employer and locals were employed in their thousands.

Fire-fighting ships

London was home to two huge steam-driven fire-fighting engine manufacturers – Merryweather, of Greenwich, and Shand, Mason & Company based in Blackfriars. By 1860, both companies enjoyed a captive market, and the growth of both Bombay and Calcutta into cities of industrial excellence created a large demand for the latest advances in fire-fighting systems, for which both companies could deliver the technology demanded.

Each then possessed Merryweather, and Shand, Mason fire engines, which were in the main horse-drawn. However, fires that occurred on both ports' waterfronts required a different engineering solution. The answer lay in creating a floating fire engine. In 1867 the Indian government ordered its first fire-fighting vessel from Shand, Mason. The vessel was constructed by Richardson, Duck & Company, of Stockton-on-Tees, her graceful

---

STEAM FIRE ENGINES

AFTER THE FIRST (HORSE-DRAWN) steam-driven fire-fighting pump from Braithwaite & Ericsson in 1829, the idea of using steam pressure to propel water onto fires caught on with other manufacturers.

A new design capable of raising steam more rapidly and built throughout in a manner suitable for hot climates was tested and accepted in 1882. For Kidderpore Docks, the India Office ordered a unit with an engine designed to disgorge 300 gallons per minute. In 1887 Shand, Mason & Co. designed a novel 'combined irrigating and steam fire engine', to supply a demand for an inexpensive engine for irrigation purposes and, in cases of emergency, to be equally efficient as a steam fire engine. The engine was capable of raising steam within seven minutes. A feature of this model 'produced for hot countries such as India' was its ability to function at maximum power on cheap fuels such as wood, straw and vegetable refuse as well as coal. Many units were sold to India and from all accounts were successful.

Merryweather, like Shand, Mason, saw its products gain worldwide acceptance; but it was to India that sales increased phenomenally. In 1891 and 1892 numerous customers received units of an improved design that had gained acceptance with the Metropolitan Fire Brigade in London. So successful was this approach that engines were sold to Kidderpore Dockyard; a government factory in Dum Dum, Calcutta; the Gordon Mills; Calaba Jute Mills; and the Rajah of Nepal.

lines designed for high-speed navigation. At 130 ft long, 16 ft in the beam and a mean draught of 4 ft, she was possibly the first floating screw-driven steam-powered fire engine.

The ship comprised four boilers, but three were found to be more than adequate for her designed performance, leaving one boiler spare for emergency service. The six steam pumps were of the bucket and plunger type. During pump trials, water was discharged through six 1.5-inch jets to a height of 160 ft. After successful completion of her trials, when she gave 10.76 knots per hour, the ship and all her machinery were dismantled into the 11 sectioned parts of her construction, then crated and shipped around the Cape for assembly in Calcutta – probably at Garden Reach. The floating steam fire engine was still in service well into the 20th century.

In 1916 the Port of Calcutta Commissioners contracted Merryweather to deliver a steam fireboat. The vessel, initially named *Merryweather* for her trials on the Tyne, was forbidden to sail to Calcutta because of the German U-boat menace and the possibility of home service. In February 1919, she was placed out of Admiralty commission at Boulogne, France, and sailed to Calcutta, where she was renamed after the city itself.

Despite all efforts to advise people of the danger of fires, fire-fighting appliances imported from Britain were simply inadequate to contain the fires in Calcutta. Her industry and population exceeded the infrastructure's ability to support the problems that surfaced. In 1920 Merryweather designed two vessels, 'a fire-float and a combined salvage and fire-tug', which were devised with Admiralty involvement. The first ships launched were proved on the Tyne and built at Armstrong's Elswick works for their own factory use. A second pair was dispatched to Calcutta, where they provided service well into the 1950s.

The *Great Eastern*

By 1850, it was to the Raj that British engineers and foundries looked for their futures. With railways actively promoted and the first batch of locomotives contracted for the inaugural train service from Bombay to Thana in 1853, Isambard Kingdom Brunel (1806–1859) – 'Britain's greatest engineer' according to the Institution of Civil Engineers (ICE) – and shipbuilder John Scott Russell (1802–1882) laid plans for the world's largest passenger and freight steamship to make the London–Ceylon run of some 11 000 miles – around the Cape – without the need for re-coaling en route.

Its maiden voyage was to ports further east than India, but it was the era when India featured prominently in all engineering managers' minds.

The launch of Isambard Kingdom Brunel's *Great Eastern* in 1857 heralded a new era in large, screw-driven vessels, although this leviathan of a ship sported paddles and sails in addition to her screws. Screw ships rapidly superseded paddle-steamer technology, with transport in up-country rivers and shallow waters perhaps the main exceptions. The efficiency of the new technology can be assessed through a single journey from London to Calcutta around the Cape, when some 10000 tons of coal would be consumed in driving the paddle steamer to its destination compared with 6000 tons for screw, provided the speed was reduced from 14 to 10.5 knots. The disadvantage of such a speed reduction was an increase in journey time from 33 to 44 days and considerable rolling in gales, requiring bilge keels. The P&O was a pioneer in swiftly changing from paddle to screw propulsion, and for all practical purposes enjoyed a monopoly well into the 1860s when applying this new maritime technology.

The gigantic vessel was contracted by the Eastern Steam Navigation Company and estimated to be 680 ft long on the waterline. Named the *Great Eastern* (or *Leviathan*), this monster of a ship displaced 19000 tons. There were many problems, and in the end the vessel saw the shores of India only once when, in 1870, she laid telegraph cables between Bombay and Aden for the Great Ship Company.

Had the *Great Eastern* served India as originally intended, it would not only have provided some stiff competition to P&O, but during the first decade of railway construction would have earned a quick fortune at a time when space on India-bound vessels was at a premium. Records reveal that the ship's cargo area was so huge that on the New York trade route it was never once used to capacity. This would not have been the case had she plied the route to India. India's demand for machinery, locomotives and general engineering products – including a huge amount of ornamental domestic and business ironwork, especially from Glasgow's Saracen Foundry – consistently outstripped the number of available vessels. P&O would have to wait until the next century to commission a ship as large as the *Great Eastern*.

Chapter 5

PORTS, HARBOURS AND LIGHTHOUSES

*It was one of the great duties which the Indian Government was
bound to discharge towards the people of India to provide
proper harbours and lights along its coasts.*
MR GOURLEY, MP, PARLIAMENTARY DEBATE, 10 MARCH 1871

In early India, little attention was paid to the construction of harbours.
The west coast was generally not considered favourable for harbour development during the early 18th century, mainly because the Portuguese
and Dutch dominated the coast from Surat to Goa and Malabar. Although
Calcutta became the EIC base, Madras was for a long time the first port
of call for Calcutta-bound ships circumnavigating the Cape from around
1680. By 1830, cargos were discharged at no fewer than 144 points on the
Madras Presidency seaboard alone. By 1850, vast sums had been spent on
developing the Madras region coastline, with the Mutlah chosen in 1855
for the next considerable amount of expenditure. Only from 1860 were
Bombay, Karwar and Karachi upgraded into harbours of strategic and
commercial importance.

The need for lighthouses or lightships became apparent from the heavy
losses of vessels suffered by the EIC. At one time the losses were greater
than could be replaced by the shipbuilders dotted along the Thames and
Medway. Drastic measures were called for, and the EIC was not exactly slow
in responding to the challenge.

Bombay harbour and shipbuilding development

By 1750, the EIC had established a small repair shipyard in Bombay to
service its west coast fleet – the first dry dock in India. Calcutta was then

still malaria-infested and many arriving in India for the first time tried to keep well away. Even so, Calcutta was preferred over Bombay for serving EIC vessels. In 1762 the EIC established a second dry dock for its rapidly expanded fleet. These docks, the Upper and Lower Old Bombay Docks, were admired by travellers into the early 19th century.

In 1807 and 1810, the Upper and Lower Duncan Docks were completed and in service, with improvements in 1841 and 1847 respectively. These small docks were often used as shipbuilding berths, and a few dozen battle-ships-of-the-line and frigates for the Royal Navy that were built there using Burmese teak were remarkable for their strength and seaworthiness. Each vessel had the benefit of a well-planned harbour with the first generation of lighthouses to guide their movements. Steam-powered cranes were in vogue – despite the cheapness of coolie muscle – making the offloading of cargos quick and relatively inexpensive. When dredging operations were undertaken on a grand scale, Bombay harbour enabled larger ships to enter without the use of intermediary vessels.

Madras Harbour

From about 1850, there was tacit competition between Bombay, Madras and Calcutta. By 1860, the Peninsular and Oriental Steam Navigation Company (P&O) was poised to monopolise the sea route to London via the Cape, so the various port authorities vied to capture its business. Madras had much to offer, with Bombay its chief competitor. The popularity of Madras Harbour received an added boost in 1890 when Sir Alexander Rendel, the Chief Consulting Engineer, launched an ambitious expansion programme for the breakwater project, as well as for added berth facilities.

Madras was enjoying not only a steady growth in trade through its port, but greater railway facilities, which were being developed in the city's environs. The city was also recognised as a tourist centre, with advertisements for its attractions displayed in Britain. Rendel selected a 42-ton Titan steam crane to serve Madras Harbour. He insisted that the entire crane be assembled in the builder's yard and thoroughly tested. With the breakwater blocks at Madras cast in 32-ton individual cubes, the test-load for the crane was settled at 40 tons over a radius of 50 ft. Shipped in conveniently sized small parts, the Titan crane weighed 152 tons. It was still earning its keep at the time of Independence in 1947.

Karachi Harbour

From about 1850, Karachi (Kurrachee) was the first port of call for some. Unlike those at Bombay, its harbour and port facilities left much to be desired. In 1856 the government approached James Walker (1781–1862), who had just completed an extensive survey of the harbours on the Isle of Man.

Walker never visited Karachi. The EIC sent Walker 'a careful survey of the whole area of Karachi', saying that they were 'desirous of ascertaining the opinion of an Engineer of experience in tidal harbours and hydraulic works in England'. Walker considered the detailed surveys in his Great George Street office and in his subsequent report stated: 'Karachi is capable of being made an excellent harbour and ... there are no very great engineering or other physical difficulties to contend with in making it work.'

Later, the Government of Bombay appointed a Captain George Parker as Master Attendant to ensure that Walker's recommendations were implemented. Today, Karachi owes her prosperity to those two engineers.

The vast number of sailing vessels that increased in tonnage yearly, as well as the opening of the Suez Canal in 1869 for steamships, prompted the EIC, and later the Government of India, to initiate programmes to install lighthouses from Karachi to Thailand to protect shipping. When Karachi port expanded further, two lighthouses were installed with a dynamo that greatly added to the harbour's safety. From about 1880, one lighthouse, Manora Point, comprised a single-flashing, hyper-radial apparatus with 4 × 90-degree optics from Chance Bros of Smethwick.

Lighthouse progress
Up the Hooghly to the Port of Calcutta

Calcutta is situated on the Hooghly 122 miles from the open sea, and the time taken to cover that distance could be anything up to a day owing to tidal fluctuations. Previously, the journey from Saugor, 81 miles from Calcutta, had to be accomplished during daylight hours, because of the fear of running aground on sandbanks during darkness. Five years later, the lower reaches from Saugor to Diamond Harbour, 44 miles from Calcutta, were illuminated by electricity and, by 1919, vessels could travel safely round the clock. Electric lighting replaced the 21 gas-lit floating lighthouses and buoys that had provided some meagre illumination and guidance since the 1840s. Ports and lighthouses benefited enormously from the advent of electricity in India, as discussed in Chapter 14.

Prongs Reef Lighthouse, Bombay

The first guides for ships entering Bombay Harbour were a group of tombstones and whitewashed houses. These sufficed until 1766, when two signal houses were established. Two years later, the Colaba lighthouse, at the southernmost extremity of the island, was erected. This was completed in 1771 and improved in 1800. The lamp was 150 ft above sea level and the tower formed a prominent landmark.

By 1841 the Colaba light was no longer considered good enough to guide ships into the harbour. In 1842 the lightship *Colaba* was placed into commission, taking up its place about 7 miles south-west of the Prongs Reef.

The first lighthouse as we know the structure today was installed to protect navigation into Bombay in 1819. By 1869 a total of 54 lighthouses were in service, stretching from Baluchistan on the Persia–India border to Mergui on the Burma–Thailand border. All were operated by oil.

Shipping accidents at Bombay increased with the growth in trade in the third quarter of the 19th century. Although in 1906 the Bombay authorities were claiming to 'have overtaken Calcutta in importance' and claiming they could 'now rival London and Liverpool in order of cargo handled in the British Empire', it was apparent that the lighthouse and lightship that had been in service for over 30 years were no longer up to the job. Vessels arriving from Britain were approaching 5000 tons in size, and when faced with an emergency through poor lighthouse facilities were incapable of pulling up in time to avoid disaster.

The new design for Prongs Reef ensured that the final construction would enable Bombay to boast that she had the largest and best lighthouse in the Raj. The range of the light at mean sea level was estimated to be 16 miles; if the observer's eye were 30 ft above sea level, the light could be seen from a distance of 23 miles, or 20 nautical miles. The tower when completed was 169 ft tall and was estimated to have weighed 5792 tons; the area of the 42 ft diameter base was 1385 sq. yards.

The lantern and its pedestal reached Bombay in late 1873 after the first apparatus was lost in the SS *City of Venice*. The renowned Chance Bros of Smethwick made all optical parts of the apparatus. Milne & Son of Edinburgh supplied the mechanical portion of the equipment, with the bulk of the remaining material, including girders, a needle crane and windows, all arriving from Stothert & Pitt, of Bath. The Prongs Reef Lighthouse entered service in 1876. The lighthouse received electric lighting in 1898 (see also Chapter 14).

Madras Lighthouse, c.1860 (Courtesy of the British Library)

The demand intensifies

The heavy loss of sailing ships and crews prompted immediate action from mariners for the establishment of more lighthouses. The EIC did not require Home Office approval to construct 'these warning towers as it saw fit'. At the estuary of the River Hooghly – noted for its treacherous currents and changing waterway – the EIC decided to site a lighthouse some 82 miles from Hooghly town at the south-west end of Sagar Island. Constructed of iron in 1808 on Middleton Point, it stood 76 ft tall. From there, pilotage continued 40 miles to the Sandheads. Iron lighthouses were also erected on shore at various points including Madras, Karwar and up the Hooghly.

Steam dredgers

As steamships grew in size with a corresponding increase in the amount of goods and passengers carried, the need for port, harbour and canal dredging, as the following chapter explains, became vital. Two shipyards in the forefront of this engineering were William Simon of Renfrew, Scotland,

and Priestman of Hull. Both firms all but specialised in this branch of maritime industry, with virtually captive markets at home and abroad. By 1890, over 20 Priestman dredgers were in service throughout India, with a corresponding number at work in Japan and the Far East.

Over the years, dredgers increased phenomenally in size as the need arose to dredge ever deeper. A good example of the increased dimensions of dredgers from the earlier converted steam tugs to custom-made vessels was the hopper-dredger *Kuphus,* one of 32 similar vessels built for the world's expanding by William Simon. Built for the Bombay Port Trust, the *Kuphus* was launched on 3 September 1888, its passage from the Clyde to Bombay achieved in 34 steaming days. Of 222 ft length, the vessel dredged 93 000 tons in 136 hours. Records testify to the vessel providing reliable service well into the 1940s.

In 1906 the largest dredger ever built was destined for Indian service. Built to the specification of the Indian Government again by William Simon, it was 250 ft long, 45 ft in the beam and 18 ft deep, with its huge shafting and control gear driving two rotary cutters. Suction pumps – the largest on record – were powered by an independent set of vertical triple-expansion engines. Four Babcock & Wilcox water-tube boilers provided steam.

The dredger was capable of cutting a canal or channel 40 ft deep, while depositing the sludge on or beyond the banks of the waterway. The vessel was dispatched to the Bengal Presidency, where it provided reliable service for over 40 years.

East Bengal State Railway dredger

The spread of railways, especially throughout Bengal, placed the onus for the dredging of harbours squarely on the railway companies. Throughout Bengal, river barges were employed to haul coal down to Calcutta in privately chartered boats. Ferry steamers proliferated. In 1908 the Eastern Bengal State Railway placed a contract with William Simon for a large dredger, which, after undergoing trials on the Clyde, was dismantled for shipping to Calcutta. On arrival at Howrah, Burn & Company (one of the oldest engineering firms in India; see also Chapter 12) uncrated and re-erected the parts for final trials. When fully assembled the dredger was named *Alexandra*. Dispatched to the Lower Ganges at Sara to combat frequent silting and shoaling of the river, she drove a channel 20 ft below the waterline.

The Priestman grab dredger

The huge requirements for dredging large harbours, both on India's coast and on inland waters, prompted Priestman Bros from the early 1900s to build twin-screw vessels comprising the firm's most powerful grab hoppers to date. One of the largest dredgers they built was the *Bhavsinhji*, which was used in the northern Indian State of Kathiawar. The vessel's overall length was 139 ft, with a hopper capacity of 500 tons.

Priestman grab-hopper dredgers were used extensively throughout India. It was reported that 12 vessels were engaged on India's coast simultaneously before 1914. Most of these dredgers were tested in Hull.

Port construction

Kidderpore Docks

A monumental task confronted the Government of India in surveying and constructing the Kidderpore Docks from 1884 to 1887. It was conceived and undertaken on a scale to parallel any of the great feats of railway engineering in the subcontinent. In 1870, when the Port Trust was established, only four jetties were in service, with a further four under construction. Ten years later, all eight jetties were functioning, fully equipped with hydraulic cranes. However, the growing volume of trade required further expansion. A team of the port's own civil engineers was appointed – without consultants – and one of its first tasks was to measure the rise and fall of the tide with a gauge installed at least a decade before. It was found in 1882 that the tide rose 12 ft at high water and 18 ft during the monsoon season.

Capital plant, comprising huge pumps, steam engines, Lancashire-type boilers, generators and the docks' massive wrought-iron gates, were awarded to Sir W.G. Armstrong, Mitchell & Company, of Newcastle. The same firm won the bid for the supply of 56 moveable hydraulic cranes. In addition to the cranes, a pair of 'sheerlegs' capable of lifting 100 tons was erected on the east wall of the dock. Operated by steam engines from a separate boiler supply, the sheerlegs, along with all engines and machinery, were constructed by Day, Summers & Company. The renowned J. & H. Gwynne of London crafted steam-driven pumping engines. Thousands of Indians were employed.

With this expansion project, Calcutta stole a march over Madras, Bombay and Karachi – but not for long. The new docks were capable of accommodating the largest vessels that Glasgow could build, with steam-turbine technology only a decade away. New East India Railway tracks laid into the jetties could connect the tea-growing areas of Assam and Darjeeling, the jute-producing mills scattered around Bengal and the emerging sugar-growing centres dotted along the Bihar–Bengal border, providing transport directly from grower and producer to awaiting cranes for transfer into a ship's hold. The whole enterprise was a triumph of brains, engineering and human energy power that stretched from the foundries of Manchester and Newcastle to the willing village muscle of Bengal.

A floating dock on the Ganges

In 1930 the long-established firm of Wallsend-on-Tyne shipbuilders Swan, Hunter & Wigan Richardson constructed in its shipyard a complete floating dock for India. It was thoroughly tested before being dismantled and dispatched to Calcutta for trans-shipment to the right bank of the River Ganges at Mokameh Ghat, about 50 miles below Patna. The dock was of the two sectional pontoon-type, being completely self-contained, with fully waterproof compartments. It was ideal as the river rose rapidly during the rainy season and enabled the dock to be floated to site. The overall length of the dock was 210 ft, with its width 56 ft. Its lifting capacity was 500 tons. The dock was fully self-reliant for power, with diesel generators, a vertical multi-tubular boiler and hydraulic pumping machinery. The dock was employed in repairing shallow-draught paddle steamers, barges and landing stages, and earned its place in local history for servicing the ferries between Mokameh Ghat and Semaria Ghat.

Stability

The EIC built harbours to facilitate trade. The building of lighthouses demonstrated an era of peace and the stability of these harbours. Though the French built some lighthouses in their colonies, they do not compare to the scale of British endeavour. Lighthouses represented both external and internal stability. As EIC rule increasingly gave way to Parliament and 'direct rule', and routes to India and a burgeoning shipbuilding and engineering industry were firmly established in the major cities of Calcutta, Bombay and Madras, focus turned to the inland infrastructure in India.

Chapter 6

CANALS AND WATER SUPPLIES

*What a wonderful change of affairs... A year of your reviewing of the great
projects now in hand or estimating will, I hope, give such a start to irrigation
and navigation as India will never forget, under God's blessing.*
ARTHUR COTTON – LETTER TO AN IRRIGATION OFFICIAL c.1864

With the exception of the Ganges, Brahmaputra, Hooghly, Indus, Beas,
Jumna and perhaps a few other larger ones, not much use was made of the
rivers in India for navigation or irrigation before the arrival of the British.
Perhaps this was because those who braved the elements were unsure of
ever returning home after confronting unknown fast-flowing currents and
allowing for the unidirectional flood waters from the Himalayas during
spring thaws. The early and medieval people of India used a few timber
and circular boats made of wickerwork covered with leather, which floated
down some of the larger streams and are now accepted as the only means
of short-distance transport by water that was attempted before the height of
Mughal rule. Boats then were hacked out of tree trunks – not dissimilar to
the European practice some 500 years earlier – and it appears that any water
trade of consequence was confined mainly to coastal regions.

British restoration begins

When Governor-General Lord Wellesley (1798–1805) advocated much-
needed improvements to Calcutta's drains, roads and river communications
in 1803, steam-driven mechanical devices had yet to arrive on Indian soil.
Time-honoured hand tools were attempting the impossible: traversing
Calcutta's Salt Water Lake with a deep canal from Dhappa to Samookpotta
where it was destined to connect Tolly's Nullah (canal) with the Bidyadhari
River. The nullah's namesake Major William Tolly has gone down in local

Calcutta history as a principal benefactor to the city. Cleared out by Tolly at his own expense in 1775 the main channel was from 13 ft to 17 ft deep at low water, with a rise of about 5 ft at high tide. At best the canal was 180 ft broad. By 1807 some 20 000 people were estimated to have been gainfully employed in commerce, river transport and general maintenance as a result of the works. As rule in India came under increasing parliamentary scrutiny and direction, Wellesley's public policy did not always win favour with the EIC Court of Directors but demonstrated an early vision of public works and improved infrastructure. In his own words he considered it 'a primary duty of the Government to provide for the health, safety, and convenience of the inhabitants of this great town, by establishing a comprehensive system for the improvement of its roads, streets, public drains, and water-courses'.

Following in Wellesley's footsteps, the early administration of Francis Rawdon-Hastings, later the Marquis of Hastings – not to be confused with Warren Hastings – deserves considerable credit for taking the first steps towards the restoration of the old Mughal canal system. Hastings' first approach was the establishment of India's infrastructure from his experiences of the sorry state of his domain when travelling the country. A tour of Britain's dominion in India opened his eyes not only to the country's wealth, but also to the crumbling conditions that had further decayed following the collapse of Mughal rule. Hastings lost no time in giving Britain's civil engineers virtually *carte blanche* to apply their expertise for the common good.

The Madras area once abounded in bridges from the days British settlers established their presence in the city. The first bridge was constructed in about 1670 across a 'stream-type canal' until the Egmore Bridge was erected in 1703. In 1818 Hastings gave orders to EIC civil engineers that all Mughal canals and roads were in urgent need of repair and action must begin. He knew that 'Hindustan was wealthy and this wealth is lying untapped for want of a proper canal system'. Plans for irrigation throughout eastern India complemented those for canal construction. Fawcett, Preston reported in about 1820: 'The sale of pots and pans to India continues with the supply of winches and tools for the excavation of canals for the East India Co.'

Canal irrigation

Southern India

The first canal undertaken for the exclusive purpose of navigation was known as the Cochrane Canal and extended from Pulicat Lake through the Ennore backwater to Madras. This canal was originally constructed with private capital, and without any influence from the EIC. Started in 1801, work was unduly slow, perhaps because of the primitive equipment used during the digging phase; it was completed in 1806 by Basil Cochrane who had taken ownership of the project in 1802. It was a great success with both communities, and the venture was eventually taken over by the government of Madras in 1837 after Cochrane's departure from India. Traffic began to flow towards Coimbatore, and the canal proved very popular. The beginnings of municipal infrastructure were taking place in Madras, and steam engines were then in vogue. In that year water flowed into the city, where boats queued up to carry passengers to Kakinada in the north and Marakkanam in the south. However, the emphasis on canal construction was changing and irrigation was coming to the forefront of the official arguments in favour of canal construction. Cochrane's Canal became one of the earliest official canal projects sanctioned and would lead to the first great irrigation works constructed on a grandiose scale in the Madras Presidency.

The Grand Anicut on the Cauvery

In 1834 repairs restoration began to the Grand Anicut (dam) originally built on the Cauvery River in the second century AD by the Chola rulers. Once the greatest engineering feat in India, the anicut had fallen into disrepair and was heavily silted up. The anicut had been constructed to divert the waters from the Coleroon river branch southwards to the arid Cauvery Delta. In 1804 an EIC survey had established that the bulk of the waters were flowing to the Coleroon branch with the Cauvery at best a 'trickle' in dry seasons. Work began to restore the Anicut but the project was fraught with engineering difficulties.

In 1836 Arthur Cotton devised a viable scheme for controlling the Cauvery River with the construction of a new anicut at the head of the Coleroon to direct the water back to the Cauvery, saving its priceless water from running to waste – a feat of civil engineering that finds no 21st-century counterpart. This achievement was the beginning of a brilliant career in civil and water engineering that had a major beneficial impact on India. The Rajahmundry District was known for succumbing to the vagaries of monsoons, responsible for causing frequent famines. The success of the scheme added an additional 250000 acres to the 150000 acres of already irrigated land and brought urgent famine relief. As the network expanded nearly one million acres of land was irrigated. Sections of this waterway survive today, as do some of the earliest masonry bridges still in daily use.

The financial returns on the project were also an outright success and provided the impetus for a novel proposal by Cotton to introduce canal irrigation to the Godavari Delta.

The Godavari Delta

After the repeated crop failure and recurring famine in the 1830s and 1840s, Cotton was given a free rein to harness the waters of the Godavari River to irrigate the impoverished coastal area. The area had already been surveyed by Sir James Caldwell of the Bengal Engineers at the beginning of the century. Work commenced in 1847, with completion of the Godavari Anicut in 1852, which successfully harnessed the waters of the Godavari to irrigate over 700 000 acres. Captain (later Major-General) Charles Orr of the Madras Engineers played a major role in the engineering works, with the full support of Cotton who was convalescing after serious illness and exhaustion. In the following decades the network was extended several times. As the largest canal in the world at the time, the scheme was heralded as the greatest engineering achievement by the British in India. By the 1890s the canal network served a large part of the Godavari Delta enabling the intensive production of sugar and rice. The magnificent 1852 headworks of Cotton's Godavari Delta irrigation scheme remains virtually as he left it.

The Kistna Canal

Canals were constructed with such success that the government undertook a similar venture for an anicut across the Kistna River, located to the south of the Godavari canal system. The Kistna flows south-east through Karnataka and Andhra Pradesh to the Bay of Bengal. Construction of its headworks at Bezweda began in 1852. The canal irrigated more than 500 000 acres and also provided navigation throughout the Kistna Delta, connecting with the *Godavari* system. Significant credit for the scheme must go to Major-General Orr who headed the construction of the weir, having learnt his trade under the supervision of Cotton on the Godavari works. No major engineering difficulties were encountered.

East Coast Canal and Buckingham Canal

From 1852 a massive extension programme was undertaken to the section of canal known as Cochrane's Canal. By 1857, then renamed to the East Coast Canal, the system extended to the Kistna Delta 69 miles north of

Madras and was quickly extended further in response to famine, with the route designers digging further northwards to construct relief work. During 1877 and 1878 the Duke of Buckingham extended the East Coast Canal with a 12-mile link to connect connected the Kistna–Godavari system with the city of Madras for the purpose of famine relief after the devastation of the 1876–8 famine. The eponymously named Buckingham Canal system was recorded as being an unqualified success. The expanded delta systems contributed much to the prevention of famine and the transformation of the deltas into fertile, 'life-giving rice fields'. During the great famine of 1876–8 the inhabitants of the Godavari and Kistna deltas were spared, and it is estimated that the food sent out of the area as relief saved three million lives. Migration to the now-abundant deltas increased steadily between 1880 and 1901.

This inaugural canal, now integrated into a network in and around Madras, grew until 1898, when its existence was threatened by the onslaught of railways. By then an estimated £930,000 had been spent. In retrospect the canal was also a success, its pioneering spirit motivating other schemes to advance with the benefit of more mechanised construction equipment. As recently as 1961 there were about 1200 boats plying the canal system in and out of the city, carrying some 19000 passengers and 190000 tons of cargo in that year. Today, the remains of this embryonic scheme for south-ern India can still be seen, but regrettably the mismanaged and neglected canal now contains little more than raw sewage and the city's refuse.

In other parts of southern India in and around Madurai, canals that were forged from 1840 greatly stimulated trade for this fertile region. Cotton, the acknowledged expert of his day for irrigation and flood control, was also in-strumental in a similar scheme in Orissa. Other areas of the Indian Empire were also embracing canal technology. Waterways in and around Mysore and Trichinopoly soon gained acceptance, the progress only checked when railways were developed from 1856 in Madras from plans formulated to connect the Madras Residency with Mysore, Bangalore and Trichinopoly.

Northern India

By 1853, when the inauguration of passenger train travel gripped India, the river navigation of the whole country had improved steadily and canals for freight traffic had been attempted with varying success on a small to med-ium scale. There were many canals constructed throughout Calcutta and the southern part of Bengal from 1822. However, early trials were far from successful and fast-flowing waters from Himalayan spring thaws destroyed many of those embryonic endeavours. By 1835 some success was assured, with canals constructed as far away as Asansol and neighbouring Bihar. By 1880, over 20000 miles of canals and distributaries criss-crossed western Bengal and Bihar.

The East and West Jumna canals

The first major work of any consequence in northern India concerned the restoration of two Mughal canals from the Jumna, which was 'undertaken with little idea by the government or the engineers of what was involved', according to Joyce M. Brown in her well-researched paper, 'Contributions of the British to Irrigation Engineering in Upper India in the 19th Century'. In those early days the British had little experience of irrigation engineering and European models were redundant in the face of the unique Indian terrain, the seasonal Himalayan meltwaters and the vagaries of the monsoon.

The canals dated back to the 14th and 17th centuries, having originally been constructed to link series of rivers and streams. They had fallen into disrepair and the last of the Mughal-built Jumna canals had collapsed 50 years before the EIC entered Delhi in 1801–3. The British started the restoration of the Western Jumna and Eastern Jumna Canals between 1817 and 1830 in order to settle war-torn districts by establishing pastoral communities. Waters had ceased to flow during the Mughal troubles of the mid 18th century. Famines were endemic and irrigation was getting special attention.

Work started immediately under the Marquis of Hastings' advocacy, with the latest machinery of its day imported from Britain. Watt-type steam engines, fuelled by wood, were summoned into service, and by 1820 water flowed again into the city of Delhi. From that date, the great system of British irrigation started with the era of canal-building that later complemented the spread of railways. India's huge untapped resources and large geographical land mass ensured that both systems of transport worked in harmony and in parallel for the better part of a century, catering for both national and local commerce.

One of the first engineers to devote himself to the canals in northern India was Captain George Rodney Blane (1791–1821). Blane joined the Bengal Engineers in 1808 at the age of just 17 and was later appointed Superintendent of Canals, Delhi Territory, and stationed at Ludhiana in the Punjab from 1814. He immersed himself in the restoration of the old

Mughal canal built by Shah Jahan on the west bank of the Jumna, which passed through Karnal to Delhi. His dedication to the task was rewarded when he brought water into Delhi in 1820.

Blane must be given credit for the initial success in canal engineering by the British in India during this period under Hastings. It was a period where there was little knowledge and no formal training in hydraulics, especially in India. Equally, it was an era given over to sheer tenacity of purpose and empire-building, where initiative, guts and determination made up for any deficiency. Regrettably, Blane's life was tragically cut short by malaria when he was only 30 years old. He is credited with restoring the old West Jumna canal that grew to 347 miles in length, with a further 1803 miles of distributaries, coming into service in 1825.

The East Jumna Canal restoration was entrusted to engineer R. Smith, who devoted seven years between 1823 and 1830 to covering the 129 miles with a further 679 miles of distributaries. A novel feature of the civil work was the use of concrete, which was applied in the well-foundation construction. The Sirsa Branch, about 92 miles long, was added to the Western Jumna Canal between 1886 and 1895. The scheme was successful in the mitigation of famine. In response to the 1837–8 famine, these early works provided the stimulus for the construction of the far more ambitious Ganges Canal.

The Ganges Canal

With the planned construction of the Upper Ganges Canal from 1842, plus two canals in Bengal, the need arose to train local engineers. This consideration led directly to the establishment of the Thomason College of Civil Engineering at Roorkee. The canal, completed in 1854, comprises 440 miles with 2709 miles of distributaries. Costing £3 million, it was then the most expensive canal works undertaken anywhere.

A civil engineer, Sir Proby Cautley (1802–1871), is credited with drawing sketches of the Doab Canal in the Punjab between 1823 and 1833. These drawings and suggestions for improvements were later acted upon and the Doab Canal was cleared and extensively renovated to become a vital means of water transport.

The Punjab government, newly formed after the British annexed the Punjab in 1849, undertook the engineering. The canal, in the tract between the rivers Ravi and Beas and completely new, became known as the Bari Doab Canal. The motive was, as on the Jumna Canal, to settle the area after the recent wars. It took nine years (1850–9) to build the canal, which was constructed on the same principle as the Jumna Canal. The builders were fortunate in having as the canal's projector Joseph Dyas – an engineer who gained his experience on the West Jumna Canal.

The construction of the Ganges Canal, which was mainly undertaken by hand, was confined to the narrow strip of country lying between the Jumna and the Ganges. At Hurdwar it received the waters of the latter river, which it spread through innumerable channels and over much countryside before finally returning to the Ganges at Cawnpore and to the Jumna a little below Calpee. By April 1861, 520 miles of the main canal had been completed with 1542 miles of distributaries well advanced. To serve the canal, a pump was manufactured at the Roorkee Workshops (see also p. 259) to the designs of the British pump firm of Whitelaw & Stuart. It was installed at Muzaffarnagar during the famine year of 1860/61 as an experiment to test the practical value of irrigating the high land. The upper headworks for the Ganges Canal were at Bhimgoda.

The Solani Aqueduct, some 20 miles from the head of the canal, required a good deal of spoil removal, and at this site it was led away in wagons running on rails, pulled by either men or animals. All rails were imported from England and assembled under European supervision. The wagons had a side tilt and 450 of these were built in India, by either Burn or Jessop in Calcutta. *Thomason*, a locomotive from Kitson & Hewitson of Leeds, was first used on 22 December 1851, and can claim the credit of being the first to enter service on Indian soil.

The *Mechanics' Magazine* had commented favourably on the 'imported' Sikh workers from the Punjab to the Ganges Canal who toiled in the extreme heat and bitter cold to complete the work.

> These hardy northern Hindoostani Sikhs have taught us what hard work really is. They speak and ask for little during their toil. They earn their privileges and whatever time is taken for prayer is quickly made up once back at work. It is little wonder that the resident Englishman in retrospect views these tall, stout sikhs with their unusually funny and colourful headgear, as a once worthy enemy who stood up to the might of the British Empire and were only beaten by sheer force of modern arms and weapon technology.

The canal was completed at a time when new canals and waterworks, such as the Dhoon and Rohilkund Canals and the huge Agra Irrigation Works, were being constructed, and the manifold benefits of this British triumph soon became apparent to all – especially the local people. The

Calcutta Engineer's Journal in 1864 summed up opinion collectively:

> It has been shown that grain has been produced sufficiently to feed a million-and-a-half hungry people for an entire year, without counting a proportion of supply of fodder for cattle, and wholly irrespective of a large crop of sugar and cotton, which is equivalent to a further addition of food. It has been shown that it caused the circulation of coin to the amount of Rs.15,122,640 or £1512,264; while it is probable that the government has been saved from making remissions of land revenue to a large amount. But the services and benefits of the canal did not end here. One of the greatest difficulties in administrating speedy relief to the famishing population of the regions, and the tardiness and cost of conveyance, has been eliminated. Along the lines of the canal, this aggravation of the common distance was not now felt. The unexpected demands produced as sudden a supply of the means of transport. The boats plying the canal were largely increased and the Ganges Navigation Co. was entitled to return a dividend of 34% for the half year.

The British India Office, 'concerned that the railways had only advanced to comprise a mere 4944 miles by April 1867', proffered a more or less blank cheque – in reality £2 million – to extend existing and construct new canals. Initially, the Punjab was singled out for special treatment. The cost of constructing railway lines in northern India was approaching £20,000 per mile: more than four times the cost of canals. Additionally, canals required little maintenance and no locomotives, and were therefore free from fuel costs. At the same time as advancing railway tracks towards Afghanistan and the Himalayas, the export trade from the establishment of new industries – especial food – stimulated the Government of India to improve all communications with new canal building and larger boats to haul 'cheap and bulky articles down the Indus'.

In addition to the newspaper's comments, Colonel Turnbull, the Superintendent General of Irrigation, observed a phenomenal change to the horizon since the diffusion of the Ganges Canal and its distributaries, saying:

> The east [of India] is becoming one huge garden due to canals and irrigation. It is abundant in wheat, lentils, mustard, rape as oil seed, carrots, coriander, cumin, tobacco, flax, all the esculent vegetables of Europe, hemp, rice, cotton, indigo, sugar and barley to mention but a few. Beautiful groves of mangoes, tamarinds and bananas all overshadow village pagodas, mosques, temples and tanks, giving the whole area from our efforts an everlasting beauty to the landscape.

The area was transformed with the removal of stagnant and wasteful marshes. The project had been fraught with engineering difficulties and needed unprecedented innovation in canal construction and meticulous planning. Social considerations were also accounted for. Construction at Hurdwar was strictly regulated to ensure the depths would not result in the drownings of the pilgrims who bathed in the waters of the Ganges.

Sirhind canal

Again in the Punjab, the Sirhind Canal from the Sutlej was constructed from scratch between 1869 and 1882. Its irrigable area of over one million acres made it one of the largest canal systems built in the 19th century and, because its line passed through native states, its building established the principle that tracts should be irrigated in the best way possible, irrespective of national boundaries. The Maharaja of Patiala, a neighbouring state, contributed to the cost of the canal's construction. Navigable between the Sutlej and the Patiala, it was designed by James Crofton and Robert Home, engineers who had worked on the Bari Doab Canal, which received its waters from the Ravi River.

In the initial proposal for the Sirhind Canal, the estimate for the first 37 miles selected advocated the use of 26 stationary engines with wagons on tramways drawn by ponies. This was later modified to four engines. The first two miles were excavated using two locomotives. On completion, the canal was 538 miles long with 4639 miles of distributaries, while the overall cost was £1.9 million.

An English supervisor working on the Sirhind Canal, Thomas Shaw from Derby, returned home on its completion. He related to his colleagues, many of whom were then departing to seek their fortunes in the Raj, that the local Sikh workers:

> require little superintendence and can be trusted to accept and carry out instructions with the minimum amount of added direction. I have never heard of these tall people once withdrawing their labour. I was always glad that our clerk of works ensured that these loyal and industrious tribesmen were paid on time weekly. To withhold any monies from their toil would be party to blatant dishonesty, which was the lot for the rest of the country when the white man was absent to direct fair play.

Up to 1900/01, the following canals (with their rivers) were built in Upper India. West Jumna, Jumna (1817–25, 347 miles); East Jumna, Jumna

(1823–30, 129 miles); Upper Ganges, Ganges (1842–54, 440 miles); Bari Doab, Ravi (1850–9, 369 miles); Agra, Jumna (1868–74, 109 miles); Sirhind, Sutlej (1869–82, 538 miles); Lower Ganges, Ganges (1872–8, 768 miles); Betwa, Betwa (1881–5, 168 miles); Chenab, Chenab (1883–92, 426 miles); Jhelum, Jhelum (1898–1901, 113 miles).

The 'Ashtitank Convict Canal'

In its 7 June 1882 issue, *Engineering* reported the completion of the Ashtitank Convict Canal in the Sholapur District. It was a project designed to connect with the Great Indian Peninsula Railway, with the principal dam being 12 709 ft long and 58 ft at its maximum height across the Ashti Nala Valley. The storage capacity was 1500 million cu. ft from a catchment area of 92 sq. miles. Two canals with an aggregate length of 29 miles were built.

The work provided employment to a large number of local people for almost the entire famine period, with British supervisors creating food halls to provide regular meals to their workers – who included women and children – with an average daily complement of 9257. The maximum number employed on any one day was 17 179. Convict labour was used on a large scale, the daily number varying from 237 in 1878 to 774 in 1880. The revenue earned from the irrigation returned about 4% on investment.

A cynical viewpoint and control of famine

London's stock market during the late 1860s was raising funds for the long-talked-of irrigation projects of which the largest then on consultants' drawing boards was for the Madras & East India Irrigation Company Terms usually favourable to railway investors with a 5% guarantee soon enabled the £2 million in shares to be oversubscribed. Railways in that year were approaching £18,000 per mile when constructed in central and eastern India, while canals were being rapidly cut for less than a quarter of that price.

Until his death in 1899 Cotton continued to lobby the administration in India to invest further in canal irrigation. Yet, with the Mutiny of 1857 and rule in India transferred to Parliament, these were times of tremendous change. In 1854 the Government of India took control of canal-building and public works, and came under increasing pressure to source private investment for further construction. However, there was always a cynical and alternative view prevailing. The journal *Engineering* in its 12 April 1867 issue was far from encouraging to investors with capital to spare: 'For our part we cannot view the case [for canals] very hopefully and at best it must be, under the present system, very many years before India is supplied as she ought to be with railways and canals.' Today, many of those same canals still function after a century and a half of reliable service. Following the great famine of 1876–8 a Famine Commission was appointed to address the need for direct state intervention and support of irrigation schemes and water management.

Clean water supplies and sanitation technology

The issue of a widespread regular supply of water has plagued the whole of the Indian subcontinent since time immemorial. The problem has not been solved entirely almost 70 years after Independence, especially in India's numerous villages. It vexed the early English settlers, who during the early 17th century sensibly confined their trading to the coast, allowing passing ships to replenish supplies more easily. Recent research on the history of water supplies has revealed ancient and medieval technology in earthen bunds or dykes from about 1500 BC at Inamgaon (Maharashtra). In Gujarat, late 6th- and 7th-century masons dug deep trenches to reach dependable, year-round groundwater. Similar excavations were noted in Bengal from that same era. However, a huge problem that confronted ancient and medieval India was that of storing water during periods of drought. Apparently, earthenware pottery was the short-term solution to the problem while wells were dug.

The Mughal period introduced some form of dams or 'tank bunds', but these crude attempts literally evaporated or, once rains ceased, gradually soaked away. One of the lasting projects was the Hussain Sagar dam fed by the Balkapur River, which branched off from the Musi River some 32 miles from Hyderabad. The dam was vital for the twin cities of Hyderabad and Secunderabad. When completed, it was 1.5 miles long and covered an area of about 8 sq. miles. Later, the British supplied drinking water from this dam in about 1889, and a regular supply to both cities was taken from the newly built Osman Sagar in 1921. This project was designed and built by British civil engineers acting for the Nizam of Hyderabad. Hussain Sagar survives today.

Calcutta water supplies

With the Raj firmly in India's seat of power and in full control of her infrastructure, not unnaturally the first consideration when it came to establishing a regular supply of pumped, filtered water in India was given to Calcutta. The administration had to look homeward for technology. Even so, Britain's own water infrastructure in 1800 was still rudimentary, and the scourge of cholera loomed continually on the horizon. In Calcutta wells were dug and a small dam created with pioneering hydraulic turbines to pump water into the city. Calcutta's population had risen exponentially from 12 000 in 1710 to 117 000 in 1752, increasing to around 160 000 in 1800.

There was extra stimulus when disaster struck in Calcutta. Cholera broke out in 1817 in the Ganges Delta because of the appalling brackish water that people were forced to use and to drink. The burgeoning city simply could not cope. The epidemic spread to Western Europe in 1823, Moscow in 1830 and London in 1832. The Hooghly River was never clean at the best of times, 'little more than a floating sewer', and the British had to act fast. The answer lay in adopting steam-driven pumping power on a large scale.

Calcutta had depended for its water needs on the Hooghly River and a few tanks and very small reservoirs outside the town limits. The tanks themselves were wholly dependent upon rainfall. The first improvement was affected in 1820 by the erection of a small pumping plant using a Watt beam engine on the banks of the river. This water was distributed directly from the river to a limited area by means of open-brick aqueducts laid along the streets, from which the fluid could be drawn and tanks replenished.

The pumping plant was subsequently enlarged in 1835 when a condensing engine from Bolton was used. Later, as the population approached the 300 000 mark, the city's fathers recognised the necessity for an improved water supply, with emphasis on drainage works; discussions went on for a number of years. In 1859 it was found that the city's finances could not support a scheme. Three years later the plans were revitalised, and orders placed for heavy machinery plus a filtering and distribution system for the supply of 3 to 4.5 million gallons daily, at an estimated cost of £135,000. The contract for the whole works was given to Messrs Brassey, Wythes & Aird based in Birkenhead. The firm had already gained an excellent reputation for building railways and bridges the world over.

Construction began in 1866. The waterworks was designed to supply 6 million gallons daily for an estimated increase in the population to 400 000. Intake works were erected on the riverbank at Palta, about 14 miles from Calcutta and practically beyond the influence of the brackish water brought in by the tide. Three beam engines pumped water into six masonry settling tanks having a total capacity of 24.5 million gallons. From these tanks water gravitated, after settling onto 12 filter beds with a collective area of 240 000 sq. ft. After filtration, the water was collected in a central well and gravitated through a 42-inch cast-iron pipe from Scotland's Glenfield & Kennedy foundry. The fall from the filtration beds was an average 1 ft to the mile – very little by modern-day standards.

At Tallah, additional pumping machinery was installed in a covered reservoir and from here the water was pumped to Wellington Square, which incorporated additional beam engines for distribution. This initial large-scale solution to the problem of water supplies to Calcutta lasted until 1888, at which point a completely new water system was installed that comprised three Worthington horizontal pumping engines from James Simpson of Newark, 48-inch cast-iron piping 66 000 ft in length, plus huge settling tanks and filters capable of handling 82.75 million gallons, with additional James Simpson pumping engines at Wellington Square. When a complete new pumping station at Halliday Street was added, Calcutta's inhabitants greeted the project as 'yet another feather in Britain's large hat of industrial progress and achievements', according to The Gazette.

However, Calcutta's population rose so quickly as a result of the established jute industry, heavy engineering and shipbuilding and the greatly expanded port facilities, that by 1891 the water system could barely cope for over a million people. For growth in the southern suburbs, a new pumping station was built at Bhowanipur, with two large triple-expansion James Simpson horizontal-type steam engines that necessitated additional engines at Tallah. The Tallah engines were supplied by Fawcett, Preston, by then well established in supplying bale presses for Bengal's jute industry.

A pumping station was quickly built at Barrackpur with direct-acting engines from Tangyes, of Smethwick. The old Watt beam engines were scrapped, the engines obsolete for an age of highly efficient and more powerful horizontal-type compound engines that had completely captured the market. Another increase in capacity was ordered in 1898 and implemented the following year, raising a further 900 000 gallons per hour with the assistance of two further engines from James Simpson, each capable of pumping 211 000 gallons per hour. Combined with a new filtered-water works, the cost of the intervention came to £3 million, but to the poor it was a lifesaver. The recurring scourge of cholera had, at least in part, been eliminated.

In 1896 the Howrah Waterworks was commissioned, with water taken from the Hooghly River via a large purification plant. Two sets of compound-duplex engines from J. Evans, with steam raised by three Lancashire boilers, pumped the river water into large filter beds. Additionally, two smaller steam engines, from the same manufacturer, pumped water from the beds to a generously sized reservoir. A further modification and increase of capacity using the proven and highly efficient three-stage expansion, duplex-vertical, direct-acting engines from James Simpson, 'requiring

WATERWORKS AND EMERGING TECHNOLOGIES

ONE UTILITY THAT PURCHASED large numbers of steam engines was the waterworks. It is believed that an engine was first used for irrigation service in Bengal in 1826. Since the first pumping engines, believed to be from James Watt, were installed on the banks of the Hooghly River in Calcutta in 1820, a continuous programme of refurbishment and upgrading in the industry was barely enough to keep pace with demand. The Calcutta Waterworks was subsequently enlarged in 1835 with a condensing engine, which served until 1867. In that year a pair of Watt beam engines were installed at the Pulta Waterworks Pumping Station that provided reliable duty until 1901, when the demand from the city was more than 6 million gallons daily.

James Simpson, of Newark, enjoyed considerable success with new and repeat orders for the water and heavy industries that sprang up throughout India, its flywheel-type engines relegating the old, low-pressure Watt beam engines to obscurity. Watt could not compete with Simpson's advanced technology, which heralded the demise of Watt's steam-engine production. The two engines James Simpson supplied to the Calcutta waterworks were capable of delivering 4000 gallons of water per minute (gpm). So successful were these engines that sales to Bombay (two units in 1889), Poona (1890), Delhi (two in 1890) and Hubli (two in 1891), along with an additional order for Bombay for two large engines capable of delivering 10 417 gpm of water to cater for the city's swollen population, enabled the firm to achieve household-name status.

By 1911, James Simpson was favoured by many municipalities over its competitors. In that year, two vertical engines were purchased for the new Calcutta drainage scheme and six other similar units were delivered to Delhi and Karachi. The firm produced a 'standard' pipeline engine for long-distance pumping when gravity could not be used. One of its largest water contracts for engines to serve India was sold to Allahabad. In 1916 five large centrifugal pumps with engines for an irrigation scheme were dispatched and were believed to have been in service as late as 1990.

huge valves of massive proportions', was able to deliver 380 000 gallons per hour against a head of 140 ft. Steam was supplied by Babcock & Wilcox boilers from Glasgow. The engines and boilers were installed in a brand-new pumping station at Mullick Ghat and were believed to be in service until the late 1930s.

The Calcutta Waterworks developed into a showpiece of infrastructure for India and a model for other utilities. In 1914 the Pulta Station of the waterworks was considerably expanded with a huge uniflow steam engine from James Simpson that pumped water through a 42-inch pipe. At that stage Pulta comprised four huge pumping engines, including an all-but-redundant vintage beam unit. The James Simpson engine was then the most powerful water-pumping engine in the whole of India. A further expansion of the Calcutta Waterworks system at Howrah was conducted in 1926 with an additional VTE-type James Simpson-Worthington engine from its extremely active Newark foundry.

The average Indian now began to see the accrued benefits that British rule was implanting. Disease was common throughout India principally because of the unbearable heat, bad sanitation and widespread rubbish, but British civil engineers constructed massive drainage systems and dams, and the first recognised refuse collection by bullock carts began in Calcutta. Incinerators were established there in about 1860, with the people paying to have their rubbish burnt. The Governor of Bengal – Sir *John Laird Mair* Lawrence – decreed in 1865 that all rats must be caught and destroyed. When British residents themselves began to implement the policy it soon caught on with the Bengalis. This was also the era when the first public toilets were built. The facilities were widespread from 1870, and in 1878 the Sanitation Bill tried to enforce public hygiene with a decree that the construction of toilets was compulsory 'even in mud huts in and around Calcutta'.

Bombay water supplies

One of the chief problems that faced Portuguese mariners visiting Bombay and Surat at the end of the 15th century was the lack of fresh water, and initially they had to beg, borrow or steal supplies until rudimentary wells were dug. It was a difficult task, especially during the dry season. The sole source of reservoir water was off Bombay Island, and that was only intermittently available. Nothing of any major or lasting consideration was achieved until the EIC established its rule from 1661, when the island was ceded to the English 'to be held at an annual rent of £10 in gold' from 1668. From 1700 a series of tanks were built, but the water stored was totally inadequate for even the few thousands then residing in Bombay. By 1800, with shipbuilding established, early cast-iron pipes carried water from the mainland, but this attempt to alleviate the problem was also inadequate. It was only with the arrival of the steam engine, according to the *Mechanics' Magazine,* that water supplies could attempt to match demand. Migrants and Europeans were then flooding into the growing metropolis, with EIC shipbuilding yards established alongside those of Parsi origin.

The first project for increasing the water supply to Bombay by means of surface collection, which was the only practical plan in the case of the town, was devised by Colonel Sykes of the EIC. He proposed in 1829 to collect and impound rainwater falling on the high ground at the south-western extremity of Bombay Island. Though inadequate because of the capricious rainfall, this was the start of better things to come. A Colonel Jarvis revised Sykes' plan in 1845, but did not increase supply to any large extent. The following year, a Major Crawford pointed out the capabilities of the Goper Valley – a natural choice for surface collection – and a storage reservoir was created.

In 1851 huge water projects were undertaken that culminated in the Tulsi and Vehar lakes schemes following an extensive survey by Lieutenant De Lisle, a superintendent for the EIC. Work started more or less immediately, with the creation of an artificial lake 14 miles from Bombay in the centre of the island at Salsette. It was designed to contain 11 million gallons for its 1300 acres. When evaluated, the area covered was four times greater than any reservoir constructed in Europe or North America. 'It was the largest overseas work undertaken by British engineers to date', according to *The Engineer.* It was assessed that for each pound spent, upwards of 35 million gallons would be supplied to Bombay. In comparison, for that amount of money, only 12 million gallons were delivered to Liverpool, Manchester or Glasgow. The waterworks were architecturally designed to be a showpiece for the empire. At the foot of the inner slope of the principal dam, the inlet tower was 104 ft tall, cast in iron by Bray & Champney of Leeds, the company responsible for the reservoir civil works and pipe-laying. All cast-iron piping was manufactured by D.Y. Stewart & Company of Glasgow. The steam-engine firm of James Simpson of Belgrave Iron Works, Pimlico, London, furnished the huge sluice valves, hydrants and a sizeable portion of the special castings.

In 1870, when the success of the Suez Canal was obvious to all and the French were busy installing a series of lighthouses along the Egyptian and Persian shores, Britain was 'over committed in Bombay', to quote *Engineering* in August of that year. Major Crawford, now Chief Engineer for the Tulsi scheme for increasing the water supply into Bombay, was granted an extra £320,000 to purchase additional steam-driven pumps and piping. Water flowed in 1872. Those schemes could not have been timelier. Textile industries flourished with shipbuilding – both sail and steam – considerably augmented by Bombay's first large engineering works in Richardson & Cruddas. Shanty towns sprang up virtually overnight, all demanding increasing amounts of water. However, the demand for water was all but matched from the huge projects conceived by the EIC. If for no other reason, the company can be lauded for bringing potable water to Bombay's inhabitants.

Beginning in the year of Queen Victoria's Jubilee, 1887, a new waterworks was installed at Rajkot to augment the main water supply for Bombay. Three small dams were created with a 9-inch main connecting the principal dam to the pumping station some 3 miles distant. A local dignitary formally opened the completed project in August 1892.

Cotton-spinning and textiles demanded large amounts of water. The wealth of Bombay abounded thanks to huge profits made in the new industries from 1850. The well-heeled not only wanted their gin and tonics, but the privilege of ice in their drinks. For this symbol of affluence, the Bombay Ice Manufacturers was formed, and it consumed large amounts of drinking water. Business must have been good and the water supply reliable, for when a steam engine was delivered to the firm from Willans & Robinson, Rugby, in 1907, the premises grew considerably. A similar machine from the same firm was also dispatched to a textile mill in Cawnpore in that year.

The next major water-supply scheme placed into service was the 110-mile Lake Tansa to Bombay pipeline project, in 1926 to 1927. The 80 000 tons of pipe arrived from Dorman Long's new Redcar Works, and was built by Braithwaite Engineering at its specially created Mulund factory, which was staffed by 12 Englishmen and 700 locals. Braithwaite also supplied some 16 000 tons of bridges, of which the largest structure, Kasheli Bridge near Bombay, today carries the pipelines and heavy road traffic. Pauling & Company built three huge dams at Lonavla, Walwhan and Shirawta for what became known as the Tata Hydro Scheme, which, aside from water, additionally provided electrical power principally to feed Bombay's cotton and textile industries.

Bombay's sewage disposal system did not receive the attention it warranted because of the emphasis on water supplies. The first major scheme was put into service with a huge government-sanctioned project commissioned in 1908. However, population growth tended to outstrip all the resources and skills that British engineers could implement. Fortunately, the reliable functioning of the railway was a principal factor in controlling famine and disease throughout the Bombay area.

Waterworks in other cities in India

The 1231 wells installed in Nagpur during the 1820s soon proved inadequate when the town became a hub of the railway industry. In about 1825 the nobility of the area had established a small dam from an ancient installation on a reservoir across a valley on the River Nag, principally to supply the palace. Waterworks were created in 1869 and expanded in 1874 when the population reached the 90 000 mark. James Simpson provided engines and Marshall of Gainsborough boilers. Large diameter piping of 0.5-inch thickness was supplied by Richardson & Cruddas of Bombay,

With a regular supply of water, Nagpur flourished. A large trans-shipping depot and foundries were established (Courtesy of Institution of Civil Engineers)

then branching into large water projects after having earned its reputation in the building of bridges. The following year, additional James Simpson steam engines arrived with huge quantities of cast-iron piping from P. & W. MacLellan. This enabled water to flow from a newly created dam capable of storing 1500 million gallons, to resolve the town's water problems. With that regular supply of water, the town flourished as a large depot for the Bengal Nagpur Railway. The railway company then established large foundries to undertake maintenance and renewal of locomotive parts (see Chapter 10).

The first major scheme for the town had operated from 1883 on the gravitation system from an existing reservoir at Ambajheri, but the daily needs of its 48 000 people and the huge requirement for the Bengal Nagpur Railway could not be met from a gravity supply. By 1900, when a large reservoir was constructed and quickly placed into service, Nagpur was more or less self-sufficient.

The City of Baroda enjoyed the benefit of the Maharaja Khanderao's wealth in 1866 when a scheme for bringing water into the area from the Nerbudda River was surveyed. Alan W. Forde, a senior English water engineer, investigated this proposal, though little is known of the outcome. Later, water was brought from the River Surya at Jafferpur in ad hoc pipes

Embankment dam at Nagpur water works, c.1900 (Courtesy of Institution of Civil Engineers)

using hydraulic turbines. Additional waterworks were created about 1868 and expanded in 1878 when the population increased to around 100 000.

The rising population and expanding industry continued to outstrip the meagre water resources. Work started on a huge new works in 1885 to afford a constant daily supply of 3 million gallons for an estimated 120 000 consumers. An earthen embankment across the Surya River, 14 400 ft long and 54 ft high, capable of storing 1287 million cu. ft of water, formed a complete new reservoir. From the main input valve house to the Mandvi Tower in Baroda, the distance was nearly 13 miles. To carry the huge amount of water, 7700 tons of piping was required. Large settling tanks, each 404 ft by 394 ft and 13 ft deep, were constructed of brickwork in lime mortar. To pump the water, four engines from James Simpson were installed. Additionally, a 4-mile canal was cut to feed the village of Sayaji Sarovar. After a most successful trial run, the Gaikwar officially opened the whole complex on 20 March 1892.

In Sholapur waterworks were conceived on a large scale to feed 16 villages. Steam engines were first installed around 1891 by James Simpson.

A waterworks was established in Poona in 1790 by Sardar Raste, using English piping and 'elementary machinery', but not engines. British water engineers throughout the Victorian era subsequently tapped the surrounding hills with steam-driven pumps that served until electricity came into vogue. A dam 107 ft high spanned the valley of the Mutha River in 1879, and was the first of the large dams in the Deccan with sufficient capacity to supply not only Poona but Kirkee as well. In 1916 the Central Water Power Research Station was established in Poona to make technology available to the rest of India.

Some 50 miles south of Poona is Nira Railway Station. Close to this area, in 1885, British hydraulic engineers began constructing a dam and a lake – Lake Whiting. It served the local people well until 1928, when a huge scheme with an initial cost of £1.25 million was budgeted for a combined dam, reservoir and canal project from the Lloyd Dam at Bhatgarh, the source of the supply. The lake had an area of nearly 15 sq. miles, and fed into the Nira Canal network over a mile long. When commissioned around 1930, over 4000 sq. miles were irrigated.

Ahmedabad built its first waterworks in 1859 when a Lieutenant Dickenson of the Royal Engineers raised water by means of four Persian wheels. It was primitive, certainly, but it far exceeded what the Mughals had devised. Improvements were made in 1864 – by which time Persian wheels were obsolete – with steam-pumping engines obtained from Britain via Nicol & Company of Bombay. Fresh distribution pipes and filters were installed. After 1873, further improvements were made as Ahmedabad grew industrially. Again that improvement proved inadequate. By creating headworks on the Sabarmati River and installing horizontal pumping engines 'from Bolton', the whole water supply was upgraded. Both engines were capable of lifting 133 000 gallons of water in ten hours.

Waterpower was conceived as a means of driving simple mechanical equipment as well as for generating electrical power. An early scheme was the installation at Gokak in southern Mahratta. The fast-flowing Ghatpraba River was capable of supplying local domestic needs as well as small industry. In 1886 it was decided to divert part of the river slightly to supply a cotton mill, using three hydraulic turbines from the firm of Escher Wyss, in Zurich, Switzerland. Power was transmitted by a novel system of wire ropes over 700 ft to the mill; it was the first of a series of mills to use waterpower. Astonishingly, each rope was over 1500 ft – a length previously unheard of. The rope speed was calculated at 5600 ft per minute. The whole plant was placed into service on 5 October 1887, earning the Swiss foundry an excellent reputation for quality work delivered on time. The project, which created much local wealth, proved an added bonus when a small dam was constructed once water was driving the turbines. The original cast-iron pipes from Kilmarnock-based Glenfield & Kennedy have provided service for over 115 years to date.

The city of Jaypore in Rajputana was founded in 1718, during the early days of the Raj. A small stream, the Amani Shah, was evidently damned or 'bunded' and diverted to the city. The slope was measured to be 16 ft per mile. Originally, wells supplied the inhabitants but English engineers supplemented these with a flow from the earthen dam. Water was then taken from the River Bandi. The dam itself was founded on wells and appears to have been built on first-rate masonry about 60 ft high and 300 ft in length. It served the populace until 1873, when steam power was applied from a pair of horizontal, high-pressure Lancashire-built engines, capable of delivering 36 000 gallons per hour to the city. In 1883 the supply was all but exhausted and a new site was selected 750 ft above the old pumping station, where an embankment was calculated to impound 148 million cu. ft of water. Work began in June 1884. Light rails for railway gauges, 16-inch and 24-inch, capable of handling diminutive double-sided tipping wagons were ordered by telegraph from England. Once on Indian soil, 129 wagons were used at one time. Extra locals were employed, with the workforce strengthened by elephants. The work was completed in September 1885, and a huge flood saw the water rise nearly 6 ft in 24 hours. Compound beam engines imported from Easton & Anderson of Erith, Kent, incorporating a rather antiquated bucket-and-plunger-pump mode of operation, delivered some 2 million gallons per day. Coal was hauled from mines near Calcutta, and extra engines were installed when consumption rose considerably. No water rate was levied on the city, the cost being met by the Maharajah of Jaypore. Two English engineers, a foreman, three native drivers, a smith, six firemen, six oilmen, four labourers and ten apprentices operated the waterworks with its steam engines.

By the 1880s, steam-pumping engines were the norm for all of India's large town water supplies. In Mysore, over one decade, the water distribution supply doubled with the installation of steam engines from Appleby Bros of London. The old existing hydraulic turbines – some from the 1820s – were of the 'Hercules' type. In Amritsar, new James Simpson steam engines capable of raising 1000 gallons per minute upgraded the water supply by drawing the fluid from 100 new wells constructed in 1904. The Kolar Water Supply contracted James Simpson for engines, with steam raised by Babcock & Wilcox boilers, not only to drive pumps but also generators to power induction motors, all capable of delivering over a million gallons per day, with the total height of lift being 550 ft. However, perhaps the largest pumping station installed during the first decade of the 20th century was for the Madras government. From that same Newark-based engine manufacturer, the first large diesel engines to be installed in any waterworks for pumping duties enabled the government to deliver a staggering 315 million gallons every 24 hours from eight engines. The James Simpson engines were found to be capable of supplying 10% more than was guaranteed.

The phenomenal growth of waterworks throughout India stimulated indigenous industry to start supplying goods and services to that utility. The Balham Dass Waterworks at Raipur in the Central Province is a good case in point. Traditional wells were established long before the British arrived, culminating, in about 1833, in the area's first reservoir off the Karoun River. In 1891 the town's population was assessed at 30 000. The English consultants drew up a plan for a reservoir to cater for 40 000 people at 10 gallons daily per person. Two pumping stations were built with triple-expansion horizontal-surface condensing engines from James Simpson. For the 624 tons of cast-iron piping, the Barakar works of the Bengal Iron & Steel Company was favoured, with all valves and fittings from Glenfield & Kennedy Company, as India then did not manufacture valves of that size or capacity.

A service reservoir holding 420 000 gallons was created and, allowing for growth, consumption was estimated to be 273 000 gallons per day. Over five years in service, only 212 000 gallons daily were drawn. From the arrival of all machinery and the start of civil works, the whole project was completed in less than 16 months – a great achievement for the combination of British design and superintendence and indigenous labour.

One London-based firm specialising only in pump manufacture was the Essex Street Works of Messrs Gwynne & Company. Its reputation was justifiably earned from its dedicating all foundry efforts to basically one engineering product – the centrifugal pump – and perfecting the design as new metallurgy developed. With outbreaks of cholera from the mid 1850s, Gwynne had the right product at the right time. Sales to India rose rapidly following unqualified success throughout Britain.

Part of the United Provinces, Cawnpore grew rapidly thanks to its surrounding fertile land and good rail connections to Delhi, Bombay and Allahabad. Its 1892 waterworks – with a large extension in 1910 capable of pumping 4.5 million gallons daily – was soon outstripped by population growth. In 1913 a large waterworks was established with a capability of pumping 7 million gallons daily. The Puech-Chabal plant was constructed within budget at £11,466. The designer, Mr W.T. Nash, blended the works into the local Mughal architecture of Fatepur Sikri, the fortress of the Emperor Akbar at Agra.

The Cauvery–Mettur Reservoir Project

The Cauvery-Mettur Dam in the Madras Presidency has a place in early EIC history. The EIC took over Tanjore District in 1801, and in 1836 Arthur Cotton's construction of the Upper Anicut greatly relieved the difficulties of water supplies. In fact, the project was so successful that it was found necessary to build a grade wall across the river in order to curtail the supply and prevent erosion.

The idea of placing a dam across the river in the neighbourhood of Mettur was an old one, its origin rooted in history, but the scheme prepared by Colonel W.M. Ellis of the Royal Engineers, and later of the Madras Public Works Department, formed the basis of the work that benefits India today. The scheme had to wrestle against opposition but was finally sanctioned in

1925. The first engineers appeared on site in 1926, building a large camp to house 14000 workers. Some 50 miles of new roads were constructed and a special railway to Salem, 25 miles away, was built with 50 miles of 2 ft track equipped like a tramway to operate 26 locomotives together with 1000 wagons for transporting materials. The engineering buildings comprised workshops, locomotive repair depots and a powerhouse. Power was obtained from Sivasamudram by means of a 62-mile transmission line.

Large areas in the Tanjore district were brought under irrigation by means of canals that resulted in the creation of a reservoir dam of 59 sq. miles. Portland cement manufactured in India was used throughout. The cost was assessed at £6 million. Labour was plentiful and the dam provided much-needed employment from construction services to locomotive drivers hauling the materials for the project. Many firms supplied capital equipment, including English Electric and Metrovick (Metropolitan-Vickers) for electrical plant. Over 100 pneumatic drills and picks arrived from Ingersoll Rand of America. To crush over 3000 tons of stone daily, three large crushing machines arrived from Hadfields of Sheffield; while to deposit large amounts of concrete, two huge distributing towers were designed and manufactured by Stothert & Pitt of Bath. These towers, standing 304 ft high and weighing 1400 tons, could handle 166 tons of cement per hour.

The dam was an unqualified success from the moment water was released. Its 94 million cu. ft capacity was sufficient to deliver water to over 1 million people. Apart from providing a continuous supply of electrical power, nearly 500000 acres of crops were watered. Lieutenant Colonel Sir George Stanley (1872–1938), Governor of Madras, officially opened the project on 23 August 1934. It was then the largest dam in India and the sixth-largest in the world.

Analysis of water supplies in large Indian towns

The British administration was doggedly determined to supply India with pure, freely available drinking water. The Chief Health Officer and a team of health and water scientists undertook a fully detailed survey in 1900/01. Its conclusion was:

> With reference to the analysis of water received from Bombay, Madras, Benares, Agra and Jubbulpore as they were given in different systems of numeration and related to different months, I have released them all to parts per 100000 and compared them with Calcutta water for the

corresponding months. Comparing Bombay, Madras and Calcutta, Calcutta shows the best results throughout. As regards bacteria, Bombay water contained 1060 whereas Calcutta showed only 164 per cubic centimetre. The absence of free ammonia and small quantity of albuminoid is a good feature of Calcutta. There is little to choose between Agra and Calcutta water when analysed and Allahabad water on the ammonia may be pronounced decidedly inferior to both of them. Jubbulpore was decidedly inferior to Calcutta as was water from Benares when similarly compared. On the whole, in summary Calcutta water compares favourably with that of other large towns in India.

Water management, famine prevention and the legacy of British rule

The North-West Provinces, with an area of 23 360 000 acres, of which some 60% lay under cultivation, were tended by an estimated 18 million of the 30 million inhabitants. Extensive irrigation works started by EIC civil engineers were considerably added to in the age of public works and were vital in a region with sparse rainfall. It was assessed that by 1869 nearly 1.5 million acres were irrigated, of which 110 000 acres were allocated to rice, 589 000 acres to wheat and 466 000 acres given over to other crops. The region was adjudged by the Lieutenant Governor of Bengal as 'the most successful in the annals of Indian irrigation that the populace must thank the hard-working Punjabis for in no small measure'. Chief among irrigation works was the Ganges Canal. Its total length was 3694 miles, then comprising 654 miles of main channel and 3040 miles of branches and distributing streams. On these branches were located the chief cities and towns of Delhi, Agra, Allahabad, Lucknow, Cawnpore and Benares.

Prevention of famine was at the forefront of the incredible endeavours by the British engineers, most of whom started out as complete novices in hydraulic engineering and were true pioneers in the field. Criticisms of their endeavours focus on problems of water logging and salinity, problems that engineers would continue to grapple with well into the next century. Most of the schemes were unprecedented and fraught with unique engineering difficulties that required the finest minds of the time, and often came at great personal sacrifice. Financing became increasingly problematic as the Government of India came under pressure to source private investment. By 1875 the boom in loan-financed state construction was over. Later efforts were hampered by tensions in India and overseas. The outbreak of World War I and World War II further set back public works with the restraint in funding and supplies. The inquiry into the Bengal famine in 1944 concluded that large-scale private enterprise was needed to supplant the public works schemes.

Yet, by 1942, five years before Independence, the area of irrigated land in India stood at 57 million acres, of which 32 million were irrigated from public works. The endeavours of the engineers who saved so many from famine and brought renewed abundance and trade to life across India attracted worldwide attention. Herbert M Wilson of the US Geological Survey was sent to India to study the British-built canals to see how the schemes could be translated to the US, where large-scale irrigation was still in its infancy. Today, water management remains one of the great testaments to British rule in India.

Chapter 7

ROADS: LEAVING NO STONE UNTURNED

In India, the roads are at best, little better than roads, and whenever deep
rivers ... chains of mountains, or other obstacles, oppose themselves to the line
of direction of the road, it is carried round.
JAMES RENNELL (1742–1830), THE 'FATHER OF THE INDIAN SURVEY'

The Grand Trunk Road from Calcutta to Delhi is a perfect specimen of a
metalled road, adapted to the rapid transport of wheeled carriages.
COLONEL PROBY CAUTLEY

'Roads, for all practical purposes, were non-existent when considering
India as a whole,' according to a Captain Hamilton, who visited Bengal on
behalf of the EIC in 1706. The Mughals offered Hamilton a proposal for
renovation, but no amount of inducements could convince him to take up
the rulers' entreaties.

Road construction was not given any degree of importance or attention
during the first 50 years of EIC's hegemony from 1690. It had received scant
attention during Mughal times and not one hard-core, all-weather highway
existed. There was some perfunctory effort to 'throw a few stones in a pot-
hole and make do', but nothing substantial was attempted. The local people
had allowed their bullock carts to traverse the same time-tested rutted dirt
tracks for centuries. Besides, with rivers the principal form of communication for the movement of goods from farm to market, there was little or no
trade that required an all-weather highway.

The Maquis of Hastings, Governor-General of Bengal (1813–1823), began road construction with a more military point of view. He had directed
that work should begin on the perennial canals from 1817 and in Bengal
advocated the development of civil engineering education, with an emphasis on road and canal construction. In later life he became patron of the new
Hindu College in Calcutta, then the seat of government, but he continued
to advocate widespread road improvements on every available occasion.

In 1835 Madras was the most advanced and best-organised city in India. Despite much upgrading to roads and what were once main highways, repairs were mainly inadequate. It was freely acknowledged that a more concerted approach must be applied. In 1831 the Madras Presidency abandoned all attempts to paper over the cracks, issuing instructions that all district superintendents should do everything to resurface and rebuild without any government grants. An era of great commercial promise for Madras was rapidly developing, with fine harbours and an expanding coastal trade with the rest of India under EIC control. The directors of the Company saw fit to stimulate this enterprise, actively encouraging the Presidency to go it alone in an era before the spread of telegraphs.

Though the EIC directors, many of whom had never set foot in India, felt it was their pockets that should benefit first and foremost, their servants in India were quick to realise that the indigenous people should be considered on a par with the Company. In a report on the famine of 1837 in the north of India, Colonel Richard Baird Smith, who directed the relief measures that reached 'some 80,000 Indians', cited the lack of roads and railways as a major factor in the severity of the famine in the United Provinces. And so, from 1830, the ramshackle infrastructure throughout its Indian Empire was given a significant boost through a grand programme of domestic projects, and funds for road construction were allocated on a regular basis.

By the 1840s road-building costs were averaging at £400,000 a year. A 'silent revolution' began in the agrarian economy as a direct result of British rule, which saw the rise of bullock carts and a shift away from the heavily burdened and slow pack-bullocks, which were then released for work in the fields. The improved road network gave rise to faster bullock carts that could carry 10 times more than their predecessors and the pack-bullocks.

The Grand Trunk Highway – Calcutta–Delhi–Lahore

In 1836, work began on a highway 1423 miles long to connect Calcutta with Lahore. It was originally the brainchild of Sher Shah Suri in the 16th century, but like the ideas of most rulers then, it was a figment of imagination to impress a downtrodden populace. It fell to the British to create this great highway, which was surveyed to follow the old route from Calcutta to Delhi. As usual there were those who scoffed at the need for an all-weather metalled road, with river transport being much cheaper and possibly free from bandits such as were met on the road. This fact could not be ignored.

However, Governor-General Lord Bentinck (1828–1835) – who established English as the medium for communication – looked to India's future and resolved to push on with the project that was to distinguish his career. During the heyday of its construction the road became recognised as the most remarkable thoroughfare in India, if not in the world, according to the London *Times*. It crept north-west, mile by mile, under difficult conditions and with many discouragements of a kind that would be inconceivable today. Raised a few feet above the plain, to save it from flooding, its massive rock foundation was laid by thousands of native workers, many of whom were landless and in need of employment. Wages compared favourably with the returns from peasant holdings. New villages were created en route, especially around Benares, that survive today.

It was known as the Grand Trunk Road, and was grander than any scheme ever before conceived, even by the Romans. This highway also incorporated the first modern masonry bridges installed in India. The EIC, using local artisans under the Company's own civil engineers, erected solid, all-weather stone bridges that have withstood the test of time. In the Bareilly district alone, a total of 78 bridges, of which 65 were masonry and only 13 of timber construction spanned rivers up to 400 ft wide. The terrain was arduous and there were many engineering difficulties to overcome.

When the road was completed, for the first time in Indian history wheeled carriages could roll across the land and as a 'consequence the map of India began to shrink', according to the *Morning Chronicle*. The Grand Trunk Road subsequently developed a life of its own: marching regiments behind the blare of trumpets and cheerful brass bands; wedding processions with the jangle of bells, laughter and ribald jokes, and a trail of scarlet litters; holy men pacing sedately from shrine to shrine; trade-carrying carts drawn by horse or bullock, remarkably travelling twice the normal distance in a day on the smooth, hard road. A legacy of Bentinck were the trees that had been planted at 60-foot intervals to provide beautification and much-needed shade to travellers.

The traffic that the Grand Trunk Road carried before railways appeared was incalculable. The construction costs had come to £1,000 a mile and a further £50,000 a year in maintenance. The whole thickness of metalling had to be renewed every six years well into the 1880s. The tarmac surface was novel in India at the time. The arrival of traction engines and steamrollers warranted a reappraisal of the road and further strengthening was undertaken. Delays were endless – lack of funds and skilled labour plus

lack of materials and transport over second-class roads all contributed to
the frustration of those who used the highway. Even so, nearly 1500 miles
from Calcutta to Lahore of thoroughfare, virtually all tree-shaded, was
described by *The Times* as 'a truly remarkable monument to early British
energy in India. For boldness and conception, worked out under vastly difficult conditions, it has hardly been surpassed.'

Road construction progress in the era of public works

In 1854 some 3600 miles of hard-core were laid, and by the end of 1856 the
Government of India assessed the road structure to have expanded to 8749
miles. Indeed, it was a great feat of civil engineering, especially taking into
consideration the fact that those small bridges were erected so quickly and
with little modern steam machinery. As yet, there were no large girders
across Punjab's main rivers to carry road traffic. However, the British had
laid on steam-powered ferries, with many run and maintained by Punjabi
Sikhs. Road building was soon to overtake the growth in maritime passenger services. At the same time as these EIC civil engineering directives,
Royal Engineers arriving from Britain were fully engaged in constructing
roads and bridges throughout the Punjab. The era of EIC rule had run its
course and direct rule from the British Parliament was firmly in place, and
with it a determined policy of improvement.

While the Grand Trunk road was being constructed, other roads – then
little more than tracks – were also greatly improved. At the same time, under Lord Dalhousie's tenure as Governor-General (1848–1856), the postal
system was being reorganised, the telegraph introduced and an extensive
programme of public works established in the hope of completely opening
up India. But without an infrastructure based on good, all-weather roads,
those programmes would not succeed. Roads were essential to any postal
system. It was also the era when steam engines were spreading throughout
India, and without solid, all-weather roads to haul the huge parts required
to raise power, transition into an industrial society could never be achieved.

From the 1860s, the central government began to devote much attention
to roads, especially of the fair-weather type. Statistics reveal that in the period 1853–4, some £582,000 was spent on main roads and bridges, rising
to £2.75 million in 1866. Notable feats of road building were highways to
bring cotton to the coast during the American Civil War (1861–5). These
were known as the Arbyle Ghaut Road and the Kyga Ghaut Road, both of

STEAM ROAD ROLLER

AS THE PRESSURE FOR ENLARGING the network of roads kept increasing from growing businesses and the civil and military establishment, a need was felt for finding new ways of laying roads. William Clark, Chief Engineer to the Calcutta Municipality, conceived the idea of laying roads using steam in place of bullocks for powering a heavy roller. He communicated the main details of his project to the engineer F.W. Batho of Birmingham, who completed the design in 1862. Local to Batho was the Birmingham engineering and machinist firm of Worsdell & Evans, who undertook the making of India's first steamroller. The finished steamroller was dispatched to India in 1863, where for the next seven years it did splendid work.

By 1902 asphalt and bituminous road surface dressings were proving their worth in Indian cities. Steamrollers were made in sizes from 6 tons to 15 tons with the first Aveling machines appearing under patents in that year. Many were shipped to Calcutta once production was in full swing. From 1916, Aveling & Porter was exporting half of all its steamrollers, in varying sizes and weights from 15 tons to 25 tons, of which nearly half went to India for permanent-way construction. An estimate from the renowned Road Roller Association states more specifically that of 350 rollers built after 1918, around 200 were exported to India alone.

From the late 1870s the Gainsborough, Lincolnshire, foundry of William Marshall enjoyed considerable success with its diverse range of steam-road machines. The firm had the distinction of rolling a smooth layer of tarmac across the huge Dufferin Bridge that spanned the Ganges.

A great many rollers were shipped to the subcontinent fully assembled, once huge cranes from such firms as Stothert & Pitt were capable of off-loading them in one complete lift. In 1985 five Marshall rollers were still in service in Chembur, near Bombay, the oldest dating from 1911. During the 1930s, a contract was signed between Marshall and Tata Industries to assemble complete kits dispatched from England. The last batch was exported around 1955, and some of these assembled kits can still be found in rural areas.

By 1935, steamrollers proliferated throughout India. Roads were metallised as city boundaries expanded.

which connected Dharwar to Carwar in North Canara. Both were metalled highways. The war in America also stimulated fair-weather road construction in Nagpur and other cotton-producing districts.

Road improvement provided a huge benefit by extending communications to areas that were infamous for recurrent famines. Long-awaited infrastructure after centuries of misrule and incompetence was quickly in place once Britain assumed full responsibility. Two areas that received considerable funds for road construction from the 1860s were the North-West Provinces and Oudh. An aggregate 4654 miles of first-class and 24104 miles of second-class roads at a total cost of £2.02 million were audited that included the Grand Trunk Road.

In the Punjab 1000 miles of metalled roads were constructed in the 1860s, which proved immensely valuable to its inhabitants. Multan was also given priority due to the demand brought about by the increase in trade from the steam navigation that now plied the Indus. In the same decade, the spread of railways throughout the Madras Presidency was all but matched by a corresponding spread of roads. A huge public works programme of road construction – along with extensive renovations to waterways including the Irrigation & Canal Company's properties – were redeeming features to the encouragement of industry in south India. By 1880, the total length of roads in Madras State was 5150 miles (8288 km). Included in this total were 25 main highways covering some 4000 miles (6437 km); ghaut or exception roads stood at 650 miles (1046 km); and 'salt roads' accounted for 500 miles (805 km). The Madras Public Works department budgeted £120,000 annually for road maintenance.

While the railways were spreading at a far greater rate than road mileage could be constructed, statistics reveal that serious efforts were made to extend the road infrastructure. From 1860 to 1880, Bengal road construction increased by 400 miles (644 km), the Cuttack coast road to Nagpur was completed, Bihar added 400 miles (644 km), and the Great Deccan Highway within the Jubbulpore territory between Mirzapur and Nagpur was upgraded to first class.

In a work published by Arthur Cotton, the renowned civil engineer and great advocate of canal-building in India, it was estimated that 'including all between the oceans to encompass the Himalayas and Afghanistan, i.e. a million-and-one-quarter miles, would require about 50,000 miles (80,467 km) of first-class highways besides nearly 10-times that distance in minor roads merely on an initial basis'. His dreams were not fully realised at

THOMSON-CROMPTON STEAM ROAD TRAIN

ONE OF THE PRINCIPAL ADVOCATES of taking steam road transport
to India was R.W. Thomson (1822–1873). Much of the progress made in
the 1860s was a result of his inventive spirit and indomitable energy. Born
in Scotland in 1822, he had never been to India, but was apparently fired
with admiration for the industrial progress – especially railways – 'that was
advancing the Indian Empire'. Barely a week passed without the ordinary
newspapers referring to 'some form of mechanical and social progress to
improve the lot of Queen Victoria's Indian subjects'.

In 1867, Thomson invented a portable steam crane comprising a 'pot-
type' boiler and India rubber tyres. The following year, Indian railway companies began using 'this novel device for off-loading cargoes that otherwise
would be the work of loyal and hardy Indian backs'. In December of that
year, Thomson devised a small road locomotive on India rubber tyres that
the newspapers pronounced to be 'in advance of everything that preceded
it'. Its first contract was for Ceylon, and was quickly followed by orders for
India. In 1869 Thomson sent out a small experimental engine to the Punjab.
Colonel R.E.B. Crompton was able to fit rubber tyres that were unaffected
by climate. In 1868 a Mr Armstrong, of Rawalpindi in the Punjab, manufactured a neat two-cylinder steam car. The carriage travelled at 12 mph on
a level road, and half that speed on an incline of 1 in 20.

Colonel Crompton (1845–1940) first had the idea of putting steam into a
vehicle and propelling it on an Indian road just before Armstrong's efforts.
One of the stipulations of the contract between Thomson and the Indian
government was that at least one engine should have a test run of several
hundred miles drawing a load. In 1870 Crompton was sent home from the
Rifle Brigade, then stationed at Peshawar, to look after the construction of
the engine. *Ravee* was the first engine to reach India in 1872 and was immediately set to work, moving stores from the Hassan Abdal camp, working
day and night for six weeks. A sister engine, *Chenab*, arrived early in 1873
and, after a few mishaps, ran day and night for nine weeks, covering nearly
2000 miles without visiting the repair shop. The *Indus* arrived in 1873 and,
although weighing only 8.5 tons, it tackled a train of 64 tons, ascending an
incline of 1 in 33 at a speed of 5 mph. When all engines were operational,
regular services were run from Jhelum up to Attock, and later a daily haulage service was maintained between Rawalpindi and Attock.

Costs were fully documented. Hauling 14 vehicles carrying 15 tons of
goods going one way, or 7 tons of passengers both ways, worked out at

Crompton's prototype the 'Blue Bell' in India, which he had shipped out to India, c.1870 (Courtesy of the Institution of Engineering and Technology Archives)

2s. 2d. per train mile or 3.45d. per ton-mile at Indian rates. The animal transport cost was found to be 5.28d. per ton-mile. In the case of bullock carts for the heavier loads, the cost was assessed at 6d. per ton-mile. Tyre costs were estimated at 1.5d. per mile.

Engines were soon carrying mail and passengers between two stations in the Punjab, some 70 miles apart. They could run on wood fuel with a large water tank for about 15 miles without stopping. The two-axle omnibuses were equipped to carry up to 65 passengers. Unlike Britain, with its severe speed restrictions, India was not subject to any regulation and speeds of between 15 mph and 20 mph were occasionally achieved over short distances. Crompton extracted the maximum haulage capacity the vehicles could manage. They could at one time haul 19 towed vehicles carrying a 40-ton payload at 5 mph up a gradient of 1 in 18 on the recently completed Grand Trunk Road.

The demand for Thomson's road steamers between 1870 and 1873 – especially from India – overtaxed the manufacturer, Tennant, which 'could not make them fast enough'.

The steam road train in India died as quickly as it was born. The inevitable progress in railway construction and its immediate acceptance by the public at large, spelt the demise of that short-lived advancement of steam technology in India. Crompton would go on to make a major contribution in electricity supply in India (see page 295).

the time of Independence. Nevertheless, Indians could travel in unparalleled comfort by 1947, whether by train, car, bus or bullock cart.

By the end of the 19th century, the mileage of metalled or first-class roads rose from approximately 37 000 miles in 1860 to 69 000 miles in 1900. Smaller, compacted roads accounted for over 200 000 miles. All major design and construction fell under the control of the central government, which was still in Calcutta. Other roads were within the sphere of various local authorities. Second-class roads were not provided with permanent bridges, and third-class roads were usually only passable for approximately eight months of the year.

The phenomenal road-building programme could not have been achieved without traction engines to haul masonry and aggregate, and steamrollers to smooth a finished surface. Just about every foundry in Britain turning out these products saw their road machines perform service in India. Right up to 1980, National Asphalt Products & Construction Company, of Chembur, Bombay, relied mainly upon Marshall steamrollers of over 50 years old.

The arrival of cars and lorries and a proposal for national highways

Until 1900, steam lorries – mostly from Sentinel and Foden – used the Indian hard-core roads, which were generally confined to coastal cities. The 20th century brought the introduction of the petrol lorry from Albion of Scotland that could travel farther afield. The only disadvantage was the lack of petrol stations, but as fuel oils became more widespread so did the internal combustion engine. Taking advantage of the demand for petrol lorries, Thornycroft, of Chiswick, London (established in 1898), had built upwards of 5000 lorries for the War Office by 1917, with 100 units, rated up to 5 tons, dispatched to India before 1913.

By 1910, a few cars were noted in Calcutta and Bombay. Only the best roads were suitable for motor traffic and distances were limited. Motor haulage then was totally unsuitable for bulky cargo, so the railways, elephants and bullock carts were still the usual means of conveyance. By 1914, motorcars and motorcycles – as well as the ordinary push-bike – were gaining widespread acceptance. During and after World War I, the use of motor cars by Europeans and India's privileged rich began to prevail in cities, while the use of lorries – mainly as feeders to the railways – increased rapidly. Statistics

Elephant Carriage, Bikaner, 1902 (Courtesy of the British Library)

reveal that imports of motor cars rose from some 3000 in 1913 to a post-war five-year average of about 8000, and to over 20 000 in 1928/29. Imports then declined to 6201 in 1932/33, but rose to 15 697 in 1937/38. Of these, 40% came from Britain and 41% from the United States and Canada combined. The importation of motor buses – especially Guy, of Wolverhampton, and Leyland, from Leyland, Lancashire – plus vans and lorries fluctuated similarly, with 15 077 imported in 1937/38; 81% of all non-bus vehicles arrived from the United States and Canada combined. From Britain, the Morris and Wolseley were perhaps the most popular models. World War II added to the number of vehicles. In 1943 thousands of chassis parts, later assembled by Indian workmen, were obtained from the US and Canada to help with the war effort. The cessation of World War II allowed renewed focus on public works and the development of road communications in India.

In 1943 Sir Kenneth Mitchell, the Controller of Road Transport in India, presented his extensive report into the unique demands of road construction in India and developed a proposal for the creation of a national network of highways. The penultimate Viceroy of India, Archibald Wavell (1843–1847) was enthusiastic about the national highway programme, which was put into action on 1 April 1947, with the Government of India taking full responsibility for its construction and maintenance costs. In the early years after Independence road construction stalled though Mitchell's earlier highway proposal would form the blueprint for the National Highways programme of later years.

Chapter 8

MAIL SERVICES, THE TELEGRAPH
AND THE TELEPHONE

*To send a telegram to England from Calcutta and receive a reply the next day is
merely one more technical achievement in the legacy of Imperial Britain.*
MORNING CHRONICLE, 1881

Possibly the first postal service in India was established by King
Chandragupta – who reigned from 322 BC to 298 BC – when he dispatched
letters to his governors in around 322 BC. Later, the historian Ziauddin
Barni described in his chronicles that the horse and the foot runner were in
existence for communication during the 13th century. Horses were used for
speedy delivery in certain parts of the country but it was really the foot runner who was the mainstay; the runner was called 'Hakara' in ancient books,
but later termed the postal runner, or dak runner. 'Dak' is a Hindi word for
post or mail. The runner, during the 15th and 16th centuries, carried a cleft
stick, and the small bag with the mail was held in this cleft. When travelling
at night, he lit resinous twigs to guide him on his way. These postal runners
had to face numerous hardships and danger, travelling through forests
inhabited by wild animals, crossing swollen rivers during monsoons and
trekking across snow-capped regions. The stick and the spear could afford
hardly any protection. However, despite all the odds, the dak runners kept
running and delivered the mail. They were recorded by an early EIC official
as 'a hardy race of people, honest and with a great sense of duty'.

The postal services

The EIC established postal runners on regular routes, setting stages for
handovers. By 1688, the company had asked its Bombay and Madras offices

to each build a post office and directed that all mail should be brought to the post office first. Robert Clive introduced the system of sorting mail with the EIC seal into different bags according to direction. When Warren Hastings took over in 1774, he introduced further reforms, providing an official postal service to the public. After the EIC fully established itself and became the *de facto* administration of the country, it decided on major reforms to the postal system. The Post Office Act of 1837 combined the presidencies and declared all private post illegal.

From the early 18th century, the EIC's letters were conveyed by sailing ship around the Cape of Good Hope, it taking the best part of a year to receive a reply from a letter dispatched from Calcutta. In some instances mail was transported to Marseilles in France and from there on horseback to Calais. The urgency of getting mail from India to London taxed for decades the minds of those engaged in surveying routes. When the route via Suez and camel overland to Alexandria was established, a package of mail in 1834 once achieved the remarkable time of 59 days. But that record was eclipsed two years later when one English mail reached Bombay in a mere 45 days.

Postal rates depended upon weight and distance, and hand-struck Bishop Marks were applied on letters at Calcutta. Little known is the Zemindari Dawk, established in 1707, which flourished well into the period of Warren Hastings. The three presidencies of Bombay, Madras and Calcutta used different hand-struck stamps.

The first Indian stamps were known as the Scinde Dawks, issued by the Commissioner of Scinde, Sir Bartle Frere (1815–1884) in 1852. Frere was an admirer of Sir Roland Hill (1795–1876), who had established the world's first recognised postal system with a letter carrying a stamp in 1840. Frere's stamps were first introduced as red on vermilion wafers, but for reasons unknown they were soon discarded. The EIC Court of Directors was keen that all stamps should be printed in India. Captain H.L. Thuillier, Deputy Surveyor General of the Survey Office, Calcutta, after some trial and error printed stamps of 1 anna and 4 annas, but from 1855 until 1926 stamps were printed in England by Thomas De La Rue & Company, which also printed banknotes for the empire. However, since 1926, when a new press was established in Nasik, all stamps have been printed there.

After the Indian Empire was consolidated, the centrally issued stamps were valid throughout the country except in the territories of the native Maharajas, who issued their own stamps; some overprinted the name of their state on the centrally issued stamps.

The post office in Calcutta's Dalhousie Square and the Lal Dighi 'tank' (or reservoir), c.1870. The post office was erected on the old Fort William site in the 1860s (Courtesy of the British Library)

Standard-sized post boxes were first installed in England around 1850. One company in the forefront of casting iron 'pillar letter boxes' for the British Post Office was Andrew Handyside at his Britannia Works in Derby. From about 1870, the firm cast a similar variety of boxes for India, with Bombay and Calcutta installing the first shipment. The construction of roads led to safer postal routes, with mail carts replacing dak runners. In 1880/1, the number of post offices and boxes was 4671, with the mileage of inland postal communication being 21 498. The corresponding figures for the years up to 1914 were 1890/1, 8048 and 25 672; 1900/1, 9927 and 27 686; 1903/4, 11 204 and 28 347; 1914, 43 668 and 31 290, respectively. River boats and the railway allowed unprecedented speed and reliability in delivering post to any destination in India.

The telegraph

A defining moment in the advancement of technology in India came as early as 1839, when an insulated wire was laid beneath the Hooghly River to connect the two banks at Calcutta by electric current. Some 12 years after this experiment, the epoch-making telegraphic trials of the American

Samuel Finley Breese Morse (1791–1872) were successfully applied in laying a cable connecting England with France. However, many of the early pioneers of the technology were unconcerned with Europe; their focus was on India. Experimental telegraphs had already begun in India in 1852, and by the beginning of 1856 about 4500 miles of electric telegraph were in operation between the principal Indian cities.

An electric telegraph system promised to be of immense value in the administration of the subcontinent, so an Indian Telegraph Department was quickly formed in 1850. Five years later, its offices were opened to the public for the transmission of private messages. Sir William O'Shaughnessy (1809–1889), head of the department, decided to introduce the Morse system instead of the needle system then in use. In 1857 he sailed to England, where he ordered 80 instruments from Siemens of Woolwich and recruited 40 energetic young men, whom he arranged to have trained in Morse-operating at Gresham House, London. His recruits were chiefly orphan sons of Indian army officers, and some were as young as 14 and 15. Despite having been told that in India they must expect years of hard work and small pay, there was no shortage of applicants for the post of Morse Assistant. The number of recruits was increased to 74. After six months' instruction, the first detachments were sent to Bombay, Madras and Calcutta, and at once began to teach local probationers. The department expanded rapidly and their positions improved accordingly.

Many companies were formed to undertake the monumental task of erecting lines across often inhospitable terrain and via states with hostile governments or simply no recognised or accountable regime at all. The support of Britain's ubiquitous gunboat policy, aided and abetted by the breech-loading gun, was a comforting factor when perhaps the telegraph company with the largest capital, European & Indian Junction Telegraph Co (EIJT), sought to connect the existing lines on the European Continent with the Persian Gulf from 1856. The Government of India agreed to provide the final connection with Karachi. The capital stock then stood at £200,000.

The land telegraph in India was gaining widespread approval from trials undertaken in October 1851, when a 20-mile link that connected Calcutta with Diamond Harbour was deemed successful. At the end of its first year of operation, the initial telegraph wire between Calcutta and Agra, a distance of 800 miles, was accepting messages. It was extended to Lahore and Peshawar by 1857.

By 1855 nearly all seats of government were in communication with one another over a network of 3000 miles at an estimated cost of £50 per mile. Within two years, the revenue from both government and private use exceeded expenses as related in the 'First report on the Operation of the Electric Telegraph in India from 1 February 1855, to 31 January 1856'. While the first batch of statistics was being compiled, Britain's telegraph engineers were earning good money (compared with working in England) erecting an overland rather than a direct sea-crossing telegraph between Calcutta and Madras. It was placed into service in March 1858. Within three months it was 'grossly overloaded'.

By 1860, not only were wires connecting up small towns with the big cities, but reliability was improving by the year as new materials and better insulators cut line losses. India had in that year 14500 miles of government-owned and 3500 miles of railway-owned telegraph lines.

In 1866 a Lieutenant Colonel D.G. Robinson began to reorganise the Department of Indian Telegraphs. Prospective young officers between the ages of 18 and 23 were asked to sit for an examination in English, history, geography, elementary mathematics and physics, classics and a modern language, and had to obtain marks of at least 50% in each subject. Successful candidates were granted £100 each to cover expenses in each subject during a course of training. Upon satisfactory completion, they would be nominated for appointments as Assistant Superintendents with pay at £240 per annum and given a passage to India.

The proliferation of telegraphs, like the rapid spread of railway lines, formed a growth industry in itself. Wire was imported by the hundreds of mile, mainly from Siemens, giving rise to an urgent need for batteries and dynamos. For the Raj, it was comforting to note that India was still at the forefront of technology, second only to Britain itself.

The length of domestic Indian telegraphs during the decade from 1886 to 1895 grew at a phenomenal rate. By the end of 1886, 27510 miles were in service; a decade later, 44648 miles served the country. The wire consumed during that period increased from 81480 miles to 138256 miles. Similarly, the number of messages virtually doubled from 2307000 to 4422000. The revenue into the exchequer in 1895 was audited as £656,335, and at the close of the year the total expenditure on telegraphs was audited as £5531,636. It was estimated that less than 1% of the population in 1896 lived more than 30 miles from a telegraph office. By July 1897 an estimated £6500,000 had been spent on installing the telegraph throughout India.

A factor in the efficient spread and reliable transmission of telegraphs from London to India and throughout India itself was the introduction of further new devices. Electricity was still in its infancy, but mechanical paper-tape punching machines were gaining widespread favour. Siemens once again was at the forefront of this technology.

The telephone

By 1873, the domestic telegraph was reliable and quick. Few believed the system could be improved on, with messages sent and replies received within one hour. However, the technology was over two decades old despite being upgraded. Britain and America were embracing a new form of electrical communication: the telephone. It was now India's turn to admit this novel form of communication, which was introduced in 1879. An article in the *Times of India*, dated 29 November 1880, details the experimental character of the first telephones put into service for use by the Madras Railway Company in order to 'fairly test its economy and advantages'. The article concluded that the experiment had been a success and plans were under way to extend the circuits to the offices at Perambore.

In 1881 the government granted licences to the Oriental Telephone Company to operate telephone exchanges in Calcutta, Bombay and Madras. Within a decade Calcutta 'had an exchange and over 150 subscribers'. By 1903 there were 524 exchanges with around 3220 telephone 'stations'. The system continued to be operated privately until 1941 when all shares were bought by the state and telephone exchanges came under the control of the Indian Posts and Telegraphs Department. Post-Independence, the effect of this transferral to state ownership was that the growth in the development of telecommunications was hindered by the insular and socialist policies that endured until the 1980s and which regarded the telephone as a 'luxury' rather than a 'necessity'.

Embracing technology

Indians embraced technological change with a remarkable degree of willingness and good spirit. When the telegraph penetrated the farthest reaches of the Punjab, Joseph Birks, the local telegraph superintendent, was almost out of a job. He commented in a report to *Mechanics Illustrated* in 1874: 'These Sikhs are worth their weight in gold. Little direction is required and it is noted that experience seems to pass from father to son. Indeed, good, reliable and hard-working fellows to have on our side at all times.' By the 1870s well-trained Indian signallers with a sound grasp of the English language became easier to source. By 1948 Indian engineers and technicians were more than capable of running the stations themselves. Telegraph communication remained prevalent until the end of World War II. The rise of the telephone would eventually see its demise. Though the early telephone was expensive and ill-equipped for long-distance communication, at the end of British rule all cities in India were connected by telephone and 83 000 were in use.

While initially benefiting British interests, the telegraph system indubitably improved the lot of the Indians and offered gainful employment during the telegraph's construction and its operation. Willing Indian hands worked in partnership with British supervision to ensure that technical progress was spread throughout the country at large.

Chapter 9

RAILWAYS: A NETWORK IS BUILT WITH INCREDIBLE SPEED

When one begins upon the fruitful topic of Indian railways, it is difficult to know where to stop!
THE EDITOR, *ENGINEERING*, JUNE 1876

The British built more railways in India alone than America, France, Germany and the other European colonialists built in all their colonies. Major highways in India had for centuries radiated from such inland centres as Delhi, Lahore, Allahabad and Agra, towards the coast. The process was reversed for railways, with the first starting from the three major seaports – Bombay, Calcutta and Madras – and extending into the interior of the country. Both as towns and as seaports, these three cities were of hardly any importance before the arrival of the EIC.

First thoughts of building railways in India emerged in 1831/32 in the Presidency of Madras. While the affairs of the EIC were being discussed in the Parliamentary Select Committee, it was proposed to 'improve the deplorable state of communication and commerce by the introduction of railways', according to the report. This was all the more remarkable in that it was proposed within a year of the inauguration of the world's first passenger train between Liverpool and Manchester.

Later, in 1836, Captain A. P. Cotton, a civil engineer resident in Madras, advocated the desirability of railways in India, emphasising their superiority over other means of communication. In 1838 Charles B. Vignoles (1793–1875) proposed railways to the EIC, the subject being taken up in 1843 by Rowland – later Sir Rowland – Macdonald Stephenson (1808–1895), who had briefly joined 'The Comprehensive Company for establishing regular Steam Communication with India' – or P&O as it would later be known

– in 1838, initially to establish better links with India. Numerous feasibility studies were conducted, with the conclusion that 'the sooner railways are established, the better for all'.

In the cold weather of 1845/46, Stephenson made a trial survey from Calcutta to Delhi to assess the feasibility and cost of a railway route to connect the two cities. With money raised in London the East India Railway was formed with Stephenson as managing director. In 1849 a railway network of about 5000 miles was provisionally given the go-ahead by EIC directors, with early trials completed between 1851 and 1855 by East India Railway and the Great Indian Peninsula Railway. In that same period, some £12 million was formally incorporated, with a standard gauge sanctioned initially. On 16 April 1853 the first steam whistles were heard along the single-line track from Bombay to Thana.

In eastern India, a railway from Howrah to Raniganj was sanctioned as an 'experimental' measure – an experimental line that, at 112 miles, was longer than the completed London to Birmingham railway! By the end of 1853, through Stephenson's efforts, the line was ready as far as Pundooah – 38 miles. Two serious mishaps prevented the commissioning of the first train for one more year, but the first passenger train steamed out of Howrah Station destined for Hooghly, a distance of 24 miles, on 15 August 1854.

Howrah Station, the Calcutta terminus of the EIR, c.1920s (Courtesy of International Railway Gazette)

Lord Dalhousie, who played an important part in shaping the early policy of railway construction in India, had doubts, as indeed did everyone else at that time, as to whether or not railways could be made to pay in India. He was most anxious that this 'experimental' line should prove successful, stating that its object 'is to prove not only that it is practicable to construct railways in India, as engineering works, but that such railways, when constructed, will as a commercial undertaking offer a fair remunerative return on the money which has been expended on their construction'.

By 1848, the Government of India had granted licences for the establishment of five railway companies: the first, Great Indian Peninsula Railway (GIPR), which placed its initial contracts in November 1849; the East India Railway (EIR), which from 1849 was owned outright by the EIC, guaranteeing to return 5% to all investors; the Bombay Baroda & Central India Railway (BBCIR); the Madras Railway (MR); and the Scinde (Sind) Railway.

Great Indian Peninsula Railway (GIPR)
– the first passenger train

The idea of a railway to connect Bombay with Thana, Kalyan and up the Thal and Bhore Ghats incline first occurred to George Clark (1809–1898), the Chief Engineer of the Bombay government, during a visit to Bhandup in 1843. A meeting of prominent citizens was held in Bombay on 13 July 1844, to consider the advisability of a railway in accordance with Clark's scheme. At the same time, the Great Indian Peninsula Railway (GIPR) Company was formed in England.

The Court of Directors controlling EIC finances recommended the English standard gauge throughout the whole of India. However, India, with its large open spaces, was different from England – the mountain areas had yet to gain focus – and Lord Dalhousie, India's Governor-General, recommended 6 ft for the country's railway network. Finally, a compromise of 5 ft 6 in. was settled on without protracted discussion and fuss. Still in service today for all India's main line traffic – where freight trains of up to 8000 tons are not uncommon – the broad gauge has more than proved itself.

Plans were drawn up and contracts placed by the GIPR. George Stephenson (1781–1848) was one of the first directors and his son Robert Stephenson (1803–1859) was appointed the first consulting engineer of the company. On 31 October 1850 construction work began and by 18 February 1852 the first locomotive was seen shunting near Byculla.

The first steam locomotive, believed to be from Leeds and named *Thomason*, started work on 22 December 1851, during the construction of the Solani Aqueduct, some 75 miles north-east of Delhi. The English engineers constructing the line selected the standard British gauge of 4 ft 8.5 in., which was then widely used throughout Britain, America and Continental Europe.

It appears that the first locomotives used solely for construction work on the GIPR, starting in Bombay, arrived from Yorkshire. The experimental line to Kalyan, begun by Messrs Faviell and Fowler in February 1851, was contractually finished to Thana in April 1853. It was decided that the terminus of 19 acres would be Bori Bunder in Bombay, with the advantage of a quay frontage to the harbour. The formal inauguration ceremony for what is now accepted as the first railway placed into service with a passenger-carrying train was performed on 16 April 1853. The train comprised 20 railway carriages carrying about 400 guests, who left Bori Bunder, Bombay, at 3.30 p.m. to the salute of 21 guns. At about 4.45 p.m. the party reached Thana, where refreshments were served in tents.

The inaugural engines to haul the first complete train were named *Sultan*, *Sindh* and *Sahib*, and were built in 1852 by Charles Tayleur's Vulcan Foundry at Newton-le-Willows near Manchester, established 1830. They were from a batch of eight contracted from the same fabricator to meet the expected initial demand. Later, the *Sultan* was named *Lord Falkland* as a token of respect for the then Governor of the Bombay Presidency. The Vulcan Foundry, in its promotional leaflets, continuously maintained that they had the distinction of exporting the first-ever locomotives to India.

The line was extended to Kalyan on 1 May 1854, and to Khopoli on 12 May 1856. The GIPR undertook a careful survey of the Thal and Bhore Ghats. Work started in 1856 to run lines from Kalyan over the Bhore Ghat to Poona and over the Thal Ghat to Bhusaval.

The Parsi entrepreneur Jamsetji Dorabji (1804–1882) was granted permission by the GIPR directors, after a competitive and public bid, to began the first section of the extension from Kalyan to Campoolee, 38 miles long at the foot of the Bhore Ghat mail road, in 1854. It was originally designed for a double line, but only a single track had been constructed by 1856. The most onerous section of that extension was the Bhore Ghat incline. Four years were spent in the preliminary surveys. William Faviell (1822–1902) took up the work in January 1856, augmented by a Mr Tredwell from November 1859. Sadly, Tredwell died within a month of his arrival.

The route was to serve as a connecting link with South India, then later with Delhi and Calcutta. The laying of tracks over these two Ghats was difficult and expensive. In 1856 the line was opened to Kasara at the foot of the Thal Ghat, and, on 21 April 1863, the Bhore Ghat incline was opened to railway traffic. The entire Thal Ghat route was completed in 1865. Some of the points and switches were supplied by the Monmouthshire Carriage & Wagon Works, established in 1850 and later to become the ISCA Foundry, which may well have delivered the firm's earliest carriages. To haul heavy freight trains over the steeply graded incline, Neilson & Mitchell, of Glasgow, supplied specially designed large tender locomotives in the 1860s. By 1859, GIPR had spent £834,000 to open the lines in the Concan and Deccan, a total of 132 miles.

At this time GIPR established a depot in Byculla, covering an area roughly the size of the Bombay terminus. The depot contained steam-engine sheds, erecting and fitting shops, smithies, iron and brass foundries, a sawmill, carriage repair and wagon-building sheds, a coke shed, stores, warehouses and a timber-preserving establishment, as well as workmen's and engine drivers' dwelling houses.

There was an urgent need for locomotives and rolling stock and, despite over 50 British companies engaging in this lucrative and buoyant field, it took Government of India pressure on Whitehall 'to serve the British Empire first' by a mandatory edict to have India favoured above all others.

In 1861 GIPR had opened only 330 miles of railway yet its profit of £36,000 was considerable for the day. This was even more remarkable when the interest paid that year was £322,907, down from £1,040,357 on 1860. In 1862 the early locomotives were finding the ascent up Bhore Ghat heavy work, with the strain on their mechanical parts resulting in failure of components. It was to Manchester that GIPR engineers turned to overcome those incline difficulties, ironically in a locomotive that Sharp, Stewart & Company's Atlas Works had yet to prove. Made to the designs of the firm's Chief Mechanical Engineer, John Kershaw, three engines proved successful for the large load hauled.

In 1865 Todd, Kitson & Laird made the first of 20 heavy banking engines to assist leading locomotives then pulling loads twice the weight of the inaugural train. A near neighbour to this firm, the Yorkshire Engine Company, Meadowhall Works, Sheffield, delivered a series of engines to the EIR at about the same time. From 1867 until 1871, the Leeds foundry of John Fowler dispatched 40 units to GIPR, with a similar large order from Neilson & Mitchell, of Glasgow. GIPR's establishment of India's railways through Bombay for the receipt of British heavy machinery exports opened up the country to thriving commerce. For the year 1858/59, trade was recorded at £60,219,600, with a population estimated at 185 million for its 1484367 sq. mile landmass. In 1858 the construction of railways in the Presidencies of Bengal and Bombay is recorded at 636 miles opened to traffic, with some 4821 miles sanctioned. For 1860 it was expected to have 765 miles in service and 864 miles for the following year. Statistics compiled for 1860 estimated the capital required to be £52,450,000 of which £34,133,330 was sanctioned by the Indian Government and £27,130,000 already subscribed.

In 1859 the opening up of rail communication to Bombay was a bonus for India's cotton trade. Some 94000 tons were exported, valued at £3,958,000. Customs also recorded that during the first five years of GIPR service its revenues rose by 100%.

In the late 1860s, an early form of steel gradually replaced iron throughout Britain as the versatile and durable metal for heavy industry. Its properties soon became universally accepted. In November 1866, GIPR contracted Messrs John Brown and Cammell & Company – both of Sheffield – to supply 22000 tons of steel rails. The former firm was then capable of turning out approximately 200 tons per week. All, however, was not quite plain sailing for the railway operator.

In July 1867 the Mhow-Ke-Mullee Viaduct collapsed, fortunately without loss of life, but the collapse was a close call as two trains were within minutes of the viaduct. The original structure comprised masonry spans that had given reliable service, although according to minutes of the Institution of Civil Engineers (ICE) proceedings there was a report of a weakness having been detected before the collapse. It was decided to replace the whole bridge using wrought-iron Warren trusses. The Dudley foundry of John Cochrane & Company, then enjoying an excellent reputation for quality work competitively priced and delivered on time, was contracted. By June 1868 wagons carrying 812 tons of ironwork had arrived via Bombay and the bridge was quickly erected ready for testing. Seven engines, each weighing 55 tons, were shunted over numerous times at 12 mph. The permanent set was a mere 0.06 in. On 1 July 1868 the service was restored. GIPR stated:

> Our workforce was magnificent, deep in the knowledge that restoration of the line would benefit everybody. It is worth noting that during the replacement many small enterprises flourished confirming our belief that the Indian is not only a grafter when required, but also a canny (clever and

shrewd) individual to boot. The loyalty in the workmen's womenfolk in supplying his food and basic needs cannot be underestimated.

The total sanctioned lines completed in 1872 were 1278 miles – 5384 for the whole of India – of which 326 miles were laid with double track. The main line was 1266 miles in length, with a spur of 12 miles to the Mhopani coal mines. On 9 October 1871, the last bridge across the Kistna – at Raichur – was placed into service. With the commissioning of this bridge, a through service between Madras and Bombay was inaugurated. George Berkley (1821–1893), the GIPR's consultant engineer, designed the Kistna Bridge, which was similar to a recent construction over the Tapti River. The bridge was the last link in the chain between Madras and Bombay – a distance of 789 miles (see Chapter 11).

In 1866 the GIPR had 699 miles of track opened for traffic, which grew to over 1400 in 1874. During that period its operating receipts trebled. Its routes had grown, with two services to Calcutta: one via Jubbulpore to connect with the EIR, and the other via Nagpur to link up with the Bengal Nagpur Railway (BNR). The remaining main route was from Bombay towards Madras, terminating at Raichur. It had built an important branch line from Jhansi to Cawnpore, where connection was made with the EIR and Oudh & Rohilkund Railway (ORR) networks, of which GIPR possessed running authority over ORR tracks from Cawnpore to Lucknow with its new, faster main-line trains.

The principal classes of goods traffic by 1900 comprised cotton, grain, seed, coal and manganese ore. Cotton principally arrived from the Bhusaval–Nagpur section and the bulk was exported worldwide through Bombay. Coal was received in huge double-bogie 20-ton capacity wagons from Stableford of Coalville, Leicestershire, with further deliveries from the Leeds Forge utilising the new Samuel Fox of Stockbridge, near Sheffield, toughened steel plate for its frames and bodies.

The most important station was the Victoria Terminus in Bombay (see p. 381), where 51 trains entered and departed daily. The busiest section of the line was between Bombay and Kalyan, and a bottleneck was formed where goods and passenger services converged. This is not surprising, as, from 1878, in excess of 80 000 tons of cotton alone passed through the junction en route to a large goods depot at Wadi Bunder. Bombay, Delhi, Muttra, Gwalior, Jhansi, Bhopal and Jalgaon were also busy passenger stations.

The longest run was from Bombay to Delhi, a distance of 957 miles. The journey was covered in 31 hours, falling to 27 hours 45 minutes in 1912. The

Punjab Mail had the longest run without stopping, the 77 miles covered in two hours. The fastest run was the Poona Race Special, which attained a speed of 47 mph and 52 mph in 1911.

GIPR rolling stock

The GIPR and its rapidly expanding network courted Britain's suppliers of locomotives and rolling stock for contracts 'that were given special treatment'. This was no doubt upon coercion from the Calcutta-based Government of India and Britain's Crown Agents, established on 1 April 1830 solely to administer the empire. One such concern that pulled out all the stops was Stothert, Slaughter & Company, from Bristol. Founded in 1837, the firm was ideally placed at the right time. With a huge port on its doorstep and abundant skilled labour on call, the four largest orders the firm received before 1870 were all for Indian customers. In 1866 and 1867, 20 units were turned out each year for GIPR. Other engines were supplied to EIR and ORR. The opening of large workshops and the abundance of relatively skilled labour following the customary indentured apprenticeships enabled the GIPR to import much of its wagon rolling stock in broken-down sections.

During the 1890s, the GIPR constructed heavy 44-ton capacity hopper wagons. These were a regular feature on the railway. It was recorded that one train through the Bhore Ghat when double-headed managed to haul a load of 1620 tons – possibly a record then for India.

The Bhusaval Marshalling Yard expanded to become one of the largest of its kind in India. Its huge engine sheds were modelled on those at Crewe. There were some 16 through lines and around 500 wagons shunted at any one time. One latecomer into the rolling stock market was Cammell Laird of Nottingham, whose tender for 200 wagons and bogie passenger coaches was accepted.

The original 20.75 mileage, opened on 18 April 1853, grew to about 1400 by 1874. In that year GIPR owned some 630 engines, 1300 carriages carrying around 16 million passengers, and 10000 wagons. In 1913 the figures were 1034 engines, 2204 carriages carrying 35080872 passengers, and 16744 wagons. The need to supplement its local delivery service with more mechanised transport than the time-honoured bullock cart prompted the GIPR to import its first petrol-driven lorries into India in 1907. All vehicles came from the Albion Company of Scotland.

The first narrow-gauge locomotive for India was made by Neilson & Mitchell. A 2 ft gauge engine was delivered to the Gaekwar of Baroda in 1863 for his private use, although the engine did not see regular service until 1865.

East India Railway (EIR)

A decade before Calcutta's dreams of steam railways became a reality, a survey by EIC civil engineers had been conducted to determine the feasibility of locomotion within the region. It revealed a mind-boggling 2226 359 tons of goods passing between Mirzapur and Calcutta, of which 94% was carried in more than 50 000 country boats, 1% on government steamers and 4% on connecting roads. Canal construction from the Marquis of Hastings' encouragement had benefited Bengal immeasurably. By 1850, with heavy iron products from Manchester, Leeds, Sheffield, Birmingham and Glasgow threatening to overwhelm river transport with its sheer volume and weight, railways were the automatic answer. Ironically for Calcutta, railways were assessed in terms of freight only – passengers were not given consideration.

The gauge initially settled on, in April 1850, was the standard British gauge, but Frederick Walter Simms (1803–1864), the consultant appointed by the Government of India, had strong doubts – especially as GIPR was settling for the broad gauge. Perhaps this dispute caused him to resign his position when a John Pitt Kennedy (1796–1879) took charge. Kennedy proposed a gauge of 6 ft, which again was not accepted. Later, a Major William E. Baker established the broad gauge of 5 ft 6 in., and in March 1851 the question was settled and the document ratified.

The first lines from Calcutta north-westwards were an unparalleled feat of civil and structural engineering. The terrain was a mosquito-infested swamp, with predator tigers and snakes adding further hazards. Many died in its construction, not least the vulnerable British who had arrived with high hopes of a career in the Raj.

To carry the railway safely, 460 bridges were required to connect Calcutta with Raniganj and a further 63 bridges to bring the line an additional 300 miles into Monghyr – an average of more than four bridges per mile. The shorter spans across streams were of masonry construction. Ad hoc workshops were quickly set up along the track to receive bridge sections, which were knocked down in manageable sections weighing up to two tons. Hundreds of bullock cart 'trains' were employed and thousands of Bengalis contributed their labour. For many of the locals in Bengal, it was the first time that remunerations were paid on a regular weekly basis. British contractors reported little difficulty in recruiting willing hands, especially when messing was occasionally also provided.

EIR was hard on the heels of GIPR, perhaps because of the rich coal-fields at Raniganj (see Chapter 13). These coalfields enhanced the ambitions and prospects of the railway operator, which was not lost on GIPR, it being denied a primary local source of good-quality steam coal. With little actual working experience from its initial success in western India, EIR immediately ordered two locomotives from Kitson, Thompson & Hewitson, of Leeds, subsequently named *Fairy Queen* and *Express*. Today, the *Fairy Queen* is preserved in the Delhi Railway Museum.

Railways throughout India were products of extraordinary human endurance, particularly that of the Indian people themselves, with the railways constructed in Bengal perhaps requiring the most in terms of sheer stamina. The logistics of such an undertaking in an era when neither the telegraph nor the telephone was at hand were staggering.

While construction work was advancing favourably for EIR, plans were brought forward for a new railway in eastern Bengal. Tender bids for rolling stock were invited, and, in 1855, a large order was placed with, Kitson, Thompson & Hewitson. An early audit for EIR was carefully documented at the end of 1859. At that time, some 678 route miles were in service,

'Imperial Indian Mail', EIR Calcutta–Bombay service (Courtesy of International Railway Gazette)

consuming enormous amounts of material from Britain. This figure rose to 1364 miles, costing £23 million, in 1862. The phenomenal total of 165 000 tons of rails, 44 000 tons of chairs and 9000 tons of bridge girders with a further 5500 tons then en route, all within seven years, had been hauled around Africa for offloading in Calcutta, using both steam vessels and large sailing ships.

The expansion of EIR lines into relatively new territory warranted the construction of three to four bridges per mile. The Jumna River crossing, at Allahabad, was to tax the ingenuity and muscles of over 3700 people for the better part of six years. Comprising 14 × 205 ft spans, the 4200-ton iron bridge was conceived on the grand scale that characterised most British-designed large river crossings until Independence. Designed on the Mohnie truss form, the bridge carried a double-track, broad-gauge line including a lower roadway 'capable of supporting two 12-ton elephants abreast'.

Even while the Jumna was being bridged at Allahabad, a bridge with 12 spans, each of 216 ft, was planned over the same river at Delhi. When it was completed in 1865, one span was tested with wagons containing 450 tons of pig iron. The girder deflected a mere inch, with no permanent set. The bridge was rebuilt around 1911 with trusses from the West Midlands and remains in service to the present day.

In 1855 EIR appointed a Mr W. Bourne as Chief Engineer for the newly established Chord Line, following finds of massive amounts of good steam coal. The Chord Line began at Barrakar, 144 miles from Calcutta, and terminated at Luckeeserai, 327 miles from Calcutta. A branch line to another newly worked coalfield at Kurhurbalee was planned, and by the end of 1866 had been placed into service. The maximum gradient was 1 in 100 passing through a ridged and difficult terrain. Some dense jungle was also encountered and held up progress as additional surveys were required.

EIR's rate of network growth soon surpassed that of GIPR. By 1862 EIR had 1364 miles of track in service of the total 2335 miles for the whole of India. GIPR in that year was operating over a network of less than 500 miles. According to *The Engineer* of February, 1862:

> Some idea of the work done by Britain in connection with Indian railways (and chiefly the EIR) may be formed from the fact that up to December, 1861, 2,459,928 tons of material, including locomotives, rolling stock, bridges, stations, track and other permanent way material, signalling and ancillary equipment etc. had been dispatched to India. On this service, 3012 ships were employed (all around Africa), of which 39 have been lost.

The value of materials sent out was about £12 million, and the amount paid for insurance about £318,756, being on an average £2 12s. 0d. per cent. The total amount of losses (with over 3000 men drowned) sustained in the transport is about £250,000, being less than 2.5% on the value of the materials dispatched. The (non-human) losses were fully recovered from the underwriters.

In 1864 EIR imported 64 465 tons of material. The rolling stock consisted of 3998 units of which 355 were locomotives.

In December 1866 Bengal coal was used extensively, with EIR cashing in on earning a tidy sum delivering this fuel to all other railway companies. Coal then cost about 10s. per ton at the pithead. English coal arriving by ship around Africa varied in price between 40s. and 70s. per ton. Australian coal was tried but found to be unacceptable. On the Madras Railway, wood fuel was still very much the norm.

Planned on a grand scale, the Chord Line was constructed with double-track working, leaving the main line at Kahnoo Junction, then going on to Luckeeserai and continuing with a new line direct to Allahabad. Bridging was not difficult, with the maximum single span being 90 ft – 84 ft clear – using Warren trusses as no large rivers were crossed. Andrew Handyside of Derby supplied these trusses, with eight over the Jainti River, eight over the Pathro River and ten over the Ajay River. The Chord Line was completed in 1870, bypassing the main line that followed the path of the Ganges.

By 1865 EIR could lay claim to having the longest bridges of all railways operating in India, if indeed not the most in terms of aggregate tonnage. In October 1860 seven bridges were erected requiring 33 × 60 ft spans; in November 1861 four rivers warranted 20 × 60 ft spans; and in February three river crossings consumed 13 × 60 ft spans, all wrought-iron plate. Between 1863 and 1867, a branch line from Allahabad was constructed to join up with GIPR 226 miles away. By March 1871 EIR had constructed and put into service 1503 miles. India was rapidly being connected up by rail, with a telegraph flanking most lines.

EIR rolling stock

EIR possessed men of great calibre and resourcefulness. No one in India had the material, foundry capacity or technology capable of building locomotives, but the company's Locomotive Chief Engineer, John Hodgson, set about designing his own carriages, which were crafted by two coach-building firms in Calcutta – Seton & Company and Steward & Company. Both firms were engaged in constructing horse-drawn coaches.

It was to Britain that EIR managers looked to place contracts for locomotives. The railway operator did not favour one firm above another unless assured of the quality of its workmanship and the performance of its goods in service, and the list of early locomotive suppliers to India's railways reads like a Thomas Cook tour of British industry. EIR's orders stimulated locomotive foundries in 1866 to produce some of the heaviest engines yet manufactured. When the new Chord Line from Barrakar to Luckeeserai (a distance of some 184 miles) was being planned by Chief Engineer William Bourne, the railway placed two large orders for locomotives. The Avondale Engine Works, of Bristol, established in 1866, was contracted to produce some unusually heavy engines with outside cylinders and eight-coupled wheels. When works tested, each engine weighed 48 tons and the tenders, capable of housing 2000 gallons of water, weighed 26 tons fully loaded.

Meanwhile, Sir W.G. Armstrong's Newcastle foundry, established in 1845, began the manufacture of the first of 130 engines for EIR for express passenger duty. In 1862 at the International Exhibition, the firm displayed a 60-ton engine and tender that captivated many a covetous eye.

As the end of the century neared, most rolling stock still arrived broken down in sections, including 114 bogie-wagons from the Birmingham Railway and Carriage Works, Smethwick, as well as 14 wooden horseboxes on steel frames from the same supplier. However, Britain's new 40-ton coal wagons, which were gaining acceptance domestically, were imported complete. One huge order was given to Stableford for 1000 high-sided coal wagons, which arrived fully assembled.

East Bengal Railway (EBR)

Railways for East Bengal were first mooted in 1851. The initial plan was to cut an 80-mile line through dense jungle and swampland between Calcutta and Jessore, with an extension to Dacca and Narayanganj. Even at that early stage, the EBR's civil engineers and planners were actively considering a line northward to Darjeeling, a distance of 326 miles from Calcutta. Coal was found in Sylhet and Cachar 'equal to the best quality Welsh or Newcastle coal and far superior to any found in Bengal', according to EBR.

The line's course was designed to pass through the thickly inhabited and very productive delta of the Ganges. British civil engineers had encouraged the newly formed company to build to the same broad gauge as the GIPR. However, in this area heavy bridging was called for, which, as auditors later assessed, virtually doubled the cost of construction per mile compared to India's inaugural railway. It was becoming increasingly difficult to proceed at less than four bridges per mile.

The work was planned to start in Sealdah, Calcutta, and end at the Ganges River village of Kooshtea. The engineers working on this line were concerned about the failure of iron rails in Britain. They fully intended that the 'deficiencies back home shall not occur in India'. They decided, therefore, to evaluate the construction and casting of the rail itself, devising a design that was to gain universal favour. They inserted sheets of zinc between rail and clamp, while all securing bolts were pulled up sharp against leather washers. Although not an outright success, EBR officials, in their annual report, related that despite its difficulties, 'the life of the track was in fact extended beyond that of our competitors'.

In 1858, with a service established to Jessore and a thriving jute industry (see Chapter 16) providing much-needed revenue for the railway operator, £500,000 was budgeted to construct an extension to Furreedpure on the east bank of the Ganges, before extending lines into Dacca.

While work was advancing on extending tracks towards Kooshtea, a grand terminus worthy of such a transport undertaking, designed by Isambard Kingdom Brunel, was being erected at Sealdah, Calcutta. The building was constructed in an Italianate style of oriental architecture. Two platforms were over 1000 ft long by 27 ft wide. Three light wrought-iron roofs 650 ft long covered eight lines of rails. The span of each roof was 53 ft. Accommodation for staff, plus a huge waiting room with ample lighting and ventilation, along with adequate drainage pumped dry by a steam engine, ensured that the EBR terminus was then the principal exhibit in India's capital city.

Bridging during the construction was indeed heavy for the first 80 miles. Tolly's Nullah (see p. 116) was crossed with a single 130 ft span. The circular canal, flanked by a road constructed in 1806, was bridged by a single 80 ft bowstring span. To bridge the Echamuttee, 5 × 80 ft plate girders supported on 75 ft cast-iron pillars were sunk 33 ft – possibly the first cylinders sunk in India using compressed air. To carry the track across the Kumar and Paillee rivers, 12 × 80 ft and 1 × 170 ft girders were required. The 110-mile line was opened for service in 1862. In 1864 EBR imported 10 342 tons of material. Its rolling stock stood at 472 units, including 20 locomotives.

Points and crossings were chiefly of the Carr patent, although some items arrived from Armstrong of Newcastle and Ransomes & Sims.

By March 1871 the company had built and operated only 159 miles, but this was constructed through some of the most difficult, mosquito-infested terrain in the whole of India. The average outlay was £17,991 per mile – a cost per mile only exceeded by certain sections of the EIR.

In 1873 all EBR's planned routes of 194 miles were completed, with the exception of a branch line of 2 miles to the Hooghly River from Chitpore. In 1872 severe flooding – on a level similar to that in the Punjab – caused damage to Goahurdo terminus and protective works around the Gorai Bridge. Perhaps it was those large inundations that prompted the railway company to construct huge embankments quickly, with a complete drainage system and some flood-control devices.

With the construction of lines to Darjeeling, the broad-gauge Darjeeling Mail was EBR's luxury train, being of corridor carriage stock. It was the operator's first train with all-electric lighting and fans fitted.

During the late 1880s and 1890s, a series of ad hoc railway companies developed a hotchpotch of branch lines throughout EBR's network, with various gauges including one of 2 ft 6 in. The first was the Calcutta and South-Eastern Railway, a 28-mile route from Calcutta to Port Canning constructed in 1862 and 1863. It prospered, mainly carrying passengers and freight to the docks, before being bought by the State in 1868. The Bengal Central Railway from Dum Dum to Khoola, with various branches comprising a total of 127 miles, was opened between 1882 and 1884, and taken over in 1905. A Dacca State Railway – from Narayanganj to Mymensingh – was opened in 1885 using metre-gauge track. Some nine others all sought to profit from the free-for-all but eventually succumbed to a state takeover, mostly in 1904. The network, after the amalgamation of all railways constructed throughout the area served by EBR, comprised 1595 miles.

Because of the mainly flat terrain that was inundated for most of the year, bridging was extremely heavy. On some lines, over five bridges per mile were constructed.

The state took over all lines from 1904 and later audited all rolling stock. By then, nearly 30 million passengers were being carried annually and around 4900 000 tons of freight hauled. To cater for this huge increase in demand, the total rolling stock taken over from EBR and its nine ad hoc lines that formed the network amounted to 472 locomotives, 1611 carriages and 9740 wagons.

EBR river ferries

Eastern Bengal was one of the most difficult areas throughout the whole of India in which to construct railways. The very nature of the land, with its myriad rivers – many raging torrents that flow from the Himalayas when winter snows melt – all but defeated most of the railway contractors and bridge erectors.

In many areas, river ferries were the only choice, and to ensure that Bengalis reached their destinations, opportunities were presented to both Britain's and India's maritime industries to devise a series of low-draught vessels for river use. Burn of Howrah (see below) was the principal local supplier and imported triple-expansion engines from Glasgow, Liverpool and Tyneside.

From 1900, EBR operated three river steam ferries between Fulchhari and Bahadurabad Ghat, Pandu and Amingaon on the River Brahmaputra, and between Godagari and Lalgola Ghat on the river Ganges. Two were capable of carrying railway wagons, but the Ganges ferry was only for passenger and light goods traffic. Of these three ferries, the first one maintained a reliable connection between the Dacca District of EBR, with its through connection to the Assam–Bengal Railway and the other metre-gauge systems reached by the Bengal & North-Western Railway.

EBR rolling stock

Offloading the weighty engines presented many problems because of the heavy cranage and special lifting gear required for locomotives arriving from Leeds, Manchester and Newcastle. Some arrived stripped down and were assembled at the docks. Others were uncrated and reassembled by the two large engineering firms, Burn and Jessop, based in Calcutta. The firms were the earliest engineering firms in India and well established (later merging, as discussed on pp. 267–8).

Later, Kerr Stuart built some heavy engines that served the broad-gauge system well into Independence. This stripped-down assembly work is confirmed from an order placed with Peter Brotherhood for 1200 sets of carriage and wagon ironwork. In common with other railways, EBR imported carriage and wagon bodies and frames, having these parts assembled either in its own workshop at Kanchraparar or by Burn and Jessop, at Calcutta.

Madras Railway Company (MR) and Southern Mahratta Railway (SMR)

In South India the first railway line opened on 1 July 1856 between Veyasarpady and Walajah Road, a distance of 63 miles, under the banner of the newly established Madras Railway (MR) Company. It took three years to construct. The first Chief Engineer was Sir George Barclay Bruce (1821–1908), who had worked on the EIR in 1852. It was proposed that the main line should run from Madras on the east coast to Beypur on the west, a distance of 430 miles, with three branches running northwards. From Arconam, a 308-mile route was to join up with GIPR tracks at Raichur. By May 1858, the mileage had increased to 96, with many branches sanctioned and started.

The main line was largely completed to Beypur by 1862, but branch work was very slow. Even by 1865 when Tadputri was reached, MR was still more than 120 miles from connecting with GIPR. Civil engineers knew the Madras Railway construction for the first 110 miles as the 'waterway of bridges'. A total of 27 individual bridges, ranging from 4 × 20 ft for a small river crossing to 20 × 70 ft and 20 × 64 ft for the longest river crossing of 2800 ft, was the principal reason for delays that occurred. In 1864, 62672 tons of railway material was imported. Of its 1685 units of rolling stock, 75 were locomotives.

From the very outset, MR decided to use its own locally recruited labour and dispense with contractors altogether. Bruce was accused of using only local construction methods when many felt that experienced contractors, such as those previously engaged on the GIPR and EIR, would benefit the fledgling railway operator.

By March 1871, MR had constructed 832 miles at an average cost of £11,716 per mile. The company's proposals for expansion appeared to have had the blessing of everyone then assessing Madras's potential to emulate the rapid progress made in northern India. In 1872, 870 route miles from the 958 miles sanctioned were opened for service. One reason for the delay was the arrival of iron girders that could not be offloaded because of the weather and were shipped on to Calcutta. Traffic increased partly as a result of supplying the Nizam of Hyderabad with the first deliveries of essential material for his track and railway ironwork.

On the south side of the Madras main line, a branch from Negapatam on the east coast (a distance of 163 miles) – built by another firm taking advantage of the relatively free-for-all atmosphere that pervaded India's railway construction – joined it at Erode, 243 miles from Madras. It was this that was the first stretch of the proposed Great Southern of India Railway. A prospectus had been issued as far back as 1858, with Bruce from MR acting as UK consultant. The appointed Chief Engineer was Mark William Carr (1822–1888), who had been resident engineer on the Crumlin Viaduct in South Wales and therefore brought a wealth of site experience to India. The early bridges were constructed mainly of masonry with plate girders for the longer spans.

MR was indeed forward-thinking in its approach to laying its first length of track. Adopting broad gauge from the outset, it projected lines through the Madras Presidency to connect with other fledgling railway companies to form a continuous service to Calcutta, Bombay and Upper India. The route to Calcutta was via the North-East Line but was not completed until 1893, when the Kistna River at Bezwada was finally bridged with 12×300 ft spans, weighing an aggregate 4800 tons, by Head, Wrightson & Company and P. & W. MacLellan, of Glasgow.

Gold was found in large quantities at Kolar, prompting MR to expand its broad-gauge tracks towards Bangalore. For Bombay, the same broad-gauge line passed through Raichur, where it connected with the GIPR. The company found it necessary to settle for metre-gauge to cross from east to west, from the port of Mormugao on the Arabian Sea to Masulipatam on the Bay of Bengal. A direct communication with Bombay via Poona was then established.

On 31 December 1907, the MR company's contract expired, and the government purchased the lines owned by the railway operator. On the following day, the then MR – with the exception of the Jalarpet–Bangalore section – and the metre-gauge section of the South India Railway from Katpadi to Gundur and Pakala to Dharmavaram were handed over to the Southern Mahratta Railway (SMR). The enlarged company came to be known as the Madras & Southern Mahratta Railway Company (MSMR) with the 'Madras' later dropped from its title – SMR.

The newly formed company continued to develop its system, and the network grew in length to approximately 3065 route miles, of which 1540 miles were on the metre gauge and 1043 miles on the broad gauge, with a further 272 miles that comprised the Mysore State lines. Statistics for the metre gauge reveal that 277 stations were constructed, of which 102 were interlocked with the standard signalling that was being imposed over the network.

The Central Railway Station, Madras, c.1880, designed by George Hardinge. In the foreground is the stone bridge over the Cochrane Canal (Courtesy of the British Library)

The railway operator soon found that wooden sleepers were being quickly destroyed by ants – a condition that afflicted many other lines where high humidity and tropical storms encouraged nature to multiply. The Leeds-based hydraulic engineer Henry Berry had already established a good reputation in the design of special high-speed hydraulic presses for the making of steel sleepers especially for India. Many machines were purchased – as they were by most other Indian railway companies – and, when fully set up and with training given, the presses could turn out four steel sleepers per minute. By 1910 most main lines on the SMR were supported by steel sleepers, with wood reserved for sidings and branches only.

The railway was a success virtually from its inception, despite the difficult terrain that faced workers and engineers for the first decade. In 1900, 6 million passengers were carried over the broad-gauge section, with some 5 million passengers over the metre-gauge tracks. In 1912, 32 143 700 passengers were carried over the entire railway. In the corresponding period freight traffic quadrupled, having been given a boost by the development of trade in manganese, with exports shipped through Mormugao. It began in 1905, with 3000 tons destined for Britain; a decade later 75 000 tons were

Madras Central Station, c.1920s. Madras & Southern Mahratta Railway,
showing Headquarters Administration Offices in background. Broad-gauge
trains of the South Indian Railway also used the station (Courtesy of Interna-
tional Railway Gazette)

exported to European ports. By 1914 the total weight of goods traffic had
risen fourfold over 1900's figure to nearly 4.8 million tons. By 1915 the total
route mileage stood at 3300 miles.

Bridging was very heavy, with 42 bridges for the metre-gauge system,
ranging from 50 ft to 250 ft clear spans, of which many dating from 1853 –
when the first bridge was imported from Patent Shaft & Axletree and erected
across Tannah Bay – were solely of cast iron. One bridge across the Poiney
River, on the broad-gauge network, comprised 56 equal spans of 30 ft using
masonry rather than iron. It still stands today. Regrettably, many of the early
bridges were swept away in huge torrential downpours and the monsoon
weather that affected the region. The largest bridge on the system was the
Chittravati River crossing, comprising 19 × 140 ft spans, the girders supplied by Head, Wrightson. The same firm combined its manufacturing with
P. & W. MacLellan to erect 14 × 150 ft spans across the Kistna River with a
new, lightweight design that was first applied on the Sind–Pishin Railway.
For the Kistna Bridge, 6300 tons of girder material was installed and the
whole superstructure was completed in less than 100 days.

The Furnace Shipbuilding Company, of Havertown, girdered the cross-ings of the Tungabhadra and Godavari rivers with 38 × 60 ft spans at each site. Similar-sized spans were built by Cochrane's Woodside Works at Dudley, West Midlands, for the erection of another bridge across the Cheyar River at Nadular to extend the metre-gauge system. On the northern branch extension, with some 3 miles erected, bridging was heavy. By 1870 the whole network had required over 6 miles of plate girder spans alone, plus over 120 masonry structures.

The Mysore State Kolar Goldfields Railway was created essentially to ex-ploit the rich gold vein at Kolar. During its ascendancy and up to 1902, its net earnings rose to 8.96%. In 1910 it earned the accolade of being the first railway in India to adopt electric traction, according to a London engineer-ing journal, with Siemens providing the locomotives. Evidence is, however, hard to find. For its duration, it paid the highest dividend of all established railway companies.

Louise Margaret Bridge, Chappah Ridge, Sind–Pishin, c.1880s. The construc-tion required immense engineering ingenuity at great financial cost. There was no loss of life (Courtesy of the British Library)

Scinde (Sind), Punjab & Delhi Railway (SPDR)
– incorporating the Delhi Railway

The particular need for a railway in the Punjab – recognised by the EIC as early as about 1840 as 'one of the most fertile areas of the whole of Hindustan' – was finally discussed fully in 1855. A company was formed that year with a guarantee of 5% return on capital invested. There were at one time up to five separate undertakings actively pursuing railways from Delhi northward: Moulton to Amritsar; Scinde Railway; Scinde Punjab & Delhi Railway (SPDR); Delhi; and the Punjab Railway. As late as 1864, these names survived in London technical journals devoted to railways and engineering worldwide.

All these railways fell under the auspices of William – later Sir William – Patrick Andrew (1806–1887), the indefatigable promoter of a railway system in the Punjab, as well as a direct telegraph to England in 1856. Andrew first mooted the Scinde Railway in 1853/54, with a company formed to run a line 108 miles from Karachi to Kotri, opposite Hyderabad on the Indus River. The firm selected Thomas Alfred Yarrow (1817–1874), who had been in Turkey disposing of surplus material from the Crimean War.

A Mr Wells compiled plans and estimates in the autumn of 1856 to establish the definitive route. However, in 1857, the ad hoc Punjab Railway was cutting sod to connect Moulton with Lahore, a distance of 248 miles, running over level ground without any deviation. Only two bridges were required. Although little is known about this enterprise, it does appear that it was short-lived, merging with others into what became known collectively as the SPDR. For this new company, the inaugural sod-cutting ceremony was held on 29 April 1858, and the first public train ran on 13 May 1861.

Steamships were already plying the five major rivers of the Punjab region that comprise today's Punjab in Pakistan and the state of the same name in India and also its neighbouring states of Harayana and Himachal Pradesh. Plans were quickly approved to construct a line from Delhi to Lahore. Not unreasonably, 'the bread basket of Hindustan did not wish to be denied the benefit of locomotion and be overtaken by others'.

By 1858, the port of Karachi had been greatly improved, with 40-ton steam cranes from Stothert & Pitt in service, principally to cater for the arrival of heavy materials for the fledgling Punjab railways. Extensive dredging had enabled the docking of larger vessels then still arriving around the Cape of Good Hope, with a clear water depth of between 22 ft and 26 ft guaranteed. Additionally, there was the discovery of good-quality steam coal in the region. At one time it had been thought that Raniganj in Bengal would be India's principal source of coal.

The first batch of bridges shipped to SPDR arrived from Lloyds, Fosters & Company in 1857. The Wednesbury-based firm received an order for 43 × 83 ft × 8 ft 5 in. deep spans to be constructed on the Warren truss principle. The rivers over which spans were installed included the Mulleer (21); Gugger (3); Dorbai (2); Runnapittiani (6); Loyach (8) and Rhodh (3). In an 1863 paper, the railway consultant William Alexander Brunton (1840–1881) was openly critical of all 43 spans, stating that he 'could not speak favourably of these girders when contrasted with plate girders, as there was an amount of vibration both laterally and vertically caused by passing trains, which had the effect of breaking and loosening the bolts'. It is apparent that riveting was not applied. Brunton's critical analysis appears to have been accepted by SPDR management. For a forthcoming bridge over the Chinnee Creek comprising 10 × 100 ft spans, elliptically profiled plate girders were ordered.

The same railway operator constructed the line to Umballa, opened in May 1868. Stations to Roorkee, Mussourie, Muzaffarnagar and Ghazeeabad were connected with branch lines. The unexpected slowness in construction was put down to want of fuel for brick burning in the Doab. However, the government had warned SPDR's directors, apparently in sufficient time that their initial supply of 22 locomotives would be far short of immediate requirements needed for the line to Umballa, 147 miles from Delhi. It was subsequently learnt that, 12 months previously, 418 engines were ordered 'but all English and Continental suppliers are deluged with work and no firm date has so far arrived to commence manufacture', according to the directors' report. It was learnt that the main object of the railway was to connect the network with Simla, 'the asylum for the British Government of India and all its residents'.

From Kotri, travellers going further inland went by water on the company's celebrated 'Indus Flotilla' the 570 miles to Multan, where a second railway – the Punjab Railway – completed the 240 miles to Amritsar, home of the Sikhs. From 1859, the Scinde Railway was engaged in constructing a line from Lahore to Amritsar, where the line was said to have few bridges larger than a culvert 'except where the railway is carried over two branches of the Bari Doab Canal' on 80 ft Warren girders.

The next logical step was to extend the railway from Amritsar to connect up with EIR at Delhi. This new stretch was called the Delhi Railway, and it was devised to establish an unbroken connection between Calcutta and Lahore – a distance of 1300 miles. Messrs Brassey, Wythes & Henfrey secured the contract in 1864 for the 303 miles of construction needed to complete the link. Henfrey arrived with a team of engineers and tradesmen from Britain in 1865.

On the southern section of the route between Umballa and Ghazeeabad, there were eight large bridges and ten crossing minor streams, comprising spans from 60 ft to 102 ft. The chief structures were the Jumna River crossing of 24 spans, each 102 ft and built by Thomas Brassey's Canada Works at Birkenhead, and a second bridge over the Markunda River with 11 spans of 102 ft each, also by Brassey.

Sir John Lawrence (1811–1879), who had obtained the Presidency of the Viceroy, performed the inauguration of the new service on 1 January 1869. Lawrence instituted extensive economic, social and political reforms throughout the Punjab to enhance the status of the Sikhs. Revered by those Punjabis, he earned the sobriquet 'Saviour of the Punjab'.

Construction of these railways that eventually formed the SPDR took place at the height of the Victorian era, when architectural aestheticism and elegance were the order of the day. A grand station in a manner never before considered was planned for Lahore by William Brunton II (1817–1881), then the Chief Engineer of the Amritsar & Multan Railway. When first discussed, it was agreed that the station should be located near the barracks. It was eventually designed like a fortress, with long, virtually impregnable walls that were pierced with loopholes for muskets and flanked by 'cannon-proof towers crowned by turrets'; heavy sliding doors were built into the structure to close the rail exits in case of attack. The station was opened in 1864.

In 1864 the railways that comprised the SPDR imported 21 678 tons of material. Its rolling stock totalled 755 units of which 29 were locomotives. By 1871, 676 miles of track were in service, with freight bringing in a good return for the operator. Equally impressive were the statistics covering the rapid spread of roads throughout the Punjab.

Road construction had advanced more successfully than railways, partly because bridging was not so severe with the light loads carried. Immediately after the annexation of the Punjab, an annual grant of Rs.5 lakhs was sanctioned for public works, with the greater portion being devoted to the formation of a military road between Lahore and Peshawar.

In the middle of all this progress, disaster struck SPDR. In June 1871 floods of gigantic proportions struck the Guggur and Sirhind bridges, which sustained considerable damage. Traffic was badly interrupted before the Beas and Jumna rivers burst their banks, with piers to some of the smaller bridges being carried away. Many railway embankments were damaged, with tracks twisted and torn up. Although most of the damage was quickly restored, in some cases repairs involved considerable expenditure. It took a year to replace the Guggur Bridge and a new bridge was erected at mile 178 from Lahore. Additionally, a new Beas Bridge was not tested until October 1873, with full service restored on 16 October.

Those ad hoc lines that eventually merged into SPDR lent consideration to replacing the 'Indus Flotilla' with a new railway link, but extended delays resulted because of the need for two huge bridges to be constructed. The first structure, across the Sutlej near Multan, was built by Head, Wrightson and named the Empress Bridge (see Chapter 11). The other major bridge, a single-span cantilever structure across the Indus at Sukker, known as the Lansdowne Bridge and built by Westwood, Baillie & Company, was not in service until 1889.

The railways, spreading outwards from Delhi, were expanding at a phenomenal rate. It is recorded that, in April 1886, a large steamer, the *Clare*, left Teesside for Karachi with a cargo solely for SPDR, composed exclusively of steel railway material that included 1225 tons of rails rolled in Middlesbrough, 748 tons of sleepers and 23 tons of rail keys – the rail keys from Darlington foundries. The SPDR was subsequently merged into the North-Western Railway.

Little known and also in the Punjab was the short-lived Multan & Amritsar Railway started on 8 February 1859; Sir John Lawrence performed the ground-breaking ceremony. Above the locomotive was a scroll bearing the motto *Tam bello quam pace* – both for peace and war. The line extended for 240 miles and was later merged into SPDR. The building and operation of the railway attracted criticism from many of the British who were engaged on the project.

Shortly afterwards, in 1862, a regular service was established that included the newly opened Lahore to Amritsar link of 32 miles: 'punctuality could be relied upon', stated Joseph Harrison (1826–1899), who replaced engineer John Brunton II (1826–1899). Harrison added:

> We Europeans were all but declared redundant due to the tall men in funny hats [Sikhs]. They have replaced most of the expatriate drivers and firemen and virtually all maintenance workmen. They learn quickly and pass on their skills. I have noted these Punjabi fellows supervise

construction gangs with little direction required from us. They are friendly and do not resent our presence. They are dependable and not prone to
taking advantage of any situation we may unwittingly create.

Similar comments were made shortly after the opening of the Kalka–
Shimla (Simla) Railway, when Sikhs took over most train management
from 1903. It was reported by *Railway Gazette* that a manager and consultant from Britain ran the line, with the remaining staff and engineers
'mainly fully qualified Sikhs and a few coolies for labouring and tea duties'.

Bombay, Baroda & Central India Railway (BBCIR)

The need for a direct rail link from Bombay to Sabarmati, Agra and Delhi
was recognised in 1853 as being of dire importance. Initially the railway
consisted of a single line running 310 miles northwards, skirting the coast
for about 200 miles; a plan to meet up with the EIR at Delhi was held in
abeyance. With the GIPR beginning to earn revenue from 'this novelty of
locomotion' and the construction of lines in Bengal continuing daily, on 10
August in that year EIC directors instructed a team to 'execute in all good
haste' a survey of the projected line to Delhi.

The brilliant Colonel J.P. Kennedy (1796–1869), acting as Chief
Consultant to the railway company, was immediately commissioned to
employ the requisite officers for the job. Following acceptance of the survey's proposed route for the projected 865 miles, detailed surveys were undertaken in the field, beginning 'in all haste' on 16 April 1855. Surveying
work began from Bombay via Surat, Baroda and Neemuch to Agra, on the
understanding of the Indian government that the BBCIR would continue
with further survey requirements. Additionally, a route from Surat by the
Tapti Valley towards Khandesh, with an extension to the valley of Narbada
(Narmada), was undertaken. A guaranteed interest rate of 5% was conceded
by the EIC on a loan of £500,000. However, with the EIC still administering
the whole of India, the BBCIR was directed to construct the northern half
of the agreed survey first.

The engineering survey party had not lost sight of connecting towns
which were not directly in line between Bombay and Delhi. By the time the
first few miles of earthworks were excavated, and following an additional
evaluation of the area, the proposed network for the railway operator was
increased to 4000 route miles. By close examination of plans collected from
all his field engineers, Kennedy, who like many of his kind had 'developed a

The 'frontier mail' – India's fastest train – leaving Colaba Station, Bombay, for Delhi and the North-West, Bombay, Baroda & Central India Railway, c.1920s (Courtesy of International Railway Gazette)

soft spot for his host country's people', persuaded his directors of the practicality and humane aspects of connecting outlying districts with the main routes.

Work was initiated with a deep sense of purpose and commitment, with Surat and Bombay – 81 miles apart – connected on 1 May 1856. BBCIR fixed its first terminus in Bombay at Grant Road, a short distance from the Byculla Club and the racecourse, with the intention of eventually extending the line through reclaimed ground in Back Bay to a permanent terminus in Colaba. Baroda to Ahmedabad (73 miles) and Surat to Broach (36 miles) were later tackled.

In June 1856 the first shipments of construction material, including rails, hand-truck irons and shop material, were en route around the Cape. In that same month, contracts were placed for ballasting engines, rails and chairs to lay down 50 miles of track. Among the designs for carriage stock with tenders was a 'fourth-class upon a new construction, including two floors with the upper floor side panelling removed to allow ample circulation of air (possibly the first ever) and all suited to Indian habits, being calculated to secure the power of conveying the poorest classes in that country for the lowest possible cost', according to *Engineering* on 20 June 1856.

However, the most formidable part of the construction was the number and width of bridges needed for the line leaving Bombay. This was one reason why the track into Bombay itself was opened later than lines north of Broach. Kennedy's additional report concerning bridging was published in the Calcutta *Engineers Journal* for October 1861 and pulled no punches:

> The rivers which are encountered along the entire length of the line are nearly all tidal, with deep sandy beds, which sometimes alternate with alluvial drift; these beds extend in some cases to a depth of 20ft, 30ft and, as in the Nerbudda [Narbada] River at Broach, to a depth of over 40ft. In many cases, however, the sandy beds terminate at a depth of from 12ft to 18ft in hard clay, sometimes approaching to the character of shale.
>
> The difficulties inseparable from any mode of securing and laying firm foundations in such strata as these require no comment, particularly when it is borne in mind that nearly all these rivers are subject to high tides and are crossed not far from their point of debouchure.

The first 29-mile stretch of the northern half – running from Tapti and including the Keem Bridge – was opened on 19 February 1860. The first large Tapti crossing was opened in November 1860. A phenomenal amount of bridging was required, comprising 95 individual river and stream crossings aggregating 477 × 60 ft spans from Millwall-based Westwood, Baillie Company.

The second section of track added to the Indian broad gauge in service was from Utran to Anklesvar, opening on 10 February 1861. By the end of that year, the line from Bulsar to Vadodara (Baroda), a distance of 123 miles, was connected and opened for traffic. In a letter the London Board of Directors of BBCIR wrote to its agent in Bombay in December 1861, it noted: 'The Directors are very gratified that a train of 72 vehicles containing nearly 4000 passengers and, including engine and tender weighing 720 tons, was drawn by a single engine at 20 mph from Surat to Baroda.'

Work advanced at a steady rate. In 1864 over 10 000 Indian workers were receiving a regular, reliable weekly wage and small service communities blossomed with rail progress. In November of that year, Bombay was connected to Bulsar. Six years later Bombay was linked to Sabarmati, a distance of 325 miles. In 1872 the Bombay terminus had shifted to Churchgate.

An audit taken in 1864 revealed that 26 235 tons of railway material had been imported from Britain that year. Its network operated with 3102 units of rolling stock, of which 53 were locomotives.

An extension of the line from Ahmedabad to Viramgam and Wadhwan was approved, along with a contract to connect Anand to Dakore and Godhra. Bridging was now becoming very costly and was possibly underestimated in the surveying costs. An order was placed with the London fabricator Westwood, Baillie for an additional 40 spans of 60 ft, and an additional 13 major river crossings, comprising 358 spans with 75 lesser bridges, were needed to complete it.

The cost of finished lines constructed and in service by 1872 was far more than could have been estimated in 1856. The principal expenditure was on bridging, which cost about twice as much as for bridges constructed throughout the marshy flat lands of Bengal. For the 312 miles constructed, the company paid an average of £23,835 per mile. It was the highest cost per mile of all seven major railway companies then constructing lines in India.

BBCIR suffered continually from being a great distance from coalfields, and consequently paid a high price for its fuel. Even as late as the first decade of the 20th century, the price of Bengal coal was quoted at Rs.14 per ton, while Welsh steam coal was Rs.22 per ton and softer-grade coal from South Africa about Rs.19 per ton.

Of all railway constructors working throughout India up until 1870, BBCIR faced the biggest challenge in the assessment of bridge construction. Thirty-five rivers ranging from the 180 ft Kaurito to the mighty 4000 ft Bassein South just north of Bombay required virtually unprecedented feats of engineering to girder within the stipulated contractual time. Kennedy settled on each span being mainly 60 ft per unit, or Warren's lattice girders when used in conjunction with Mitchell's screw piles. There were also many small stream bridges with single spans.

Some idea of the speed of construction and the tasks placed upon indigenous workers can be assessed from two bridges of 600 ft and 450 ft just north of Baroda. The first was constructed in three months and the latter in two-and-a-half months, both undertaken during the rainy season. Testing of each structure was very thorough, although perhaps somewhat rudimentary. For the Mahi Viaduct to bridge the 2000 ft river, two huge engines were coupled together at their chimneys and rolled downhill at speeds of up to 20 mph 'with no permanent set and with the most satisfactory results'.

Many fabricators were hard pressed in Britain to supply an aggregate 6 miles of bridges. BBCIR's initial contract for structures went to South Wales' Crumlin Foundry for 5 × 60 ft plate girders to span the Keem River, delivered between 1856 and 1859. This was followed by the largest contract so far placed for girders that went to Westwood, Baillie for 477 individual spans, with piers from Derby's Eastwood, Swingler Company and the Horseley Ironworks. The order was placed in 1856 and the last shipment of ironwork arrived in 1866. In all, 30 of those spans were used across the Tapti River, the whole contract being valued at £900,000. For the Tapti–Orunga 43-mile link, Westwood, Baillie delivered complete ironwork and fittings for 18 bridges comprising 127 spans, each test-loaded to 130 tons with no permanent set.

The last delivery of girder work, also from Westwood, Baillie, was to cross both the North and South Channels of the Bassein Creek some 29 miles north of Bombay. All material was delivered between 1863 and 1864. The following year the line was made into a double track, with 150×60 ft spans from London Engineering & Iron Shipbuilding Company, which grew into one of the largest foundries in the British capital during the latter part of the 19th century.

Perhaps the first indigenous foundry of any significance to be established in Bombay was the Parel Ironworks. Sir Guilford Lindsey Molesworth (1828–1925) was engaged in designing bridges throughout India from the 1860s and was eventually responsible for the huge bridge to cross the Narbada River in about 1876. The establishment of the Parel Ironworks was most timely. British bridge-builders, stretched to overcapacity, presented an opportunity for the Parel Ironworks. Molesworth preferred to dispense with the standard 60 ft span and opted for a structure comprising 25×183 ft girders of reinforced ironwork. The bridge took three years to cast and construct, opening for railway traffic in 1880. Today the bridge is in full service for road transport and forms the main highway from Delhi to Bombay and the south-west of India.

A new Narbada Bridge was constructed in 1935 with a double-track structure from Braithwaite Engineering, of West Bromwich. This West Midlands foundry constructed 15×288 ft , one 246 ft and one 63 ft spans for the 4600 ft crossing at a cost of £400,000 for the 13 000 tons of steel required. The old and new that flank each other are a tribute to good design, supervision and excellent local endeavour.

In 1872 the total route mileage of BBCIR's network stood at 389.5, of which only 23 miles were running double-track. The system as originally planned and approved was, like GIPR and SPDR, completed that year. A small extension was added from Patri to Viramgam, and a narrow-gauge branch of 20 miles from Meagaum to Dubhoi, the property of the local dignitary but worked by the company, was re-opened after initial teething problems. A further branch line was planned in 1872 from Anand to the vicinity of Dakore (about 17 miles) on the broad gauge but using rails of

60 lb per yard to enable the firm's rolling stock from main-line services to be used. Surveys were then undertaken to extend the whole BBCIR network from Sabarmati to Ajmer, with a view to connecting Bombay and Delhi to Agra via Rajputana, rather than 'the inconvenient route as now in service'. It opened in 1876, saving 340 miles on the previous journey.

The monsoon of 1871 was particularly destructive, taking a heavy toll. The bridge over the river Par was swept away and bridges over the Orunga and Damaungunga were severely damaged. However, with 'a loyal and hardworking indigenous workforce, equally keen to see the service restored as was the British, temporary communication was restored across these rivers within 45 days and the permanent bridges all re-opened by May 1, 1872', according to *Engineering*. Just as GIPR was affected by a reduction in revenue, BBCIR found traffic receipts were down: 'the half-year under notice fell in the periodically recurring 12th year, which is deemed by the Hindu community as unpropitious for marriages and festivals', according to that same journal.

As the network expanded with further branches approved – the company constructed the Patri branch with funds supplied by the government – the broad gauge was adopted for most tracks laid. However, towards the end of the century the section from Viramgam to Wadhwan was converted to metre gauge in order to provide through passage between Rajputana and Kathiawar. The longest engine run was between Nagda and Muttra, the 273 miles being covered at nearly 40 mph.

In 1885, under a contract with the Secretary of State for India, the metre-gauge system known as the Rajputana–Malwa State Railway, was handed over to BBCIR. The operator thus inherited a large mileage of track once owned by the State. The railway was completed at different periods between 1873 and 1881, with the route from Delhi to Ahmedabad having been shortened by 41 miles. In 1876 various branches, aggregating 83 miles, were completed. At the time of handover to BBCIR, the network stood at 580 miles – longer than from London to Aberdeen. It was perhaps felt that, with so many other more pressing matters to consider, the State was unable to devote to the Rajputana–Malwa Railway the attention warranted.

BBCIR rolling stock

The first type of broad-gauge engine weighed about 31 tons, while those after 1890 weighed 71 tons. The first passenger train hauled 20 carriages at 25 mph, while the 'latest engines imported from Yorkshire and Glasgow hauled 16 bogie vehicles at 45mph in 1900', according to *The Engineer*. The earliest goods trains were capable of pulling 50 wagons with a total load of 650 tons, while 65 of the latest wagons could carry in excess of 1000 tons a decade later. The first metre-gauge engine weighed 20 tons, as against 34 tons from 1895. The first metre-gauge passenger train hauled 20 carriages at 25 mph, compared with a train comprising 26 wooden-framed carriages in 1892 that could exceed 38 mph.

As the network expanded so did the number of different manufacturers' engines running over its tracks. Neilson & Mitchell – later Neilson Reid – who had supplied some of BBCIR's earliest engines, continued its commercial relationship, delivering a few dozen locomotives from 1880. The Glasgow engine works of Dübs & Company, established in 1863, was soon recognised for its excellent workmanship, turning out more than 50 engines for the BBCIR from 1867. A locomotive crane for the same railway company followed a few years later.

Sharp, Stewart, which had transferred its facilities from Manchester to the Atlas Works, Glasgow, was chosen for very powerful engines that were usually found on heavy goods or medium–fast branch services. At the time of its amalgamation with Dübs & Company and Neilson Reid to form the North British Locomotive Company in 1903, this most enterprising foundry had built 5088 engines from 1833, with over 370 exported to India alone. From 1880, Sharp, Stewart developed a superheated tender engine that ran well on express passenger services from 1885.

The Yorkshire Engine Works, which in 1865 had secured large contracts for India within its first five years of manufacture, sold at least two dozen tender engines to BBCIR, principally for use on suburban services.

By far the largest supplier of locomotives to BBCIR was the Vulcan Foundry in Lancashire. In an advertisement in 1933 the firm boasted that it 'had built over 2800 locomotives for India', which works out at one engine every fortnight for 81 years. The engine maker's records reveal that over 300 were delivered to the BBCIR alone.

The Ajmer Railway Works (see p. 228) was the first workshop in India to assemble locomotives from parts imported from Britain. The works built a standard fast mail and passenger train in its Central Workshops, a model that captured the eye of its rivals. In a publicity campaign, Ajmer compared its product with the original mail and passenger engine built by Dübs of Glasgow in 1874.

Twenty-four heavy goods and express passenger engines were later delivered by William Beardmore of Glasgow, a late player in the market for steam locomotives. Having excelled itself since 1835 in the casting of marine engines, the foundry later produced its first design for an electric locomotive. Two were sold to the railway company in 1928.

From 1880, numerous firms delivered wagons and coaches to the BBCIR including Teesside Bridge & Engineering Works, Stableford (over 600 units), Cravens, and Leeds Forge (around 1000 units). The little-known Clayton Wagon Company delivered bogie timber wagons 45 ft long. When the Ajmer Locomotive & Wagon Works started production of rolling stock, the BBCIR ordered 171 steel-covered wagons.

When the combined steam locomotive complement had reached 399 broad-gauge and 591 metre-gauge engines from 54 running sheds, the carriage-building shop at Lower Parel (see p. 224), which assembled bogie units in parts from Britain, braced itself for the arrival of BBCIR's first suburban electric units. Cammell Laird, of Nottingham, not renowned for the manufacture of rolling stock despite supplying more than 700 units to India, completed 160 all-steel coaches that were stripped down in shells and re-assembled at the railway operator's rolling stock assembly works. They were in service well into Independence.

BBCIR enjoyed the benefits of good advertising, nowhere better displayed than in the *Railway Gazette*. In 1929 the journal featured BBCIR's Viceroy's train at Kotah, hauled by one of many Kitson locomotives.

The Viceroy's train on Chambal Bridge near Kotah, BBCIR, c.1929 (Courtesy of International Railway Gazette)

Oudh and Rohilkund Railway (ORR)

By 1867 every titbit or rumour of railway progress in India was being published in the two principal London-based engineering journals that were then devoting more space to Indian industrial progress than that in South America, the United States, Europe and Africa combined. India was viewed as 'more of an extension of Britain's railway line', to quote *The Times*. On 12 April 1867, *Engineering*, in an issue that published columns of railway extension matters in India, compiled yet another expansion of railway statistics throughout the subcontinent.

> We see in the *Homeward Mail* that the Secretary of State for India has granted to the Indian Branch Line Company a guarantee of interest at the rate of 5% for their railways in the provinces of Oudh and Rohilkund. The entire project contemplated by this company comprises a line of railway from Surampoor, on the Delhi Railway, passing along the north side of the River Ganges, to Benares and Buxar. Their line from Lucknow to Cawnpore, which has already been undertaken, will serve as a branch to their main line, which will afford a main trunk line of communication directly through the heart of the Central Provinces, the importance of which cannot be over estimated.

In reality, ORR started off as a small branch line that left the EIR to Azimganj – 27 miles, opened 11 November 1863 – on an unusual 4 ft gauge. It was merely a trial, as it was a spur little used by the East India Branch Railway Company that, after 1865, became the Oudh and Rohilkund Railway. It was worked as ORR for 26 years, until it was taken over by the State in 1889. The fledgling company went on to build a large network of broad-gauge lines, with 672 miles sanctioned in 1867 providing a 5% guaranteed to investors, and all lines then constructed on the north side of the river Ganges. Within a decade the towns of Benares, Faizabad, Lucknow and Bareilly had been linked up with the EIR.

In 1871 the total route miles sanctioned amounted to 695, of which 295 miles were opened by the end of 1872. On 1 March 1873 a further 40 miles were placed into service, connecting the two important towns of Hurdui and Shahjehanpore. Track laying pressed on at a feverish pace, and within the next 14 weeks a further 40 miles had opened and were carrying passengers. Various branches were constructed, and it could be safely claimed that very few people lived more than 30 miles from a railhead.

The ORR enjoyed popular passenger traffic services thanks to the fondness of Indians for festivals and the large number of pilgrims attending religious fairs or 'Melas'. With Benares recognised as the Hindus' holiest city, this area not unnaturally enjoyed one of the best railway services on its system. A large amount of freight was carried, principally grain and pulses, plus coal, sugar, oil seeds, salt, wood, cotton, oils and metals – all good revenue earners. Over 1 million tons were carried by 1890.

As routes were dug out, bridging continued to be very heavy, with many wells being sunk to depths of between 50 and 85 ft – and on one occasion 100 ft – below low-water mark. The foundations were sunk into clay or firm soil before being concreted. By far the most difficult structures to erect were the various crossings of the Ganges needed to link Benares, Faizabad, Lucknow and Bareilly with the EIR. The first bridge was at Cawnpore, erected between 1870 and 1874 and comprising 25 × 100 ft spans with all girders from the London foundry of Campbell, Johnstone & Company. It took four years from the receipt of order through works testing and shipping before it opened for service in January 1874.

The second and third crossings were at Rajghat (35 × 80 ft spans) and Balawali (11 × 284 ft) respectively. The longest distance over the Ganges, at Benares, comprised a bridge with the principal river-crossing spans 7 × 356 ft and long approach spans of 9 × 114 ft, built and erected by Patent Shaft & Axletree Company between 1881 and 1887; the piers were from P. & W. MacLellan. The whole bridge was 3518 ft long and was tested by rolling 58-ton engines back and forth over the completed structure. Each river span weighed a colossal 746 tons, including the rails and walkways. Tarmac was rolled over the roadway for the first time in India. The specification stated that the roadway 'must be capable of accommodating two huge elephants abreast leading the pack'.

ORR rolling stock

The first engine to run over the ORR's tracks was built in 1867 by Sharp, Stewart of Manchester; eight were delivered between 1865 and 1868. So successful was this 'A' class locomotive that it continued in service until 1903, when the last one was broken up after finishing its shunting duties in Lucknow station yard. The next class of engine imported was a unique design from Hunslet Engine Company, established in 1864.

Freight traffic grew at a phenomenal rate and the need arose for powerful heavy-duty slow-speed engines that could sustain continuous arduous service over the whole network. The Bristol engine builder Stothert, Slaughter

& Company had established its reputation supplying the EIR and success-fully bid for 15 engines in 1870 that were dispatched within a year. In the previous four years, the foundry had delivered 70 engines to GIPR and EIR.

As demand for more powerful engines grew, especially to haul pilgrim trains to Benares, ORR was found wanting as regards rolling stock and motive power. It contracted Robert Stephenson & Company to build a se-ries of very powerful units, which gained equal popularity with the Bengal Nagpur Railway. They were still in service at the time of Independence.

At the time of takeover by the State, ORR possessed around 200 engines, which were repaired and maintained at Lucknow. Its last delivery of loco-motives appears to have been from Armstrong of Newcastle.

Carriages and wagons were initially all of the four-wheel variety. Until 1895, all wagons were limited to 11 tons capacity; after this date the capac-ity increased to 16 tons. Most carriages and wagons arrived from Bristol, Gloucester, Birmingham and Sheffield. The emerging Birmingham Railway Carriage and Wagon Company of Smethwick constructed some of the earliest 20-ton wagons for the railway company. It also supplied axles and wheels for assembly by others. Pickering of Wishaw, Glasgow, delivered over 200 covered goods wagons rated 12 tons, along with carriage and wagon under-frames.

The Oudh and Rohilkund Railway retained its name even under new management. This was confirmed when the firm placed its largest-ever con-tract for 120 bogie carriages with the Leeds Forge in 1912. Fully assembled in Leeds, each carriage was brightly painted with ORR across the carriage body. The same supplier built 200 40-ton bogie ballast wagons that survived well into the late 1950s. In 1910 ORR imported electric trolleys operated by batteries for the first time. It is believed that they were used principally in the company's railway stations.

South India Railway (SIR)

The South India Railway (SIR) system was created partly by amalgamation and partly by new construction. When it was floated on the London Stock Exchange in 1862, £417,319 was raised – £1,220 of it in India. This compared with £11 million for GIPR and a total then of £30,533,374 for all railways throughout India. The first SIR line built was from Negapatam to Erode in about 1863, while lines from Negapatam and Trichinopoly to Erode were completed in 1868. About that time, a firm called the Indian Tramways

Coleroon Bridge on the chord line from Villupuram to Trichinopoly, SIR,
c.1920s (Courtesy of International Railway Gazette)

Company was formed to build feeder lines, but in 1869 it was wound up and
taken over by the Carnatic Railway Company. In 1864, after only two years
in business, the SIR imported 4797 tons of railway material from Britain. Its
rolling stock was a mere 200 units, of which 11 were locomotives.

In 1870 Carnatic was authorised to build a railway from Madras towards Tanjore to join up with the Great Southern of India Railway, which
was then building a line from Trichinopoly southwards. The difference in
gauges led to considerable trouble, and it was finally decided that the SIR
should have two gauges on its system from 1874. Considerable extensions
were quickly constructed from Trichinopoly southwards and Tuticorin
northwards, along with lines to Pondicherry. These extensions were placed
into service in 1879. For the Pondicherry route, an ad hoc company, the
Pondicherry Railway Company, was formed but it was soon absorbed into
the SIR, whose staff had been engaged in the venture. None of these small
companies possessed workshop or overhaul facilities and their demise was
merely a matter of time. By March 1871 SIR estimated that for the 168 miles
constructed the cost had averaged £8,658 per mile – the cheapest of all railways constructed in India in terms of price per mile.

SIR had Ceylon in its sights. The track connected Maduri with Manda-
pan, along with the largest extension of 134 miles in the Tanjore district.
Meanwhile, small steamboats were plying between northern Ceylon and the
southern tip of India. It was not long before huge screw ships belonging
to the railway operator meant that through tickets from Madras to Ceylon
could be bought.

SIR was fortunate in laying its tracks mainly through fertile agricultural land that was flat and dry for most of the year. However, only single-track working was adopted and very early on the stations were incapable of handling the huge populations that found rail travel to their liking. Junctions were similarly crammed with both people and freight, quickly coercing the railway company to re-model its stops to suit traffic requirements.

The growth of SIR led to rubber being planted in the Travancore Hills, resulting in the migration of Tamil labourers to cultivate it. With the opening up of a through rail–boat service to Ceylon, much rice from the Tanjore district was exported. Other principal freight carried was grain, pulses, groundnuts, timber, salt, cotton, kerosene and over 56 000 tons of fruit and vegetables annually. The total freight carried rose from some 630 000 tons in 1866 to over 1 million tons in 1880. By the end of the century, in excess of 2.2 million tons of all products were carried.

SIR also worked the defunct Cochin State Railway, a 64-mile line from Shoranur to Ernakulam, with Shoranur the junction using the SIR broad gauge track. At its peak, 12 engines, 28 bogie coaches, 119 bogie goods wagons and 54 four-wheeled goods wagons served both passenger and freight customers. A small workshop at Shoranur was established, with all castings and heavy forgings being supplied from Negapatam. Steam engines drove the machine tools.

Theobald's train key token instruments were installed throughout the main metre- and broad-gauge lines, as well as the Tuticorin branch. Other branches from the first lines installed were operated on the Morse line clear system.

From 1886 the longest and fastest run on the metre-gauge track was between Tuticorin and Madras Beach, and was known as the Ceylon Boat Mail; 447 miles was covered in 22 hours. On the broad gauge, the 328 miles from Madras to Mettupal iyam was achieved in 12.5 hours.

One phenomenal feat of railway engineering 'barely surpassed in the world', according to *The Engineer,* was the construction of the Nilgiri Rack Railway, completed in 1899. Small hill tribes had lived in Nilgiri, untouched by external influence until the British opened up the area and planted tea.

While SIR was constructing landing stages and ports for its export trade, the Clyde shipbuilder Messrs A. & J. Inglis was building three large Parsons-type steam-turbine-driven ferries to connect India with Ceylon. Named *Curzon, Elgin* and *Hardinge,* the vessels were each 250 ft long and 38 ft in the beam, with a maximum draught of 6 ft, and capable of 20 knots.

Ceylon Boat Mail train at Dhanushkodi Pier, SIR, c.1920s (Courtesy of International Railway Gazette)

Accommodation for both first- and second-class passengers was excellent. Each vessel handled cattle cargo.

Bridging was heavy for SIR. The first structure across the Palar River failed, but was subsequently rebuilt to comprise 18 spans of 120 ft, the ironwork coming from Patent Shaft & Axletree. A second large bridge at Nandyal, known as the Dorabhavi Viaduct, required 1 × 250 ft, 2 × 145 ft and 1 × 65 ft spans and was erected in one of the most difficult and isolated places in India, about 200 miles from Hyderabad. The bridge was converted to broad-gauge service but quickly abandoned when an alternative route was commissioned. It is now preserved as an industrial monument.

The inadequacy of the metre gauge was soon criticised by SIR's own engineers. Despite some 2 ft 6 in. track and over 1000 miles of metre-gauge service, a hasty programme was initiated to replace some metre gauge with broad gauge. By 1900, about 300 miles of broad-gauge track was in service, which necessitated the construction and refurbishing of existing locomotive workshops (as detailed in the following chapter).

Development of the Indian railway network

According to the reports from Juland Danvers of the Indian Office, 842 miles of railway was open in India at the end of 1860, and of 2932.5 miles then in progress, 1353.5 miles were expected to be open in 1861. The total railway guarantees had been for £56 million, but with construction of certain lines and portions of lines postponed, the amount expended under guarantee was reduced to £49 million, of which £34,396,445 had been raised up to 30 April, the end of the Indian official year. Danvers' report continued:

Nothing like the amount of line expected to be opened this year has been completed. The East Indian Railway Company had 458 miles open at the date of their last report, *viz*, 248 miles in Bengal and 210 miles in the Northwest Provinces. Mr Turnbull, the company's engineer in Bengal and who has, from the first, been most punctual in keeping his engagements with the shareholders, had promised to open 50 miles to Colgong and 24 miles further to Bhaugulpore, in the course of the year just expired, besides 33 miles to Monghyr in the course of the present month, and 106 miles more to Patna in June next. The Great Indian Peninsula Railway Company had 437.75 miles of line open, including the Bhore Ghat incline. The opening of the 16 miles of this incline was equal in importance to that of any 300 miles of the rest of the line. The Madras Railway Company operated 252 miles of line comprising 224 miles eastward from Madras, and 28 miles eastward from Beypoor, on the Malabar Coast. The Bombay, Baroda and Central India Railway had 132.25 miles from Doolia to Bulsar in service. The whole line of 313 miles cost £3,130,000, or £10,000 per mile, which Robert Stephenson deemed impracticable. The East Indian Railway, of the practicability of which there has never been any doubt, is now estimated to cost £16,000 per mile. The Scinde Railway, 114 miles long, is open throughout and the Great Southern of India was opened for a length of 14 miles. It appears, therefore, that up to the date of the last advices 1408 miles of railway were open in India, and we have reason for supposing that at least 110 miles more are now open.

Danvers summarised by adding: 'The Eastern Bengal line is expected to be open early this year. About one-half of the Calcutta and South Eastern, a line about 30 miles long, will be opened in January 1862 and the whole line to be opened in the course of the spring. The Indian railways to date are of 5 ft 6 in. gauge.'

To compare Britain and India over the first 30 years of railway construction, Britain (1830–1860) possessed 10 433 miles, while India (1853–1883) operated services over 10 882 miles.

London–Calcutta – a proposal by through train in 1865

In 1865 most of the wealthiest families in Britain had ties that linked them with India, according to *The Times* in London, and her rising indigenous middle class, along with the cream of English aristocracy, looked anxiously for better communication with the seat of Empire. Not unnaturally, with many fearing the average hazardous 80- to 90-day voyage around the Cape, entrepreneurs began to view a direct rail link with London as a practical proposition. Numerous proposals were surveyed but abandoned, although the hope was to connect India to Britain in days rather than weeks. The answer lay in rail.

The scheme that was considered feasible was to start in Calais. Lines from Ostend to Cologne with a route direct to Augsburg were already in service, with an ad hoc rail system constructed throughout Lombardy's provinces and principalities up to Orsova. From Orsova another 345 miles of track was required to bring the line into the Ottoman Empire's capital of Constantinople. From Constantinople, it was 1355 miles to Basra on the Persian Gulf. On leaving the Persian Gulf, it was intended to traverse the low plains near the side of the Gulf through Baluchistan before bridging many branches of the Indus into India.

The *Calcutta Englishman* in July 1865 sounded a strong note of caution as to the engineering difficulties facing such an undertaking. Fully aware of the numerous rivers and nullahs that rushed down from the Beshun Kard Hills which could rise 6 ft in as many hours, the paper warned of the considerable bridging required. A question arose regarding whether or not the railway would pay. When it was hammered out in government circles, the general consensus was that 'the line would unite the two richest countries in the world, [but] the business between the two is now crippled for want of a quicker and less expensive communication'.

There were many eager to subscribe to the venture. The survey concluded that a through line from London to Calcutta would be 5075 miles long. At the time, by rail and sea from Marseilles to Alexandria and from Suez to Calcutta, the journey totalled 5600 miles and took some six weeks. Sir Rowland Macdonald Stephenson was entrusted with the construction project on an urgent basis, partially because of the unreliability of telegraphs through Arab countries and Turkey. Two months later the British had opened the first railway in Turkey – between Smyrna and Aydin – with Manchester's Beyer, Peacock locomotive factory supplying the first steam engines. A few years later the steel rail had reached the Afghan border from Karachi.

In 1882, with project work well advanced, the survey reported that should the through railway from London to Calcutta be completed, the whole journey could be achieved in less than seven days at an average speed of 33 mph, though that might be regarded as wishful thinking. An estimated four bridges per mile with an aggregate length of 186 miles was calculated.

Enthusiasm east of Constantinople soon died a natural death but the diplomatic moves continued. Consultants backing the 'Tigris Railway across Turkish Arabia' – albeit with trepidation – assessed that London to Bombay might be completed in 14 days 4 hours, of which 9 days 20 hours would be occupied by the sea portion and only 4 days 8 hours in steam-hauled comfort. However, it is highly unlikely that travellers would have wished to risk their lives through Arab territories when the benefits of unashamed luxury could be had in either P&O or BISNC liners, with the knowledge that Royal Navy gunboats were poised to broadside any aggressor.

Luxury and security at a relaxing pace won the day. Some security reassurance, had the project gone ahead, was given in *Engineering* of 18 August 1871: 'Should hostile fleets attack our interests, the navy shall simply close the Persian Gulf ... always practical by means of [Britain's] naval forces constantly maintained in eastern seas.'

Early guarantee system 1850 to 1868

The government was anxious to invite private capital into railways but private companies could hardly guess the prospects for their investment. Each was trying to bargain to its best advantage and, since it was at the instigation of the government that the companies launched into this field of activity, the government adopted a liberal attitude. It guaranteed a minimum percentage of return to the shareholders, usually 5%. As an added incentive, the government had to offer certain other concessions such as free land.

However, in order to keep private companies under proper check and control, the government had to stipulate certain protective clauses in the contract. For example, if the percentage of profit exceeded 5%, the excess amount should be apportioned equally between the government and the company every half year. The government also retained the right to purchase these railways at the end of either 25 years or 50 years on payment of all shares of capital stock in the company concerned. In essence, the government relieved shareholders of all risks by giving them some expectation of profit over and above the guaranteed interest, claiming in return reasonable powers of control and the ultimate right to purchase.

The wording in the contract was uncertain and contradictory, leading to interpretations to the advantage of the companies. In 1862 the Government of India attempted to give contracts to firms by subsidising them and not by guaranteed fixed rate of return. The government's attempt to attract capitalists by this method failed and it was thought that it would be advisable to adopt the policy of direct construction and ownership of railways through direct borrowing. Throughout that period, as will be demonstrated from the tabulated construction statistics, the growth of railways was exceeding the expansion of paperwork guidelines in a country ripe for industrial change.

State construction and the new guarantee system

In 1868 the Secretary of State for India, Sir Stafford Northcote (1818–1887), felt all future railway projects should be classified as either commercial or political; for commercial, the guaranteed system, and for political, a direct government agency, were recommended. On the other hand, Lord Lawrence (1811–1879), the Viceroy of India, argued that railways, being commercial and profit making, should be completely taken over by the government, with the profit derived ploughed back into the system for further extension. This policy was adopted from 1869 to 1879.

However, the outbreak of dreadful famines between 1874 and 1879 and the Second Afghan War created financial difficulties that forced the government to entrust the construction of new railway lines to private companies once again. A guarantee system, with certain changes now more favourable to the government, was forced upon the new enterprises extending lines throughout the country. The unusual feature of company-worked railways operating with state-managed railways was set up, and it appeared in the end to work well and for the benefit of all. Over both types of railways, the government exercised a considerable measure of control. After 1870, railway development was more rapid.

The Kalka–Shimla (Simla) Railway (KSR)

The idea of a railway line to Simla was mooted as early as 1847 and recorded in the *Delhi Gazette*. As Simla was as remote and isolated as could be imagined, it is remarkable that the first railway line in India entered service only six years later.

It all began in 1816. The dust of the recurring Gurkha War had finally settled and a victorious British army tucked into their war booty – in this case a vast chunk of hillside, which included the deodar forest and Simla. Initially of no great interest to the Raj, little did the British realise at that time that the deodar forest, annexed to India, would soon become a most coveted hill station.

In 1821 Simla was merely an innocuous, sleepy native village called Shyamala consisting of a few log huts surrounded by a dense forest where bears and wild boar roamed. A few years later, Captain Charles Pratt Kennedy (1796–1879), the political agent, was smitten by the secluded charms of Simla and built himself a grand house there. Simla's cool climate soon became famous and invalids seeking comfort from the blistering heat of the plains and turmoil of India's capital, Calcutta, began arriving in large numbers.

The next Governor-General, Lord Bentinck, was so impressed with Simla's fresh air that he declared the place a summer capital. However, getting there from Calcutta or Delhi was a strenuous ordeal until a cart road – originally called the Grand Hindostan and Tibet Road, and fully British-built – was finished in 1856. Britain's road-building engineers had much experience in constructing roads through difficult terrain, gaining from the ordeals of carving out the military road to Darjeeling in 1830.

In 1856, 272 miles of railway were in service, and someone connected with railways who had visited Simla perhaps dreamed of a line into this area of tranquillity once again. As tourism and nostalgia had yet to feature throughout the Raj, Simla must have seemed the last place to consider for a fast return on capital outlay. Be that as it may, the established railway companies were looking for profit and growth,

Many years elapsed before construction began. It was during the first year of the tenure of the Marquis of Dufferin (1826–1902), who was Viceroy from 1884 to 1888, that a survey was begun. Using the trusty donkey, English civil engineers took about 18 months to examine the feasibility of the proposed route. The survey plans were not approved until 1897 as more important routes throughout India were under construction. Deeds for building the line were finalised and accepted the following year, while a team of Welsh miners and local labour set up camp when the first dig began.

On 29 June 1898, a contract was signed between the Secretary of State and the Delhi–Ambala–Kalka Railway Company for the construction of a 2 ft gauge line from Kalka to Simla. The contract stipulated that the line was to be built without any pecuniary guarantee from the government, but the land would be provided free of charge. In November 1901 the contract was amended to call for a gauge of 2 ft 6 in. Kalka had already been connected to Delhi in 1891, when the first train covered the 161 miles on 1 May of that year.

Construction was under way in 1899 (some sources say 1900), and the first portion opened for traffic in 1903 after massive civil works. Originally constructed by the Delhi–Ambala–Kalka Railway on the 2 ft gauge with single track only for a distance of 59.915 miles, it provided an extension from its northern terminus at Kalka (connected to the EIR) to Simla. It was reached on 9 November 1903. A subsequent extension from Simla passenger station to Simla goods station, a distance of about half a mile, was completed seven months later.

The civil works involved were little short of a miracle. Kalka is 2152 ft above sea level, whereas Simla is at a heady 7116 ft. For its short length, the railway had the distinction of comprising the largest amount of tunnels and bridges on any system throughout India. The train meanders through 103 tunnels, of which three are of considerable length. The Koti, 2270 ft, was driven through a shale hill, and a good deal of trouble was experienced with pressure on the heading timber used during the construction. The second major tunnel, the Barogh, 3752 ft, was driven through basalt and trap by pneumatic drills; the train takes about three minutes to pass through. The third tunnel, Tar Devi, near Simla, is 1200 ft long.

According to one tale from Simla folklore, when a tunnel was dug below the famous Taradevi shrine the hill people declared that the goddess would never allow it to be completed. When the tunnel was half bored through, shouts of great excitement suddenly stopped all work. 'A huge serpent, several hundred feet long is lying across the tunnel,' whispered the crowd. When examined, this turned out to be an iron pipe placed in the tunnel to convey fresh air while it was being dug. Work restarted, and it would seem that the goddess of the hills was pleased as the precious garnet stones were found studded in the rocks.

Bridging complemented the stupendous feat in tunnelling. In spanning scenic mountain gorges and ravines, a unique feature was the complete absence of girder viaducts: only masonry structures called 'galleries', which resembled Roman aqueducts, were erected. These consisted of tiers of arches rising one above another until the rail level was reached. Most were constructed on a curve, the curvature being formed by making the piers wedge-shaped. The retaining walls were made of dry stone and varied from 10 ft to 15 ft in thickness.

Along almost 60 miles of some of the most difficult terrain on the Indian subcontinent, 869 bridges were constructed, and this bridging represented just over 3% of the total route. Most of the other railway lines in northern

India averaged about four bridges per mile, with more in the swamplands of Bengal. It is not often noted that the Kalka–Simla gained the distinction of averaging 29 bridges for every two miles constructed – a world record that stands today. Only the Kangra Valley Railway (KVR), completed in 1926, contained a greater number of bridges than the Kalka–Simla route. For its 102 miles length, the KVR comprised two tunnels and 971 bridges, including the stupendous 260-ft-long Roand Nulla single-arch bridge containing 230 tons of steel from Braithwaite Engineering.

After opening, the Kalka–Simla line was worked by the Delhi–Ambala–Kalka Railway Company with some four trains each way daily up to 1 January 1906, when the Secretary of State purchased the firm's shares for £900,000.

The most important stations after the Simla terminus were at Summerhill, the station for Viceregal Lodge; Jutogh, a military hill station; Kandaghat, the station for Chail – the summer residence of the Maharaja of Patiala; Solon, a military hill station; and Kumarhatti, Dharampur and Kalka, which was the joint station with EIR tracks. At its peak the train served 21 stations. The operator also constructed 9.61 miles of sidings.

The railway continued to develop under EIR control and made a profit from its first year. From 1903 the Sikh workforce took over most of the management. Potatoes were grown in the highlands and provided a nice little freight earner for the railway. In 1908 some 100 000 passengers were carried annually along with about 47 000 tons of goods.

Simla grew to become the summer capital of both the Punjab and India, as well as the all-year-round headquarters of the Indian army. Passenger traffic over the KSR was therefore of considerable importance. The principal goods carried within two years of opening were: coal, grain, piece goods, molasses, kerosene, oil, steel bars and cut sheets, salt, stone, lime, bricks, sugar, provisions and luggage (up); and potatoes, ginger, borax and luggage (down).

The KSR consisted of a single track only throughout its life, and the general method of signalling adopted was the electric telegraph. The passenger train-miles from 1900 totalled 135 000, and those of goods trains 140 000. The longest run on this railway is 20 miles, and the maximum speed then was 15 miles per hour. The gross ton-miles of goods for that same year were 12.2 million, and of parcels and so on carried by passenger trains 164 000 tons. The average distance run per engine per annum in 1913 was 11 245 miles, while for goods wagons it was 19 776 miles.

Viceregal Lodge, Simla, 1895 – the official summer residence of the British vice-roys was completed in 1888 (Courtesy of the British Library)

In 1921 it was suggested that the line be electrified. Then 22 steam loco-motives were employed, though only 15 were serviceable at any one time. When electrification was completed, only ten electric locomotives were re-quired. The journey time was reduced from approximately eight hours to 4.5 hours in 1932.

The Government of India purchased the line outright in 1926, transfer-ring the management to the State-controlled North-Western Railway.

Rolling stock

The first locomotives to be introduced on the KSR were built by Sharp, Stewart to suit the 2 ft gauge, but were altered in India soon afterwards to suit the wider gauge. These engines were very similar to those used on the Darjeeling–Himalaya Railway from 1879. A later type, consisting of ten locomotives from their Atlas Works in Glasgow, could pull a load of up to 65 tons – 10 tons more than the first engines. Introduced five years later, 30 engines weighing 35 tons from the North British Locomotive Company – an amalgamation of Sharp, Stewart and Co., Dübs and Co. and Neilson, Reid and Co. – in Glasgow were used right up until electrification. Despite the use of more powerful engines, the train load very rarely exceeded 80 tons. The running of passenger trains at night became popular when electric lighting was installed in carriages and all engines on night passenger trains were equipped with electric searchlights.

The historical importance of the Kalka–Simla line is not to be judged from its length or the amount of the traffic. It was the only line – with the Delhi–Ambala–Kalka Railway – that connected Simla with the rest of India, and its passenger traffic was therefore of the highest importance.

THE PINTSCH GAS LIGHT SYSTEM FOR CARRIAGES

THE DISADVANTAGES AND DANGERS of gas lighting for passenger coaches were well known, especially as gas was derived from coal. However, although India had experienced the benefits of electric street lighting from about 1885, the railways were yet to adopt this novel form of illumination. It was the era of the Pintsch gas lighting system. An administration report on the railways by Lieutenant Colonel R.A. Sargeaunt RE for 1892–93 clearly indicated the great strides taken by the industry to improve the lighting of carriages:

> On the East Indian Railway the Government of India have sanctioned an estimate for lighting 180 coaching vehicles by gas, on Pintsch's system, in the chord and loop line mail trains and the joint stock for service to Bombay. The building for the gas-producing plant at Howrah is well advanced and that at Allahabad commenced. The fittings for carriages have not arrived. On the Oude [Oudh] and Rohilkund—State—Railway, the Government of India have approved of 571 coaching vehicles being lighted by gas on Pintsch's system. In April, 1892, Pintsch's system of lighting carriages by compressed oil gas was introduced as an experiment on the Bombay, Baroda, and Central India Railway, the expenses being borne by the proprietors of the patent. One local train and one bogie carriage of the mail train were supplied with the reservoirs and necessary fittings, the gas works being erected at Parel. On the Madras Railway one of the company's saloons having been experimentally lighted with Pintsch's gas for a period of six months with highly satisfactory results, an indent has gone forward for sanction for a complete set of gas-making apparatus and carriage lamps, and reservoir fittings sufficient for introducing this system of gas lighting into the majority of the company's passenger stock. An indent has been sent forward for the necessary apparatus for manufacturing and supplying Pintsch's gas

on the south Indian Railway. At first 100 bogie coaching vehicles will
be fitted up, and the remaining stock next year.

Materials for making the gas itself were readily available in India as
many Manchester and Oldham fabricators were building town gas plants,
and according to *The Engineer* in 1894: '[T]he safety and cheapness of the
light makes it well suited for the long distance runs of the Indian lines.'

Railways in Mysore

Mysore was an important native state of India and once comprised
29 475 sq. miles with a population of 5.8 million, according to a census of
about 1890. The whole state was on an undulating tableland some 2000 to
3000 ft above sea level and bordered by considerable ranges of mountains
rising to over 6000 ft – the Bababuduns to the north-west, the Biligirirangan
on the western portion of the southern border, and the Ghats along the
western border – rendering railway access to the sea most difficult.

The system of railway in Mysore was mainly the property of His Highness
the Maharaja of Mysore, who began the first construction in 1881. It grew
to include 10 miles of broad gauge in Bangalore, 557 miles of metre gauge,
102 miles of 2 ft 6 in. gauge and 36 miles of 2 ft gauge. Soon after its formation, the Mysore Railway, in a fledgling state with further construction
somewhat haphazard, relied upon the Southern Mahratta Railway (SMR)
to work 270 miles of mixed-gauge track. This was a natural state of affairs
as one of the first lines in service extended westwards from Bangalore City,
which was then a junction with the SMR.

The Bangalore–Mysore–Chamarajanagar section was quickly constructed to connect with Seringapatam, once the capital of Tipu Sultan (*c.*1749–
1799). From the railway plans, a branch line was built to Nanjangud, noted for its ancient temple. This service gave access to the Cauvery Fall at
Sivasamudram and the British-built electric power transmission line from
Maddur. The Mysore–Arsikere section traversed the lush paddy fields of
the Cauvery and Hemavathi valleys, joining the SMR at Arsikere. The line
was popular with tourists for it passed near Sravanabelagola, the site of a
gigantic statue that is sacred to the Jains.

The railway consultants working for the Maharaja of Mysore were quick
to sense the needs of locals and visitors alike and took small diversions to
the villages of Belur and Halebid, which were of great archaeological interest. The Birur–Shimoga section took off from the Bangalore City to Poona

line at Birur, which provided a connection to Shimoga, then the third most important town in the state – an outlet for the mineral and forest produce of the Malnad. The huge Bhadravati Iron Works, which was one of the pioneer industries in Southern India, was situated on this line. One of the last lines to be constructed before 1910 was a branch line from Chikjajur to Chitaldroog, noted for its historical ruins and recognised for its cotton crop.

By 1909 there were 462 miles of railway in Mysore State; of these, 61 miles were standard gauge and 401 miles metre gauge. The Government of India later took over the whole of the standard-gauge mileage with the exception of the 10-mile branch from Bowringpet to the Kolar Goldfields, but those lines of the metre- and 2 ft-gauge within the state borders belonged to the state. The only important bridges were those over the Tungabhadra River near Harihar on the Mysore frontier and over the Cauvery near Seringapatam. Braithwaite Engineering constructed the latter bridge. The longest bridge on the network was on the Hassan–Mangalore line and comprised 8 × 80 ft and 4 × 15 ft spans.

His Highness the Nizam's Guaranteed State Railway (NGSR)

Up to the end of 1878, the Nizam's first line was worked by the GIPR using its own rolling stock. From January 1879 until 31 December 1884, it was worked by the State Railway Agency, and from January 1885 by His Highness the Nizam's Guaranteed State Railway Company (NGSR), with all land provided by His Highness the Nizam's government free of cost to the firm.

The Nizam adopted both the Indian broad-gauge and the metre-gauge systems for his network – the former line extending about 350 miles from Wadi Junction to Bezwada Junction. This included a 16-mile branch line from Dornakal Junction to the Singareni collieries. The Nizam was fortunate in having his own coal mines.

Additionally, the railway company worked an extension 21 miles in length into British territory. The Nizam recruited the best English consultants and engineers to further his network. He approved a broad-gauge line that extended from Hyderabad via Secunderabad to Manmad, a distance of 391 miles, with a branch line 50 miles in length from Purna to Hingoli. The branch line was opened for public traffic in 1901. The broad-gauge line connected to GIPR tracks at Wadi Junction and to the SMR at Bezwada. The metre-gauge line connected with the GIPR at Manmad.

The Singareni coalfields, 1892. In 1888, the Nizam's Guaranteed State Railway opened a six-mile-long broad gauge section for the transport of coal. By 1911 the Singareni coal mine had an annual production of nearly half a million tons (Courtesy of the British Library)

The Nizam's government guaranteed interest in sterling at 5% per annum (£1 million) and debenture (£1.5 million) capital for 20 years from the date on which such capital was paid up. The guarantee in the case of share capital ceased on 25 June 1904, but termination of the guarantee in respect of debenture capital expired on various dates from 30 June 1904 to 31 January 1928. There were no further issues of debentures, which amounted in all to £200,000, and on these no guarantee on the part of His Highness the Nizam's government exists.

At its peak, 110 Europeans, 269 Eurasians and 1761 Indians all earned their living working for the railway; whole villages depended upon those serving the NGSR. The Nizam appointed two Englishmen to administer control of the whole operation as well as be responsible for the regular payment of wages. Today, Secunderabad is the busiest railway station on the old NGSR system, renamed the Central Railway.

The broad gauge carried castor, til (sesame) and linseed via Wadi and Bezwada for export from India, with salt, piece goods, timber and miscellaneous commodities for local consumption received from neighbouring lines. Coal from Singareni colliery to southern and western India was one of the main sources of goods traffic. This colliery produced about 400 000 tons from 1890, rising to some 500 000 tons per annum in 1910.

The metre-gauge network freight was principally devoted to cotton, cottonseed, mohwa seed and linseed via Manmad for export from India. Food grains were imported and transported locally. The NGSR also built some strong, stone rural stations, mainly for second-class passenger transport.

Assam–Bengal Railway (ABR)

This construction of this railway began in May 1891 as a State line, and the Assam–Bengal Railway Company proper was formed in England in April 1892, taking over the whole works started by the State. The fledgling Noakhali–Bengal Railway Company, which once served with a few miles of track in the same area, was worked up to the end of 1895, when it was purchased by the government and amalgamated into the Assam–Bengal Railway (ABR) from January 1896. ABR was purposely constructed to open up the Province of Assam, which by means of this railway was directly connected to the rapidly growing port of Chittagong.

The port facilities were quickly dredged and expanded to handle steamers of 6000 tons. Additionally, ABR engineers dredged 9 miles up the Kornafuli River, achieving additional navigation from the Bay of Bengal. Warehousing and berths were constructed. By 1902 Chittagong Port was equipped with four complete jetties incorporating the latest up-to-date hydraulic cranes and electric light; a further four jetties planned and executed in the next decade. Today, huge anchors from Sunderland Forge, once used in the initial construction for pontoon bridges to offload locomotives from English steamers, can be found lying scattered in secluded offloading areas along with the remains of many early cranes.

The line was initially a single metre-gauge track constructed through some of the worst mosquito-infested swampland ever encountered, although typical of railway construction throughout Bengal. Nevertheless, the railway operator was doggedly determined to reach Assam, with its rich tea-growing areas and recently developed coalfields, while simultaneously importing cranes and other mechanical handling equipment to bolster the fledgling facilities at the port of Chittagong.

In 1902, when some 438 miles were constructed, the ABR had grandiose plans to construct 100 miles of branch line yearly. By 1906 the 576 miles from the Chittagong to Assam were in service. Feeder services were constructed at the same time.

ABR was indeed fortunate in being able, once the line reached Assam, to tap the rich coalfields, although with oil found in Badarpur and Bigboi and the Burma Oil Company active and keen to see a rail link between the oilfields and Chittagong, there was a strong sense of urgency in pushing through the railway line northwards. From its inception, ABR carried tons of grain, its lines traversing the great grain-producing areas. Jute was an early source of income, with the commodity hauled to Chittagong for final conveyance to the mills in Calcutta. There was no rail connection between east and west Bengal then, only a steam ferry served the local people. Once wrapped in bales at the packing factories, the jute was carried on BISNC steamers to Dundee for final processing. Later, mills were established in and around Narayanganj.

At the end of 1912, the route mileage was 805 miles, with two branches being sanctioned for construction: one from Sylhet to Fenchuganj and the other from Bhairab-Bazar to Tangi. This most enterprising of all eastern Indian railway systems had grandiose plans that were successfully implemented, and ultimately led to its profitability and large dividends being paid out. To connect the ABR with the ad hoc Dacca & Mymensingh Railway and link up with EBR at Tangi on the Dacca–Mymensingh branch of that system, 'no expense was spared with foundries in Britain directed to produce the goods at a fair price for prompt payment', according to a letter sent to its London-based consultants by the railway's chief engineer.

An intriguing feature of the railway was the hill section, which ran for over 100 miles through the North Cachar Hills – an outlying foot range of the Himalayas. The river and mountain scenery on this section was unequalled anywhere in India. The extremely heavy civil works – including 32 tunnels, gigantic cuttings and steel viaducts – were immensely interesting from the engineer's point of view, exciting considerable admiration for those who carried out the vast undertakings in a district devoid of inhabitants and practically without roads or communication. To the north of the hill section, the railway passed through 100 miles of primeval forest, then very sparsely populated but containing relics of temples and buildings dating back to the Kachari occupation.

The number of passengers carried rose from just over one million in 1897 to 4686000 in 1912. The goods traffic reached 720000 tons in 1912 with the expansion of the port of Chittagong for the export of jute, mostly, and tea, plus the import of heavy machinery. The share capital of ABR was £1.5 million, on which a government guarantee interest of 3% per annum was paid; up to 30 June 1908, interest was allowed at 3.5%. Further funds for the railway were provided by the Secretary of State, either from the general funds allotted for railway construction in India or by raising debentures on the security of the property. The total amount expended up to the end of 1912 was Rs.1,504 lacs.

The principal stations on the company's system during the first 30 years were Chittagong, Chandpur, Akhaura, Badarpur, Lumding, Gauhati and Tinsukia. All construction was fraught with dangers, including swamps, monsoons and the Bengal tiger, that might have been enough to deter even the most intrepid – but not the Victorian British.

The line extended from 576 miles in length, or 805 miles including branches, in 1906 to 1152 miles in 1923, and ran from the port of Chittagong to Assam, connecting at its northern terminus with the Assam Railways & Trading Company's line at Tinsukia Junction. There was a branch 112 miles long running in a westerly direction along the foot of the northern slopes of the Kasheah Hills, from Lumding Junction to Gauhati on the Brahmaputra, where it connected with EBR's metre-gauge system by wagon ferry. Other short branches ran to Noakhali on the estuary of the Meghna, and to Chandpur, Bhairab Bazar, Fenchuganj and Silchar – all of these stations being also on the Meghna River or its tributaries.

The bulk of the line travelled over a level plain, although there was a Ghat section at about the middle of the length some 75 miles long. The line rose from 117 ft above sea level over two saddles, each about 1860 ft above sea level, before descending into the plains of Upper Assam. The principal bridges on the ABR network were Barak, Dehing and Kopili, each erected with 60 ft spans; Teesta with 250 ft girders; and Feni with mainly 125 ft plate girders from Patent Shaft & Axletree Company. Many viaducts with 100 ft spans and up to 121 ft in height were erected on hill sections. Bridging was heavy on leaving Chittagong itself; most were of short-span plate-girder fabrications from the Calcutta foundries of Burn and Jessop.

Rolling stock

A maximum 108 locomotives served the ABR in 1914, rising to about 185 engines by 1929, with an additional ten on order. Of these, the latest 48 engines were built to the Standardisation Committee's standard-designed locomotive. Most engines were from Vulcan Foundry, with the heaviest locomotives of the Garratt-type built by Beyer, Peacock of Manchester and weighing some 90 tons.

Little-known railways

Bengal–Dooars Railway

The Bengal–Dooars Railway system comprised 153 miles on the metre gauge, of which 116.5 miles were ad hoc extensions. The lines were constructed for opening up the Western Dooars region and for the development of the tea industry. In the first instance the original 31-mile line from Barnes Ghat on the east bank of the Teesta to Dam Dimwas opened in early 1893, and the 5.5-mile Lataguri–Ramshai branch later that year. The southern extensions (66 miles) were opened in 1900, the western extensions (6.5 miles) in 1901/2, and the eastern extensions (44 miles) mostly in 1903.

Land was provided by the government free of charge and the railway worked by the company, which received all the profits. The Secretary of State reserved the power to purchase the original line and all extensions on 31 December 1919, and at the end of any succeeding seventh year, by giving 12 months' previous notice. For the year 1912, the proportion of expenses to earnings on the original line was 23%, and on the extensions 44%, while the percentage of total income on capital outlay was 13.12% in the case of the original line and 5% in the case of the extensions.

The Barsi Light Railway

With a total capital outlay of Rs.7014,477, the Barsi Light Railway system opened in 1897. Engineered by a Mr E. R. Calthorp, it consisted of 116 miles on the 2 ft 6 in. gauge, partly in British territory and partly in Hyderabad State. The Barsi Light Railway Company worked the system. The main line of 21.5 miles ran from Barsi Road Junction on the GIPR network to Barsi Town, with an efficient system of trans-shipment between the broad and narrow gauges at the junction maintained throughout the life of the firm. On this section, which was opened in March 1897, the railway operator was allowed use of part of the road, with any land outside the road being acquired at its own expense. All profits went to the company.

The British government upheld the right to determine the contract with the firm on 1 January 1944, or at the expiration of any subsequent period of ten years on 12 months' notice. The Nizam's government had the option of purchasing the length of the line – excluding rolling-stock, workshop machines and stores – in Hyderabad in May 1931 on 12 months' notice.

Bukhtiarpur–Behar Light Railway

This railway was originally constructed in 1903 from Bukhtiarpur, a station on the EIR, to Behar, a distance of 18.5 miles, and ran along one side of the District Board of Patna road. In 1909 it was extended by 9.5 miles to Silao, and in 1911 by a further 5 miles to Rajgir, a sacred town at which a well-attended religious festival was held every third year. There were four engines in service, 20 coaching vehicles and 60 goods vehicles. The train mileage in 1911 was 44 000. The number of passengers carried in 1912 was 706 500 and the amount of goods hauled was 33 000 tons. This railway's principal traffic was in goods, the district through which it passed being extremely fertile; the chief commodities carried were grain of various kinds and potatoes. The most important station was Behar, where heavy goods traffic was received.

During the triennial religious festival, which lasted for a month, there was usually a tremendous rush of passengers to Rajgir. During the festival in June and July of 1912, over 300 000 passengers were carried. The trains ran on the 'line-clear' system. The usual number of trains run was six a day, but during the festival period 20 trains per day were all crammed to capacity.

Baraset–Basirhat Light Railway

This railway was constructed in 1905 from Baraset, a station on EBR central section, to Basirhat, the headquarters of the subdivision of that name in the district of the 24-Purganas. The contract was under the District Board guarantee, with all rails laid along the existing District Board Road. The original length was 26 miles. In 1909 an extension of 8.5 miles was constructed to Chingrighatta, a village situated on the Ichamati River. In 1910, to cater for the increasing traffic and to avoid trans-shipment of goods, a chord was built from Pattipooker, on the outskirts of Calcutta, to Belliaghata Bridge Station, 8 miles from Baraset. This chord was 17 miles in length and worked as the main line, having proved itself of great advantage to the public by allowing direct communication with Calcutta.

There were seven locomotives, 44 coaching vehicles and 35 goods vehicles in service by 1912. The number of passengers carried in that year was 771 800 and the amount of freight hauled was 27 000 tons. The only known locomotive manufacturer to have supplied the railway was Hunslet, which recorded in its archives that 'our 1000th engine was the first of a batch for the Baraset-Basirhat Railway and ordered through T A Martin & Company, of Calcutta'.

The main traffic was in passengers, many of whom attended offices in Calcutta daily. In the season considerable jute traffic was carried, with some 22 000 tons hauled in 1912. Merchants did not dispatch until a favourable market was obtainable in Calcutta. In consequence, when the time was right the stock had to be moved as quickly as possible, and it was found necessary to make every wagon perform two complete trips in 24 hours. Two English managers ran the network.

Arrah–Sasaram Light Railway

This railway opened for traffic in March 1911. It ran from Arrah, a station on the EIR main line, to Sasaram Station on the EIR Chord Line – a length of 60.5 miles. This line was constructed alongside the District Board Road and guaranteed by the District Board of Shahabad. There were five engines in service, 23 coaching vehicles and 51 goods vehicles. Two large bridges from the Howrah Ironworks, with sufficient headway for country boats, were constructed over two main canals, involving considerable earthwork in each approach.

The number of passengers carried in 1912 was 290 000 and the amount of goods conveyed estimated at 18 000 tons. Its traffic was never fully developed, but the line carried much heavy grain as the country through which it passed was well cultivated and irrigated by canals; freight operations made up for passenger losses. Four trains ran daily at its peak with the train mileage in 1913 logged at 73 000 miles.

Shahdara (Delhi)–Saharanpur Light Railway

This railway was constructed in 1907 under an agreement with the local government of the United Provinces. No guarantee was given but land was provided free. The line ran from Delhi-Shahdara Station, on the EIR, to Saharanpur, with a connection to the North-Western Railway. The total mileage was 92.63, passing through rich country irrigated by canals.

There were eight engines in service, 35 coaching vehicles and 189 goods vehicles. Little difficulty was encountered as the terrain over which the rolling stock travelled was flat and fertile and irrigated by numerous canals that British hydraulic engineers had built in the previous century. Train mileage during 1911 was 137 000. The number of passengers carried in 1912 was 994 100 and the amount of goods carried was 106 000 tons. The main traffic on this line was freight, which showed a steady increase, indicating that the network had considerably benefited the local economy. The chief goods carried were grain and raw sugar, which were exported, mainly to Britain.

The most important stations were Baraut and Shamli – well-developed market towns that provided very heavy traffic in goods. The usual number of trains run daily, exclusive of freight, was four, and these were monopolised by locals. Over 100 employees earned a steady wage, with many others relying upon the railway workers for their livelihoods.

Jodhpur–Bikaner Railway

The Jodhpur-Bikaner Railway network ultimately comprised 1219 miles of open lines on the metre gauge, of which the Jodhpur section was 525 miles and the Bikaner section 470 miles, as audited in 1910. An extension of 79 miles to the Jodhpur section, from Jodhpur to Phalodi, was sanctioned in August 1912. The Jodhpur section was the exclusive property of the Durbar of the Native State of Jodhpur, in whose territory it was situated; the Bikaner section was the property of the Bikaner Durbar. All profits from operations belonged to the respective owners. These sections were worked by the Jodhpur–Bikaner Railway Administration, which also operated the Jodhpur–Hyderabad Railway, 124 miles in total, as well as the Mirpur Khas–Jhudo and Mirpur Khas–Khadro lines, totalling 100 miles.

The Jodhpur–Hyderabad line was the property of the Government of India, which made an allowance to the Jodhpur–Bikaner Administration for the provision of rolling stock in addition to working expenses, the balance of earnings being paid to the British government. The Mirpur Khas–Jhudo and Mirpur Khas–Khadro lines were the property of the Sind Light Railways, having been constructed and paid for by the Jodhpur–Bikaner Administration.

Southern Punjab Railway

This company constructed 424 miles of railway on the broad gauge, of which 401 miles were of main-line track from Delhi via Bhatinda to Samasata, the remainder being a branch from Narwana to Kaithal. The government managed, maintained, stocked and operated the railway as far as practicable as part of the North-Western Railway system, retaining 52% of the gross earnings. The remainder, plus certain rebates, was the net earnings of the firm. Surplus profits in excess of 3.75% on capital expenditure in sterling were divisible between the company and the government.

The Southern Punjab Ludhiana Extension of 152 miles was also worked by the government through the Agency of the North-Western Railway, being part of the Southern Punjab Railway.

Rohilkund and Kumaon Railway (RKR)

In 1912 the Rohilkund & Kumaon Railway (RKR) system covered 592 miles, of which the Rohilkund & Kumaon Railway proper represented 256 miles on the metre gauge and the Lucknow–Bareilly Railway 296 miles on the metre gauge, while the Powayan Light Railway adopted the 2 ft 6 in. gauge for the remainder.

All systems ran throughout the United Provinces, with connections to the Rajputana–Malwa section of the BBCIR, the Bengal & North-Western Railway (BNWR) and the ORR. Most of the system was constructed in single line. On the Lucknow–Bareilly lines the net earnings for the same period represented 7.45% on the capital outlay, while on the Powayan Light Railway the corresponding percentage was 4.49.

The original main line started from Bhojeepura near Bareilly and ran for 54 miles in a north-westerly direction to Kathgodam. It was opened in 1884. For this part of the line, land was granted free by the government subject to the condition that the company paid on demand the cost price of land purchased by the government for the purposes of the railway. The government guaranteed interest at 4% on £200,000 capital of the original line until

The headquarters station of the BNWR, Gorakhpur, c.1920s (Courtesy of International Railway Gazette)

its opening, and thereafter paid a subsidy of Rs.20,000 half-yearly for ten years until the end of 1894. After that the company received no guaranteed interest from the government, except in the case of the Lucknow–Bareilly Railway for which there was a guarantee of the principal and interest in respect of debentures for £147,000.

Any surplus over 6% on the paid-up share capital of RKR in respect of the original main line and additional main line works was divided equally between the government and the company. For 1912 the net earnings of RKR were 7% on the total capital outlay.

The government, if required, could terminate the RKR and the Lucknow–Bareilly contracts on 31 December 1932 by giving 12 months' notice, but the government was contracted to purchase the various portions collectively and not singly. The greater part of the RKR network was not opened until after 1905. In that year, only 54 miles were in operation. Of the Lucknow–Bareilly lines, a considerable portion (about 142 miles) was opened between 1884 and 1887.

The principal items of goods traffic carried by the entire system in 1912 were grain and pulses – 254 607 tons, with receipts amounting to Rs.680,871. Oil seeds, sugar and unwrought timber also contributed substantially, with receipts of Rs.116,595, Rs.151,811 and Rs.166,675 respectively.

State assumes control

The railway entered a new phase of development in 1922, when the Railway Board was reconstituted, and the railway finances were separated from September 1924. The separation of railway finances marked a revolutionary change in policy and afforded all railways considerable financial and administrative autonomy to conduct their own affairs and to initiate and carry out future policies on sound business principles. The policy lasted a mere three years.

On 1 January 1925 the State took over the management of the EIR and on 30 June 1925 the GIPR was also brought under State control. Both somehow retained their names, if not in official circles then certainly in the eyes of the public. Under State control, the railways had a period of exceptional prosperity up to 1930, followed by an era of unparalleled depression in the years before World War II. State-encouraged electrification came to Indian Railways on 3 February 1925, beginning with the harbour branch of the GIPR. The BBCIR electrified its suburban section soon afterwards in 1928.

Electric all-steel suburban train, GIPR, c.1929 (Courtesy of International Railway Gazette)

The Madras suburban lines were electrified early in 1931. The first batch of very powerful electric locomotives arrived from English Electric, of Stafford, and Metropolitan-Vickers, of Trafford Park, Manchester.

According to a census in 1904, over 1.5 million of the native population were supported by the earnings of railway servants. Of the servants, 207 814 were male and 3325 female. In the year these figures were compiled, there were 6293 Europeans employed on India's railway network. In 1907 an estimated £242 million was spent on railways throughout India 'or about 18s. per head of population', as *The Engineer* stated.

During 1951 and 1952, after Independence, the old familiar names such as the 'Great Indian Peninsula' and the 'Bombay, Baroda & Central India Railway' passed into history. Railway construction continued to expand, with both private and State lines seeing no horizons for their endeavours.

AWE-INSPIRING RAILWAY STATISTICS

FROM THE CONSTRUCTION OF THE FIRST RAILWAY in India until 1914, there are some mind-boggling statistics that today defy all logic. Coupled with Britain's involvement in building railways, docks and harbours, waterworks and sugar plants on a global basis, these statistics are all the more phenomenal. They show the sheer drive and dynamism that gripped the era of railways and steam power in a period of relative tranquility with no major military conflicts. The growth of railways up to 1922 was as follows:

Year	Mileage	Year	Mileage
1853	21	1877	7322
1854	66	1878	8212
1855	89	1879	8492
1856	272	1880	9308
1857	288	1881	9891
1858	429	1882	10144
1859	626	1886	12897
1860	839	1887	13390
1861	1587	1888	14456
1862	2335	1889	15226
1863	2512	1890	16404
1864	2966	1891	17283
1865	3372	1892	17776
1866	3408	1893	18459
1867	3465	1894	18841
1868	4016	1895	19466
1869	4283	1896	20133
1870	4840	1897	20577
1871	5205	1898	21522
1872	5370	1899	22491
1873	5695	1900	22941
1874	6227	1901	24305
1875	6519	1902	25826
1876	6833	1903	26378

Year	Mileage	Year	Mileage
1904	26881	1913	34656
1908	28794	1914	35823
1910	32099	1920	37029
1912	33510	1922	37266

The statistics for early railway construction are equally staggering. By July 1870 a total of 4653 miles were in service or under construction, averaging £12,367 per mile. The most expensive was the EIR at £16,862 per mile because of its all-year-round mosquito-infested jungle, whereas the least expensive as a result of favourable conditions was the Great Southern (South India Railway) at £8,000 per mile – less than half the cost of the EIR. Surprisingly, the GIPR's building costs were only £9,476 per mile.

STEAM ENGINES FOR THE RAILWAYS

FROM THE OUTSET, THE PRIVATE RAILWAY companies were not slow in adopting stationary steam engines for their workshops, water and oil pumping services. Most were of small horsepower and were compact units of low efficiency. By the 1890s, over 125 firms in Britain were casting steam engines, with some 18 foundries in the Manchester area alone. Once local manufacture of rolling stock was established, many units were exported to the numerous railway workshops. The Indian Midland Railway, founded in 1884, invited tenders for four compound-condensing engines, the award going to James Watt. The Lincolnshire engineer Marshall, Sons & Company designed a neat, compact, semi-fixed, non-condensing engine fitted with a Hartnell patent governor, which gained popularity with the Indian State Railway. However, the railway industry was quick to grasp the manifest benefits of induction motor drives and from 1895 gradually began rejecting the steam engine.

In 1976 there were estimated to have been some 9000 steam engines still in service and, in general, well maintained by local endeavour. Altogether, nearly 24000 steam locomotives served India under the Raj, starting in 1851 with a small contractor's engine named *Thomason* at an aqueduct site 90 miles north-east of Delhi.

Chapter 10

LOCOMOTIVE WORKSHOPS AND THE MANUFACTURE OF ROLLING STOCK

If thee want the best machine tools, engines and wagons,
thee needn't look any further than Manchester.
We build owt worth having except glass and ships, but we fix the latter.
—LETTER IN THE *MANCHESTER GUARDIAN*

When the GIPR and the EIR started service in 1853 and 1854 respectively, it soon became apparent to them both that a rapid expansion of rail travel stretching into the remotest parts of India was 'imminent'. The Indians 'took to train travel like a duck takes to water', commented the *Bombay Gazette*, and within six years, eight companies had established their presence.

The route mileage had grown to 429 miles with over 800 miles sanctioned for immediate construction. These companies were GIPR, BBCIR, EIR, MR, EBR, SR, SPDR and the Calcutta & South-Eastern Railway. In 1863, 2512 miles were in service with over 80 engines hauling some 250 000 people daily.

Britain in that year was constructing railways on five continents, including America. However, her engineering workshops could not deliver replacement items for worn-out parts. In India much rolling stock lay idle for want of an occasional boiler valve, wheel, bearing or axle. This prompted the railway companies to set up shop themselves to make spares that would otherwise have taken at least four months to arrive.

The locally created repair shops and foundries stimulated an unprecedented bonanza for Britain's machine tool industry and also an equally unprecedented boom for the employment of local skilled and unskilled labour.

Great Indian Peninsula Railway (GIPR)

The GIPR established three main workshops for the repair and overhaul of rolling stock and for the assembly of carriages and wagons. The first was at Parel, the second at Jhansi and the third at Matunga. GIPR also operated repair facilities at Bhusaval, Lonavia and Igatpuri, employing a total of 7226 workers, all but 180 of whom were Indian.

Parel

Parel, 5 miles from Bombay, was the chief workshop for the railway, having been transferred there in 1878 from Byculla. The Parel plant grew to cover an area of close on 2 million sq. ft in the early 1900s. The workshop undertook repairs to locomotives and initially assembled carriages from imported parts. Teak was used exclusively for the bodies while the frames were made from iron, and the sides and roofs were fastened to a wooden structure. In 1887, 3000 men worked on locomotives and about 2000 in the carriage and wagon department. Additionally, 50 Europeans were engaged as draughtsmen and supervisors.

From the plant's establishment until 1905, locomotive, carriage and wagon repairs were undertaken under one roof. From then on only locomotives were serviced, with the carriage and wagon facilities transferred to Matunga. Parel specialised in the repair and reboilering of engines and, from around 1889, assembling new engines crated from Britain. In 1890 some 886 locomotives served the GIPR, a figure rising to around 940 in 1900. In 1913, 1036 engines were in service with an additional 73 on order. Most of the machine tools came from well-established Yorkshire foundries that furnished the majority of India's other railway repair facilities, with Dean, Smith & Grace a principal supplier.

Jhansi

The Jhansi locomotive workshop was put into full service in 1895. Considerably expanded, the three main buildings covered an area of 2140 400 sq. ft. In 1913 electricity took over from steam, with all machines driven by overhead belting from a central powerhouse. The 30 bays, with two overhead cranes from Higginbottom, of Manchester, could handle 47 locomotives at any one time.

Matunga

The newest facilities for rolling stock comprised five workshops at Matunga, 7 miles from Bombay's Victoria Terminus. Fitting shops, foundries, machine shops, a finishing and painting shop, and a main repair shop with an 800 ft testing pit, all complete with electrical overhead cranes and lighting, allowed round-the-clock working from the day the complex was opened. Belliss & Morcom steam engines, driving Lancashire Dynamo & Motor Company dynamos, provided the electrical power. A complete telephone system connected the Works Manager to each foreman.

East India Railway (EIR)

Already a household name within the Indian industrial community, Belliss & Morcom supplied the railway company's premises at Jamalpur, Delhi, Lillooah, Lucknow, Giridih, Asansol, Ondal, Tundla, Dhanbad, Gya and Mogul Serai with a total of 40 engines by 1920 for driving generators, compressors, pumps, machine tools and water installations. EIR was the firm's principal customer in India, with the Bengal Nagpur Railway second.

Jamalpur

Jamalpur started the manufacture of locomotives, with all main parts imported from Britain, as far back as 1868. For over 20 years, the railway companies had witnessed the success of Ajmer for the BBCIR, whose locomotives were notching up considerable mileage with no more than the usual routine maintenance between major overhauls. In 1899, Jamalpur 'built its first complete locomotive, appropriately named *Lady Curzon,* after the wife of Viceroy Lord Curzon'. British visitors, Rudyard Kipling among them, referred to Jamalpur as the 'Crewe of India'.

Jamalpur began by servicing locomotives and rolling stock before assembling carriages and wagon parts imported from Britain. Later, only the chassis arrived in Calcutta, with all wooden bodies made locally. The first major shops to expand at Jamalpur were for the fitting of wheels and bogies. At the same time, a fully equipped carpenter's facility was installed with the latest machine tools belt driven from a separate steam engine.

EIR was the first railway company to create its own steelworks on European lines. The British management was determined to employ all-Indian labour, both skilled and semi-skilled, with its workshops fully fitted

Interior of the EIR rolling mills, 1896. Built at Jamalpur in 1862, these were the main workshops for the EIR, designed to undertake every aspect of the over-haul and repair of the EIR's locomotives. From the 1880s they began to build new locomotives (Courtesy of the British Library)

Boiler shop, west bay of the EIR rolling mills, Jamalpur, 1896 (Courtesy of the British Library)

Rows of turning machines at the EIR workshops, Jamalpur, 1896 (Courtesy of the British Library)

with machine tools from England. In 1911, Jamalpur employed approximately 11 000 indigenous workers, which included some 400 apprentices. The workmen came from far and wide, and the EIR also provided cheap housing. For those who travelled from distant villages, special workmen's trains were laid on at no expense.

During World War I, Jamalpur's tool room supplied 33 complete sets of gauges required for the manufacture of 13- and 18-pdr high-explosive shells. The additional production of 24 armoured cars, 118 oil-tank wagons, 43 transport and ambulance cars and over 1 million fishplates for the railways of Egypt, Palestine, Mesopotamia and East Africa virtually exhausted the workshop, which produced war material in conjunction with Lillooah.

Lillooah

The central rolling-stock workshops were at Howrah, built in 1863. As Calcutta quickly outgrew these facilities, a larger complex to cater for all rolling stock overhauls was rapidly constructed at Lillooah that same year. The Lillooah Carriage & Wagon Workshop, located about four miles from Calcutta, specialised in the assembly and overhaul of carriages and wagons. Later, the workshops assembled chassis and wheels with bodies made from

Burmese teak. In 1895, some 5000 workmen were engaged in assembling and repairing carriages and wagons. The complex soon outgrew itself, and the facilities were updated with a new foundry, iron and brass shops, and a huge sawmill 'the largest of its kind in the East', capable of turning out 336 tons of teak wood scantlings monthly. When Lillooah finally closed in 1972, the workshops' archives claimed the impressive record of having manufactured some 6000 coaches and over twice that number of wagons.

Lucknow

The little-known facility at Lucknow was set up a stone's throw from where the first iron bridge was constructed. The principal work undertaken in Lucknow was repairs to locomotives running on the Moradabad, Lucknow and Allahabad Divisions.

Bombay, Baroda & Central India Railway (BBCIR) – Ajmer

The Ajmer Locomotive Works was the brainchild of the short-lived, metre-gauge, state-owned Rajputana–Malwa Railway (RMR). Construction began in 1873, with the first line opened in August 1876. By January 1881, 580 miles were in service between Delhi and Rewari, and then through the Rajputana Agency via Bandikui, Phulera and Ajmer to Ahmedabad, where the railway joined the BBCIR's broad gauge. Later a new route was started, shortening the distance between Delhi and Ahmedabad by 41 miles. Branch lines of some 95 miles were constructed to Phulera and Agra, with other branches completed in 1876 aggregating 83 miles.

The foundation of the prestigious Central Workshop was laid in 1876 and it opened for the first overhaul of rolling stock the following year. It was meant to undertake repairs and later to manufacture locomotives. Because of the increasing volume of maintenance work, the locomotive department was later split from the carriage and wagon overhaul shops in 1884. The following year the works was handed over by the state to the BBCIR to run under a contract with the Secretary of State for India.

Ajmer stole a march on its rivals by producing its first complete loco-motive in 1895/96. The workshops were steam-driven at that time but elec-tricity gradually phased out reliance on steam engines shortly after 1900. The main mechanical workshops, such as wheel assembly, machine shop

LARGE MANCHESTER WHEEL-TURNING LATHES

NO RAILWAY WORKSHOP COULD FUNCTION without large wheel-turning lathes. Each Indian railway company was spoilt for choice when from the 1860s Manchester could offer three competing firms devoted to this production – William Muir, established in 1841; Craven, established about 1853; and Hulse & Company, established about 1834. All machine tools were belt-driven from an overhead shaft, steam-engine powered. Craven was the largest of the firms, while Muir diversified to manufacture steam hammers, boilers and forges; India took much of its production.

and locomotive erection, comprised the same manufacturer's machine tools that were installed in others throughout India. Craven Bros, J. Buckton, Loudon Bros, Armstrong Whitworth and Dean, Smith & Grace each supplied heavy-duty wheel lathes and drilling machines. When further expanded to accommodate up to 40 locomotives, Ransomes & Rapier of Ipswich furnished four overhead cranes. The main forges were from B. & S. Massey, T. Ryder and Defries & Company. In its heyday of locomotive production, Ajmer delivered 467 engines, including 20 broad-gauge units, before steam locomotive fabrication closed down for good in 1950, on the opening of Chittaranjan Works in Calcutta.

Bengal Nagpur Railway (BNR) – Kharagpur

Kharagpur's emergence as a major engineering works can be traced to the 1860s, when it was set up for the repair of rolling stock. The whole works was remodelled in 1902 and expanded to cover nearly 150 acres. The new works employed upwards of 7000 men, many of whom were retained to operate the new all-electrically driven machinery. A huge woodworking shop was created that was estimated to use over 5000 tons of timber annually in both the repair and new construction of carriages and four-wheeled wagons. A 100 ft 3-ton gantry crane from Manchester was installed and many of the latest machine tools were belt-driven from electric motors. There was a wagon and machine shop, an impressive wheel shop and a smithy with ten steam hammers.

Engineers with a 2-4-0 type engine of 1874 compared with latest 4-6-2 type superheated locomotive, BNWR, c.1920s (Courtesy of International Railway Gazette)

Bengal & North-Western Railway (BNWR) – Sonepur

BNWR, established in 1882, extended from Sonepore – as it was known before Independence – almost opposite the city of Patna, to Bahraich in the North West Provinces, a distance of 275 miles. A 20-mile branch line linked Mankapore to Nawabgunge near to the ORR. In 1891 it took over the operations and maintenance facilities of the Tirhut State Railway, which comprised 738 miles. By 1895 the network stood at 1640 miles, and 2079 by 1920. The railway management was far-thinking in not relying entirely on others for rolling stock wooden-body manufacture and locomotive overhaul. In May 1883 it constructed temporary workshops at Sonepur to serve the assembly of rolling stock and plant imported from Britain through Calcutta.

Three buildings were erected, comprising a machine shop, a smith's shop and foundry, and a carriage department 204 ft long. The buildings themselves are documented as costing Rs.19,000. By September 1883 two locomotives and 150 wagons were received in parts and assembled, with some erected at another workshop of smaller dimensions in Nawabgunge.

To facilitate further branch extensions, 35 wagons were connected together to carry a completely assembled 1.25-mile length of track. By November 1890 the Sonepore Workshops were in full commission, with sufficient material and tools to erect all wagons and coaches imported in broken-down sections from Britain. However, one problem that dogged the firm was an acute shortage of skilled labour, which had to be imported from other states.

By 1886 the workshops were considerably expanded, with new machine tools from Keighley, Halifax, Liverpool, Glasgow and London. The company could then attract much extra work including contracts from local entrepreneurs as well as those from the EIR. Many of the blueprints for the improved facilities came from Sir Alexander Rendel, who designed much of the rolling stock. A Mr H. Prince, Consulting Engineer to the BNWR, was also instrumental in specifying the railway operator's new ferries plying the Ganges and Gogra rivers.

Eastern Bengal Railway (EBR)

The Kanchrapara workshop was set up in 1908, 28 miles from Calcutta. Fully equipped and powered by electricity from the Calcutta Electric Supply, along with stand-by generators, the workshops expanded at regular intervals until the company reached its peak of efficiency in 1914. During the 1870s, around 500 people were employed, increasing to some 850 a decade later. By 1914 double that number served the complex. Apprentices were taken on with the stipulation that 'at least 12 hours of the working week of 46 hours be devoted to classroom training'.

A separate facility was built at Saidpur, about 242 miles from Calcutta. The complex, though not so comprehensively equipped as Kanchrapara, served the EBR with distinction. Established during the 1870s, Saidpur was limited to handling small jobs, as it had no foundry facilities. It served an area of high unemployment, and in 1880 some 1200 people were employed, a figure that grew to over 2100 by the end of the century.

A small workshop was also installed at Dacca. As traffic grew, especially in the hauling of tea and jute (see later chapters), a large contract was given to the Crown Agents for a complete machine shop to perform major repairs to all locomotives. Despite the absence of an iron or brass foundry, the Dacca shops expanded to employ over 400 men and could handle up to 50 locomotives annually.

Stores and rolling-stock wheels and frames were, in the main, purchased through the India Office. Carriage wheels and bogies were bought in Britain, with most carriage and wagon bodies locally made for fitting in the workshops. Frequently, both Burn and Jessop (pp. 267–8), who assembled the parts for final inspection by an EBR engineer, supplemented the workshops.

Madras Railway (MR) and
Southern Mahratta Railway (SMR)

Although the Madras Foundry of the MR was not strictly a rolling stock workshop, it produced 10 000 tons of Greaves-type cast-iron sleepers to replace 600 miles of wooden sleepers that were being systematically destroyed by white ants. Another workshop, specialising in metre-gauge lightweight rolling stock construction and repair, was at Hubli, a centre for the cotton trade.

South India Railway (SIR)
– Negapatam and Trichinopoly

The SIR company was formed from the amalgamation of numerous ad hoc lines that served only local needs. The requirement for main workshop facilities soon became apparent when the Madras Railway was unable to service other railway companies' rolling stock. A maintenance workshop was therefore established at Negapatam in 1866.

The introduction of broad-gauge rolling stock prompted the SIR to construct additional workshops, including a complete new facility at Trichinopoly. Occupying 760 acres, it cost an estimated Rs.315 million and the most up-to-date all-electrically driven machinery was installed. By 1915, the Trichinopoly workshops had 13 cranes capable of lifting locomotives of up to 100 tons. The massive Class XE engines and tender weighing just less than 200 tons required the combined lifting capacity of two such cranes.

As SIR's operations continued to grow, the old workshop facilities at Negapatam, Podanur and Erode were remodelled to reflect the increase in rolling stock being operated. At its peak, some 5000 people were fully employed at Trichinopoly, with a further 1500 at other service depots.

Assam–Bengal Railway (ABR) – Pahartali

From its inception, the ABR never undertook any work or projects in small measures. Its plans were quickly transferred from the drawing board into reality and its construction projects were undertaken with vigour, and from most accounts little expense was spared when a goal was in sight. Such was the case when the ABR built a fully equipped locomotive, carriage and wagon workshop at Pahartali, some 2 miles north of Chittagong, in 1898.

The central workshop at Pahartali was planned to overhaul all types of rolling stock, with fully equipped brass and iron foundries to manufacture duplicate parts as required. It comprised three principal buildings – a saw-mill and carriage shop, a foundry and smith shop, and a main machinery and erecting shop that embraced two bays. All the main buildings were placed side by side some 80 ft apart. The centre line of a 40 ft steam-carriage traverser extended 800 ft east and west.

When first in service, all prime movers were steam driven from an engine house. The total cost of the buildings, engine pits, steam traverser, turntables and so on was £69,373; the most expensive item, the machine and erecting shops, was audited at £12,691. All labour employed in 1898 was imported: mechanics and fitters arrived from western Bengal and the Central Provinces.

By 1920 all carriage bodies were manufactured at Pahartali and only the steel frames were imported. The workshops and maintenance facilities employed over 4000 men as the complex grew. Many of the original buildings exist today, the complex now serving Bangladesh. However, much of the machinery and facilities has either rotted away or been stolen.

Chapter 11

BRIDGE BUILDING

There can be little doubt that in many ways the story of bridge building is the story of civilization. By it, we can readily measure a progress in each particular country.
FRANKLIN D. ROOSEVELT

There are no exact details of the first bridge constructed by the English settlers in India. Certainly, Madras was settled before Calcutta, and it is possible that the structures across the myriad streams that make up the Madras area were masonry bridges, as recorded in documents existing from the 1680s. An artificial 'cut', which later became part of the Buckingham Canal (see Chapter 6), was made to link the Cooum River with the Elambore River. A bridge was constructed of local stone in about 1670, while the more substantial Egmore Bridge was erected – also with local materials – to ford the 'cut'. Reconstructed in 1728, the Egmore Bridge acquired the name St Mary's Bridge.

As British settlers dispersed throughout India, they could not have failed to recognise the civil engineering achievements in masonry bridge construction from the earliest times, especially in and around Hyderabad. Apart from the remains of small mud and stone structures from about the 14th century in Orissa and Bengal, the earliest bridge of any substance surviving anywhere in the Indian subcontinent is that referred to affectionately as the *Purana Pul* ('Old Bridge'). Built in 1575, 14 years before the founding of Hyderabad by Mohammed Quli Qutub, it is the oldest of four structures that span the Musi River, a few miles from the centre of the city. The *Purana Pul* comprises 22 arches for its 600 ft length; it is 36 ft wide and stands 54 ft above the riverbed. The beautiful stone structure, in use and crossed by thousands daily, got its name, it is said, because Quli

Qutub Shah, Prince of Golconda, fell in love with a dancer, Bhagmati, from Chichlam on the other side of the river. More than a decade later, in 1591/2, Quli Qutab Shah (1565–1611) founded a city named 'Bhagyanagar' after his love. 'Bhagyanagar' later became 'Haiderabad' (Hyderabad) when the title of 'Haider Mahal' was conferred on Bhagmati.

Subsequent bridges across the Musi River were to follow: in 1777 at Saak; in 1801 by the British civil engineer de Havilland – this early bridge suffered a partial failure in 1937; and in 1831 by Colonel James Oliphant of the EIC. Another significant masonry bridge is the Peripatam Bridge (1802–04), constructed over the south bank of the Cauvery River at Seringapatam, some 48 miles from Bangalore, and paid for by the Rajah of Mysore. This bridge might have been known as the Wellesley Bridge, from an old inscription when Lord Wellesley, Duke of Wellington (1769–1852), visited India during the first decade of the 19th century. Wellesley is credited with, in 1803, ordering the construction of a pontoon bridge to allow entry to the EIC's naval dockyard at Bombay. In 1821 at Kapti, some 530 miles from Bombay, an EIC official remarked: 'a handsome bridge spans the River Kanhan'.

EIC civil engineers not only strengthened existing bridges but also built new structures, of which the most widely known were those across the canals on the western face of Black Town, Calcutta, built in 1805; over the Authara Nala at Puri (1814); Perambur Nara, Madras (1816); on Cooum River at Chintaripettah (1816); Canara District, Madras (1819); and across the Wotari Nala, Madras (1821–23). Rope and wooden bridges found a valuable niche in mountainous districts, especially in the Himalayan regions. A touch of English nostalgia must have surfaced in naming two bridges 'Shakespeare' – one near Madurai (1824) and the other over the Kowar Nadi in Hazaribad (1825).

First iron bridge

Probably one of the last designs for the Wilson-type iron bridge – installed in both North America and Jamaica by 1810 – was that made by an engineer in India. Captain D. McLeod was entrusted with designing and constructing the first-ever iron bridge of the Raj across the Gompti River at Lucknow in the province of Oudh. In 1811 he made a model to illustrate the principles of the Sunderland Bridge across the River Weir, England, to Wilson's successful designs, and was asked by the Nawab to provide a similar model for the Lucknow site.

After surveying the river, McLeod produced an elevation drawing of a 200 ft span arch with a 28 ft rise broadly on Sunderland lines. A wooden deck would be unsuitable, not only because of the climate but because 'elephants are a common mode of conveyance in this country', to quote McLeod. The final design for the bridge was worked by EIC's London consultant, John Rennie (1761–1821), in conjunction with Butterley, of Derbyshire. The iron-work was cast in 1814/15 and shipped out to Calcutta around the Cape the following year. At Calcutta the various parts of the structure were loaded onto barges, which then sailed upstream on the river Ganges to Lucknow. The bridge, when offloaded in Lucknow, was then the largest single manu-factured export from Britain. It contained 2627 individual pieces, of which only 19 arrived broken in Lucknow. With the death of the Nawab and lack of interest by his son, the bridge was not finally erected until the 1840s. When eventually constructed the bridge had a centre span of 90 ft, flanked by single spans each 60 ft.

Railway bridges

India has been described as 'the land of remarkable bridges' in Frederick A. Talbot's book *The Railway Conquest of the World*. Talbot backs up this statement with excellent examples of British engineering. The first major bridge to be constructed was put into service for the inaugural train be-tween Bombay and Thana in 1853. The Dapoorie Viaduct for the GIPR, which links Bombay Island with the mainland, comprised 22 stone arches of about 33 ft each span and carries main-line traffic today.

The longest bridge on any railway system by 1858 was EIR's Soane River crossing near Arrah, with iron girders supplied by Newcastle's Sir W.G. Armstrong foundry. It was 4700 ft long, or just under one mile, with a large space between the double track 'for the passage of elephants and pedestrians'.

For the BBCIR, Westwood, Baillie & Co furnished 477 individual 60 ft spans for crossing the North and South Bassein Creeks, plus another 350 spans for the line to enter Bombay. They were replaced only in 1929, with steel girders from P. & W. MacLellan's Clutha Works of Glasgow. As the railway network expanded and new bridges were built, artistic skills also flowered. Some engineers, such as Granville Mills (1858–1915) were also accomplished artists, transferring their deftness with a sharpened pencil in their engineers' details to canvas in some cases. Comprising 20 × 40 ft,

Bridge over Jumna at Allahabad, c.1860s (Courtesy of the British Library)

14 × 62 ft and 5 × 142 ft girders weighing an aggregate 850 tons for a total length of 2530 ft, this river crossing for the GIPR at Bhusaval was subjected to the most rigorous testing. Five locomotives aggregating 175 tons were shunted back and forth and resulted in deflection of a mere 1.006 in., with no permanent set. Westwood, Baillie supplied the ironwork.

The demand for larger and longer individual spans was demonstrated over two crossings of the Jumna River – at Allahabad and at Delhi – with 14 × 205 ft and 12 × 216 ft respectively for the EIR. With an aggregate of 10000 tons of cast iron from Thomas Brassey's Canada Works at Birkenhead, and Ormerod, Grierson of Manchester, one span was tested with 450 tons of scrap pig iron. In service by 1865, the Allahabad crossing was eclipsed by the Koilwar River structure comprising 28 × 150 ft spans between Asansol and Mogul Serai.

Crossing the Ganges

The Ganges was a further challenge to railway engineers projecting the railway into the far reaches of Britain's Indian Empire. Before the first Ganges crossing was completed, British bridge builders had successfully constructed three crossings of the Jumna River, all by the EIR. Like the Ganges, it was mighty in name, flow and width. The ORR, established in 1865, operated mainly on the north side of the Ganges. The company

Construction of the Curzon Bridge over the Ganges, Allahabad, 1903 (Courtesy of the British Library)

was entrusted with erecting its first bridge across the river at Cawnpore between 1870 and 1874. *Engineering*, of November 1870, stated in its usual bold terms: 'Considerable interest attaches to this bridge, inasmuch as when completed it will be the first bridge built across the Ganges, which is prominent alike in the religion and geography of India.'

The bridge was a formidable undertaking, of double-girder construction and with a single-line roadway 9 ft wide: the little-known fabricator-ship-yard Campbell, Johnstone of London more than played its part, with the 25 × 100 ft wrought-iron double girders each weighing 140 tons, plus 2 × 41 ft girders of similar width for that inaugural occasion. All piers were of local brick and timber construction. It was the first bridge in India where an early form of hydraulic machinery was employed for riveting. A second crossing of the Ganges, at Rajghat in 1874, comprised 35 × 80 ft spans, with a third structure at Balawali in 1875 containing 11 huge girders each 248 ft.

By far the most spectacular of all the crossings for its day was the contract won by Patent Shaft and Axletree Company, of Wednesbury, in 1880. Opening in 1887, it comprised 7 × 356 ft + 9 × 114 ft for an all-steel structure at Benares, the Hindu holy city, and it was perhaps a fitting tribute for this holy city that size and greatness should be salient features of its design. The specification warranted the largest single girders ever then built, with each 356 ft span weighing 746 tons when fully erected with its rails and walkways. A further bridge across the Ganges was built at Garhmukhtesar, comprising 11 × 200 ft equal spans. By 1910, the ORR had the distinction of claiming that, on its network of 1700 miles, 17 miles comprised bridges.

The last great crossing of the Ganges was at Sara, before the river enters the Bay of Bengal. Named after Lord Hardinge, this magnificent structure comprised 27 500 tons of steelwork for its 15 × 345 ft + 6 × 75 ft girders.

The Kistna Viaduct at Raichur

From 1869 to 1872 the Indian railway network grew from 4283 miles to 5370 miles – the largest expansion for a single country east of the Bosphorus. One bridge that was urgently required was a crossing of the Kistna River near Raichur. The specification called for some of the deepest piers ever sunk on the GIPR network, and tendering was fierce in Britain to secure the contract. Skerne Ironworks, of Darlington, won the contract for the 36 equal girders of 107 ft, weighing an aggregate 2500 tons, while Cochrane's Woodside Works in Dudley secured the award for the cast-iron piers, which aggregated 1200 tons.

The Empress Bridge

The Empress Bridge on the Indus Valley State Railway (IVSR) across the Sutlej River, near the village of Adamwahan, was for its day one of the most unusual structures erected. Conceived on a grand scale, with 16 girder spans each of 264 ft, its foundations were more than 100 ft below low-water

Formal photo of the engineers who built the Curzon Bridge, Allahabad, c.1902–5. From left: Mr R.R. Gales, FCHM, Inst CE, Engineer-in-Chief; Mr L.F. Jackson, Assistant Engineer; Mr R.A. Delanougerede, Executive Engineer; Mr S.P. Flowerdew, Assistant Engineer; Mr E.B. Robey, Assistant Engineer; Mr N. Pearce, Assistant Engineer' (Courtesy of the British Library)

level. The wrought-iron girder trusses of the double-N or Murphy-Whipple type were shared between Head, Wrightson & Company and Westwood, Baillie. Great urgency prevailed when ironwork was being ordered, and the Siemens electric lighting apparatus from Woolwich enabled the IVSR's workmen to continue construction late into the night during the winter of 1876. There is no conclusive evidence of an earlier use of electricity, despite a vessel launched at the Garden Reach Shipyard in 1861 being fitted out 'with a searchlight'; therefore this dynamo must be accepted as India's introduction to electric power.

The method of well sinking followed the same pattern as for other Punjab bridges, but the increased depth brought its crop of difficulties. The entire work on the foundations occupied more than three working seasons. At one time, 300 miles of rails were 'blocked up in loading the wells'. Not infrequently, dredging tools would be lost in the sand or silt that had entered a well during a 'blow'.

Men and materials came from far and wide. From Calcutta, material consignments came 1500 miles on the EIR; from Bombay, ironwork arrived over 1800 miles to site; from Karachi, girders and Portland cement were hauled some 600 miles by ferryboat. The formidable task of hammering home the thousands of rivets and 30 000 service bolts enabled families to travel from Calcutta and Bombay to secure employment. 'These people are hard working and earn their daily bread but for sheer quality and quantity of work where little supervision – if any – is required, we look to the Sikhs,' commented James Bell, the erection supervisor. Such faith was not misplaced, when each girder required 35 000 rivets to be driven home. Most were of 1-inch diameter, and the best Sikh team could manage about 60 to 80 red-hot rivets per day. So experienced were these Sikhs that Bell related: 'the last span was erected and riveted, so far as the trusses were concerned, in 45 working hours and the span was completed in eight days'.

When fully erected, each span weighted 419 tons, with the whole bridge aggregating a little under 7000 tons. Opened in 1877, it was the largest, but not the longest, bridge in the world. A special telegram arrived from Queen Victoria congratulating the Government of India on the completion of so grand a work and signifying a wish that the bridge be named 'The Empress'.

It has been suggested that Rudyard Kipling was thinking of the erection of this bridge when he wrote *The Bridge-Builders*, the first story in his book *The Day's Work*. Kipling refers to a 'great Kashi Bridge over the Ganges' with two decks and a roadway. The Agra capping stone seems to be the only real connection between Kipling's fiction and the Empress Bridge: Agra stone was commonly used in most EIR bridges built around this time.

A second generation of bridges incorporating steel

As a second generation of heavier and more powerful locomotives began to replace old timber-framed carriages and wagons, increasing the load on the bridges, the need arose for a complete reappraisal of most bridge structures. At the Kistna River at Kudchi, the MR erected 14 × 150 ft spans and replaced the old Chittravati Bridge with 19 × 140 ft. The same railway company successfully erected its largest and most impressive structure at Kalpi with 10 × 250 ft all-steel girders for yet another crossing of the Jumna River. All over India now, cast iron was out. New structures were built of mainly Sheffield, Teesside and Glasgow steel.

New and renewed structures on the
Bengal Nagpur Railway (BNR)

The BNR embarked upon a huge programme from 1896 that cost untold lacs of rupees. This outlay was not only to strengthen or replace the first generation of bridges, but also to invite tenders for a host of new structures for a vastly expanded network that catered for the spread of the permanent way into newly established coal mines. The bridging for its day was monumental, with four bridges in excess of half a mile each, dwarfed by the crossing of the Mahanadi River comprising 64 × 100 ft – over 1.25 miles. So large was the specification for this bridge that the contract was shared between three structural engineering firms: Braithwaite & Kirk, Horsehay Foundry of Shropshire, and the Horseley Ironworks of Tipton, Staffordshire. The bridge was constructed in the record time of 25 months.

Jessop of Calcutta secured one bridge on the BNR network. The Burubalang River crossing comprising 2 × 150 ft + 13 × 60 ft on brick piers established Jessop as structural engineers capable of competing against British companies for single girders in those span ranges.

It was a hectic period, with nine large and six medium-sized river crossings started in 1896, totalling over 5 miles of bridging. All work was completed in the first half of 1900. Archive records show that during the last four years of the 19th century, 68 structures exceeding 2000 ft were under construction in India.

The Kistna River Bridge at Bezwada

Perhaps the most impressive – and certainly the most expensive – bridge to be completed at the end of the 19th century was the crossing of the Kistna River at Bezwada on what was then called the East Coast Railway. For years Madras had remained cut off from northern India. All tracks stopped at Bezwada, where the Kistna had to be crossed by ferry. When work at the site began on 19 September 1890, the first task was to 'train' the river – reduce its width – to a little over three quarters of a mile. The actual distance trimmed at the time of sinking the caissons was 1264 ft.

Once this had been achieved, caissons for the well foundations arrived from Richardson & Cruddas, of Bombay in the winter of 1890. Masonry work began immediately, with many labourers and their families well experienced at the task from previous service with British supervising engineers on other projects. Each well was sunk 82 ft below low-water level. A whole community grew, with an estimated 10 000 people enjoying a regular weekly wage. In 15 months, wells and caissons were made ready for

Construction of the Kistna Bridge – view of the inside girder, c.1890s (Courtesy of Institution of Civil Engineers)

Construction of the Chenab Bridge at Sher Shah. The designer, James Bell, also supervised the construction of the Empress Bridge over the Sutlej and received much praise for both engineering feats. Over 5000 men were employed on the Chenab site, c.1889 (Courtesy of Institution of Civil Engineers)

girder erection, with the help of electric light for working at night. When fully erected and bolted into place, each 300 ft span weighed a staggering 535 tons. The railway company erector-supervisor, a Mr E.W. Digby, maintained that each of the nine girders was constructed in just 67 days.

The first train over the new bridge was driven by Lord Wenlock (1849–1912), Governor of Madras, on 17 March 1893. On the same day, the Nizam's coal trains passed over the metre-gauge line to connect with the SMR that delivered coal to the southernmost tip of India.

The skill of the hard-working Punjabi workforce was praised. Digby wrote in his final report, which was quoted in *Engineering* in 1896:

> There were at various times between 1500 and 3000 skilled men on the girder work, chiefly men from the Punjab, about 1200 miles away. The best of these men, and indeed the majority of the Punjabis, had recently been employed on the Chenab Bridge (1888–91) with all 28 × 145ft spans. Many Telugu local workmen were employed ... Wages ran from 4 annas to 12 annas per day, but the Punjabis earned at least three times that amount and were worth every penny.

Godavari River crossing at Basa

There was one bridge erected by the Godavari Valley Railway as part of a service for the Hindu pilgrims so that they could go 'to pray at their temple in the middle of nowhere'. For many years the faithful had battled the elements, as well as the rough tracks and inhospitable terrain, to reach the ancient temple of Sri Gnanasaraswati. The well-established civil and bridge engineer Granville Mills (1858–1915) – who had worked with the ABR and in Burma – was entrusted with the project that included planning and constructing much of the permanent way to the temple itself. Darlington Wagon & Engineering Works won the contract with a bid of £204,441 for the 1040 tons of material delivered to site. Mills, a quintessential – if not totally eccentric – Victorian engineer, carried canvas, paint and brush with his toolkit. An artist of considerable merit, Mills painted the various stages of construction while his wife, Cordelia, a painter in her own right, portrayed the temple that was the object of their construction work to Basa.

The Nilgiri Mountain Railway

The Nilgiri Railway is notable as being the first Abt-rack railway constructed in India. When started, it was the longest in the world. All the equipment came from England, with rails from Cammell's of Sheffield. The line started from Mettupalaiyam, terminus station on the MR, and ascended nearly

---

INDIA – 'THE LAND OF REMARKABLE BRIDGES'

DERBYSHIRE FABRICATOR BUTTERLEY, which cast the first iron bridge for India in 1815 for the Nawab of Oudh, is also credited with commissioning the first major bridge of the 20th century – a structure 9092 ft that is still in use today. The bridge crossing the Godavari River at Rajhmundry – an area where Arthur Cotton performed his finest civil and flood-control works – contained 56 spans, each 150 ft, plus a walkway and telegraph circuit. The year 1862 saw the EIR reconstruct what became India's longest bridge, the 93 × 108 ft spans (total length 10 082 ft) across the Soane River in Bihar, in north India. All steelwork arrived from Dorman Long. The original cast-iron bridge had provided faithful service until 1862. (It is worth noting that the longest bridge in South Africa, across the Orange River, is a mere 3615 ft.)

5000 ft within the first 15 miles. Tea and coffee planters, along with other settlers, had agitated the Madras government for many years for a railway.

Work started in 1891. The latest machinery was used, including high-explosive dynamite for tunnelling. A single metre-gauge was selected. Bridging and tunnelling was heavy, with the most troublesome place being the Benhope Cliffs, where the line passes for 1000 ft along the face of an almost vertical cliff 2000 ft high. For its 28 route miles to Ootacamund, nine short tunnels were hand-dug, the longest being 325 ft. The railway's final elevation was 7220 ft, with much of the gradient being 1 in 12.

Bridging was exceedingly difficult for the short length of the line, comprising 23 medium-sized bridges and 113 smaller structures – an average of nearly five bridges per mile. Most girders, all plate constructed, arrived from Teesside Bridge & Engineering Company, of Middlesbrough. The longest bridge, over the Kullar River, was 450 ft while the highest was at Burliar at 120 ft. Of the larger bridges, only eight were over rivers. The remainder crossed deep gorges. Most spans were 60 ft in length, with 100 ft spans only adopted for the longer crossings. The cost of the line was approximately £15,000 per mile, which compared favourably with others of a similar character.

The first batch of special locomotives capable of carrying 625 gallons of water in side tanks and a ton of coal arrived from Beyer Peacock, of Manchester. When the Nilgiri Mountain Railway was opened amid great jubilation at the end of 1899, the Indian railway network stood at approximately 22 491 miles, with a further 2369 miles under construction.

Pamban Viaduct

If ever a bridge was constructed in idyllic scenery, in what is still one of India's most tranquil settings, it was the one at the most southerly tip of India. The SIR had planned an important link in its system to 'bring Ceylon nearer to India' by train, rather than depend upon the 12-hour sea journey from new turbine steamers purchased on the Clyde. The Pamban Viaduct across the submerged reef was a single metre-gauge line planned with a rail level throughout at only 12.75 ft above mean sea level. Site work began in August 1911, when the first of 145 spans, each 40 ft, arrived from Teesside. Construction progressed well until a bad storm in May 1912 inflicted serious damage to the temporary timber works for nine foundations that were all washed away.

Work was interrupted twice in the same year when cholera broke out in the neighbourhood, which frightened away all labour. Later, when British doctors rushed to the area and successfully controlled the epidemic, a workforce had to be imported from different states and Ceylon.

To facilitate free access to shipping, a Scherzer-type rolling bridge was erected over five months, being completed in December 1913. This important link in communication between India and Ceylon was opened for traffic in February 1914.

Lower Ganges Bridge at Sara

The British had documented the flow of Ganges waters since Sir Thomas Roe was appointed Ambassador to the Mughal Court in 1604. Between 1764 and 1791, when reliable surveys were undertaken, the river had moved eastwards by about a mile. When borings were taken in the Ganges lower region at the village of Sara in 1868 to construct a bridge for the EBR, surveyors noted that a further change of eastward movement of about 1.75 miles had taken place. The project was shelved.

The next serious proposal was undertaken in 1902. Later, the Secretary of State sanctioned construction of 'a mighty bridge' in 1908 with Robert Gale (1864–1948) as Engineer-in-Chief. The bridge was opened on 1 January 1915, by Lord Hardinge, the Viceroy, after 41 months' hard toil. He gave his name to the bridge. It was in full use until August 1947, when the break-up of India saw the bridge become a political pawn and it was thrown into disuse. During the Bangladesh War of 1971, Pakistan Air Force bombers attempted to destroy the whole structure but failed in their efforts.

Pedestrian, animal and cart-wheeled traffic bridges

Along with the civil and railway contractors that developed India's infrastructure, the Royal Engineers and other military units constructed roads and bridges where once mud tracks terminated at the bank of a swift current. Where steel could be hauled to site and erected, it was automatically favoured. However, in most remote areas masonry, timber and rope bridges were used.

Perhaps the first use of iron for bridge construction is recorded in a letter to a Kathmandu newspaper from the British Embassy on 2 December 1994, in an article entitled 'Rising Nepal'. In 1810, with 'ironwork imported from England, a General Bhimsen Thapa, on orders from a Sundari Devi, constructed a bridge in a remote district. It was replaced by the Royal Engineers in 1905 and finally dismantled in 1995. The site is commemorated by a pillar surmounted by a lion'.

History recalls a little-known endeavour of the people in the Saugur region of central India, who between 1828 and 1830 smelted sufficient iron to construct a 200 ft suspension bridge, designed by one Major Duncan Presgrave. It was experimental, and Presgrave decided to support it with at least double the iron's weight (14.8 tons) in wood (36 tons). In his final report he stated that it was a 'good and cheaper bridge than those in Calcutta made with English materials'.

The role of the Royal Engineers and Corps of Engineers

At the height of the EIC's influence, the need to rebuild India's infrastructure completely from the decaying mess that characterised the remains of Mughal Empire rule was recognised. The Royal Engineers, along with a separate Corp of Engineers, were dispatched far and wide to construct hard-core, virtually all-weather roads, especially in northern regions.

Throughout the Punjab, the Royal Engineers were constructing road and masonry bridges virtually as quickly as blueprints left its survey office. At Markunda, near Umballa, some 27 arches with spans of 80 ft using brick lining were constructed in the 1840s. At one time 'Delhi and its surroundings began to resemble a large construction site', according to Captain Grindall, attached to the local government.

The beauty of Agra created a mini tourist industry for resident British settlers. Aware of the need to bridge the Jumna in that town, the Corp of Engineers constructed its largest structure to date. The ironwork from Dudley comprised 1414 tons to complete the crossing, thereby allowing visitors from Europe to view one of the great wonders of the world.

Occasionally the Royal Engineers and Corp of Engineers would combine their expertise to construct roads and bridges of a military nature. The Lahore–Peshawar road passed over numerous streams and culverts, all spanned with masonry. One bridge of significance was the crossing of the Sohan River that warranted 10 equal spans of 100 ft. It was thought too large for masonry as no span of 100 ft had ever been considered for any bridging in India except in iron. The design was altered to 15×63 ft, entirely of masonry and floored with timber throughout. A special tramway using animal power was built to facilitate the haulage of stone. Drainage was provided and a hard stone road was constructed. The bridge opened for traffic in 1862, and still serves today with tarmac that merely disguises the original hard-stone surface.

Continuous improvements were made to the Peshawar road and, with rivers constantly changing course, a new bridge was called for at Hurroo. Its principal dimensions comprised 10 × 40 ft spans, and all piers and super-structure were of deodar timber with compacted rubble masonry for the abutments. Pine tar was used for all touching surfaces. The bridge, opened in 1864 at a cost of Rs.34,000, is still in service, supporting lorries of up to 15 tons fully laden. The Punjab 'got a Rolls-Royce for the price of a cheap Ford'.

The bridge over the Jumna River near Kalsie on the Saharanpur–Chakrata road was a highly complex project. About 20 years earlier, a light foot and animal suspension bridge had been constructed in iron with a central span of 200 ft, plus 2 × 100 ft spans flanking, but the huge floods of 1873 had undermined two piers. A brand new bridge of overall length 500 ft was designed slightly downstream with a roadway width of 14 ft. The finalised dimensions were for a central span of 250 ft plus two side spans each of 130 ft. The greatest depth of water was 12 ft. The wrought-iron gird-ers, believed to have been made in Manchester, were shipped to Karachi in sections. The bridge, weighing a total of 298 tons, with a 150-ton centre span, was opened for public use in June 1878. Its final cost was audited as Rs.298,700 – Rs.15,400 below budget.

The last major bridge for pedestrian and animal traffic built by the Corp of Engineers at the end of the 19th century was across the Indus at Bunji. It was a 337 ft suspension structure with steelwork from Bullivant, of England, and was opened in late 1895. From that year until 1900, Indian Professional Papers documented over 160 bridges of all shapes and sizes expertly constructed along empirically proven military lines throughout the Punjab and Kashmir. One, a walkway suspension bridge 337 ft long in the Punjab, erected in 1899, was perhaps the longest of its type in the world.

Initial setbacks

Steel pontoon bridges were tried but success was a long time coming – perhaps because of the use of cast- and wrought-iron materials when their properties had not been fully assessed in tropical climates. In 1852 a pontoon bridge in the Darjeeling district buckled, while a year later two failed in Bengal. In 1871 a large iron pontoon bridge failed at Muttra – fortunately with no loss of life, despite the fact that many pedestrians were in mid-crossing. Weakness of the wrought-iron material and fast-flowing currents were to blame.

A pedestrian bridge was built in the Bombay Presidency across the Bassein River in 1869. Comprising 2 × 50 ft and 1 × 60 ft spans and weighing 15 tons, the whole structure was erected by the British Army Corp of Engineers to replace what might have been a pontoon bridge. Built on the Sedley system, the total cost was a mere £300. It was opened, to the delight of locals, in March 1869.

A bridge across the Bunnehulla (Benehalla) River, also in Bombay Presidency, was built to connect cotton-producing villages in the Dharwar district in 1864, and another example was constructed over the Quoina River, at Kurar, on the Bombay–Madras trunk road, to enable pedestrians and animals an uninterrupted passage between Sattara and Kolapoor. Comprising four spans, each 116 ft on masonry piers, the total weight of the completed bridge was 258 tons. It was opened for service in 1868.

Pedestrian bridges in Calcutta & Bengal

An early iron suspension bridge, which survived into the next century and must have been traversed by millions of feet, was the 120 ft single-span bridge that brought workers into Kidderpore Docks at Calcutta. It was believed to have been cast and erected by Burn & Company. It had a width of 24 ft, so the designer certainly allowed for passage of the masses in the briefest of time.

The extensive canal works and rivers that flowed through and by Calcutta warranted a complete re-appraisal of the need to bridge together isolated communities. One of the largest road bridges was contracted to the Crumlin Ironworks, in South Wales. Erected in 1862, the 10 × 150 ft was then the longest iron road bridge in Bengal. By 1868 Calcutta was bursting at the seams. Records indicate that some 22 steel road bridges, many incorporating cylindrical piers and ornamental trusses, were built in the following years to link isolated parts of the city.

From 1900 to 1902, pontoon bridges in and around Calcutta were much in vogue. Most were designed to carry loads of 15 tons, safely accommodating the numerous traction engines and steamrollers then in use. To allow river traffic to pass through, 10-ton hand-operated cranes manufactured by Herbert Morris, of Loughborough, were employed. The longest pontoon bridge in the outlying districts, about 590 ft, was across the Maghmati River.

Perhaps the most famous of all Calcutta's pedestrian bridges was the pontoon floating bridge over the Hooghly River. Ironically, while pedestrian crossings spanned various canals and small rivers such as the Myapore Regulating Bridge over the Ganges Canal, the Hooghly was given scant consideration perhaps because of the numerous flimsy craft that carried the capital's citizens across this slow, sewage-ridden, meandering waterway.

A steel bridge was ordered from a Derbyshire firm in 1873. When steelwork arrived and erection began, the floating portion of the bridge was assembled on 28 pontoons coupled together in pairs to secure stability. After many difficulties in bolting the steelwork portions together, the pontoon bridge, at 1530 ft in length, was inaugurated in October 1874. The total cost of all steelwork and supporting chains from Derby was £56,810.

A 200 ft opening for the passage of ships was one of the most difficult problems in designing the bridge. Vessels of 200 tons or more were moved by stream against the tide and the bridge was generally opened twice a week at high water. The opening was achieved by removing the two centre portions of the bridge bodily.

The aggregate ironwork of the pontoons was 1650 tons while that of the girders comprised 875 tons. A considerable amount of teak timber from Burma was used, assessed at 1500 tons. On its inauguration there was a daily traffic of about 6000 tons, which was conveyed in bullock carts, besides an estimated 100 000 passengers. The pontoon structure, despite various deficiencies, survived until the famous 1500 ft Hooghly Suspension Bridge was opened in August 1942.

Of all Indian cities, Calcutta can lay claim to having the greatest number of bridges solely for pedestrian and animal use.

New Howrah Bridge in Calcutta

The last major bridge of the British Empire was built during World War II, when Japanese military forces looked poised to enter Burma and Bengal. Since 1884, Calcutta residents had had to make do with the floating pontoon bridge to cross the Hooghly River. Contracts for the new bridge had been drawn up in 1937. Orders for 23 500 tons of steelwork were placed with Tata, at Jamshedpur (see the following chapter), to roll the girders, with the fabrication work undertaken by Burn, Braithwaite of India and Jessop at four different Calcutta workshops. The 3000 tons of rivets arrived from Braithwaite & Kirk and certain specialist steel fastenings from Cleveland Bridge, of Darlington.

Japan's rapid march towards the Bengal–Assam border was gaining momentum and demand for the bridge on the Hooghly was insistent.

Sabarmati River crossing in Ahmedabad

The EIC had built a masonry bridge across the Sabarmati River at Ahmedabad in the 1760s but it was carried away in a flood of 1875. A whole new steel bridge comprising 14 × 110 ft spans was paid for by the India Office in London, with a contractual clause that must have caused amusement to many in West Bromwich: 'The bridge must be fully capable of safely supporting a herd of elephants in columns of two abreast.' The bridge was exported to Bombay and erected in 1891. Today, the same bridge carries six-wheeled lorries that when fully laden weigh over 15 tons.

Rope bridges

Efforts were made by the British administration and its military engineers to connect communities isolated by gorges and rivers using every means at their disposal. When iron, steel, masonry and wood were not feasible, the last resort was a rope bridge. In 1866, to bridge the Chenab, the Royal Engineers shot across the river a single wire that eventually formed part of a rope bridge 195 ft long. According to military papers published by the Roorkee College in 1899, the rope bridge cost a mere Rs.664, while the benefits accrued to the local community were incalculable. Records indicate that by 1867 at least 200 rope bridges had been built by the Royal Engineers and the Corp of Engineers. One bridge at Kilar over the Chenab was designed for 'coolies, sheep and goats'.

The success of rope bridges stimulated what is now the Royal Corp of Engineers to consider yet grander schemes. What was once credited as being perhaps the longest ropeway bridge in the world was erected by the Royal Corp of Engineers near Darjeeling in the Himalayas. The ropeway ran to Biban Bari in the Little Rangit Valley, 4300 ft below, with one span of 4680 ft.

Another rope bridge once brought engineers to install water turbines at the Gokak Falls, at a height of 176 ft, which fed water into numerous hydraulic turbines to operate cotton mills overlooking the fall. A suspension bridge at the turn of the century replaced the precarious rope bridge that had served for at least a decade.

Overcoming more difficult tasks

Girder sections were shipped around the Cape in crates that weighed usually 4–5 tons. These were then raised, pushed, drawn and dragged by cranes, ropes and tackle, plus elephants, section by section to site, with plenty of supporting 'platform' wood. Later, steam cranes and huge hydraulic jacks supported by indigenous muscle all contributed to completing the structures.

As early as 1900, the Government of India proposed a railway line through the Kangra Valley in northern India, but as traffic prospects were not sufficient to warrant the expensive work needed, the project was put on hold. When the Uhl River Hydro Scheme was being built by the Punjab government, the Government of India, then based in Calcutta, was induced to carry out this work as a State railway.

In 1926 work began on a narrow gauge line of only 2 ft 6 in. – a decision based on the difficult terrain, summer rainfall of between 60 in. and 100 in., and the high incidence of earthquakes, the last recorded having been in 1905. To serve the construction, a huge 260 ft three-pin spandrel-braced, riveted-steel, single-arch bridge had to be erected at an altitude of 7000 ft across a huge gorge spanning the Roand Nullah in the foothills of the Himalayas.

This single-arch bridge is perhaps the most remarkable of all India's railway structures. It was one of the 971 bridges and two tunnels to complete the 102-mile Kangra Valley Railway (KVR). An aerial ropeway was built to carry men and materials, with steam engines driving huge stays into solid ground that were then sealed with concrete. A motley assortment of pulleys and tackles were used, with many men precariously suspended to bolt extension girder steel sections into place. Much temporary supporting steelwork was used to ensure that added sections did not put the structure out of balance, causing the whole assembly to cave in.

The British empirically proven apprenticeship system was all-pervasive on the KVR, as it was then affectionately known. Certificates awarded to those who stayed the course 'were so highly prized that one would think a pot of gold had been dropped into the young man's lap', commented a

Braithwaite erector from Birmingham. Indeed, such an award was a passport to a future job and the recipe for a lifetime's success. Another aspect of the British system was a remarkable reduction of accidents despite the construction methods then used.

Standing the test of time

Up until Independence, the British in India installed more than 175 000 railway bridges, excluding culverts – an average of a little over 4.6 structures per mile. Some of the original masonry bridges are in constant service today. Many of the original road bridges from the 1830s – such as on the military road to Darjeeling – are virtually as the British installed them.

The renewal and re-girdering of railway bridges was undertaken to accommodate the third generation of locomotives, including massive Beyer-Garratts, from Manchester, during the early part of the 20th century. By 1930, it was estimated that every town of importance had a railway station and that less than 1% of all villages were further than 50 miles from a railhead.

Chapter 12

FOUNDRIES, IRON AND STEEL: THE RISE OF INDIAN SELF-SUFFICIENCY

It is unsustainable for too many people to work in factories because the 'real' jobs are in farming.
A CRITIC OF THE INDUSTRIAL REVOLUTION

Over the ages some of the highest- and purest-quality iron deposits known have been widely extracted in central and southern India. Despite problems with fuel and obtaining the high temperatures demanded for smelting, small mines and forges were scattered throughout the country forming an indigenous iron industry with significant diversity and evidence of early European, Chinese and Persian influence. Some of the finished product was turned into wire for musical instruments. However, Indian ore and the skill of Indian smiths also extended beyond southern India and gained a reputation for quality, particularly in the manufacture of weaponry and armour. Assembled in Thanjavur, wootz, a high-carbon crucible steel, had been exported to Roman legions from about AD 300, and continued to be dispatched to Mysore and Hyderabad up until the 1830s.

The furnaces producing iron for domestic consumption were small, mainly family businesses. Despite the primitive state of these installations, the impure iron was of such an acceptable quality that they could adequately serve local village blacksmiths' needs, as well as the iron workshops that produced simple agricultural implements, carpenters' tools and other craftsmen's devices. It has been stated that some form of rudimentary boilers for sugar-making were built from this iron. The local enterprise ran well into the 1860s.

In western India there were few iron mines to speak of, however a small industry of indigenous village smelting furnaces survived until the late

1850s. A pre-industrial iron industry in Kathiawar comprised two large iron foundries – one at Ranavav near Porbandar and the other at Ranpur in Navanagar – and there were also some good furnaces in the Ratanpur region of Rewa Kantha. In Maharastra, the iron ore deposits were largely worked by a semi-nomadic Muslim class known as the Dhavads, who specialised in smelting. In Karnatak smelting was usually undertaken by workers from the Kudivakkalgeri Lingayat caste. Such smelting was often fuel-heavy and the resulting quality poor but sufficient for the manufacture of tools and cooking utensils.

The Nizam of Hyderabad and the Frenchman Raymond

From the early 1700s British iron, and later steel, was in great demand, especially for casting weapons. However, the Dutch and French could rival England in the art of weaponry, and this trade caught the eye of the Marathas, who regularly purchased cannons and cannon balls from European peddlers. In India itself, only rough cannon balls could be produced.

The Nizam of Hyderabad and his successors were a dynasty of astute policy builders. During the period of French influence (1750–78), Parisian generals took an active part in the War of Succession, attaching a part of their army to the reigning Subedar of the Deccan. In effect, the French Corps became an integrated part of the Nizam's army. In 1775 the young Michel Joachim Marie Raymond (1755–1798) arrived with his father, a merchant, to trade spices and other wares.

Raymond was a mere 20 years old when he landed at Pondicherry in 1775, three years after the town had fallen to the British. He journeyed to Mysore, joining the service of Hyder Ali (1722–1782), the 'Tiger Chief ', and rose to the rank of captain. When Ali died and the French Corps was subsequently disbanded, Raymond entered the service of Nizam Ali Khan (1734–1803), the second Nizam of Hyderabad, in 1785. Within a year, the Nizam had placed Raymond as head of his Ordnance Department, and from that time gun founding was established in Hyderabad.

Despite British domination in the area, there seemed to have been no conflict of interest with Raymond producing cannon. He set up various other ordnance factories for his employer and hundreds of cannon were cast from 1786.

That the Nizam thought highly of Raymond, then a legendary figure in the history of the Deccan, can be attested by the magnificent tomb erected in his honour. Only one gun foundry remains, located opposite the Mahboobia Girls' School, but its ruins are preserved for posterity. Specimens of Raymond's superb craftsmanship – along with numerous cannonballs – have been tastefully preserved throughout Hyderabad, nowhere better than in the city's Public Gardens.

Foundries for the EIC

Once having made its presence felt as the governing body of India, the EIC had to initiate the production of usable iron in large quantities virtually from scratch. It can be assumed that the company's officials, who wandered throughout the land and penetrated villages where family concerns made iron in limited quantities solely to serve local requirements, decided that 'a more effective manner of manufacture in workable quantities had to be found'. Some officials may have thought that iron production in India existed on a scale similar to that back home, but they were soon to be disillusioned.

The EIC recruited iron founders from England in about 1760 to augment its plans to establish a viable foundry industry, without any prior knowledge of major ore or fuel reserves throughout India for its ambitions. Geologists were hired expressly for that venture. As early as the 1770s, attempts were made to replace coal with charcoal, despite the fact that this consideration had not gained favour in Britain. Improvements in blasting techniques were sought, but the steam engine was yet to arrive.

Perhaps the most sustained effort to establish a viable foundry was the Porto Novo enterprise in South Arcot, founded in 1826 by a former Company servant named Heath, who obtained substantial support from the EIC and the Government of Madras. The firm undertook production at both Porto Novo, a small seaport south of Madras at Palampetti near Salem and at Beypore on the Malabar Coast. Two years later, a foundry was established at Trincomalee. Charcoal was the fuel used and bullocks were employed to power what primitive machinery was used. It was at Porto Novo that the Bessemer process of steelmaking – an inexpensive technique of mass production – was first introduced in India. However, the company could never get off the ground and was declared insolvent.

In 1859 British foundry expert William Sowerby visited all four works of the EIC, now added to by a wholly new enterprise at Poolamputtee. He said after his visit: 'The iron is very good, and would always command a good price, were the supply regular; but it arrives in England by piecemeal and is

CALCUTTA AND BOMBAY MINTS

THE EIC INVITED TENDERS in or around December 1809 for two separate mints to be built at Bombay and Calcutta. Boulton & Watt's Soho Works was successful with its offers on both occasions.

It was decided to set up the Calcutta Mint first and the whole engine was shipped out in 1810 around the Cape. Lieutenant W.N. Forbes, of the Bengal Engineers, was a natural choice to supervise the erection of all five engines as he had spent part of his recent home leave at Boulton & Watt's Birmingham factory. The works was considered to be the best training school in Britain for acquiring a practical knowledge of steam engines.

When placed into commission, the Calcutta Mint was successfully stamping out 200000 pieces of coin every eight hours. Two years later, the output from those Watt machines increased to 310000 coins in a seven-hour day. Thus the Watt steam engine may be regarded as the first machinery operated by steam on Indian soil, although its date of arrival cannot be confirmed.

The EIC decided to replace its pioneering mint at Calcutta with a larger, better-equipped establishment on the banks of the Hooghly River. Behind a colonnaded façade – inspired by the Temple of Minerva at Athens – room after room housed apparatus such as Mughal mint-masters had never before seen. There were special furnaces for smelting gold, silver and copper, with rolling mills, circular cutting presses, milling and coining apparatus, lathe-laps, triturating mills and proving machinery all shipped out from England.

It turned out to be one of the most impressive overseas orders ever received by Boulton & Watt: 'five engines and over 100,000 pieces of machinery for the Calcutta Mint, 1825', to quote the firm's manager.

New Boulton & Watt machinery was introduced to the Bombay Mint in 1832. Ardaseer Cursetjee Wadia (1808–1877) the aforementioned (Chapter 4) and somewhat overlooked great Parsi engineer transferred his services to the EIC from shipbuilding to a position at the Bombay mint 'for the purpose of devoting myself to the study of steam machinery and the foundry business'.

On a visit to England in the 1840s – where he was elected a non-resident fellow of the Royal Asiatic Society of England and associate of the renowned Institution of Civil Engineers (ICE) – Cursetjee noted that he found the Royal Mint much inferior to the mint in Bombay.

not therefore valued as it should be.' It is interesting to note that in his report, cited in *Engineering* in 1867, reference, is made to pig iron exported to
Britain for use in the then largest and most prestigious bridges of their time.
'A portion of the pig iron from Porto Novo,' said Sowerby, 'has been sent to
England where a large quantity of it has been used in the construction of
the Britannia Tubular Bridge and Menai Bridge.' Both bridges were built in
1846. It is perhaps surprising that the EIC should have found its products
hauled thousands of miles around the Cape to be used in these structures.
Porto Novo's iron must have been of excellent quality: surviving the test of
time, spans of 460 ft and 230 ft supported 600-ton trains until 1970.

Gun casting

One of the earliest known foundries for the EIC was established at Fort
William, Cossipore, near Calcutta. On the banks of the Hooghly, about
4 miles from Calcutta, the EIC also established a large brass foundry in
1834. The British were still sceptical of any lingering French presence
and were firmly of the opinion that the establishment of a local gun
foundry would be preferable to awaiting shipments of arms around the
Cape. Lieutenant Colonel George Hutchinson (1796–1859), of the Bengal
Engineers, was appointed in 1822 as Superintendent and Director of the
EIC's gun foundry, which had been established at Fort William from about
1770. In 1834 the foundry was rebuilt in Cossipore to Hutchinson's designs,
with all the machinery steam-powered. It grew to become the largest
foundry for ordnance in India. In 1893 the Cossipore Gun Factory, as it was
named, then under government control, produced steel for the first time.

By 1900 the Cossipore Foundry had expanded to produce shells that
could be used in small warships. Still steam-powered, the foundry imported the latest hydraulic machinery for pressing out this ordnance. One
machine, consisting of two tandem compound engines, arrived from
James Simpson. This Simpson hydraulic engine was the model for other
armament foundries and was preferred by the Indian government in other
installations.

Saugar and an early Calcutta foundry for iron bridges

The iron-smelting region around Saugar in central India was little known.
In 1833 the *Journal of the Asiatic Society* wrote that many cottage industries were given over to iron smelting purely for domestic consumption.

However, the region can lay claim to fame in the significant triumph for its efforts achieved in the construction of a 200 ft suspension bridge – 'from people who had never seen iron in large quantities before', as that same journal quoted. Perhaps EIC guidance was at hand to steer this enterprise into smelting enough iron to bridge the Beosi River.

For many years the EIC had experimented with iron founding, and after much trial and error had failed to locate the secret of success. That it was in the Government of India's interest to establish iron founding on a large scale to reduce the amount of finished castings imported from Britain explains the desire to take over all EIC operations and establish additional ordnance-producing plants.

Recent research has revealed that a third foundry was established in Calcutta around 1845 solely to cast and build bridges. The Calcutta Public Works Department had embarked upon the grandiose scheme to cut canals throughout west Bengal and create ad hoc dams to catch monsoon floodwaters. The foundry, called the Iron Bridge Yard, was the brainchild of one of the Brunton family of engineers who settled in Bombay and Bengal. As canals were quickly being hacked out, an urgent need arose for bridges to keep communities intact. Henry Prince (c.1830–1906) obtained an appointment as assistant engineer to William Brunton, who was then attached to the Calcutta Canal Division.

The Iron Bridge Yard experienced a chequered career. During its heyday, it cast many bridges and roofs and much general ironwork for Calcutta and the new town of Muttra, before closing its works for good in 1863. Prince's duties were then confined to completing the Barrakur Bridge in Calcutta before being transferred to the Andaman Islands in charge of the penal colony at Port Blair. However, as a going concern the foundry supplied a few needs for the day, further reducing the reliance upon imported British ironwork.

The Roorkee Foundry

The demand for iron castings of all descriptions could not be met from local endeavour, and in the 1840s Britain was still the principal supplier. In 1843 the EIC began the erection of the Canal Foundry & Workshops at Roorkee. It was ideally sited alongside the Ganges Canal, which included the Solani Aqueduct. In 1852 the works was separated from the canal as demand and therefore the physical size of the complex grew. Initially the foundry was designed to manufacture government orders only, but private parties found the products of such good quality that non-government orders were also taken.

In the first decade, however, its financial condition was sadly neglected and a loss of Rs.424,455 was sustained. Auditors were called in, but by 1864 the foundry had returned some small profits to the state. In the following year Rs.335,382's worth of work was undertaken, returning 3% profit. By 1869, 11% profit was achieved on sales of Rs.476,041. Ironically, the steady growth in sales saw the foundry reduce the price on each casting sold, perhaps because of increased competition.

The foundry was well equipped with a 20 hp engine, a smith's shop with two Bradford steam hammers, a carpenter's and woodworking shop, furnaces, a pattern shop and a mathematical instrument shop where surveying instruments were made and repaired.

The horrendous events of the Indian Mutiny of 1857 prompted the government in 1862 to commission Colonel H. Yale RE, of the Public Works Department, to design a memorial to that tragedy and those who perished in the carnage. The stonework and plinth were constructed at Allahabad, the stone obtained from a quarry of hard white sandstone situated on the right bank of the Jumna River near the town. The gate of the screen was cast in gun metal in Calcutta with the inscription 'There be they who came out of a great tribulation'. Around the pedestal's base was a touching and poignant dedication to the dead with the date 15 July 1857, saliently displayed. The screen stood within an ornamental garden enclosed by an iron railing designed by a Captain Allen. The whole ironwork was cast at the Roorkee Foundry, as it was later named. Ironically, the cost of the garden and screen was defrayed out of a fine levied on the native city of Cawnpore. The memorial was completed and consecrated on 11 February 1863.

By 1870 the EIC was no more – at least in name – but its legacy for the people of Roorkee cannot be dismissed. In a professional paper issued by the Corps of Engineers, the range of work executed by the Roorkee Foundry was shown to be very great, and in a country such as India highly prized for the economy. 'The diversity of its product range was astounding for its size,' according to the paper. 'Steam engines of all kind from locomotive to stationary; pumps, printing and hydraulic presses; planing, slotting and drilling machinery; lathes of all kind; levels, prismatic and surveying compasses, scales and mathematical instruments; as well as a range of scientific apparatus' are listed.

Madras Railway Company's foundry

The demand for castings and materials to sustain railways nudged many transport undertakings into creating ad hoc foundries to serve their own needs. The Madras Railway (MR) was no different. In late 1867 the MR's system stretched over 600 miles – including the Bangalore branch – with some 268 miles for proposed construction on architects' drawing boards. The lines were laid with wooden sleepers and ordinary chairs, which started to fail after 12 months in service. A Greaves-type pot sleeper was installed early in that year, with a reduction of maintenance estimated to be from 70s. to 65s. per mile. The installation of cast-iron sleeper material was an outright success, but supply soon failed to match demand.

MR established a contract with Messrs Hopkins, Gilkes & Company, bridge builders and general iron founders of Middlesbrough, for 10 000 tons of Greaves-type sleepers to be cast in Madras from redundant old railway chairs. Local coal was available. The Middlesbrough foundry shipped out two Woodward steam-jet cupolas, then an 'acceptable invention in favour of iron-founders'. The foundry was placed into service in June 1868, and served the railway company for the next 20 years.

Calcutta-based iron and engineering industries

By the time Queen Victoria ascended the throne in 1837, Calcutta was irrefutably the 'Jewel in the Crown'. Once shunned by Mughal rulers as a mosquito-infested mud swamp unfit for human survival, a little over a century and a half from the time Job Charnock arrived in 1690 this inhospitable land was dotted with magnificent palaces, emporiums and three huge foundries and engineering works. 'The plumes of smoke, which meet the eye on every side, recall my visit to Manchester,' quipped one visitor on a trip to the Raj. The spread of railways and maritime commerce stimulated at least three huge foundries and numerous small engineering shops in India's capital city. All enterprises were heavily committed to casting beam engines and building both steam and sailing ships – many ocean-going; there was also iron smelting in two different locations towards Asansol. Additionally, other foundries were scattered around Howrah and Fort William.

This concentrated activity was the brainchild of a General Watson from the EIC who, with a grant of land from his employer, established a marine yard in 1781. The wet docks were commissioned the following year.

Calcutta had developed into a city of diverse industries by 1910. Gold and silver was worked, with many blacksmiths' shops hammering out iron. Stamping machines and steam forges served the small but expanding cutlery industry, although this played a totally second- or third-class role to imported Sheffield cutlery. However, the crafting of guns was a feature of Calcutta that attracted much foreign interest.

From the 1860s, the city's speciality was making shotguns, using small furnaces and the redundant iron and steel that was virtually discarded as scrap by others. The industry flourished until about 1901, when records indicate that only 463 guns were manufactured. This was only a sixth of the output in 1895. There was a lucrative export trade in 1903/4, when some 899 firearms were documented as 'sold abroad'. This number is by no means large, and can perhaps be attributed to stiff competition from European arms manufacturers when rapid progress in the crafting of rifles – tried out in the Boer War – had reduced the price of ordnance following cessation of hostilities in 1901. The British authorities then attempted to reduce the number of gun licences issued.

The rise of the iron and steel industry stimulated the growth of small foundries that serviced the large concerns. One such enterprise was Messrs John King of Howrah, engineers and founders, which profited so much that it set up shop in Barakar to undertake engineering maintenance services. Perhaps there was a connection with the small Barakar Iron & Steel Works that by 1904 had turned out 40 000 tons of pig iron and 15 000 tons of castings.

According to statistics compiled by the Government of Bengal, the number of iron and brass foundries in service in the province, but mainly centred on Calcutta, totalled four in 1881, 15 in 1891, 25 in 1901 and 38 in 1903. By 1914 over 50 were established, which stimulated a corresponding rise in rope manufacture and engine repair shops. In 1914 most foundries used steam engines for main drives although electricity (see Chapter 14) was making considerable incursions.

Unbridled optimism – the rise of Indian self-sufficiency

When railways began to take shape from 1853, there was unbridled optimism regarding the industrialisation of India. The long-held view that Britain kept India in total poverty without any form of industrial capacity is not borne out by the evidence at hand. Granted, the demand for railway material continued to outstrip Britain's capacity to supply well into the late 1900s, but those in India then looked to self-sufficiency as the most viable alternative.

It must have been to the dismay of the huge foundries rolling out railway lines – principally in Middlesbrough, Sheffield, Glasgow and Workington – that *The Engineer* as far back as August 8, 1856, wrote: '*The Bombay Telegraph* states that "Messrs Hunt and Elmsley, the great contractors, are about to establish an iron foundry on an extensive scale at Jubbulpore for the purpose of making rails for the proposed line of railway between Bombay and Mirzapur".' This proposal was for the GIPR. Regrettably, nothing more is known of the venture, although huge railway works to build wagons and coaches were later established at Byculla, near Bombay, in 1878 and at Jhansi in 1895 (as detailed in Chapter 10).

In 1848 the firm of Parry crafted its own iron machinery for sugar crushers, since it felt that the production of sugar was not profitable enough to warrant the importing of sugar manufacture machinery from foundries based in Glasgow, Liverpool and Derby.

In Salem and Bellary, pig iron and iron manufacture was reported among the main local industries as late as 1851. Although the local iron that was used was more expensive than imports from Britain, it was found to be more malleable and hence better suited to local needs. This industry survived into the 1890s, having imported many British furnaces from Muir of Manchester along with some small blowing engines from Birmingham for forcing air to increase efficiency. At Mogul Serai locomotive workshops, forges from Muir of Manchester and Scott of Glasgow were still in use into the 1990s.

Bengal Iron & Steelworks

The early indigenous projects, such as the Porto Novo Company, were – surprisingly, according to Dharma Kumar in his excellent book *The Cambridge Economic History of India Vol. 2* – designed to produce iron mainly for sale abroad. At a time when the demand for iron exceeded supply throughout the settled parts of India, this is indeed a strange assessment. With a huge railway, industrial, canal and commercial buildings, civil works including water pumping stations and agricultural projects outstripping the supply of materials and expertise, India had become the greatest importer of iron and steel east of the Bosphorus by 1870. Not unnaturally, the rising

Indian middle class questioned the need to rely upon Britain and diverted their thoughts to building their own foundries and steel works.

The only large-scale steelworks successfully established in India during the 19th century were those of the Bengal Iron Works Company (BIW) founded at Barakur, near Raniganj, in 1875. The BIW immediately began producing pig iron in that year. A capital of Rs.1 million proved to be a serious under-funding. The BIW's first blast furnace and foundry was commissioned in 1877, with most of the heavy plant arriving from Head, Wrightson & Company, Teesside Engineering and the Sheffield steelworks. The company was forced to borrow Rs.400,000 at 10% to finance the material.

Renamed the Bengal Iron & Steel Company (BISCO) and incorporated in England with a capital of £150,000, the firm held property on land bearing large coal and iron deposits, as well as two blast furnaces with an annual capacity of 7000 tons; a foundry was also included. Shortly after iron-making began, it was proposed to increase capacity to 20000 tons per annum.

BISCO offered to undertake steel production, provided that the government would not construct a steelworks in competition to its own venture, and that the government would agree to buy 15000 tons of steel rails yearly for five years.

Steel was produced in 1901–2, but BISCO abandoned the manufacture within a year, having lost heavily. However, the firm was ideally sited on a coalfield, which it owned outright. Rail transport connections to all parts of India were excellent and every order could be delivered 'within a few days once loaded onto an East India Railway freight train'. Then India produced some 80000 tons of pig iron of a quality almost equal to some of the best Scottish brands. In 1902 steam-blowing engines were replaced with steam turbines believed to be from Fraser & Chambers.

In 1919 the firm was reorganised, with enlarged capital, as the Bengal Iron Company (BIC). The steelworks also produced huge quantities of coke. All foundries were equipped to produce every size of girder required for bridges and the structural steel industry, from modern blast furnaces and rolling mills – the majority supplied by Davy United of Sheffield and Head, Wrightson & Company. British Thomson-Houston supplied many switchboards.

BIC produced armour plate for military purposes. One firm that was actively engaged in the production of machine tool bending rolls for heavy armour plate was Scriven & Company, of Leeds. Designed to the specifications of Newcastle-based Armstrong, Mitchell in 1895, it could bend 5 in. thick hot steel. A pair of vertical-inverted steam engines powered the machine. Having proved their worth in England, one complete unit was shipped to BIC, with another believed to have been delivered just over ten years later to Tata Iron & Steel. It was massive, to the extent that huge concrete foundation blocks were required to support its 98-ton weight.

India – developing as a great iron and steel exporter

At a speech given before an invited audience of engineers and iron and steel manufacturers before the Staffordshire Iron & Steel Institute in Dudley, West Midlands on 29 September 1911, Isaac E. Lester, formerly works superintendent to the EIR, gave a very interesting account of 'Indian iron' that must have sent warning signals through the British iron and steel industry.

Despite the high volume of imports to India from Britain in the year 1909/10 – 602 282 tons, valued at £5,893,933 – Indian foundry industries were rapidly becoming self-sufficient, stated Mr Lester. Each large railway company had its own foundry and workshops, and Calcutta- and Bombay-based rolling mills were producing large bridge girders up to 200 ft in length. At this time India's extraction industry was gaining prominence, with figures for manganese ore of some 500 000 tons, worth £527,358, being exported worldwide. A new plant for Tata Iron & Steel at Kalimati in the Bengal–Nagpur district was shortly to be commissioned and export markets were already established, according to Mr Lester. He continued his lecture by reminding Britain's iron and steel industry that complacency in the export markets must be checked. Germany and Czechoslovakia had already made inroads into India, with America having secured the Gokteik Viaduct in Burma in 1899.

Although the coal industry was mentioned, with further large deposits employing some 16 000 in mines owned by the EIR, Britain's coal exports to India by 1910 were for all practical purposes nil. Mr Lester rounded off his speech by highlighting India's enormous and mostly untapped wealth: 'In the study of geology, mineralogy and the development of [India's] resources it is interesting to note in this connection that the Indian and home governments are more and more realising the immense wealth of this portion of the Empire.'

Tata Iron & Steel Company (TISCO)

Jamsetji Nusserwanji Tata (1839–1904), whose career provides a true example of industrial romance, was the founder of the Indian steel industry. Tata graduated from Elphinstone College in 1858. His passion for learning and his vision were all but limitless. Tata was probably the most creative of the first generation of Indian industrial entrepreneurs. A member of a family of wealthy Parsi Bombay merchants, his first industrial successes were cotton textile mills in Bombay and Nagpur, as discussed in Chapter 16. Many Parsis who had established cotton mills from 1855 made money, although none was as successful as Tata. His interest in iron and steel was apparently fired when he came across an official report on the Chanda district, which identified large deposits of high-quality iron but also noted a lack of suitable coal in the region.

By the 1880s Tata had 'set his heart' on building a steelworks that would rival the best in the world. Tata brought over American and European expertise to undertake pioneering survey work in Bengal and Bihar – both states rich in raw material and excellent for transport connections – with the object of establishing iron- and steelworks on a large scale, utilising the latest scientific methods. He did not live to see the realisation of his steelworks; his successors, his sons Dorabji Jamsetji Tata (1859–1932) and Sir Ratanji Tata (1871–1932), ensured his legacy, and Tata Iron & Steel Company was officially incorporated in 1907.

From 1902 Tata, sought foreign expertise and, selecting the Jherra Coalfield for its fuel, Tata established a steelworks at Sakchi, a small village in Chota Nagpur some 155 miles west of Calcutta. Tata was in the right place at the right time for serving the huge market of Calcutta – rapidly expanding with thermal power stations, an upsurge in shipbuilding and the ever-increasing railway network – with a sea outlet for exports.

Tata was additionally fortunate in obtaining cheap and excellent-quality iron ore at Gurumaishini, which when evaluated by British metallurgists was found to contain over 60% of pure metallic iron. A railway line was quickly driven to the source of this wealth. The plant was soon completed, and production of iron began in 1911 and of steel in January 1918. Later, the name of the village was changed to 'Jamshedpur' in honour of the pioneering work of Jamsetji Tata himself.

Excellent pig iron was turned out from the very beginning and initial difficulties with the latest state of British furnace manufacture – still in its development stage – were soon overcome. With a special railway station constructed at Jamshedpur and subsequent expansion of the works, production rapidly increased from a designed output of 120 000 tons of pig iron, and for the conversion of 85 000 tons into 72 000 tons of steel. This was at a time when no less than 450 000 tons of iron and steel goods of a similar class were imported annually. Up to the end of 1913 a profit of Rs.858,583 was made, with a complement of 125 European – mainly British – engineers and skilled supervisors, plus about 9000 locals.

Orders flowed in thick and fast, not only from domestic markets but from Japan, China, Java, Ceylon, Burma, the Straits Settlements and Australia, and also from South America and the west coast of the US. The horizon looked extremely bright for the new phase of industrialisation that India was embracing.

The imported plant for Tata's steelworks came from both America and Britain. Initial electrical equipment arrived from both General Electric Company and British Thomson-Houston; firms in Cleveland and Pittsburgh supplied the furnaces and major mechanical equipment, with steam hammers and forges coming from Muir of Manchester and Thwaites of Bradford. To commission the plant a huge workforce was required, comprising about 325 Europeans – again mainly British – and 4000 indigenous workers. In 1924 only 229 foreigners were serving the complex, after which time their numbers declined rapidly. One of the huge direct current switchboards rated 800 volts from British Thomson-Houston survived well into the 1970s.

Between 1920 and 1937 pig-iron production in India grew by about 400% and steel even more. One firm that contributed to this increase was Davy United of Sheffield with its steel plant products. The English Steel Corporation, also of Sheffield, supplied much of the new technology. Almost the entire output of iron and steel came from TISCO's Jamshedpur complex near Asansol.

OLDEST ENGINEERING FIRMS IN INDIA

BURN & COMPANY'S HOWRAH IRONWORKS

The *Railway Gazette* in November 1913 featured the foundry enterprises of Burn, Jessop and Richardson-Cruddas in its special comprehensive book devoted to Indian railways – described by the editor as 'the oldest engineering firms in India'. The exact origins of the firm are unclear, with some sources citing a Colonel Swinton as founding the firm in 1781, when Warren Hastings was in residence as Governor-General of the three Presidencies, with a Mr Burn later noted in 1789. What is clear is that the Howrah Ironworks marked the beginning of the engineering industry, as we know it today in India. The firm was in the right place at the right time. Its early products were domestic utensils and ornamental cast-iron work, plus some collaboration with Kyd & Company's shipyard. There is evidence that the second generation of Indian-made paddle steamers received their engines from the Howrah Ironworks. Certainly boilers were either made from local iron ore or assembled from parts shipped from England.

The spread of the railway from 1853 motivated the firm to supply goods and services that British industry would occasionally fail to deliver on time. Sometimes, too, ships were unfortunately lost at sea. Cast-iron bridges for the EIR were built, along with cast-iron sleepers for imported rails from Workington and Sheffield. Proficient under its British management, the firm was entrusted by consultants to cast caissons for deep river crossings that a host of railway companies required to support spans up to 200 ft in length. Railway wagons were turned out, and by 1895 some 2000 units could be produced, including the casting of wheels. Mill and marine engines with their associated gearing gradually nudged out the smaller British specialists. By 1905 Burn was supplying steel girders of up to 350 ft per single span.

From 1880 the company began to build complete paddle steamers, initially with engines imported from Scotland. When demand started to exceed supply, the foundry cast its own engines, mainly to British patents. By 1890 the first complete Burn paddle steamers began to ply Indus and Brahmaputra waters. Although the foundry built steam and later diesel railway cranes and every other item of ancillary railway equipment – much still in service throughout India and East Africa – the firm never designed or constructed steam locomotives. Today, the renowned foundry is merged with Jessop and Braithwaite, under the BBJ name.

JESSOP & COMPANY

There is evidence that this historical firm, founded in 1799 in Calcutta, was connected with the same Jessop who was dispatched with the Butterley castings in 1815 to Lucknow to construct the first iron bridge in India. At first Jessop was a smaller player to Burn, producing similar products such as railway wagons – many in service in Kenya and Uganda in 2005 – railway cranes, steam engines, bridge spans up to 250 ft, and structural steel work for railway and heavy industrial use. Jessop, from around 1859, embarked on the production of small machine tools, many in collaboration with Alfred Herbert of Coventry. The demand for turret lathes and drilling machines saw the firm enjoying a healthy business with the local jute mills.

RICHARDSON & CRUDDAS OF BOMBAY

Not much is known about this firm, established in 1858 in the old railway works at Byculla. Growing from small beginnings during the period when the BBCIR was merely a fledgling company, like Burn and Jessop, the partnership saw a niche in the construction of railways that their expertise could profit from. Initially, the building of Bombay's tramway system stimulated the firm into large-scale construction projects when steel bridges were required, albeit of small-sized spans. Warehouses, railway station footbridges and roofs, and some power station and jute industry steel buildings, all provided the firm with urgent work, until after stiff tendering it was awarded a bridge of 10 × 100 ft to span the Kalyan River in around 1889. At the time this was the longest bridge entirely made in India.

Expansion of the Bombay Port Trust docks and a new powerhouse for the Bombay Tramway & Electric Supply Company enabled the firm to expand considerably its relatively modest premises to cover 14 acres by 1910. Most of its staff was British.

The enterprise kept a large stock of material that by 1912 amounted to some 10 000 tons, replenished through the company's London office. Success followed success, and the enterprise was noted for quality work at a competitive price. It was to its credit that from the first decade of the 20th century, government and municipal offices alike favoured the firm for many concrete and steel-framed buildings. The enterprise also undertook the erection and sometime equipping of complete hospitals under a British consultant. The ever-expanding railway system enabled the firm to supply and build railway stations, goods yards, and signalling and engine sheds to cater for the Indian State Railway enterprise that gradually took over many earlier and now loss-making railway companies.

Chapter 13

EXTRACTION INDUSTRY DEVELOPMENT

There is no likelihood that India will ever be a
great coal-producing or even coal-consuming country.
ENGINEERING, Vol. 62, 1895

By 1900 India's principal power resources were coal and wood, with petroleum and hydroelectricity (detailed in Chapters 6 and 14) beginning to emerge. Fortunately for Bengal's jute and iron industries, a plentiful natural resource was immediately at hand – coal, which was mainly concentrated in one great series of deposits in western Bengal. The large tea estates that were well developed in Darjeeling, Assam and the Nilgiris (see also Chapter 17) relied on cheap hydropower and stimulated that industry. Whereas, the bulk of petroleum used was imported from British Burma. Calcutta reigned supreme, as less than 120 miles to the north-west lay the largest coalfield in the country, as it still is today. So acute was the need for cheap fuel for the Bombay Presidency's cotton and other large industries that, after 1920, coal was occasionally imported from Europe and South Africa. Later oil was imported in large quantities from Burma, the Middle East, Russia and the United States.

India's industrial engine was at one time thought likely to outgrow the amount of indigenous coal that could be mined. The extensive use of steam-engine machinery and the emergence of turbo-alternators demanded large amounts of coal, in which most of India's large towns and cities were lacking before World War I. However, there was no attempt to check industrial expansion. Locomotives arriving from Britain as early as 1910 were built with sectionalised tenders capable of carrying both oil and coal, especially for services in the North-West Frontier and towards Afghanistan

Sind–Pishin Railway (Northern Division) group of engineers, c.1890–2 (Courtesy of the British Library)

– the Sind–Pishin Railway. By 1914, transporting coal to the large industrial centres such as Calcutta, Bombay and Madras, whose large-scale factories produced the nation's goods, was profitable for all railway companies involved, as well as for coastal steamers and those vessels plying Hooghly and Ganges waters.

Mining history

India has a long tradition in the mining and smelting of gold, copper, lead, zinc and iron ores and the mining and cutting of diamonds. However, it had not been in the interest of Indians to consider the mining of coal for profit. The British mined India's first ton of coal in 1775 from Raniganj. British geologists in the service of the EIC reported that there was 'no evidence whatsoever to indicate that any indigenous workings of that commodity could be seen'.

The history of India's coal industry begins in 1774 when a Mr S.G. Heatly and a Mr J. Summer applied to the EIC for the right to dig coal at Raniganj, north-west of Calcutta. In 1777 six mines were worked and 90 tons extracted. Nothing further was undertaken in substantial quantities until about 1815, when the enterprising William Jones (the independent mechanic aforementioned in Chapter 4) mined coal from adjacent pits and was the first man to sell the commodity on the open market.

The initial attempt to exploit coal in substantial quantities was made by the British magistrate of Chota Nagpur, who obtained the right to mine from the Marquis of Hastings in about 1816. He then turned to EIC funds for a grant to expand his coal interests, and the company promptly advanced him Rs.30,000. Later, a Captain Stewart worked the Raniganj Coalfield for two years before it was taken over completely by Alexander & Company. It was this mine that introduced steam-engine power to the industry. In 1831, with the back-up of steam power, Alexander's was producing around 15000 tons of coal yearly that was recorded as being hauled down the Damodar River in some 350 boats.

The first recorded extraction of coal in Burdwan was in about 1816. Mines were opened up from where coal was floated 60 miles down the Damodar River to Calcutta. It was estimated that the quality was only 75% as good as that of Newcastle coal, then imported for the numerous metal-working forges.

When a regular steamer line came into operation after 1834, the Calcutta Marine Board invited tenders to establish coal depots at Ramahal, Colgong, Monghyr, Barh, Dinapore, Gazipur, Benares, Mizapore, Allahabad, Kulna, Berhamporte and Samkar Bazaar. The large Calcutta trading house of Carr, Tagore & Company, which was jointly owned by Indian and British expertise, was given the controlling interest in 1836 of the mines at Burdwan, Raniganj and Pachete. Its founder Dwarkanath Tagore – another prolific and historically overlooked entrepreneur in Calcutta – owned the Calcutta Steam Tug Association (see also Chapter 4) and was quick to recognise the opportunity for controlling the supply of coal.

The rapid spread of steamboat services stimulated the need for further coal exploration in the upper reaches of the Ganges. In 1828 the Asiatic Society's Physical Committee requested that a Captain J. Franklin, in the pay of the Bengal government, be allowed to carry out geological explorations in winter that year. This was necessary to spare the cost of hauling huge stocks of coal hundreds of miles upstream. Other officers were dispatched across the country towards Patna to gather rocks, observing the strata and outcroppings as well as chemically analysing their finds. All samples were hand-dug using simple spades. These men were the predecessors of the Geological Survey of India.

An unknown Englishman travelling upcountry in 1830 through the Palamau noticed that several coal layers were exposed where a river course had cut off a portion of a hillock. He assessed that by constructing a couple of ad hoc engine works, a canal could be made to reach the Ganges at Futwah, a little below Patna. Later, the Steam Department of Calcutta sent out its superintending engineer from Dinapore to explore exposed beds along the Soane and Amanath rivers and send a few gunnybags back for examination. Within two years these beds were worked, and although the coal seams were not 'rich' by English standards, the 'black gold' was usable.

About the same time as those beds were being exploited, the British Political Agent in Kasayah Hills discovered at Cherrapoonjee in Sylhet a very superior coal assessed to be some 15% richer than that from the mines at Burdwan. A leading Bengal Hindu merchant, Babboo Juggernath Dasa, who held the Dinapore depot contract, was granted a four-month option to farm the region's coal – and later stone – mines. Within ten years of steamboating on Bengal rivers, local – mainly Burdwan – coal was generally in use. By then these coalfields were attracting much migrant labour, despite appalling working conditions – although these were no worse than the horrendous conditions back in Britain.

Bengal

The Bengal coal industry progressed slowly until 1840, when shipments to Calcutta were estimated to have reached 36 200 tons. In 1843, when the group of ad hoc workings amalgamated to form the Bengal Coal Company, production had expanded to around 55 000 tons. Progress using steam-driven mine winders from Lancashire increased rapidly and by 1845 output had reached 62 400 tons.

The Raniganj coalfield contained two valuable seams, separated by iron-stone shales 1000 ft thick. Exploration in the Raniganj area progressed at a feverish pace. A new seam at Giridih was found in 1857 and worked until 1861, when it was felt to have been exhausted. A further geological survey was undertaken in the same field in 1871, following which it was re-opened and systematically worked until 1903. The nine mines of Giridih employed at their peak some 10 700 people producing 767 000 tons of coal. It possessed two valuable seams in the lower coal series, and one of the shafts fell to a depth of 640 ft.

Despite the choice of employment available to workers from all over India, the coal industry managed to retain its human resources. The Bengal Coal Company created villages and housing complexes that guaranteed a roof over their workers' heads.

The reliability of Indian labour encouraged further geological surveys. These proved positive in and around Jherra (Jharia). A mine was opened there in 1894, and as coal was being extracted further seams were found, enabling Jherra to compete with Raniganj. By 1903 Jherra worked 115 individual mines, employing 28 000 people who produced an impressive 2746 000 tons. Many mining engines arrived from John & Edward Wood of Bolton and Fraser & Chalmers of Erith, Kent, serving for at least 50 years.

Private companies proliferated. Competing against EIR mining operations were the Equitable, New Birbhum and Barakar coal companies, each extracting over 300 000 tons by 1886. By 1900 the European-owned collieries produced between them in excess of 4 million tons, and those owned by indigenous firms exceeded 1.5 million tons. In 1903 the total output of all coalfields in Bengal had risen to 6566 000 tons from 272 mines, with nearly all now using steam-engine-driven mine winders. Most engines came from Lancashire firms, with Walker of Wigan a principal supplier.

Coal was found in many other areas of India and by 1905 the country was more or less self-sufficient – with 282 mines working in Bengal alone – employing some 84 000 people and producing a staggering 7 million tons. The railways then consumed about a third of all output. British imports fell from 70 000 tons through Calcutta in 1880 to 2000 tons in 1901, though coal was still imported via Bombay and Karachi. Local coal at this time sold openly in Calcutta at Rs.7 per ton, compared with a price of Rs.15 per ton for English coal arriving at Bombay.

Mine owners exploited more and more coal reserves. The demand for Bengal coal increased further again, with 8418 000 tons mined in 1906. Exports of coal through the Port of Calcutta increased tenfold from 1895 to 1906; 2851 888 tons passed through the port, with about 55% loaded onto coastal vessels for domestic uses, 851 000 tons used as bunker coal and the rest dispatched to East Africa and the Malaya–Singapore area. Some coal even found its way into locomotives on Egyptian railways. Between 1909 and 1910, the Giridih and Kurhurbaree collieries were producing over 1 million tons annually, providing gainful employment for an expanded workforce of 16 000.

Assam

On 25 November 1837 the EIC's Captain Vetch stated in a letter to the Commissioner of Assam that he had found detached specimens of various kinds of coal in the Jellundee, Belseeree and Booroolee rivers. All these rivers eventually flowed into the Brahmaputra River from the Bootan Mountains. Further exploration along the banks of the Teesta River proved positive. Many strata examined showed a seam some 3 ft thick.

In the next two years a Captain Hanay and a Captain Jenkins, also in the employ of the EIC, noted extensive coal seams close to the channel of the Disung River. Again, the tests were positive. By 1863 some 102 mines in that region were producing good-quality coal that found favour with steamboat operators and tea plantation managers alike.

The expansion of paddle-steamer services to Assam stimulated much enterprise. Most vessels travelled from Calcutta almost empty against the tide. On return, each vessel was loaded to the gunwales, carrying a full cargo of coal and, when space was available, tea for ocean-going steamers to transship to Europe. According to the *Colliery Guardian* of 12 September 1863, the pithead cost of Assam coal was between Rs.55 and Rs.70 per 100 maunds. (The maund varies in weight across India, ranging from 25 lbs to 85 lbs.)

India was rapidly approaching a period when it would become virtually self-sufficient in coal, and a great deal of coal from the Assam region would be destined for the future Assam–Bengal metre-gauge railway starting in Chittagong. En route to Assam from Chittagong, copious quantities of good steam coal were exploited from 1866 in and around the Sylhet area.

Welfare of the coalfields' managers and employees became of paramount importance. Conditions were far from ideal, and this aspect was not entirely overlooked by British superintendents in charge of operations. Houses were built and some ad hoc clinics with locally trained nurses were in attendance.

Most of the coal from Assam from around 1870 appears to have been destined for riverboat services, hauled to Patna and Calcutta to fuel the three railway companies operating steamers based in India's capital. In 1895, with the railways hauling tea and coal out of Assam and machinery and tourists into the district, the coal mines were working at virtually full capacity, producing an average of 180 000 tons annually. Although this coal was of a softer form and 'caked' easily when burnt, it benefited from having a very small amount of ash. 'It is equal to Welsh coal,' according to *The Engineer* of September 1895.

Later, Assam coal was in big demand to fuel jute mills, tea factories, local railways and ocean-going steamships. However, the introduction of small hydraulic-turbine-driven dynamos and a few oil engines coupled

to mechanical drives into Assam tea estates, gradually checked the rapid
growth of coal usage for non-railway and heavy industrial consumption.

The Warora Coalfield

While the Warora Coalfield in the Central Provinces was being developed,
Engineering in October 1873 reported:

> The total value of commerce in the Lower Provinces was £2,090,813,
> principally due to the policy of a free export trade. There was a compar-
> ative absence of machinery exports being 'only £310,000'. However, only
> 54,000 tons of coal and coke was imported [from Britain], pointing to the
> fact that the country is already commencing to rely upon her own fuel
> resources as new mines are being exploited.

In October 1873 some 400 tons of machinery were hauled from
Lancashire foundries to Birkenhead for the Suez voyage to Bombay. On arrival, it was transferred into wagons of the GIPR for the 30-mile journey to
Warora. There, it was offloaded and hauled in bullock carts to a new mine,
where one shaft had been sunk to a depth of 170 ft. The bullock carts – '60
yokes and 30 drivers to haul the first load comprising 100 tons', according
to a correspondent of *The Engineer* in November 1873 – 'dragged the machinery to site without damage'.

Work progressed at a feverish rate to exploit the Warora coalfield complex. Two modern winding engines from Bolton when placed in service
consumed up to 400 tons of coal daily. Then the shaft was sunk to 210 ft.
Two additional Bolton engines were installed the following year, rapidly
increasing the mine's output. A complete workshop was exported from
Manchester, to be operated by both English and native tradesmen. During
its first four years of operation, not one man was lost. Minor accidents occurred but a mine clinic kept casualties to a minimum.

Geologists were brought to Warora to examine the extent of the field's
seams. After a year's evaluation, in the report to the management, it was
conservatively stated as being about 1000 acres and to possess not less than
'20 million proven tons'. Nearby, the Bandur Coalfield, in full operation,
had proven 10 million tons of reserves, with the whole area assessed as
providing some 200 million tons. The GIPR was unquestionably delight-
ed with this news. For years the GIPR was unfortunate not to possess a
good, reliable local source of coal. It was initially hauled by sailing ship
from Wales and Newcastle around the Cape until Bengal fuel arrived in

sufficient quantities. It was merely a matter of time before the company connected a branch line to Warora from its mainline network.

It was to India's gain that the rapid spread of railways enabled the highly profitable EIR, with its rich Bengal coalfields, to connect up with lines constructed by the GIPR to haul 'black gold' to its transport neighbour based in Bombay. All coal wagons belonged to the GIPR.

In 1895 a government category of comparative coal efficiencies in equivalent British Thermal Heat Units revealed that Giridih best coal topped the list at 1.0; Barakar in Bengal was assessed at 0.9, while Warora was somewhat down the league.

Mhopani and Umaria mines

The two principal railway companies – GIPR and EIR – were fortunate to have their tracks running through main coalfields. In 1874 GIPR had 1872 miles in service, with 326 miles of that double-track. Having relied on a division of coal from both domestic and South Wales sources, the railway company ran a branch line 12 miles to the new Mhopani Mine, where over 1000 tons was extracted monthly. In 1889 the Umaria Coalfield was supplying GIPR locomotives, together with the Indian Midland Railway, which consumed 1600 tons monthly, and the BNR, taking at least double that quantity. All three companies paid Rs.5 8 annas per ton at the pithead.

Increasing demand and alternative fuel supplies

In 1888 the Indian railway network stood at 14 456 miles, with nearly 1200 miles sanctioned for construction. Geologists were busy seeking out additional coal mines as well as looking into alternative fuel sources. The proliferation of huge steam engines, especially in the cotton, textile and jute industries, consumed thousands of tons daily. All this power demanded increasing amounts of coal. The era of diesel internal-combustion technology was still some 15 years away.

Over the previous decade numerous new coalfields had been exploited as well as further seams worked from existing mines, especially throughout Bengal. The EIR could rely on its own mines alone in Bengal, and had a nice little earner in selling its coal to 13 other railway companies. Trial pits were exploiting the new Rampore coalfield. The Jherra Coalfield was on the verge of being connected with a branch line to the BNR, as original estimates of its potential were 'grossly underestimated'.

Coal was found the year before in the Kali Valley in Upper Burma in a seam 10 ft thick, which regrettably was found to dip at an angle of 45 degrees. It was Burma's vast oil wealth that claimed the attention of government, railway officials and geologists alike.

From the Warora Mine 113 073 tons were extracted in 1887, while the Umaria Colliery produced 25 548 tons in that same year. The Dandot Colliery was started in 1888, and special inclines with steam-winders were constructed to haul coal down to the main line at Kalapani Station. Three winding engines arrived from John & Edward Wood, of Bolton. A railway line was rushed to the Singareni Coalfield in 1890, where one mine was quickly commissioned into production and two additional shafts sunk by 1893.

The BNR also owned collieries. One, at Argada, adopted electric working as soon as coal was extracted. The colliery also purchased the latest machinery for driving dynamos and compressors, which was installed by 1905. In each case, all machinery was supplied by Belliss & Morcom.

While this activity was reaching its peak, a more concerted approach to extracting oil from Burma was gaining momentum. Scottish industrialists established the Burma oil industry in 1886 to exploit concessions negotiated in that country. Oil exploration machinery was arriving from Britain, Canada and America 'before Indian coal is exhausted'. Simultaneously, geologists were at work in India in the hope that their efforts would be well rewarded by oil finds.

There was hope of fuel oil for railway purposes in the petroleum-bearing area of Khatun. It was computed that any of the wells already sunk would supply enough oil for the Sind–Pishin section of the North-Western Railway. Boring tools were imported from Canada and attempts made that year to locate light oils for lubrication purposes. The oil when extracted at moderate depths was heavy, and there was some doubt that it would run freely through a pipeline. Geologists felt that an alternative proposal would be to construct a new branch line to Sibi from the main route – achieved later at a cost of a little over £250,000.

During the building of the Sind–Pishin Railway, petroleum was found in the Bolan Pass and a pipeline laid to supply the Khojak Works, whose oil-burning locomotives used an estimated 3 million gallons yearly. Coal began to lose its prestige in that area, which came under military restrictions when British Intelligence discovered threats of 'another invasion from Russia's Tsar'. During that period the first large shipments of Burmese oil arrived in Calcutta.

Arching a length inside Khojak tunnel, c.1880 (Courtesy of the British Library)

By 1925 India relied exclusively on Burmese oil for its petroleum requirements. In 1926/7, 138 million gallons were imported, reducing to 127 million gallons the following year 'due to a price war'. By 1935, 201 million gallons were imported – 183 million from Burma, the rest from the Middle East – mainly to fuel oil-burning locomotives and the large number of stationary engines, many from Stockport and Lincoln, 'that were cheaper to run, cleaner, and easier to maintain', according to *The Statesman*.

The Indian coal industry by Independence

In 1895 locomotives running throughout India consumed only 145 213 tons of British coal, but a staggering 1 116 481 tons of Indian coal and 311 512 tons of wood. Additionally, small quantities of coke and patent fuels were burnt. It was obvious that India's railway companies were gradually ridding themselves of English and Welsh coal. In that year, the railway network operated over 19 466 route miles. In 1900 the network had increased to 22 941 miles, with another 2300 miles on consultants' drawing boards.

The Nizam of Hyderabad was fortunate during the building of the huge Kistna Bridge, which when completed in 1893 enabled a through train service from Calcutta to Madras to be established. When Lord Wenlock, Governor of Madras, took the first train over the bridge on 17 March, it signalled the start of many coal trains from recently discovered coalfields within the Nizam's territory that would pass over the bridge to serve the metre-gauge Southern Mahratta Railway.

The Hyderabad Deccan Mining Company worked these coalfields, and its coal was distributed throughout the whole of southern India – an area devoid of any substantial workable deposits. Bolton-built steam engines once again played their part.

From 1895 to 1900 a phenomenal increase in coal output barely caught up with demand. Steam turbines had been introduced at the Bengal Borrea Coal Company. This, coupled with larger and more powerful locomotives – industrial horizontal-type steam engines exceeding 2000 hp for the new cotton mills that competed with Lancashire – and India's entry into the coal export markets – Malaya, Thailand and Ceylon – meant that the future for the industry looked decidedly prosperous.

The EIR worked collieries at Kurhurbaree and Serampore, drawing its entire supplies from them. It had the cheapest coal in India at a little over Rs.2 per ton at Giridih. The total output of these pits at the time exceeded 550000 tons. Two of the EIR collieries were so expansive that they were virtually one. Both fields comprised 25 mines, including the Jubilee, which was sunk to 650 ft – the deepest mine in the whole of India. These fields yielded 282000 tons of large coal and 109000 tons of small coal. In all, the EIR extracted over 2200000 tons from its collieries.

The Assam Railways & Trading Company worked four pits, producing some 205000 tons of soft and coking coal with a very small ash content. The Central Provinces extracted 160000 tons, the Punjab 70000 tons and the Nizam's territories 260000 tons – second only to the Bengal fields. The Indian government had taken over a number of collieries including Warora (six shafts producing 120000 tons) and Umaria (four mines producing some 130000 tons).

One of the largest mines in India was the expanded Singareni Colliery of the Hyderabad Company. Between the years 1893 and 1898 its output rose from 293000 tons to around 310000 tons. Two additional pits were sunk in 1899 which, with additional winding, hauling and screening machinery installed, enabled a further 1000 tons to be extracted daily.

The North-Western State railway could rely upon the Dandot Colliery, which, although only of small stature when compared with any of the Bengal 'giants', nevertheless raised over 50000 tons in 1901. The same railway operator also had at its disposal the diminutive Bhaganwala Mine, which extracted a mere 7000 tons per annum. The coal had to be hauled long distances on pack animals, which accounted for the mine's small production. Even so, the cost of hauling this coal to the North-Western State Railway over its railway counterpart's tracks would have been costly. In addition, two other mines, at Khost and Sharigh, produced coal to feed hungry locomotive boilers.

The Sind–Pishin Railway, with its line terminating about 100 yards from the Afghan border, found a new coal seam at Mach, which also served the line running through Bolan.

Both oil and coal were now consumed, with many locomotives capable of being dual-fuelled. In western India coal seams were actively exploited during the last decade of the 19th century. The Harnai Valley developed from 1895 and good steam coal was mined near Gundak, north of Quetta, in Baluchistan.

The government produced some statistics that occasionally made horrific reading. Despite all the safety measures installed, the safety of underground workers varied considerably. By far the worst record was at Sharigh. For every 3131 tons raised, one Indian paid with his life. At the other extreme, the Kurhurbaree Mine managed to extract 147500 tons before a fatality occurred. The weight of coal raised per employee varied from 7 tons at Bhangawala, Bengal, to 147 tons at Umaria, but the time for this feat was not given.

Most collieries employed up to 110 horses and ponies. A man would cut about 1.25 tons daily with the traditional English pick in an eight-hour shift. Five-day working was the norm in 1901. Whole families sweated in those satanic conditions, and a government report assessed that throughout all the Bengal coalfields an average family earned about Rs.18 per month. While British working conditions were exported to the tropics, India was a 'virtue of efficiency, safety and good housekeeping' under British colliery managers compared with conditions in Russia and China. The new Mining Rules promulgated in 1899 were augmented by the first known guidelines on child labour. The British Administration 'laid the law down about the minimum age and number of hours that a child could work', but parents flouted all regulations.

The GIPR was fortunate in having its patience further rewarded. Geologists found coal near the Nerbudda River at Mhopani and immediately sunk a shaft in about 1890. In 1902 the GIPR mined 90 000 tons from the Warora Mine at Rs.4.8 annas per ton until the new Nerbudda Coal & Iron Company, having begun operations in 1894, produced 83 000 tons at approximately Rs.4.5 per ton. In 1908 nearly 96 000 tons were mined. Several new coalfields were also opened, with GIPR being the principal customer. Once again, the Lancashire steam-engine foundries were favoured for additional mining machinery.

The number of coalmining concessions granted under the new Mining Rules rose from 60 in that year to no fewer than 400 in the first nine months of 1907. Those concessions were in addition to the concessions granted to the Indian (Native) States and in the permanently settled zamindars (landowners) districts. In some parts of India mineral rights were included with surface rights by the terms of the settlement, but elsewhere the government possessed all mineral rights and granted concessions for mineral exploitations in accordance with the Mining Rules as laid down in 1899.

Many British firms rushed to gain contracts to serve collieries engaged in opencast workings. One firm from Lincoln, Ruston & Hornsby, established in 1857, was fortunate in having a branch factory in India manufacturing small pumps and horizontal engines. Diversifying into large steam-engine-powered excavators at the turn of the century, the firm designed and built possibly the most powerful excavators for Indian mines in 1901.

In 1907 the combined coal output as supplied for railway usage was estimated at 2447 341 tons. Most was delivered from Bengal with steam-powered winders and a few turbines, by now much in vogue. The Erith, Kent, firm of Fraser & Chalmers was rapidly gaining a good reputation for its early turbine products, although the lack of expertise in India checked what could have been a monopoly market for its technologically well-advanced prime movers.

In the coal industry right up until Independence, huge winding engines were regularly commissioned with all machines imported from Britain. Perhaps one of the largest to be placed into service upon the outbreak of World War I was a pair from Sandycroft Foundry near Chester. In 1910, with railway growth exceeding 32 000 route-miles, the network consumed over 3 million tons of coal. Steam turbines, horizontal engines and steamships accounted for another 1.3 million tons.

Coal exports

The railways consumed over a third of all coal produced. Imports of foreign, mainly Welsh, coal into Calcutta – which was the chief distribution port, with most of its mechanical handling equipment from Stothert & Pitt of Bath – dwindled to a mere 2000 tons in 1901. Exports of Indian coal were a modest eight tons in 1880, 26000 tons in 1890 and 250000 tons in 1897, rising to more than 500000 tons in 1901. In Bombay, Welsh coal competed favourably with Indian up to 1902 as regards price, although the latter could be bought in Calcutta for Rs.7 per ton. However, steamer freight costs and other charges raised the price to Rs.15 per ton. Indian coal was exported through Suez to the west and Singapore to the east, where it competed with supplies from Japan.

Indian coal had a virtual monopoly in the construction of the Uganda Railway from 1895 to 1901. Huge amounts of coal were shipped out in specially converted BISNC vessels for offloading at Kilindini Docks, Mombasa. Interestingly, in 1951 the SS *Verala* discharged 2744 tons of Bengal coal loaded at Calcutta into South Wales. It was the first known shipment of coal from India to Britain. Britain's coal exports to India by 1910 were for all practical purposes nil.

Diesel-generated power

By the time the Prince of Wales (later King Edward VIII) inspected part of India's infrastructure in 1927, steam-driven mechanical drives were gradually being displaced by diesel-electric propulsion. The prince inspected digging machinery for the new irrigation canals in Madras, which were provided by Ruston of Lincoln and consisted of oil-electric drag lines each with a 250 hp engine driving a British Thomson-Houston Company 240-volt series-wound motor, the controls being of the automatic contactor type. These machines were cheaper to run and did not require coalbunkers, and the fuel consumed was governed by the power output. As technology improved, so did the size of the machinery. Opencast coal mines and especially limestone quarries were ideally suited to diesel-generated power.

Engineering and mining education

The British were quick to appreciate that no industry could survive on sound lines unless trained and experienced technical personnel were continually available to service it. Although the Indian mining industry progressed rapidly from 1900 to 1920, the availability of trained personnel was unsatisfactory. There was then no college or institution in India solely devoted to training these engineers. In 1901 the Indian National Congress advocated a Government College of Mining Engineering strictly along British lines, after the model of the Royal School of Mines in England. A school was established in Dhanbad, which performed excellent work in its pioneering role. Other schools surfaced mainly in the mining areas of Asansol, Assam, Nerbudda, Sylhet and Calcutta. However, it was not until 1927 that the Benares Hindu University started courses in mining and metallurgy to the equivalent of British degree standard. At first, British tutors were hired to impart their learning to an eager audience of young Indian hopefuls.

Mining colleges of all descriptions sprang up, until by 1936 classes in aluminium, manganese, copper smelting and coal were freely admitting Indian students into the faculties. By the outbreak of World War II India was self-sufficient in training her own people to tackle mining duties, even though the lecturers were still principally imported from Britain.

The power requirements for Indian mines increased the demand for diversity in engineering courses, where steam mechanics went hand in hand with the recognition that electricity was the engineering subject of the future.

Chapter 14

ELECTRICITY GENERATION

Better the steam engine devil you know
rather than the complicated turbine monster you don't.
SAYING IN BENGAL AT THE TIME OF TURBINE
INTRODUCTION FROM PARSONS OF NEWCASTLE, c.1895

In India as elsewhere in the world, acetylene gas and oil were employed to light public roads and houses before the advent of electricity. When a Mr A.J. Kennedy, of the London-based *Gas World* journal, travelled through India, he documented his findings from many cities that he studied in depth. He wrote:

> Very remarkable from this point of view is Madras, the oldest city in India. For lighting purposes, the municipality levy a rate that brings in £4,500 per annum – very small indeed – for an area covering 27 sq. miles. All the artificial lighting is done by means of oil lamps, of which some 6000 are in use. The lamps, with their 1.25 in. wicks, are fixed in square lanterns of ancient design on the top of iron posts, also of an old pattern. In the less important thoroughfares the lamps are about 150 yards apart. In the important thoroughfares the distance between each lamp is less, being more numerous at road junctions. What I have said about Madras applies also to other cities that I have visited. However, from Tuticorin in the extreme south, to Cashmere in the far north, there is not a single town or city that is really well lighted (by gas or oil). Bombay and Calcutta are the best-lighted cities in India and both with room for improvement. Delhi is wretchedly lit by oil. Jeypore, situated 200 miles south-south-west of Delhi, is one of the most beautiful and interesting cities in one of the largest and most important Rajpur States. The city is laid out with much regularity and is, in fact, the best planned city in India. I was rather surprised to find a gasworks, which was erected in 1878 by order of His Highness Maharaja

Sawai Ram Singh, costing Rs.210,205. It has since been expanded and now occupies a site of about four acres. An Englishman, John Dominy, runs the gasworks and the waterworks as well as three cotton presses. He is 55 years old, hale and hearty, having been in India for 22 years and managing the gas works for 11 years. The gas is made from kerosene of the cheapest kind imported from America. It was found that Russian oil would not suit the purpose. The oil arrives in tin cases containing 65 lbs or eight American gallons. The gas is conveyed from the retorts to the two gas holders each 45 ft diameter. These feed the street lighting of which there are 729 lamps with glazed lanterns, each containing a batswing burner. The lamps are from 80 ft to 100 ft apart with the city itself well illuminated. The cost is borne by the Maharajah, who also supplies the inhabitants with water free of charge from hydrants. Those fortunate enough to have water laid on pay a water rate. The Maharaja's palace is lit by oil gas, as are also the houses of the nobles. Nearly all the shops and private houses use oil. The cost of making the gas is Rs.7 8 annas per 1000 cubic ft including one rupee on each case of oil imported. The state has to pay duty on everything imported, which amounts to 4%. Inside and outside the gasworks there are about 70 hands employed, the stokers earning about 2s. per week and lighters about 1s. 8d. per week. Common labourers earn between 2d. and 2½d. per day.

When coal gas engines, invented in Germany by Nicklaus Otto (1832–1891) in 1867, came into vogue at the end of the 19th century, India was quick to grasp the benefits of oil-engine-driven dynamos. Lighthouses switched over to the new technology and Bengal jute mills reduced their reliance on steam. Bombay Municipality opted for Hornsby's engine, and the firm was particularly noted for the contract of illuminating the Taj Mahal in about 1902.

The first time electricity was used in India was during the construction of the Punjab Northern State Railways' Empress Bridge from December 1875 onwards. The small Siemens of Woolwich dynamo, which allowed round-the-clock working, was introduced during the winter of 1876 with considerable success, enabling the workmen to continue their activities well into the night. The dynamo was then transferred onto the next bridge constructed for a Punjab Northern State Railway contract.

In 1880 a bridge lit by electric light was built in Bombay, and several Burmese rice mills were lit by electricity in that same year. Sir Richard Temple, then engaged in constructing a bridge across the Jhelum on the Kandahar line, employed the fledgling Indian Electric Light Company to provide night-time illumination to advance progress on a contract 'of dire military consequences'.

Lighting

On 20 July 1879, an Englishman, Mr Flurry, demonstrated the benefits of an electric bulb to a select audience in Calcutta. The technology used by Flurry was simple. A dynamo driven by a small steam engine generated electricity and the illumination it gave dazzled everybody in attendance. This new invention was urgently required to replace inefficient oil lamps, which then illuminated the streets of Calcutta. However, the cost proved prohibitive.

At the same time as Flurry's trial-and-error experiments, a report on electric light experiments for Howrah, published in 1877-8, was implemented on 31 May 1880, with the embryonic lighting of Howrah's goods shed. A steam engine drove four dynamo-electric machines that powered four carbon-arc lamps on the two platforms near the cargo shed for two hours. This pioneering event was carried out on the EIR's premises by Louis Schwendler (1838–1882), later Director General of Government Telegraphs in India and formerly of Siemens. It registered favourably with EIR's engineers and management. The main fuel used for illumination then was coal gas, although this was potentially dangerous even at the best of times.

The four lighting reflectors used in a second experiment were of zinc lined with silver glass, with a wire gauze screen to intercept any burning particles of carbon that may have fallen from the light filaments. Three Siemens dynamos and two Gramme machines were used, driven by the same steam engine rated at 25 hp. Calculations revealed that the lighting gave at its most brilliant 'about 9000 candles with a consumption of 12.5 hp'. Later, the current from the generation package was conveyed over 4 miles of cable to supply the premises of the Calcutta Telegraph Office.

The Electrician of 16 April 1881, stated quite boldly: 'Adoption of electric lighting of railways in that country [India] is perfectly practical, and might be attended by considerable saving.'

The success at Howrah motivated both municipalities and industry in India to make a rapid transition to electricity. In September 1881, Muir Cotton Mills in Cawnpore replaced all its gas lighting with electricity, reporting that 'output has all but doubled'.

In May 1882, Queen Victoria's birthday was celebrated in grand style in India, and nowhere more so than at Indore and Mhow. With many nobles and military and state dignitaries in attendance, electric lighting from Bombay and dynamos from the newly established Eastern Electric Light & Power Company illuminated the lawns and gardens along the riverbanks. Two months later, 16 Brush of Loughborough lamps, supplied by the same power company, lit the whole of Bombay's Princes Dock. It was a two-month trial scheme that 'simply continued'.

The firm of Dey, Sil & Company, of Wellington Square, Bombay, started a business of renting out dynamos in 1885, and was a pioneer of sorts in this field. It was responsible for providing electric lights for a dinner hosted on 20 December 1886, in honour of the delegates to the Calcutta Session of the Indian National Congress. The Maharaja of Bikaner, in Rajasthan, started using a steam-driven dynamo for his palace as early as 1886. This was possibly the only instance in those days where electricity was generated by such an expensive method for day-to-day use.

In 1899 Bombay Municipality installed electric lighting 'throughout the principal streets and where people congregate'. In that same year Calcutta decided to 'dispense with punkah-wallahs and used electric fans as well as to illuminate St Paul's Cathedral'.

Electrical lighting technology was applied early to the Prongs Lighthouse built at the entrance to Bombay Harbour. The harbour authorities decided in 1898 to adopt electric lighting for use with the Chance optical apparatus, considerably increasing the range of light at mean sea level to 16 miles, or 23 miles from the optical equipment itself. An unqualified success, it was still in service after World War II.

Hydroelectric power: Darjeeling and Nilgiri

The first hydroelectric power plant in Darjeeling was opened in 1887 at Sidrabong, established by the Darjeeling Municipality. Following further UK success with its hydraulic machines, work started in 1895 on a hydro plant near Sidrabong, and Gunther & Sons placed a bid for the prime movers. Work at Sidrabong was somewhat delayed by a lack of technical details on the rivers and streams in and around Darjeeling. Also there was no decent road by which machines or construction equipment could get to the site. The town of Darjeeling commissioned Gunther in that same year for two Girard turbines to be supplied from a waterfall of 270 ft. The turbines were directly coupled to two Crompton of Chelmsford single-phase alternators generating 2300 volts.

The power plant was an instant success, but electricity generation was still very much a hit-and-miss affair and the demand on both generators soon dragged down the voltage to a level where the carbon-filament bulbs refused to glow. Small units driven by petrol were installed privately, but that approach failed to overcome the problem. In 1906 the Darjeeling town fathers again contracted Gunther & Sons to extend the power station through an additional machine coupled to a single-phase generator constructed by the General Electric Company (GEC) of Witton, Birmingham, the turbine also of the Girard type.

When the Nilgiri region was opened for tea-growing (Chapter 17), tea planters flocked to the area and brought their lifestyles and technical progress with them. A rack railway was introduced in 1899. The area abounded with running water, so not unnaturally engineers assessed the region as favourable for hydropower. In March 1905 the government installed six hydraulic turbines from Gunther & Sons. Using a 600 ft head of water from the Kartari Falls, power was transmitted to the Wellington Cordite Factory as well as to local consumers for lighting only. The powerhouse was constructed of local stone with a hand-driven overhead crane rated at 5 tons that ran the full length of the building. Insulators were of porcelain from the Potteries area of England. GEC's Witton, Birmingham, electrical factory supplied all alternators.

In late 1906 the government commissioned the firm for a large machine that could be installed in the same building as the original small units. Both turbines were fed by a penstock from a fall of 630 ft. The following year a hydraulic machine was installed at Aruvan Kadu, near the Nilgiris, to meet the rapidly growing demand. Gunther used the latest technology, employing phosphor bronze – developed by Britain's maritime industry – and steel alloys along with self-oiling bearings. Governing control was by a direct-acting chain gear rather than the customary belt drive. The turbine was directly coupled to a three-phase GEC alternator. When in service, both turbine and alternator were found to provide a continuous 10% increase in output without any appreciable increase in winding temperatures.

The success of that installation received glowing praise from the technical press of the day. *The Engineer,* consistently championing British industry, boldly stated in its 8 February 1907 issue: 'We have been informed by our correspondent that the most satisfactory results have been obtained. This is one of the most powerful turbines made up to the present time by any British firm of hydraulic engineers.'

Unlike the railways and the textile, mining and shipping industries, the first power station in India was developed in the public sector under state patronage.

Ever-increasing demand and innovation

The success of Darjeeling and Sidrabong created a sensation all around: it was widely reported in all the leading newspapers. Princely states in different parts of the country as well as the Government of India felt impelled to replicate the example demonstrated by Darjeeling and Sidrabong. The Maharaja of Mysore set up the Shivasamudram Hydro Plant in 1912, using water from the Cauvery River to supply Mysore City as well as the Kolar Gold Mines. A plant of capacity similar to that at Aruvan Kadu was installed in a large tea estate in Travancore State in 1906. Two years later electricity came to Srinagar in the Kashmir Valley on the Jhelum River. It was the largest installed power plant to date. Other hill stations with nearly year-round water flows were Mussorie (1901) and Simla (1913).

The Tata Hydro-Electric Supply Company (see below) brought electricity into Bombay to service the huge demand for power at a time when the central cotton mill steam engine was facing gradual retirement. Delhi (1908) and Madras (1909) were forced to rely upon thermal power generation, as transmitting power over long lines was not then economical for the small loads required. Calcutta had a distinct lead in the new electrical technology, with growing public consumption as well as its tramway. In 1899 two generators driven by conventional steam engines illuminated the city's boulevards from its Imambagh Thermal Plant.

The first steam-turbine-driven alternators to be installed came from Parsons of Newcastle in 1895. The Borrea Coal Company, of Bengal, purchased two sets. That order was followed by a similar-sized turbo-alternator for a jute mill in Calcutta.

Calcutta Electric Supply (CES)

After Darjeeling, Calcutta was one of the first municipalities to establish an organised electricity service. In 1897 the Calcutta Electric Supply Company (CES) was formed. The machines were steam engines from Belliss & Morcom, and later Willans & Robinson of Rugby, all driving dynamos supplied by Crompton and Dick, Kerr. The company was formed with local enterprise, and Colonel Crompton, who acted in the main as consultant – with an eye on supplying the utility from his Chelmsford works – secured the first large base-load generators to be installed in the utility's new central power station. With their installation, the cost of generation was reduced to 0.7d. per kilowatt-hour. So successful were these dynamos that CES engineers decided to increase the output of the new station. By 1914 CES had become India's largest city-based utility.

From 1911 the load grew far quicker than consultants had estimated. The need for bigger and faster clearance of fault levels was catered for by British Thomson-Houston Company, of Rugby, in a new range of combined AC and DC switchboards, installed at the new Howrah North Substation to provide feeds for EIR motors. By 1930 CES had received five new English Electric turbo-alternators at its new Mulajore Power Station, then the largest power plant in Bengal.

The huge demand for electricity from the utility service providers, railways, mines, industries and middle-class households in cities and towns spurred a boom in the power equipment industry. A host of small engineering companies soon joined the bandwagon to compete for the new electrical technology. One such company was Chippenham-based Peter Brotherhood, among whose earliest export orders in 1883 was one to an unknown customer in Calcutta. Another was Willans & Robinson, who have not survived for posterity. Research into the company by Dr Allen, of Droitwich, reveals that between 1888 and 1914, 1253 engines were produced for electrical power generation, stationary, traction and marine drives in 25 countries throughout the world. It would be fair to state that some 25% of all that output would have seen service in India.

Yet another firm was Scott & Mountain, which supplied India with a large number of locomotives. The company's range of electric fans caught the eye of expatriates in India. The market was buoyant for this product, and the only impediment to a massive sales drive was the limited amount of power available from municipal power plants. The jute industry turned to the firm with various contracts for dynamos and motors as well as complete lighting installations powered by steam-engine-driven dynamos for 'one of the largest jute mills in Calcutta' – the name is not recorded. The mining industry in Asansol took delivery of various Scott & Mountain pumps that provided reliable service well into the 1930s. In Bombay's Nehru Museum lie the remains of scrapped motors. One such relic is very similar to a Scott & Mountain product manufactured around 1914.

Hydroelectricity turbine suppliers

While British government ministers viewed the Raj as solely a British domain and a captive market for British industry, contracts placed from the fourth quarter of the 19th century show that they could not keep competition out. This was more so when a capital plant was selected by the Indian government or by private industry, especially the emerging utilities. The entrepreneurial Swiss firm of Escher-Wyss, founded in 1805, was an early supplier of hydraulic turbines to India. The firm had penetrated Britain's captive market in 1866 when it supplied ten locomotives to the EIR at a time of industrial strife throughout the engine-building industry in Britain.

From the 1880s, Escher-Wyss supplied water-powered turbines to drive various cotton mills, and in 1909 its first Pelton wheel order for a power plant; some 84 Francis turbines were supplied from 1911, and 69 Kaplan and Axial turbines. In 1928 Escher-Wyss was contracted, along with the resources of Metropolitan-Vickers and British Thomson-Houston, to build the Pykara Hydro-Electric Development Project in the province of Madras.

Gilbert Gilkes & Gordon's hydraulic turbines

The demand for small hydraulic turbines to power both mechanical drives and dynamos in Indian industry grew phenomenally. This growth in demand from private power generators can be attributed to India's geography and the distances involved in constructing a reliable and affordable transmission and distribution network. For example, the CES before 1914 had barely designed a distribution system that extended beyond the city's environs. Gilbert Gilkes and Gordon, a British company based in Kendal, in the Lake District, came along at the right time with a proven product.

Its first order to the Raj in 1900 was for His Majesty's Government – possibly through the Crown Agents – for a Girard-type wheel of a mere 12 bhp. The site of installation is not recorded. During the next decade only private industry was served, with its first contract to a utility in 1915 for a Pelton-type wheel driving a British Westinghouse generator for Darjeeling Municipality.

By then many cotton mills, tea estates and a flourmill in Cawnpore were relying upon Gilbert Gilkes and Gordon's quality hydraulic turbines. The next decade was very much the same. Only larger machines found favour with utilities, the biggest turbine being supplied through Wardle Engineering for Jammu. Tea estates were quick to adopt hydraulic turbines.

A typical unit was supplied to a Mr Forbes of the Pashok Tea Estate in 1923. Capable of custom manufacturing its products to any order, the firm in the following year noted supplying perhaps its smallest unit ever to Machagong Engineering Company.

In 1945 Gilbert Gilkes and Gordon delivered its largest hydraulic turbine yet to an unknown Calcutta customer. A Major H.M. Banon, residing in the Punjab, purchased a Virgo Impulse turbine. By then, Gilbert Gilkes and Gordon had manufactured 5024 machines.

Hydroelectric plants were rapidly gaining acceptance, especially in northern and southern India. In Shillong a scheme to deliver cheap electrical power was backed by the British government. After tendering, Gilbert Gilkes and Gordon was selected to design and build its largest hydraulic turbine to date, which went into service in 1959. But an even bigger hydraulic turbine was built by the firm for India in 1994. That year, three Pelton wheels were also delivered to the Eastern Overseas Corporation for Likim Ro – the fifth of seven orders to the same customer.

Rapid progress from 1900

The first large hydroelectric scheme was a joint venture with the United States, which in the 1900s was the world leader in hydraulic turbines, high-voltage transmission and the building of huge dams. Not unnaturally, for the Cauvery Dam project the Government of Mysore turned its attention to America and Switzerland, rather than to Britain, for empirically proven experience in the building of dams and high-voltage networks.

In July 1900 a contract was entered into with General Electric, of New York, for all electrical plant; with Escher-Wyss, of Zurich, for the hydraulic turbines; and with Ingersoll & Sergeant for all electrically driven compressors. The Glasgow fabricator Mechan & Company was subcontracted for the complete penstocks portion of the work, duly dispatching two engineers to oversee erection.

Power was required for the Kolar Goldfields, some 92 miles away, and it was assessed that the transmission voltage should be 33kV. The goldfield had then placed orders for 6000kW of generation equipment from a scheme initiated by Diwan Sir Seshadri Iyer and carried out by Colonel Joly de Lotbinière, with all machines in service by 1902.

The six horizontal-shaft turbines of 80% guaranteed efficiency were built in Zurich in less than a year. The transportation of heavy plant to site brought out the ingenuity that characterised British engineers. The nearest railway station was 30 miles from the headworks. Transporting the heaviest items that could not be hauled by traction engines presented initial problems for the American engineers. Some loads weighed up to 14 tons. Eventually, a combination of elephants and bullocks was found to be the most satisfactory means of hauling plant. Ascending the hills, the bullocks pulled in front while two elephants pushed from behind.

In 1906 a hydroelectric plant was planned for Kashmir to harness the Jhelum River and export current for 200 miles of electric railway linking Abbottabad with Srinagar. The generating capacity allowed sufficient reserve to power a large fleet of dredgers, which were to be used in safeguarding Kashmir against the disastrous annual floods as well as reclaiming valuable rice-producing land from the marshes. The power plant's distribution scheme showed provision for an electric tramway, mills, silk factories, a foundry, mines and workshops. The power supplier raised £2 million in London.

The use of heavy monsoon rainfall in the Western Ghats for power generation was one of Jamsetji Tata's principal projects, though he did not live to see his favourite achievements placed into service. In 1907 Tata's sons obtained a concession and licence for the supply of 30 000hp (22 000kW) of electricity to Bombay. The Tata Hydro-Electric Supply Company was founded specifically for this project with Rs.1.75 crores to work the agreed licence. Three huge dams were built at Lonavla, Walwhan and Shirawta, plus a hydroelectric power station above the Bhore Ghat. The idea was to catch this water and from Lonavla generate power to feed Bombay, principally for the textile industry. Even before these works were completed, Tata received applications for the supply of power to most of the cotton mills, enabling the company to dispose of all the power it could generate.

By 1910 Bombay had expanded not only to challenge Calcutta industrially, but also to become the country's principal centre for textiles. Steam-engine-driven dynamos had secured a firm foothold over steam engine prime movers when used for small mechanical drives, but were rapidly assessed as being insufficient to cater for the enlargement of the 'British factory system' then gripping Bombay. The city's flourishing textile industry in 1913 comprised 83 cotton mills with in excess of 50 000 looms and 3 million spindles and was still expanding. In that year, coal cost approximately £1 per ton delivered to Bombay and the demand for electrical power was deemed of paramount importance.

R.E.B. CROMPTON'S (1845–1940) CONTRIBUTION

CROMPTON'S FAME IN TRANSFORMING India was sealed with his steam-road locomotives of the early 1870s (described earlier in Chapter 7), but the advent of early steam-driven electrical dynamos steered him away from road transport to found a purpose-built factory to produce electrical machines and lighting, albeit with dynamo technology initially imported from France. Having returned from India, in 1878 he founded the firm of Crompton & Company in Chelmsford. It was the dawn of the electrical supply industry.

In 1879 Crompton exhibited his first portable electric lighting set driven by a Marshall of Gainsborough traction engine at the Royal Agricultural Show at Kilburn. He also demonstrated the first arc lamp of his own manufacture. It was an unqualified success, and it was only a matter of time before this combination was exported to India.

Crompton went to India shortly after producing his first series of dynamos. His first installations were at Karachi, and included a supply of direct current to the docks around 1879. Later, in about 1900, a hydroelectric station was installed in Darjeeling at an altitude of 7000 ft. Other important cities such as Calcutta, Madras, Cawnpore and Allahabad ensured that Crompton became a household name throughout India.

In 1899 Crompton left England for Marseilles to join the SS *Arabic*, bound for Bombay. He was to set up shop in Calcutta. While the factory was being constructed, he travelled to Darjeeling to advise on extending the electric lines he had previously constructed, and also made a visit to Shimla to design a lighting scheme for the town.

Little difficulty was encountered in obtaining finance for these projects. There was capital from the rising Indian merchant class, which had complete confidence in Crompton and his products as well as in his engineering skills and integrity.

Crompton established an agent, Messrs Kilburn, to further his business in Calcutta. On his return to London, Brown, Boveri & Company was successful in tendering for Indian installations to combine its Swiss-made turbines with Crompton's alternators, as alternating current was now superseding dynamo generation.

Today, Crompton's company is still a leading power equipment supplier in India.

A huge powerhouse was built at Khopoli, some 43 miles from Bombay, with turbines from the Zurich factory of Escher-Wyss. Four turbines were each directly coupled to American General Electric generators. Two stand-by Willans of Rugby diesel generators were coupled to Siemens alternators for emergency service.

The success of Khopoli quickly outgrew itself, and by 1919 the Andhra Valley Power Company, in collaboration with Tata, was planned at an esti-mated cost of Rs.2.1 crores. Thus another 90 000kW was added to the sys-tem. Stafford's English Electric Company, established in 1904, supplied all five generators with switchgear from British Thomson-Houston, founded in around 1885. Even that increase in capacity was, by 1924, rapidly becoming insufficient to meet Bombay's insatiable demand for power, mainly for the textile industry. Two years later, with electric traction actively pursued for the GIPR's Bombay to Poona service, it was obvious that this requirement could not be drawn from the existing services.

A new power plant was construct-ed at Kalyan comprising four Parsons steam turbines. Metropolitan-Vickers of Manchester, and English Electric provided transformers and switch-gear respectively, with boilers and the coal-handling plant from Babcock & Wilcox, of Glasgow. Kalyan was lo-cated 33 miles from Bombay but had to deliver power to Poona 86 miles away. By providing a separate power plant for railway traction, the load to Bombay's industrial and domestic consumers was secure and free from the severe fluctuations associated with delivering traction requirements.

Transmission line construction, Punjab, c.1920s. Messrs Kennedy and Donkin are noted as the Consulting Engineers (Courtesy of the Institution of Engineering and Technology Archives)

In 1919–20, the great Indian entrepreneurial family Tata founded a third company, Tata Power, to undertake the so-called 'Nila-Mula' scheme, with capitalisation of Rs.9 crores. The project was completed in 1927 with an installed capacity of 185 000kW. Tata was a major provider of electricity and controlled virtually all central station power generated and transmitted to Bombay by 1930. The firm supplied not only the cotton mill and engineering industry but most current consumed by Bombay's tramway and the new suburban lines operating at 1500 volts DC.

In Mysore, in addition to the Cauvery River project, two new ventures – Shimsha and Jog Falls – were quickly sanctioned. Planned on a grandiose scale, the transmission system was designed to carry power to supply 350 towns and villages, thereby raising Mysore's capacity to 67 000kW. In Kashmir, the Jhelum River was, from 1925, used to generate power and feed both Srinagar and Baramulla. Installed at Kashmir Durbar, the hydrostation gradually developed to reach an installed capacity of 16 000kW, which was used extensively to illuminate the town as well as powering a nearby silk factory. Electricity was here to stay.

Siemens-Schuckert of Berlin

Germany's electrical industry was not slow in exploiting the British Empire. Werner Siemens had perfected the dynamo machine in 1866, and the Germans lost no time in transferring their prime movers from steam engines to turbines – and very shortly afterwards, diesel engines – with Siemens-Schuckert at the forefront of this transition. The firm's introduction to India was a project in Khopoli in 1912, but little is known about this as the company lost its archives after 1945.

The Lahore Electric Supply Company acquired a licence to supply electric current to the city of Lahore in 1912. The original plant consisted of a non-condensing steam-engine-driven dynamo system from Belliss & Morcom. As the load increased, similar sets were added. In 1924 tenders were invited for a complete new station on a site to be constructed some 4 miles outside Lahore. The Berlin firm, despite intense competition, won the contract for a new coal-fired boiler house. German Babcock & Wilcox supplied the steam generator. A single impulse-type turbine from Escher-Wyss drove a Siemens-Schuckert generator. The whole power plant was accepted after extensive testing in January, 1927. Siemens-Schuckert again competed favourably against British manufacturers when the firm supplied electrical equipment to the South Indian Railway, Madras, in 1930–1.

General Electric Company (GEC) England

GEC was established in 1886 in London as the General Electric Apparatus Company. Its first lamp bulbs were produced seven years later. In 1903, the firm changed its name to the General Electric Company so as to avoid confusion with General Electric of America – there was never any corporate tie between the two firms. In that year, in Calcutta, it established its presence in India. It was one of the first British electrical companies to reside permanently in India, ostensibly to create business for its Manchester and newly built Witton, Birmingham, works to undertake small repairs to machines and switches in India (mainly Calcutta) as well as to sell its range of bulbs.

GEC styled its offices after the Magnet House names it gave its sales outlets in England. By 1918, with business buoyant, a huge new head office was built in Calcutta and regional offices were established in Madras, Bombay, New Delhi, Karachi, Lahore, Cawnpore, Bangalore, Trivandrum, Coimbatore and Hyderabad (Deccan). The firm's engineers descended upon the coal-mining industry – an industry riddled with fatal accidents despite strong government legislation on safely procedures – successfully persuading many mine owners to rid themselves of steam winders in favour of the new machines coming out of Witton.

In 1935 GEC won a tender to electrify the Calcutta factory for Carreras Tobacco Company. An entire new plant incorporating high-tension switchgear, transformers, motors and the new GEC Osram lighting was installed, and 12 new cigarette machines were capable of turning out 6 million cigarettes daily.

GEC, along with many large plant manufacturers from Britain engaged in power production, supplied complete generating plants and substations to the state electricity authorities from the 1930s. The firm was one of the first to supply base-load generators rated in excess of 50MW. The largest turbo-alternators GEC delivered to India were in the late 1980s to Lake Rihand, with the remaining equipment, including transformers and switchgear, from Northern Electrical Industries, of Newcastle.

Railway electrification

The first railway to be electrified was not in Bombay, as most publications on Indian railways have suggested, but in the little-known Mysore Kolar Goldfields, in Mysore State. It imported two electric locomotives from Bagnall of Stafford, with overhead electrical equipment from Siemens of

Berlin, Germany. Electric battery-operated road vehicles – trolleys – were brought into use and operated by the EIR, ORR and EBSR about the same time, 1912.

Until 1914, with an abundance of coal and water – plus the ability to train local people with the mechanical skills required to keep more than 100 000 steam locomotives fully operational – India saw no need to adopt electric traction in a big way. In 1923, British Thomson-Houston designed a special range of robust traction motors from its Rugby factory. These were installed in trolleybuses for Wolverhampton and found to be 'highly suitable'. A larger version was developed that was to earn the company much credit. Then BBCIR embarked upon changing its suburban network out of Churchgate Station from steam to electric traction. British Thomson-Houston's motors were upgraded for heavy main-line traction use.

The GIPR in 1922 opted to electrify the line from Bombay to Poona, a distance of 192 miles, initially as a trial run. If successful, it was to serve as a model for the rest of the country. The complete electrification of the two railways was undertaken between 1927 and 1929. This programme had become a key local issue. Bombay's population had swollen, mainly as a result of the success of its British-installed industry. Even when steam traction was actually quadrupled from the early 1920s, the trains were still crammed to capacity – as they are today, despite the frequency of service under electric traction. The work of converting GIPR rolling stock from steam to electric traction was begun in May 1922, continuing until February 1925, when the Bombay Harbour section was opened for traffic under the new traction system. A few months afterwards, electric operation was extended to Kalyan, some 33 miles from Bombay. There, the main line via Igatpuri, approximately 52 miles away, and a spur to Poona, 86 miles further on, diverge. On 5 November 1929, the Governor of Bombay opened the Kalyan-to-Poona section. Initially, current was taken from the Tata Hydro-Electric Group, but for the extensions a new steam-turbine power station was built by the GIPR at Kalyan.

The electrification programme involved an interesting experiment in the transport of fully erected rolling stock from England to India. Previously, coaches from British suppliers had been built at the works, and then dismantled for packing and shipping – a procedure that was not only time-consuming but very costly. For the new rolling stock to both electrified railways in Bombay, it was decided to have the coaches fully put together in England and to ship them complete to India in a specially chartered boat.

Unloading coaches for the opening of the electrified train service on the Bombay suburban section (Courtesy of the Institution of Engineering and Technology Archives)

However, at 12 ft the extra-wide coaches appeared impossible to transport from the manufacturers, Cammell Laird of Nottingham, to Hull. They were eventually transported on special bogies from the works alongside the River Trent where, from a wharf built for the purpose, they were transferred onto flat-bottomed barges to Hull.

Meanwhile, the coach bogies, electrical fittings and miscellaneous parts were crated and sent on the same vessel to Bombay. At Bombay the bogies were unpacked and placed on the track at the quayside. The coaches were then swung from the ship direct onto their bogies and conveyed by steam train to the workshops to be assembled for service. The electrical equipment, including switchgear, was already fitted and tested, and the main motor cables already run to the bogies as 'flying leads' that only required terminating. In all, the whole operation, planned 'like clockwork precision', was achieved with few problems.

Both railways when electrified installed a local service running every ten minutes during peak periods. British Thomson-Houston and Metropolitan-Vickers were subsequently favoured for a large base-load generating plant.

Enter the diesel engine

When Rudolf Diesel (1858–1913) invented the diesel internal-combustion engine, and the German company Maschinenfabrik Augsburg-Nürnberg (MAN) started manufacturing reciprocating diesel engines, Indian industry was again quick to adopt the new technology. MAN sold its first diesel engine to the Central India Spinning & Weaving Company, at Nagpur, in 1902. A year later, the Himalayan Glassworks at Rajpur installed a small unit. Then two larger diesels were ordered by the Calcutta Tramway in 1908 for driving dynamos.

Before the outbreak of World War I, Ceylon Tramway purchased the firm's largest sale to the Indian subcontinent. The firm then sold nothing to India for over ten years before being contracted through its Winterthur agent. During the next two years, MAN sold 15 diesel engines, all to utilities. In 1932 MAN sold its largest engine yet to India, to the Trichinopoly Electric Supply Company. In 1933 and 1934 the firm sold mainly small-capacity machines, principally to utilities and private industry powerhouses, until in late 1934 the Jaipur Central Power Station purchased a huge unit. A sister unit was sold to the same customer in 1937.

When Hitler assumed power, he actively encouraged German exports. AEG, Siemens and MAN launched a huge sales drive in India. MAN's busiest period for installations to India was from 1935 until the outbreak of World War II. A total of 96 engines were secured under Hitler's demands for exports, at the expense of British industry. From MAN's first sale to India, in 1902, until the end of 1939, 163 engines went to industry and central power stations. While the Germans had stolen a valuable march on British manufacturers, it was merely a matter of time before home industry caught up. In 1897 Dr Rudolf Diesel accepted a visit from the board of Mirrlees, Watson & Yaryan Company, of Glasgow, and an exclusive agreement was signed to produce diesel engines in Britain. One of its first diesel engines was supplied to Baroda in 1906 from Mirrlees, of Stockport. In that same year, a similar-sized unit was delivered to the Bombay Dockyard. In 1910 three diesel generators were installed for Manochji in Bombay.

The company's archives reveal phenomenal orders worldwide, with India the principal overseas market. By 1935 a total of 1243 diesel engines were manufactured at the Mirrlees' factory, of which 151 units operated in India. The largest engines then produced by the firm were for the David Mills of Bombay and for the Guma Waterworks in Simla, with at least 30 machines rated over 350 bhp mainly for utilities.

Remote tea estates turned to Mirrlees from 1909 for small dynamo and machinery prime movers that lasted well over 30 years. Indian customers ranged from the Indian Radio Telegraph Company, of Poona to Gingia Tea Estate Assam, the East India Distilleries in Nellikuppam, cotton factories in Punjab, the Karachi Steam Roller Flour Mills, and most railways, with small utilities making up the remainder. An encouraging reference was wired to the firm around 1930 from the Rajkot State Electric Supply Company in Wahiawa. 'Our engines are working splendidly since being installed nine years ago ... only a little wear on the bearing is noticed.'

Today, the engineering training college in Poona retains an excellent selection of vintage British diesel – and early aircraft – engines. A unit from Mirrlees of about 1925 is used to illustrate diesel engine technology to aspiring students. Also, a huge Mirrlees engine is preserved in Bangalore.

British market domination

America's and Germany's leads over Britain in electrical generation were quickly narrowed. From an emerging industry of medium-sized, though formidable, firms, Britain had developed its own technology by 1900. Despite aggressive American and German competition, the five large British electrical manufacturers continued to dominate the Indian market from 1919 onwards. Well after Independence, India still relied on British technology and finance to keep her head above water.

Chapter 15

INDIA ADOPTS THE TRAM

*The great advantage of the tram is that it will rid our streets once and for all
from the foul smell of horse droppings if nothing else.*
MANCHESTER CORPORATION OFFICIAL, *c.*1895

Madras: considerations for the rest of India

It was not until 1874 that horse-drawn trams made their entry into Madras
when 11 miles of metre-gauge track, laid by J.E. & A. Dawson's patent
Meccano-type rail, carried its first fare-paying passengers. By 1888 the
line was assessed as a dismal failure and narrowly escaped being scrapped.
In that year the *Indian Engineer* reported moves to construct an electric
tramway, but nothing further happened until 1891.

The municipal authorities extended a concession to Messrs Hutchinson,
of London, who promoted the Madras Electric Tramway Company, registered in London on 2 April 1892. The prospectus spoke of 18 miles of track
to be laid at a cost of £5,000 per mile, with the municipality having the right
to purchase the concern after 21 years on payment of gold to the amount
of the gross capital account, plus 25% as compensation. Capital was fixed
at £100,000 as it was hoped to raise most of the money in London, with the
remainder in India. The directors included William Digby, Companion of
the Most Eminent Order of the Indian Empire (for famine relief), while
S.A. Chalk of Chalk & Digby, partners in Messrs Hutchinson & Company,
became managing director of the Madras Tramway.

The firm was to operate under the Indian Tramways Act 1886.
Comments on the flotation were scathing, such as: 'We have seen some

curious prospectuses in our time, but apparently this stands alone. The last Madras Tramway was a dismal failure, and the chances of the new one now proposed seems to be about the size of a piece of Chalk.' (No doubt an intentional pun!) Nevertheless, the Madras Tramway was to earn the distinction of being the first to run electric tramways in the east.

The Electrical Construction Company (ECC), of Wolverhampton, was awarded the contract for building the Madras Tramway in 1893. The system was to be powered by an overhead source, but the plan immediately ran into problems. One was the submarine cable coming from Penang, 1500 miles away, and belonging to the Eastern Extension & Australasian Telegraph Company, which feared interference with their line. Another difficulty surrounded the onshore Government of India telephone line running along the main street, which led to severe conditions being imposed on the tramway company by the Telegraph Department of the Government of India.

In Madras, faced with a virtual ban on overhead construction, the tram operator decided to use conduit. Thomas Parker, of ECC, designed a special system as a trial run to circumvent the technical and legal problems. In August 1893, the British India Line steamer *Muttra* sailed with the first shipment of machinery and material. The building of the depot and power station began on 18 September 1893, on a site at Randall's Road, Egmore, just off the proposed main line along Poonamallee Road. The depot was built to hold 30 cars, but could be enlarged for 50.

The conduit was built up of cast iron, rather than being packed with sand, as was more usual. All insulators were suspended at 8 ft intervals, supporting a rigid conductor. Unlike the bipolar conduit systems of Europe and North America, the Madras version apparently used the track rails for a return supply of electrical current. Track laying started on 10 January 1894, along Esplanade Road, Madras.

Experiments continued at Wolverhampton, and on 22 May 1894 a car was tested on part of the track filled in to road level only, without its passenger compartment. This is understandable as the car bodies were constructed in Madras at the Perambur Railway Workshops. In all 50 cars were assembled, according to the press release – although company papers mention only 32.

A Mr C.H. Gadsby took over the tramway in December 1894, got it running and remained until April 1896. Trial runs began in February 1895, and public service started on 7 May with seven cars. The vehicles were 24 ft long and 8 ft wide, and were meant to have first, second and third class, but this system was apparently dropped. Fares were fixed by the concession at half an anna per mile, with the native princes having special cars for joy riding.

Trouble was immediately apparent. The Hindus could not travel with the Muslims, and the Christians would not travel with anybody. The company surmounted the problem by introducing a lottery based on ticket numbers. The Christians approved of the way that the company had repaired the previously neglected road, as well as the left-hand rule of the road, which the trams introduced. The drivers of ox-carts, jutkas, shandrijdans and carriers of sedan chairs thought otherwise and learned how to stuff iron bars into the conduit. One spectacular short circuit stopped the entire line.

From 1900 the only way in which the unwilling contractor-turned-operator could get back his working capital was to make the system profitable and then float a new company to buy it. ECC bought out the other shareholders, becoming sole owner on 31 May 1900, and placed William Thom as manager. Shrewd management and a rising population turned the scales. On 16 March 1904 the ECC registered a new company, Madras Electric Tramways (1904), to take over 9.25 miles of route – 2.75 miles double track, 6.5 miles single track – a 3-acre depot site, 45 motor cars and two trailers on a 21-year concession, with a further concession for 3 miles of extensions. The price was set at £120,000, but such a sum could not be raised in cash. As a consequence, the ECC was obliged to take £70,000 in shares and a further sum in debentures. Like it or not, they were in Madras to stay.

Expansion and new rolling stock

By 1905 the route mileage had risen to 13.25 miles and its rolling stock to 51. The new cars were cross-bench four-wheelers by G.G. Milnes. Their number and fleet numbers are uncertain, but a 1935 report records that the original 32 four-wheeled cars were written off in that year, which would fix the Milnes' class at 19 cars – 13 in 1903 and six in 1904. In 1907, the overhead system of collection was applied to the whole network. Later, the firm imported Brill trucks and built its own car bodies. A landmark was the first bogie car in 1911.

By 1924 the system had grown to 26 miles; the concession was extended and new capital raised to modernise the rolling stock. The new cars, built in Madras, were long centre-entrance saloons on maximum-traction trucks. The first post-war trucks came again from Brill, but when Brill ceased to make maximum-traction trucks the ECC turned, in 1932, to English Electric. Two more sets were bought in 1935, by which year the Milnes' four-wheelers had been rebuilt as short saloon cars and the last of the 1893 cars had been withdrawn, although one or two survived as works cars.

However, the tramway began to feel the effects of competition from diesel buses. In 1926 the Madras General Omnibus Company was formed, with the tramway firm managing the affairs of the bus side of the business. It was, to all intents and purposes, a monopoly. It had a fleet of 100 buses, which were linked with tram termini, and tram-cum-bus tickets were issued for the convenience of passengers. As the scheme was found uneconomical, the running of buses was stopped in 1929.

Calcutta
The Calcutta Tramway Company (CTC)

The tramway era in the British Empire was still in its infancy when the Government of India decided that Calcutta should also enjoy the advantages of this new mode of transport. Calcutta itself is a flat city and therefore ideally suited to horse traction. Ironically, it was freight, rather than passengers, that motivated the government to consider the metre-gauge tramway 'to remove the country produce from Sealdah Station to the godowns situated in the vicinity of Strand Road and Sobha Bazaar', according to the Justice of the Peace appointed by the tramway commission.

The inaugural omnibus service in Calcutta ran between Dharamtala and Barrackpore on 22 November 1830. Presumably this took the form of a horse or pony and carriage, similar to that running in England. The first tramline proper was opened on 24 February 1873, at a cost of Rs.150,000. It was not a success, quickly losing Rs.500 per month. Even so, the network over the next decade was gradually expanded to cover the principal streets in the city. But it was a time when electricity was being experimented with at Howrah Station. As better forms of tramways spread across Asia, many questioned the value of this decidedly slow – and frequently foul-smelling – means of conveyance. Additionally, the freight carrier had been usurped by an extension of the EBR and rendered all but superfluous.

Nevertheless, by 1885 traffic had increased to about 13 million passengers with some 2 million car miles run each year from 186 cars hauled by 1000 horses over 19 route miles. All the horses used were imported, yet despite screening and training, Calcutta's punishing conditions pushed many of them into a premature grave. The quick changeover to electric tram operation was inevitable.

The District Board of Calcutta, keen to see a mechanically propelled tramway that horse- and bullock-drawn carts failed to provide for the city's rapidly rising population, was well aware of the increasing popularity of steam tramways in Britain, as well as other parts of Asia. Approval for such a system was quickly given by unanimous vote. The board guaranteed a 4% dividend on all light railway lines constructed. One was the Howrah–Amta Light Railway tramway that was opened in stages between 1897 and 1908, and – rather surprisingly as Calcutta then had electric power in most government buildings – favoured steam traction initially over direct current. Numerous lines on a 2 ft 6 in. gauge track were opened to serve local communities, but none then inside Calcutta's city limits. Many people thought that the new tramway would adopt the same gauge.

The Howrah-Amta Steam Tramway (HAT)

The District Board of Howrah established the HAT with a guaranteed interest on the capital cost at the rate of Rs.1,100 per mile opened, but limited to Rs.28,000 per annum. In consideration of this, investors received a surplus fund, or bonus, slightly in excess of 4% on their capital. Construction began in 1895 with an approved gauge of 2 ft over a total length of 28.62 miles. The permanent way consisted of flat-footed steel rails weighing 25 lb per yard on cross sleepers – 5 ft × 6in × 4in – nine being laid to each rail of 24 ft in the straight and extra for sharp curves. One problem faced was the amount of civil works involved to keep out the spread of jungle growth. To check this spread, additional maintenance workmen were required, which added to the overall costs.

The line was ballasted throughout. The only gradients – 1 in 100 – were on the approaches to canal bridges, which required good headway for passing steamers with their large funnels. The line was part designed and constructed throughout by T.A. Martin & Company – later to merge with Burn & Company, once India's largest engineering firm on behalf of the ad hoc-formed Bengal District Road Tramways Company, Howrah-Amta, under the provision of an order by the Government of Bengal dated 26 March 1895.

There were many construction delays, according to official viewpoints. From January to April 1897 only 9.5 miles were opened, and by 31 December

1897 a total of 16.5 miles were in operation. The net revenue amounted to Rs.23,967, equal to 5% per annum on total capital. By June 1898, revenues had increased substantially. On gross earnings of Rs.77,000, the net profit was 7.23%.

The rolling stock consisted of tank locomotives especially designed and built for the tramway by Sharp, Stewart of Glasgow 'being admirably suited for the work required of them'. They had four wheels coupled, with a radial tank in the rear to carry 0.75 tons of coal and 250 gallons of water. Stephenson-type valve gear was incorporated with all parts concealed. All four engines imported cost Rs.20,702. Additionally, 40 coaches and 12 goods wagons at a total cost of approximately Rs.280,000 served the system. Fares charged ranged from 18 pies per mile first class to 6 pies per mile intermediate class and 4.5 pies per mile third class.

The whole line, as initially planned, was opened on 1 June 1898. Later, trains made their entrance into Howrah Station over the streets, but this practice was abandoned in 1939. The HAT's life was indeed short. By 1900 electric traction was deemed the answer to Calcutta's transport problem, and the Calcutta Electric Supply Company was placing newer and larger generators into service on a regular basis. The days for steam trams were thought to be numbered, but cynics were proved wrong.

The operation, known as the Howrah–Amta Tramway, was for the most part unsatisfactory. By 1900, however, horse-drawn trams ran alongside steam vehicles on some 30 miles of track, with 186 vehicles in operation.

The steam tram, for all its deficiencies, had the advantage of speed and endurance over India's trusty four-legged beasts of burden. There were many proposals to open up rural areas for localised steam tramways, mainly where the major railway companies had no service, but little documentation is available.

Although the HAT system closed down, in name, around 1917, entrepreneurs after 1918 viewed the redundant lines as ripe for a revival. From Amta Station fresh rails were laid to Sheakhala, with a branch line to Autpur. Strangely, steam traction rather than electric motive power was adopted and the Leeds firm of Hunslet favoured for engines, which provided a reliable service until 1970. The whole system was closed down on 1 January 1971. Manning Wardle – also from Leeds – supplied engines from about 1918 that survived until closure.

Other steam tramways in Calcutta

There is evidence from the Institution of Civil Engineers' archives in London that Calcutta possessed other steam tramways. In 1881 Merryweather, the London-based manufacturer of steam-driven fire engines and early trams, received its first tram contract for Calcutta, comprising three units. Another successful firm in the tram market was W.B. Dick of Kilmarnock, established about 1850, which supplied two units in 1890. It is not recorded whether these were steam-powered. W.B, Dick later became Dick, Kerr of Preston, a major supplier of electric trams and electrical machines from 1900.

It is known that a contract was placed in the pre-electric era for a fully enclosed steam-tramway locomotive, and in May 1882 the Calcutta Tramway Company (CTC) was allowed to try out the steam tram on the Chowringhee line for one month. Despite six accidents during that period, the residents of Chowringhee resolved in favour of the continued operation of their solitary steam tram, subject to stringent regulations relating to its speed, noise, hours of running, the length of trains and the conduct of the driver. The tram did not operate after 5.30 p.m. However, the dominance of steam on Chowringhee was short-lived, and within a year the experiment was discontinued. The steam tram was relegated to specials for the transport of pilgrims to Kalighat during the Durga Puja. History reveals that this steam tram later found regular employment on the Kidderpore line.

In 1905 two small tramways or light railways were opened, between Barasat and Basirhat and between Tarakeswar and Magra, both believed to be steam-powered. While several steam tramways were opened in rural areas, most lay within a short distance of Calcutta.

Very few details on India's steam tramways survive today. In 1894 a book entitled *Light Railways for the United Kingdom, India and the Colonies* states that '51 miles of steam tramways outside municipal limits are in service', but nothing further is added.

Work begins on electrification

By the end of the 19th century, Calcutta had begun a programme of complete reorganisation of the means of transport. Work on electrification began in 1900 and the first line was placed into service in March 1902. By December of that year, virtually the entire system had been converted to electric traction. The success of that trial led to considerable expansion, with new lines laid to connect the rising suburbs in the north and south of the city. This expansion accompanied new routes in city streets to galvanise the emerging business section of the city. In reality the new lines were barely quicker than walking.

In 1901 a new agreement between the Calcutta Corporation with the private company that ran the horse-drawn trams stipulated that electric traction must be employed and horses dispensed with. Current was to be collected from a single overhead wire, with the return path through the wheels and tram lines. From 1905 the tram company was obliged to pay the Howrah Commissioners a fixed rent of Rs.35,000 per year, until 1931, when the city had the right to purchase the whole system.

The first complete section of the newly expanded electrified system was opened in June 1905, and the whole network as then planned placed into service in October 1908. One of the most beneficial aspects of the change from horse to electric traction was the contractual stipulation that the metre-gauge service be changed to the British standard gauge of 4 ft 8.5 in.

For the initial electrification of the system, single-ended four-wheeled trams on Brill 21E short-wheelbase trucks were supplied by Dick, Kerr & Company. That choice of single-ended cars was dictated by the availability of cheap land in Calcutta. By 1905, 171 cars had been delivered of which 96 were open-sided and 75 were enclosed. A year later a further 45 cars were added to the fleet. However, the service life of many of the earliest cars was not long, and withdrawal appears to have begun in 1911 to enable reconstruction into more suitable vehicles. Cross-bench cars were found unsuitable in monsoon weather and dispensed with.

New routes were quickly opened, and a double-ended shuttle service operated between the High Companyurt and Dalhousie Square and between Dalhousie Square and Nimtollah. The Chowringhee Road service was extended. With the building of the extension to Rajabazar in 1910, the growth of the system paused for some 15 years.

Surprisingly, while Bombay was experimenting successfully with double-decker cars, the concept was never applied in Calcutta.

An assortment of rolling stock

Up until 1931 all electric trams comprised a 'train' of two single-deck coaches, each carried on a four-wheeled truck. The leading coach incorporated the motors and was reserved for first-class passengers, while second-class passengers travelled in the trailing coach. From that year the tramway company undertook the replacement of its old-type rolling stock, introducing six articulated cars from English Electric – Dick, Kerr works – which was no doubt an innovation from Continental Europe. They were well upholstered, better lit and radically more comfortable than previous stock. The English Electric Company also supplied all trucks and electrical equipment for an additional order. However, Indian craftsmen, some from the company and some from outside contractors, constructed the bodies.

Also from the early 1930s, two principal local engineering firms, Burn of Howrah and Jessop of Calcutta, competed with the established players in tramway engineering. Initial success favoured Burn, with a small order to be followed by an additional 37 more cars in 1933. Over the next three years, Burn delivered 70 units from its Howrah works.

In 1938 Jessop & Company built 36 cars, which were the first tramcars to be fitted with the new Westinghouse air brake made in Chippenham, England. They must have been highly successful, for 34 more cars, identical to the firm's first delivery, were added to CTC's fleet the following year.

Service across the Howrah Suspension Bridge

The only road connection between Calcutta and Howrah was the 28-pontoon floating bridge built in 1874. It was impossible to run trams across the structure, but even so it served the population reliably. At the height of World War II, when Japanese military forces were poised to strike at the very heart of the British Empire, the citizens of India were not let down in their daily requirements and needs by the British government. The tramway was a service 'that must be kept going at all cost', according to the English manager.

When the new Howrah Suspension Bridge was opened in 1942, tram tracks were laid immediately and the structure was opened for traffic. The first Calcutta tramcars trundled across its 1500 ft high-tensile steel span in February 1943.

The emergence of the diesel bus – a chequered beginning

The first diesel bus began service in 1918. During the 1920s the tramway company was faced with troubles of traffic congestion. It decided to experiment with its own bus services and accordingly in 1921 inaugurated a route between Park Circus and the pontoon bridge to Howrah, using Thornycroft single-deck buses. However, it found that this merely added to the problems of traffic congestion, stating: 'The inadequacy of buses demonstrated the superiority of the trams for carrying large numbers of passengers to their destinations more quickly and at cheaper fares.'

The bus experiment was ended after five years. During that time, the CTC opened a tramway extension to Park Circus in 1925. It was confident that trams were the answer to all Calcutta's transport problems, and right up until at least 1977 did not operate any further bus services. The company's further faith in the tramway over buses was demonstrated in 1928 with the opening of the Rash Behari Avenue line in the south of the city.

A rather unusual form of double-decker bus was tried out and placed in operation during the 1930s. Somewhat weird and wonderful by today's standards, the vehicle comprised an ad hoc upper storey built upon a light commercial chassis. Apparently, this mode of travel was not popular and the CTC abandoned the double-decker bus, concentrating instead on its tramway service.

However, the tramway firm's confidence in electric traction alone for Calcutta was not shared by other entrepreneurs who persisted with buses, and now it is the bus, rather than the tram, that handles the greater portion of the city's passenger travel.

Bombay

Until the arrival of horse-drawn tram on the island on which the city of Bombay developed, horses were principally for the well-heeled, and the poorer indigenous people jostled with bullock carts that provided the main means of conveyance for Indian families, as they do today in all rural areas.

In January 1865 an American import–export firm, Stearn Hobart & Company, applied to the Bombay Municipality to lay and operate a tramway system within the city, and was granted a Deed of Agreement on 28 February 1865. However, the end of the American Civil War had plunged Bombay's textile industry into crisis, and the financial crash stopped all progress on the tramway scheme. Five years later, the American firm took issue with the municipality when it commented that the agreement was *ultra vires* and not binding.

In the meantime, English firms got wind of this tramway proposal and lodged keen interest to build and run the system themselves. Ultimately, Messrs G.A. Kittridge and F.W. Stearn secured the concession on 1 March

1873. The contract stipulated the construction and maintenance of either single- or double-track operation at fares not to exceed 3 annas over 3 miles. The Bombay Tramways Company (BTC) was floated in New York with Rs.2.4 million raised. The rent was assessed at Rs.3,000 per mile of double track and Rs.2,000 per mile of single track.

The English firm of Glover & Company was employed to construct the track and the first sod was cut on 1 January 1874 at Colaba. After only 19 weeks, the opening ceremony took place for the two services: Grants Buildings to Pydhonie, 2.52 miles; and Bori Bunder via Kalbadevi to Pydhonie, 1.25 miles. On that auspicious day the company operated six cars and carried 451 passengers over the 3.77 route miles.

The Bombay Tramways Company (BTC)

Expansion in terms of route miles advanced rapidly as the BTC found its system regarded as acceptable, although very slow by public opinion. Over the 22 years to 1896, 13 routes were added, bringing the now standard gauge all double-track to a total route mileage of 17.377 miles.

The first 50 cars were imported from America and most probably from the John Stephenson Company, of New York. Single, short cars required one horse, while two horses were required for the 23 longer cars and four horses for the eight-window closed cars seating 24 passengers with 12 standing. Even with improved ventilation, many of the passengers sweltered in the heat and the cars known as the 'Bombay Roof' were soon discarded.

By about 1895, many of the new cars were assembled locally at well-equipped workshops in Colaba Causeway, with the castings and wheels imported from America. In 1905 the fleet comprised 195 one- and two-horse cars that cost locally from Rs.950 to Rs.725, with over 100 horses purchased from the Bombay Omnibus Company. Later, a further 100 horses were purchased to start additional services, bringing the total number of these trusty beasts of burden to 1160.

Electrification of the BTC

The BTC applied on 19 July 1899 for sanction to convert the whole system from horse-drawn to electric traction on the overhead system, as was then the technology in common use worldwide. The cost was estimated at Rs.1.5 million and the company stipulated that Bombay Corporation should not exercise its right to purchase at its first option date or for the next 14 years.

By then two electrical firms, Crompton & Company, of London with its considerably enlarged Chelmsford electrical works, and the British Pioneer Electric Light Company through its agent who was acting on behalf of Brush Electric Company, of Loughborough, both offered the same rental terms.

After protracted negotiations, BTC was wound up on 1 August 1905 and sold for Rs.9,849,990 to the British Electric Traction Company, which had proffered additional inducements over Crompton. The new owner, with worldwide interests including tramways in Athens, Indonesia and Singapore and profitable systems in Australia and New Zealand, had absorbed the Brush Electric Company, thereby adding manufacturing facilities to its strength. The Corporation of Bombay had in August 1902 set its sights on purchasing the tramway system in its entirety. Although the tramway company was entrenched in its determination not to be taken over, the issue went to arbitration. Mr H.V.R. Kemball, the Executive Engineer for the Indian Public Works Department, was employed as the arbitrator.

Among the terms laid down were: a concession for 45 years; speeds not to exceed 12 mph; 1 anna maximum fare for any part of the journey; supply of all power requirements; maintenance of the roadway up to 18 in. from the outer rails; all cars to be well-lighted at night and carry lamps of distinctive colour to indicate direction; and services to operate from 6.30 a.m. to 11.30 p.m. Once the agreement was ratified, the Bombay Electric Light & Traction Company (BELTC) was established with a capital of £1 million.

Horse-drawn tram at time of the plague exodus, Bombay, c.1896–7 (Courtesy of the British Library)

BELTC took over 17.377 miles of double-track tramway, 195 single-deck tramcars, 1385 horses and 18 bullocks on 2 August 1905, together with the various depots and stables. Work on conversion was started within the year and the company also applied for some 5.7 route miles of extensions. Some of the extensions were deferred because of the narrowness of the streets – subsequently widened. The sale price was settled upon the profits for the previous three years at Rs.6,199,990. The contract for track reconstruction and extensions was awarded to J.G. White & Company, of London, which had already completed the first power station at Wari Bunder in 1905, with an electricity service established on 11 September of that year. Belliss & Morcom, using its ubiquitous and proven steam engines, provided most of the generating plant.

A formal opening of the substantially completed extensions and improvements, all now electrically powered, took place on 7 May 1907. Four tramcars ran in public service from the firm's offices and people jostled on board for the occasion. 'The whole of the electrification construction work was energetically proceeded with, while at the same time traffic by horse traction was well maintained,' commented an English visitor, later endorsed in similar fashion by *The Times*.

Horse-drawn trams still had some work to perform over extended lines that were not yet electrified, but the whole conversion was completed by 16 May 1908, with the tramway network extended to 20.58 route miles. The citizens of Bombay immediately took to the novelty of mechanical conveyance within their city, with receipts taken – from those that paid their fares – of Rs.2.94 to Rs.4.90 per mile in today's money equivalent. At the end of that year, the number of passengers carried annually had exceeded 30 million, with some 3 million tramcar miles travelled. By 1914, the figures were 40 million and 3.75 million respectively. The purchase and electrification of the tramways had taken nine years to complete, mainly thanks to the long drawn-out negotiations regarding the purchase and leasing of the system. However, once in possession the new company carried out the conversion within the three years stipulated by the agreement.

From 1920 the BELTC decided to totally refurbish its electrification system, with much of the original equipment antiquated and burnt out. Inviting tenders for substations at Byculla, Albert Road, Baboola and Lamington Road, British Thomson-Houston Company won all contracts placed for the 44 units of truck-type switchgear. Oil-filled, they served well into the first decade of Independence.

Rolling stock

The first modern cars for electric traction usage were imported from Brush Electric Company in 1905 but few details have survived. Of the two cars sent as samples, one held 52 passengers while the other held 50 passengers. They were approved after successful trials and Brush was subsequently contracted to supply an initial fleet of 150 cars.

The Brush orders excluded seating, which was made and fitted at the Bombay workshops. Seats were of the slatted variety 'providing excellent accommodation for lice' – replaced in due course by solid wood. At this time Bombay was capable of undertaking rolling stock manufacturing work to a high degree of competency, with the Parel Railway Workshops having provided coaches for the major railway companies since the 1880s.

By 1923 the emphasis was on double-deck bogie cars with their increased capacity, and a total of 59 were in service by 1929. From 1920 most were equipped with English Electric motors mounted on Brush maximum traction LCC-type bogies. The cars could accommodate 86 passengers – 36 in the lower saloon and 50 in the upper deck. In 1937 the Kingsway (Bombay) Workshops established by the company assembled its first car, and 23 were in service by 1939. They had much in common with the London Metropolitan and Blackpool double-deckers of 1934/35, known as the 'Pullman' type.

The demands on engineering and power sources

The engineering side of converting from horse-drawn to electric traction was enormous. Three years was stipulated in the agreement for this conversion, and work was undertaken at a feverish pace. Rails were to be 90 lb or 96 lb per yard, with many arriving from Workington and Middlesbrough. Special castings for points and junctions were supplied from Edgar Allen of Sheffield, which had delivered similar products to most of the world's tramways. But it was delivery of the electrical generating plant that caused the main delays. With the original coal-burning station erected on land at Wari Bunder in 1905, most of the electrical equipment was from Brush. Its output was 3340kW, which was increased to 5960kW by January 1910. Even this was not enough to supply the tramway, and so a new coal-burning station at Kussara was built alongside the harbour and opened in late 1910. The equipment comprised, by 1917, eight Babcock & Wilcox water tube boilers, three Brush vertical reciprocating engines each of 1000kW, two Parsons steam turbines of 1000kW each – later replaced by a British Thomson-Houston

Company Impulse-type turbine rated 6000kW – and two 2000kW turbines also from Parsons. In 1922, one of these Parsons units was replaced with a Belliss turbine of 3000kW.

In 1922 Tata Hydro Power was able to supply energy from the Western Ghats and the tramway operator decided to take electrical supply in bulk rather than depend upon the Kussara plant, which was closed down on 11 January 1925. From that date all power was taken from Tata and the Andhra Valley hydro plants. Two substations were opened to convert generated power to the 550–600 volts DC overhead system to drive the trams and meet the needs of the expanding tramway network. Motor generators, later to be replaced with rotary converters, served until static conversion equipment was perfected. In 1930 a mercury-arc rectifier substation was installed at Colaba and a larger-capacity unit built at the Lalbag Substation in 1931.

Maintenance facilities were not neglected, with large workshops on a site of nearly 400 000 sq. ft opened in 1917. Many apprenticeships were undertaken in all aspects of engineering, these opportunities being snapped up overnight. 'The young Indian is quick to learn and is capable of giving us a good day's work for his wage,' wrote Alan Parker, the Workshop Superintendent. All rolling stock was hand-painted and the manager recorded that some 700 people of all disciplines were employed. Each car was subject to a thorough overhaul every 18 months and was off the tracks for only 21 days.

The spread of Bombay's tramway network

The BTC had applied for various extensions in 1914, but the Great War that gripped Britain was more concerned with men, weapons and transport than the 'insignificant Bombay tramway network'. The four extensions planned in early 1914 were placed on hold. Once the war was over, Bombay received the consideration for her infrastructure then long overdue.

The textile industry – now the city's principal employer but being challenged by the likes of Richardson & Cruddas, structural engineering builders – expanded to such a degree that the municipality's transport system was approaching obsolescence. To cater for this upsurge in employment and mobility, one of the first schemes to be approved was the doubling of the track in Colaba Road.

The next principal extension to be opened was from Wari Bunder northwards along Real Road to the Victoria Road Bridge in 1921, which provided passengers with a connection for main line train services. With Bombay's prosperity principally dependent on textiles, work started on a new cotton depot at Sewri in the same year.

The Bombay Harbour Trust, anxious for transport links to be improved, then proposed a new line to connect their dockyard with the city centre. The trust advanced the money and a new track was opened in October 1923. The loan was repaid by 1927. In that year, the system was considerably expanded and continued to grow until 1935. Fares increased as the network was expanded: from 1 anna in 1901, to 1.5 annas in 1921, to 2 annas in 1935, when the tramway network had a route length of 30.87 miles.

Further extensions were discussed from 1924 to as far northwards as Worli but using the new trackless trolleybuses from Guy Motors, of Wolverhampton. Nothing came of these proposals. A tramway to Worli was considered at that time to be un-remunerative compared with motorbuses that were not restricted by the limitations of overhead cables. Many other proposals were discussed to support an expanding population and the rapid growth of industry and to cater for Bombay's diversity of industrial and domestic life. However, the awkward narrow streets and cost of projecting further tramways began to signal that the apogee of the tram had past. In 1926 the company set up an omnibus service, which soon proved popular and at the time of 'municipalisation', 242 buses were running in Bombay.

The new Bombay Central Station, constructed in the main by Braithwaite Engineering of West Bromwich and its subsidiary Clive Works, Calcutta, was opened in December 1930. The planners maintained that locomotion should still be steam rather than electric traction. As the new station initially accommodated only eight express arrivals and departures daily – though this was soon to be considerably increased by BBCIR – the tramway company considered that insufficient passengers would use its services and elected not to project lines to the new railway terminus. Other extensions from the General Post Office that were also considered would have necessitated a reappraisal of an existing siding. By then an 'adequate bus service was established'.

The town corporation from 1933 suggested the construction of new lines such as from Sewri Station to Parel, as well as other projected routes, but the tramway company steadfastly refused on straightforward economic grounds. Its revenues were still healthy but with no spare cash for new projects. The company must have been acutely aware that throughout Britain bus services were competing with railways, especially in fare structure, but felt that larger vehicles to hold twice as many passengers were warranted before the outright adoption of the diesel engine. Eventually, these vehicles were supplied locally on imported chassis. By 1938 the tramway operator was making a reasonable profit, and the job opportunities that surfaced throughout Bombay, especially in the docks, harbour industries and transport, attracted many migrants from other Indian states.

Financial and technical restraints

The government's electrical engineer had complained that the trams' brakes were inadequate for 12 mph and as a result the average speed was further reduced to 5.75 mph. With fierce competition from the BBCIR with its suburban service from Colaba using 1500 volts DC and the GIPR using a similar electrification system, the tramway was quick to point out that only increasing its speed would provide the recipe for survival. New magnetic brakes and sanding gear were fitted so that speeds of 18 mph could be attained. The savings were dramatic, with the number of cars reduced from 237 in 1923 to 178 by 1935, each car running an average of 90 miles per day. However, passengers decreased from 101 million to 96 million in the same period.

The Bombay Municipality assumed ownership of the combined tram, bus and electricity undertaking on 7 August 1947. The system had been run down and neglected during World War II. The new undertaking acquired a fleet of some 426 trams and 242 buses, many of which were in a dilapidated condition through lack of spare parts and material imported from Britain as a consequence of the global conflict. Over the next few years, the tramway was restored to its pre-war efficiency, with cars overhauled and re-painted in the crimson and cream livery as before and new rolling stock added to the fleet.

Delhi

Delhi was the last city in India to consider the benefits of a tramway. Having never adopted horse-drawn transport, the city plunged into electric traction from the start. The Delhi Electric Tramways & Lighting Company was opened for public service on 3 June 1908. As Delhi was in transition to becoming the nation's capital in 1911, it was a surprise to many that this expanding city had to wait so long after Calcutta and Madras to experience the benefit of an electric tramway.

Delhi Electric Tramways & Lighting Company (DELTC)

The network was perhaps better planned than that of either Madras or Calcutta, and no doubt benefited from their experiences. Ten miles of track were laid running practically to all parts of the city as well as to the outskirts of Subzee Mandi and Sudder Bazaar. Planners from Britain also drew from home and Continental European experience, adopting track layouts on the European plan. The track comprised the usual concrete bed and single line with turnouts, while the overhead equipment consisted of the side-pole arrangement with bracket arms or span wires. When fully operational, 24 cars were planned to cover the 10 route miles of service. Each car was of the convertible type so as to meet summer and winter conditions of service.

On each car end there was a reserved first-class compartment for which passengers paid an additional fare of 1 pice per mile. The ordinary fares were calculated at about 0.75d. per mile up to 1.75d. per 3 miles. There were three main routes on the system, but all cars passed through Fatehpuri Junction. Unlike the ad hoc stopping arrangements of India's earlier tramway systems when passengers, in collusion with the conductor, could board and alight at will, in Delhi a fixed stopping-place stage system was adopted, indicated by white bands around electricity poles with clearly displayed notice boards on each fixed bracket.

Especially for the tramway, the DELTC erected a new electricity-generating station with reserve plant for lighting and power as well as for traction. It was conservatively planned, the company anticipating the large demand for traction loads as well as power for fans and other outlets.

A power station was constructed at Tajewala, the head works of the Western Jumna Canal, from a survey undertaken in 1903. The evaluation of this site for hydraulic generation was assessed eventually to supply Umballa, Saharunpore, Delhi and other towns in the vicinity with electrical energy. However, at the opening ceremony of the tramway network the hydraulic station was not completed, and it is believed that power was generated in a coal-fired plant. Bruce Peebles of Edinburgh constructed the power plant and most of the electrical system. Some 700 poles were erected to carry the 60 miles of overhead wire and lighting cables and a well-equipped workshop was built. However, the local contractor went bankrupt and his failure meant that Bruce Peebles benefited considerably from the liquidated damages paid.

The tramway was to advance the city 'with the expeditious and cheap delivery of parcels and goods'. The cotton mills at Subzimundi and the large wholesale trade of the Sadar Bazar, along with the corn markets, all came to rely upon the tramway, if only for the arrival of their workers. When the network grew in popularity, the DELTC received many enquiries for the use of its electric power to drive corn-crushing machinery, as well as local workshops turning out small engineering pieces. Some were delivered with power 'upon reasonable request'. However, the company intended to start an electro-plating department and could not entertain any further demands on its limited power resources.

Rolling stock

Originally there were 24 tramcars, which were supplemented by two additional units from America in 1924. These were delivered by J.G. Brill and were of all-steel construction. They each had an 8 ft wheelbase and 26 in. diameter steel-tyre wheels. The construction resembled a tramcar of the Blackpool design with a centre entrance. The small motors were from General Electric of Schenectady, with motor-driven air compressors operating the brakes. A sliding partition inside the car separated first- from second-class passengers. Both cars were painted in aluminium. Seating for second class was the conventional, uncomfortable, wooden arrangement, but at least sunblinds were fitted to relieve some heat discomfort.

Post-World War II

The DELTC handed over its entire assets to its successor, the Delhi Central Electric Power Authority (DCEPA) on 1 April 1947. Exactly four years to the day later, the Delhi Road Transport Authority took over from the DCEPA. A total of 26 tramcars were in operation until 1954, when six were scrapped. In 1958 the authority had only 14 tramcars in a roadworthy condition. Four years later two cars were condemned, with four others under maintenance for a complete overhaul. In that year the tramway system catered only to the needs of the most important localities of the city of Old Delhi. The area of operation had been Jama Masjid to Sadar Bazar and Jama Masjid to Sabzi Mandi (renamed from when the line was inaugurated) from the inception of service until 1950, when another re-appraisal of this vintage transport was undertaken. Then, the route mileage was severely truncated to a mere 5.69 miles.

As with Britain's transition from trams to diesel buses, it was inevitable that Delhi would succumb to this change. In 1963 the last tram gracefully left the stage and they have never been seen since. Today, the trusty Morris

Isis taxi has all but total control of Delhi's streets, augmented by a host of clapped-out – but surprisingly fully reliable – Leyland Ashok and Tata buses to cater for Delhi's swollen population.

The Delhi trolleybus system

Delhi was the first city in India to introduce experimental trolleybuses. There was some similarity to the tramcar in their construction, the main differences being rubber tyres and two booms. Three trolleybuses were provided in February 1934 from Guy Motors, of Wolverhampton. The trolleybuses operated until 1954, when one was scrapped. The trolleybus was initially successful in Delhi, thanks to the inability of trams to negotiate narrow streets. Slow-moving bullock carts were the principal obstruction to the progress of the trolleybus throughout India.

Delhi is a flat city and favourable to both trams and trolleybuses. The city fathers set a maximum speed of 20 mph, although these Guy vehicles could accelerate to 60 mph in less than 30 seconds. Despite the fact that each trolleybus was designed to accommodate 27 passengers, frequently over 100 people crammed in, with the majority 'finding no funds for their ride', to quote the English manager. And yet the vehicles weighed only 4.5 tons. Because of the narrow streets, with their 15 ft wheelbase and 23 ft overall length of chassis they were much smaller than similar trolleybuses in Britain. The trolleybuses operated between Tis Hazari and Pahar Ganj, but complaints from the diesel bus operator resulted in a change of route from Lahori gate to Triploia.

In 1977 Bharat Heavy Electrical Industries – established during Britain's Harold Macmillan government and set up by Associated Electrical Industries (an amalgamation of British Thomson-Houston Company and Metropolitan-Vickers), Parsons and English Electric – developed a prototype trolleybus to attempt to compete with diesel buses. It was tried out in Delhi, but from all accounts the venture was unsuccessful and nothing further ensued.

Cawnpore

The penultimate city to adopt a tramway was Cawnpore, in 1907. Cawnpore, one of India's smallest cities, is situated in the North-West Provinces, on the right bank of the holy river Ganges, 42 miles south-west of Lucknow,

266 miles south-east of Delhi and 628 miles north-west of Calcutta. The Ganges was recorded as being 300 yards wide here. On reflection, it is ironic that the Cawnpore city fathers should have elected to install a tramway when larger or more industrialised cities such as Karachi, Lahore, Nagpur, Bangalore, Dacca or Lucknow did not.

In 1907 Cawnpore was comparatively neglected, and deficient in the ancient palaces and historical buildings that characterised neighbouring Lucknow. Its tourist industry was all but nil. However, the city had grown as a manufacturing and commercial centre, thanks to its chief industry of making leather goods that achieved a measure of popularity in Britain. Cawnpore earned a good reputation as a grain market, perhaps as a result of its position on the Ganges and its having good main-rail connections.

Cawnpore Electric Tramways (CET)

The town's tramway was first electrified in 1907, with power supplied by Belliss & Morcom steam engines driving 500-volt dynamos. Despite the old part of the city's famous narrow streets, it was not quite as difficult to run lines in as Delhi. Its cantonment population was considered to be a good source of revenue for the tramway company. Only two major routes were constructed, with one originating on the banks of the Ganges and, via the large cantonment, terminating at the principal tram shed, with a spur line heading northwards. The second and main route started at the tram shed and headed south to the main railway station, coming to a halt on the Grand Trunk Road. A canal had to be crossed. The whole electrical system was designed and built by Crompton & Company, using Belliss & Morcom steam engines. The CET was an immediate success, with only the horse- and bullock-drawn carts for competition. Fares ranged from 1 anna to 1.5 annas – affordable by most people.

Chapter 16

THE TEXTILE AND JUTE INDUSTRIES

Cotton and textiles made Manchester and Bombay.
Equally, it was the jute industry that made Dundee and Calcutta.
ENGINEERING, 1895

It is often said that textiles made Manchester and Bombay as did jute Dundee and Calcutta. The two Indian port cities, one on the eastern and the other on the western coast of the subcontinent, had already established flourishing maritime and engineering industries (as discussed in earlier chapters) long before textiles and jute entered the picture. However, it is jute and textiles that launched them on the course of becoming the two largest industrial, business and financial metropolises east of Suez. The two industries made rapid strides after their creation and soon overtook established enterprises, employing thousands of workers who collected the raw material – cotton – from fields scattered throughout central and western India; cleaned, ginned and baled the cotton; wove it into grey fabric at their numerous mills; and then stretched, dyed and shipped it to different parts of the world. Cotton, however, was not unique to India. Many other countries were growing the crop and making textiles.

What was unique to India was jute. Nowhere else in the world was this fibre being produced. And when the first jute mills began to be established in Calcutta, no other country, including Crimea, had a jute industry. As for Bombay and Calcutta playing both a competitive and a complementary role with Manchester and Dundee, it is an unquestionable fact that the Lancashire city could not have become the cotton and textile capital of the north-west of England in the 19th century without shipments of raw cotton from Bombay; nor could Dundee have risen as the jute city without the bales of fibre shipped from Calcutta.

The first cotton mill in India at Calcutta

Contrary to much current industrial history assessment, India's entry into cotton and textile production did not begin in Bombay in the 1840s or 1850s. The clock must be turned back nearly three decades to the pioneers who sailed up the Hooghly River in around 1817 to build India's first cotton mill. Sited about 15 miles from the centre of Calcutta as we know it today, the original mill still stands where British textile merchants worked and lived in harsh conditions.

The textile mill buildings were modelled on the then established Lancashire pattern of rigid foursquare-sided, four- or five-storey high, 'soulless towers of incarceration', constructed of burnt brick and timber instead of local stone. For lighting, they relied upon the sun's rays, with ventilation comprising wooden-framed windows. The walls were up to 3 ft thick, 'almost like the ramparts of a medieval fort'.

According to the *District Gazette,* 'cotton spinning and weaving of cloth in Howrah dates back to the early days of British administration'. Many years ago, enquiries were made of the old residents of Bauria village, whereby some of the retired workers revealed that the entire estate belonged to the Dutch and was later purchased by Captain Alexander Kyd, of the prodigious Anglo-Indian Kyd shipbuilders.

The spread of textiles throughout Bombay

The impetus for the founding of India's cotton industry in Bombay came from Indian entrepreneurs. Cowasji Nanabhai Davar opened the first Bombay cotton mill, the Bombay Spinning Mill, in 1854. Naturally, there was antagonism from Lancashire mill owners, who saw their virtual monopoly under severe threat from India's plentiful resource of cheap labour. However, this opposition was soon tempered and eventually offset by the support of British manufacturers of textile machinery – especially Pratt Bros of Oldham – and the numerous foundries devoted to the manufacture of steam engines, of which Lancashire, and in particular Bolton, took the lead. By 1870, Bombay was home to 13 mills all powered by steam engines, mostly from Bolton, Blackburn and Manchester. Electricity was merely two decades away.

On 23 August 1879, Nowroji Nusserwanji Wadia (1849–1899) established his textile enterprise, the Bombay Dying & Manufacturing Company.

INDIGO PRESSES

DYES, ESPECIALLY INDIGO, were a favourite with Indian consumers, and the smaller foundries in England lost no time in seeking commercial opportunities. Early models of indigo presses were not successful. Occasionally, blocks of indigo were broken by the strain of the rebound of the press beam or of the platform when released as a result of uneven surface pressures. One firm that successfully overcame this problem was Owens & Company, Engineers, of Whitefriars Ironworks in London's Fleet Street. From 1872 the foundry exported to Bombay and Calcutta a series of wrought-iron presses that with the addition of 'production rails' could complete the entire factory work with little labour in attendance.

These Owens' presses were also applied to compression of other substances such as in the extraction of oil from seed and the production of oil cake. In 1992 a unit was still in service in Dacca, Bangladesh.

Certainly the most famous and perhaps the most successful of the Wadias, he was educated in England. His first textile interest specialised in Indian spun cotton, which was dip-dyed by hand and laid out in the sun to dry. From these modest beginnings grew one of India's largest textile producers. In 1883 the huge Hick, Hargreaves foundry of Bolton, was supplying steam engines to Wadia mills. So successful were the engines from this Bolton foundry that in that year alone, two horizontal Corliss condensing engines were installed in the Crown Spinning & Weaving Company, with a further two units going to E.D. Sassoon's enterprise.

From its establishment in Bombay, the cotton industry spread rapidly. In 1858 the Oriental Mill was in production. This was followed by the Maneckji Mill, the Victoria Mill, Coorla Mill and the Bombay United Mill all in 1860; the Albert Mill – next to the Parel Works, then building bridges and assembling imported rolling stock – in 1867; the Alexandra Mill in 1868; Morarjee Goculdas Mills in 1870; and both the Sassoon and Khatau Makanji Mills in 1874. Most of these establishments were in the hands of Parsi merchants.

Statistics from 1875 reveal that export of textiles to India from England increased from £16 million to £20 million between 1866 and 1868. However, all was far from rosy for Indian cotton mills. Between 1859 and 1882 imported cotton piece goods, mainly from Lancashire, paid 5% in duty, with yarn carrying 3.5%. But fear of competition from Indian mills led to a great agitation in Lancashire, which resulted in the removal of practically all India's import duties between 1882 and 1894.

By 1900, more than 100 mills were in production throughout Bombay, including the National, Nerlad, Dhun, Presidency, Calicut and the Century. It was again to Bolton that Wadia turned when all those mills required steam engine power. Other firms local to Hick, Hargreaves such as Dobson & Barlow, E. & J. Rigby, and John Musgrave supplied large numbers of engines, transmission equipment and textile machinery to the rapidly expanding Wadia enterprises. Indeed, Bolton Archives recall that in 1883 Hick, Hargreaves exported the most powerful steam engine ever made to a Bombay textile mill.

The spread of India's cotton and textile weaving industry was on a parallel with the diffusion of railways and electricity. Other towns, aware of the huge employment that was nudging Bombay into the forefront of industrial supremacy – still only exceeded by Calcutta because of her heavy industry and shipbuilding – stimulated the rise of textile production in such places as Indore. In 1866, having established its presence in cotton manufacture a mere two years earlier, the Nandlal Bhandari Mills bought a steam engine from Higginbotham & Manock of Manchester. While 50 years earlier in Lancashire cotton had been king, it was now the turn of India to 'challenge the might of Manchester'.

Statistics reveal that Bombay's cotton and textile industries boomed from 1884 to 1895 when 70 mills were in production – a factor not lost on Lancashire industry.

The textile industry arrives in Ahmedabad

The year 1859 was the year of rebirth for Ahmedabad. In that year, Sheth Ranchhodlal Chhotalal laid the foundation of the first power-driven spinning mill there. The railway line BBCIR had not yet progressed far enough north to embrace the city, so bullock carts from Cambay hauled all Chhotalal's machinery for erecting a mill, including 2500 spindles. This cartage is recorded as costing him a mere Rs.170.

Success of the first pioneering textile venture in Ahmedabad led other entrepreneurs to establish mills, and by 1878 four mills were employing hundreds in the city. In 1900 the number of mills had risen to 27. All spun yarn and were not manufacturing cloth. Later, Ahmedabad enjoyed healthy exports to China. Additionally, new mills in Gujarat and the Deccan area competed in that vibrant market.

The number of mills exceeded 20 by 1890 and reached 52 in 1910. One began the manufacture of fine and superfine fabrics, which were suited for the middle and upper classes. Diversification had created jobs in abundance – a blessing as Ahmedabad's population, like the rest of India, had threatened to upset the stability she was enjoying, and without employment 'anarchy was deemed to reign supreme'. By then, Indian merchants had become relatively rich and their wealth was created directly as a result of the Raj, Britain's inventive spirit and her industrial achievements.

While Bombay slowly declined as India's textile centre, Ahmedabad threatened to overtake it in 1925 with 77 mills to the former's 58. The town's textile industries had grown phenomenally after World War I with a batch of large steam engines from John Musgrave of Bolton. A brand-new mill for Haravalabad was equipped with an engine in 1915. In 1920 three mills were expanded to provide employment for over 5000 workers. Two years later, the Asoka Mill imported from the same foundry an engine that survived well after Independence. From humble beginnings, Ahmedabad grew into a major north Indian industrial city.

Nagpur and southern India

The great entrepreneur Jamsetji Tata built a factory in Nagpur in 1887. The benefits of creating a thriving textile industry were not lost on South India. Coimbatore, today the second largest industrial city in Tamil Nadu after Madras, began with the British importing textile machinery from Platt Bros, of Oldham in the 1880s, and the Bangalore Steam Woollen Mills Company was founded in about 1881. When Binny & Company took over this enterprise, the mills were expanded with 1500 woollen spindles and 50 looms for supplying blankets to the government. The outfit diversified to produce cotton yarn when, in 1916, cotton cloth production was started on the first batch of Northrop automatic looms from America.

Cotton hosiery production had begun as early as 1895, with silk hosiery a few years later. Having run on steam power since its inception, the company changed over to electricity for the whole of its production in 1905 when hydro dams were brought into service. At its peak, what is now known as the Bangalore Woollen, Cotton & Silk Mills Company employed nearly 7200 workers with 43 680 cotton and 8100 woollen, union and silk

Machine room at the Government Hosiery Institute, Ludhiana, Punjab, c.1920s (Courtesy of the British Library)

spindles. Many other mills were established throughout Coimbatore and South India, including an early factory in Madurai, with 83 looms in 1929 and in Travancore, with 11 904 looms in 1931.

India's cotton spinning and textile industry grew at a phenomenal rate. Statistics compiled and published in *Engineering* reveal that from 1880 to 1900 the number of mills increased by 206%, with the number of looms up 186% and spindles 218%. Then, the Bombay Presidency possessed 73% of all mills, 72% of the spindles and 78% of the looms. The amount of cotton consumed was assessed as 1424 300 bales of 400 lb each.

In 1900, when the first reliable statistics that included manpower appear to have been compiled, a daily average of 156 039 people were employed, comprising 99 697 men, 31 247 women, 15 564 'young' persons and 9531 children, who worked 40 542 looms and 4 932 602 spindles. In that year, India's textile industry covered many areas of the country: Bombay City, 84; Bombay districts, 54; Calcutta, 10; Madras City and districts, 11; North-West Provinces, Cawnpore, 4; North-West Provinces, Agra 2; Punjab Delhi, Lahore and Amritsar, 5; Ajmer, Indore, Berar and Travancore one each; Mysore 2 and Pondicherry 4. By 1914, India had become the fourth-greatest cotton manufacturing country in the world.

Machinery for the cotton/textile industry

There were some wonderful and fanciful ideas to reduce manpower within the textile industry. A Major Hassard came out with a cotton press in 1870 that adopted a lever principle in its simplest form. It was designed so that local workmen could manufacture it cheaply. Hard on the heels of Hassard's invention was the application of hydraulic power. An engraving from *The Engineer* of 1870 shows the general arrangement of two machines that were conveniently worked by one accumulator, each press having a separate differential apparatus. As cotton arrived from the villages and was taken to the building's upper floor to be examined and sorted by women – and, regrettably, children – pumps were placed into service. The loaded accumulator then rose and the machine was ready for action. With one machine, between 15 and 20 bales per hour were packed.

A report on exports of cotton and textile machinery to India was compiled in 1894. The chief imports from England were the cotton-spinning machines themselves, engines and boilers – India had no foundries of significance then capable of producing large flywheel steam engines – shafting and gearing, roller gins and the early steam-engine-driven dynamos. Most other ancillary parts were made in Bombay. In that year, the value of British exports to India's cotton and textile industries was running at £80,000 per month, according to an official survey. 'Although some of the smaller types of engines are being increasingly made in Calcutta, Madras, Bombay and other Indian towns, England still retains the supremacy for motors of high power,' the report concluded.

Unquestionably, the renowned machinery manufacturer Platt Bros secured the lion's share of spindles and looms that served India. Its output must have been phenomenal, with few textile mills in Bombay or Ahmedabad functioning without some machinery from the Oldham firm. Most steam-driven plants came from Bolton, with Hick, Hargreaves the largest of the British suppliers. By 1862, some 40 mill engines were installed in Bombay, with double that amount in the next decade. The firm had delivered over 150 units by 1890.

The biggest steam engine that Hick, Hargreaves installed in an Indian cotton mill was for the Manockji Petit plant in Bombay in about 1885. The *Textile Manufacturer* of 15 February 1890, a Manchester-based publication, heavily criticised the Bombay mill for ordering such a large engine, feeling that it was 'imprudent', but later retracted and gave its blessing to the mill, probably when the installation proved a success. The *Textile Manufacturer* commented:

> Mr Wadia of the mill is to be congratulated on the successful results which have been obtained and the courage he displayed in the erection of such large engines long before anything of the size was attempted in this country.
>
> Much imported cotton was used, including bales from Jinja and Kampala in Uganda, Egypt and America.
>
> All the factories at Cawnpore convey to the visitor the impression of cotton mills in Lancashire, with home architecture of four and five storeys and spacious mill yards, all kept scrupulously clean and tidy by Lancashire managers. Such a contrast exists to most indigenously run mills; filthy and unhygienic from all accounts. A much larger percentage of Lancashire inside men (weaving and spinning masters) is employed at Cawnpore than anywhere else in India.
>
> In Cawnpore several British-run mills have a mail-order business, besides placing part of their production through selling brokers, who guarantee the account and receive 1.8 per cent to 1.12 per cent commission. Workers are well treated and receive generous product discounts, which no doubt they sell on to their friends. The mills are well ventilated and generously windowed for natural light; the contrast with Indian run mills again noted. Roughly speaking, Cawnpore represents about 10 per cent of the total Indian cotton industry.

A report by A.S. Pearse stated that coal from Calcutta cost Rs.14 per ton, although Bombay mills were noted as using mainly crude oil to raise steam. Although women normally attended to their children before starting work, he observed that in the Indian-run mills many very young children were employed in reeling rooms. Pearse summarised: 'Work in the cotton mills is lighter than in the jute mills of Calcutta, which is the great industry of Bengal.'

The little-known firm of James Howorth & Company, founded 1858 in Farnworth, near Bolton, was unusual in providing early air-conditioning systems for cotton mills to prevent decolourisation of yarn by atmospheric pollution. Both industries in India benefited from the firm's development of its filtered air-conditioning systems. Records indicate that at one time, the Farnworth factory was totally committed to Indian orders.

From about 1910, diesel engines gained a foothold in the textile industry. One firm at the forefront of this embryonic technology that secured orders for their engines to power dynamos and alternators to Indian utilities was Mirrlees of Stockport. Its first large contract to the textile industry was for two engines for driving machinery and an alternator at the Khatau-Makanji Spinning & Weaving Company in Bombay. Successful in service, Mirrlees was subsequently favoured for four engines that provided main drives in textile factories in Madurai and Gulbarga and for the prestigious Manockji Petit Mills, Bombay. The firm is now part of a German–Danish combine at the same Stockport factory that once served the Empire.

The Finlay connection

James Finlay & Company started business from a Glasgow office in 1750, establishing its presence in India from 1812. The firm began trading with Ritchie, Steuart & Company in Bombay from 1816 to 1828. It took an important interest in shipping. Finlay opened up branches in Calcutta and Karachi, and a cotton mill agency in Bombay in 1902. A new firm, Finlay Mills, was established, with the Swan Mill floated as a public company. The mill commenced operations with 30 000 ring spindles and 600 looms. To compete in the highly volatile textile market, most mills – including some known as Finlay Mills – were heavily modernised and survived well into the 1950s.

The early jute industry and the Dundee connection

According to James Finlay, 'It's Dundee jute that placed our town on the world's industrial map'; and it was a well-known saying in Britain during the 1940s that Dundee was built on jute, jam, rich fruit cakes and toffees as well as journalism – notably the *Dandy* and *Beano* comics.

Yet the jute industry centred on Bengal was by no means established solely at the behest of British merchants. Jute was originally a cottage industry. In pre-biblical times, it was used for cordage, fabrics, flooring, decorations and roofing. In Bengal, where the fibre is grown, it formed the basis of hand-spinning and hand-weaving of ropes, screen and matting, plus some coarse gunny clothing for garments and bedding materials. Later, it was used for a number of diverse items including bags for packing grain and various other agricultural produce, particularly during the 16th to 18th centuries. In villages, jute clothing was common. Almost every family in Bengal raised some jute on its land, and the sack-weaving caste were called *kapalis*. The only other area in the world known to have produced some form of jute fibre was southern Russia.

FINLAY JUTE MILLS

THE FINLAY FIRM ESTABLISHED its presence in Calcutta in October 1870 by installing John Alexander Anderson, a Scot, who also became a partner in the Bombay branch. In Calcutta, Finlay's business centred on the disposal of piece goods and in operating an agency for Scottish Imperial Fire & Life Insurance Company. In 1873 the Champdany Jute Mill was built with presses from Fawcett, Preston, with a Mr P.S. Murray from Dundee nominated to take over and run the mill. However, while the surroundings of mills in Calcutta today are reasonably healthy, in 1875 the Champdany Jute Mill was 'surrounded by malarial swamps of the worst type', according to Murray who packed up and left in 1877.

Finlay's shipping interests in the Clan Line enabled bales of jute to be hauled from Calcutta to Scotland, further securing Finlay's expanding interests in eastern India. Its business agreements with Manchester industrialists, not least for large Lancashire steam engines and ancillary machinery, were given generous support by the city, and trade was noted as being 'in both directions'. In 1881 the Champdany Jute Mill bought out the Wellington Jute Mill, which was sited in the grounds of Warren Hastings' former country seat, and for a time the mill's staff resided in Hastings' former bungalow on the banks of the Hooghly River.

Finlay mills were quickly modernised when new technology was in the offing. Steam turbine power was introduced in the Champdany Jute Mill when the company purchased a turbine from Belliss & Morcom in 1909.

The processing of raw jute through various stages at that time was the result of indigenous exploration. However, there is little evidence that the growing of jute was undertaken on any organised scale until late in the 18th century when, as a result of the trading enterprise of the EIC, possibilities for the fibre and fabric came to be known to the outside world.

There is a touch of irony concerning the first shipments of jute to Britain. The British government were in urgent need of cheap, coarse linens to supply naval and military requirements when the EIC directors were exploring new outlets for this produce of Bengal. Warren Hastings' name is connected with a jute factory in 1781, no doubt with backing from the EIC's Board of Governors. Two letters written in 1791 throw some light on jute's first arrival in Britain, showing it to be the result not so much of the flax merchants' search for new fibres as of the EIC promoting its own products.

On 11 March 1791 the Calcutta Board of Trade representative wrote:

> We are continuing our researches for the new Articles for Export to Great Britain ... We sent a number in the Packet Ships, samples of clean hemp of the Country, one of the rough Hemp and one of Jute (we have no English name for this) the material of which Gunnies and the Ropes used in cording Bales are made.

In 1793 a small quantity, 100 tons, of jute fibre was exported from India to London by the company, as it became vitally important to find a substitute for Russian flax, which was traditionally used in the western countries through machinery for turning out ropes, sail canvas and sacking. Until 1796 samples of jute were sent by the EIC to London but it was not received with any enthusiasm until recurring Continental European wars interrupted Baltic flax. One shipment of 1580 cwt was received from Bengal labelled 'jute', but it was not distinguished from flax. However, a William Roxburgh of the Calcutta Botanic Garden (see also Chapter 21) was enthusiastic about the possibilities of jute, putting much energy into persuading EIC officials to continue sending samples home if only to publicise the commodity.

To many people interested in the processing of jute, the choice of Dundee on the River Tay in Scotland, some 460 miles north of London, to complement Bengal in finishing off the raw material may at first seem strange. Many reasoned that it should be a town on the Thames from where most EIC ships sailed. Or perhaps Liverpool, Hull or Manchester – even though the latter had no port until the building of the Manchester Ship Canal in 1894 – would seem a more natural choice. However, Dundee was chosen for a very good reason. Fishing was important to Scotland from early times and led to the development of one of the country's largest whaling fleets. Women were employed in the spinning and weaving of local flax. This trade gradually developed into a textile industry that became closely linked with whaling in the 19th century after the discovery that jute fibre, when mixed with whale oil, could be woven into sacking for bags and carpet backing. From a population of some 35 000 in about 1820, the town's inhabitants increased to 130 000 in less than half a century.

The first major consignment of jute arrived in Dundee in 1822. It seems unlikely that Dundee was in a position to start a mill dedicated to jute, given the early difficulties manufacturers in Dundee faced when processing the raw fibre. In 1818 there were only five mills in Dundee, rising to 17 in 1822 with 33 others established in the surrounding countryside. Spinners were in demand and were working flat out to fulfil the manufacturers' clamour for flax yarn. The first steam-powered jute mill was set up in Dundee in 1830 but the raw jute exports from India to Britain by the EIC remained low for a number of years, as attempts by the company to use the jute fibre extensively in modern industry were thwarted by technical difficulties in bleaching and dyeing. It was only around 1832 and using whale oil that pure jute could be bleached after spinning 'with modern machinery'. The first weaving mill for jute was set up in the town in 1838. In that same year the Verdant Mill was constructed and was considerably expanded over the next 26 years until, in 1864, with jute fibre arriving by the shipload, three steam engines were installed capable of driving 70 power looms and 2800 spindles.

The rising demand for jute as a result of the Crimean War added impetus to the industry in Bengal. With supplies disrupted from Russia, the EIC concentrated on exploiting this trade. By 1860 Dundee enjoyed a near monopoly of the world's factory-made jute cloth trade based on cheap Indian supplies of raw jute. Figures compiled by the EIC speak for themselves. From 1828 to 1833, 1000 tons were exported, rising to 11 700 tons between 1838 and 1843 and peaking by the start of the Crimean War in 1854 at 73 900 tons. Between 1863 and 1868, using a mixture of steam and sailing vessels around the Cape to Dundee, Bengal exported a phenomenal 262 800 tons of raw jute. In return, heavy machinery for the emerging jute industry was carried to India. Like most enterprises in India from those times, trade was a two-way street.

Emergence of jute machine manufacturing in India

As Scotland's jute manufacturing industry prospered, India's cottage-industry jute hand-looms' days were numbered. Machine manufacture of jute products based on steam power and steam-operated baling presses for packing as devised by Fawcett, Preston's Phoenix Foundry, Liverpool, under its 'Cyclone' trademark, put the final coffin nail in local family enterprise. Scotsman George Acland set up a steam-driven mill with a modest capacity of 8 tons per day at Rishra, near Serampore, on the western bank of the Hooghly River in 1855. He brought over machinery from Dundee – some of which was hand-powered only.

The Bengal jute mills found a ready market for their products although initial difficulties of financing and obtaining the required equipment prevented what should have been a rapid growth of India's jute manufacturing industry. In 1869 only five steam-powered mills, comprising 950 looms from Platt Bros, of Oldham, were in operation. Perhaps this slow development may be attributed to the huge increase of Bombay's textile industry when Britain's machinery and steam engine manufacturers were heavily engaged in providing plant and services for this commerce. At one time, the major Bolton engine producers all had a backlog of orders destined for cotton mills in both Bombay and Ahmedabad.

However, the rise in demand for engines for jute production stimulated Lancashire engine producers to enlarge their foundry capacity, thereby ensuring that others would not 'grab business by the back door'. Irrespective of an attempt to stifle competition, many new foundries courting business from Bengal jute producers noted that prices were trimmed from the larger manufacturers. The phenomenal rise of Bengal's jute industry contributed immeasurably to Britain's machinery exports. Hick, Hargreaves estimated that 'by 1913 India shall account for over one seventh of all Britain's machinery exports and 38% of India's imports of electrical apparatus and machinery; a much higher proportion than in other parts of the Empire'.

Fawcett, Preston – known locally as 'Fossetts' – exported its first hydraulic bale press to Bombay in 1863. Between 1863 and 1905 over 100 such presses were shipped to Bombay, Madras, Karachi and Calcutta, especially for the jute industry. 'These orders from India taxed the utmost resources of the establishment. They had to be turned out complete with their system of pumps, engines and boilers. Before being dispatched, each was tested at the Phoenix Works by pressing cotton or jute into a bale as if it were already in Bengal,' stated a senior manager at the factory. The most famous of these presses was the Watson Fawcett 'Cyclone', which had a capacity of up to 60 400 lb bales of cotton or jute per hour. A catalogue issued about 1890 describes how a customer erected one of these jute presses in India in 1889 and wrote to the patentee stating:

> our press, within three months of it being set to work, had reached an output of 629 bales in a little over 11 hours, and that it often worked at a speed of 63 bales per hour; and that judging from the way the press was working then, though in the hands of men who had never seen a 'Cyclone' press before, we expect an average turn-out exceeding 60 bales per hour during the next season.

The inventor of the 'Cyclone' press and of earlier grid presses – 12 to 15 bales per hour – was a former marine engineer, James Watson, who had been associated with Ralli Brothers in Bombay. The merit of 'Cyclone' technology was that it compressed bales to a greater density and much more quickly than had been possible before. Increased density cut down shipping space and also reduced the risk of fire.

Once enjoying a virtual monopoly to the jute and textile industry, Fossetts' dominance was eclipsed when Henry Berry started, through local agents in Calcutta and Bombay, to produce and sell larger and more powerful hydraulic presses for both Bombay's textile and Bengal's jute manufacturers. A varied range enabled both industries to handle 35 000 to 40 500 lb bales per hour. The machines were an instant success. However, within three years of entering the Indian market, Henry Berry redesigned its Indian presses at the Leeds factory to cater for the larger bales that Egyptian merchants packaged. Presses were sent out to Alexandria that could comfortably deal with 65 000 to 70 800 lb bales per hour. India maintained that 500 lb was sufficient for its workforce to handle, but the marketing ploy in trade magazines was convincing publicity for Henry Berry.

By far the largest supplier of steam engines to the jute industry was Hick, Hargreaves, of Bolton, which had built locomotives from its Soho Works from 1833. Between 1889 and 1912 Hick, Hargreaves constructed 32 engines, ranging from a small version for the Karmahatty Mill to its largest for the Barnagore Mill. The total horsepower exported to Bengal's jute industry during those years – in excess of 50 000 hp, was an inimitable achievement from England's biggest foundry engaged in the production of stationary steam engines. The Bolton Iron & Steel Company, local to Hick, Hargreaves, forged many semi-mild-steel crankshafts for the engine builder.

It was not only Bolton engine foundries that were dependent upon the Indian market. A host of smaller firms had tailored their products to India's cotton, jute and electrical supply industries, the competition ruthless to the point of driving cut-throat tender bids into virtual bankruptcy should delivery date penalties be invoked. Daniel Adamson, of Duckinfield, near Manchester, established in 1851, equipped at least 23 mills with engines and boilers, including a 'Lancashire Witch' portable engine. Its first triple expansion mill engine in 1863 went to Sassoon Cotton Mill in Bombay. Daniel Adamson was well ahead of many of its competitors in technology and mechanical efficiency before the firm abandoned steam engine production in favour of turbine power, of which many went to the Calcutta Electric Supply. By 1900 some 48 engines and turbines from Daniel Adamson were scattered throughout Bengal, with many installed in the Dacca–Narayanganj jute-growing area. Ashton Frost & Company of Blackburn, established in 1870, began production of engines from the

1880s. Its products were used as pumps and jute mill drives, with over a dozen supplied to East Bengal's jute industry. There is evidence that many of its products survived well after Independence. The Burnley Iron Works began business in the 1830s, casting beam engines a decade later. Technical improvements and the changeover to horizontal engines enabled the firm to supply four jute mills along the banks of the Hooghly River from 1872. The firm ceased business in 1927. Through agents Messrs Felber, Jucker & Company, of Manchester and Bombay, Blackburn's Phoenix Foundry, of William Dickinson, Loom & Machine Makers, exported jute and textile loom machines to Bombay in 1860 and the jute industry in 1869.

Another Blackburn foundry, Yates & Thom, whose complete records have not survived today, was known to have supplied many engines and gearing and ancillary equipment to mills in Jessore, Dacca and Calcutta between 1902 and 1936. John Petrie's Phoenix Works at Rochdale, established about 1819, exported its first engine to Russia in 1836. Soon afterwards, Bombay cotton mills benefited from its products before engines were shipped to jute mills along the Hooghly. It appears that its last export to this industry was around 1909. Preston possessed only a few small foundries compared to Blackburn or Bolton, one being Joseph Foster. Up to 1900 this firm shipped out 18 engines to India, including one of 800 ihp to the Kilburn Brown Jute Mill in Calcutta.

The Castle Ironworks of Buckley & Taylor in Oldham was established in 1861 to produce beam, horizontal and vertical mill engines, as well as gearing. Juxtaposed with the world's principal supplier of looms, Platt Bros (of Oldham), the two firms occasionally combined their resources to supply a mill's main drives and spinning machines. This was the case, first in Bombay around 1865, then later for equipping a jute mill near Narayanganj in 1870. Buckley & Taylor expanded to produce huge horizontal cross-compound engines, receiving an order for Calcutta around 1908. However, Bolton's principal steam engine foundries then all but dominated the market and the firm withdrew from producing steam engines, remaining in business as general engineers. Its last export to the jute industry was in 1920.

Electrical generation

Electrical generation was installed in some jute mills before 1900, but solely for lighting and office fans. One firm that found a secure niche for its products was the ubiquitous Belliss & Morcom. The firm never competed in the large steam engine prime-mover business, preferring to specialise in smaller units that drove pumps, generators, dynamos and so on, rather than the whole mill or mine complex. It appears that the first mill to install the firm's steam-engine-driven dynamo was Calcutta's Serampore Mill in 1893. In 1904 a 240 bhp generating set driving a Clayton Engineering alternator was the largest engine installed to date by the firm in the jute industry. Most installations by 1914 were small at the 25-plus jute mills that benefited from this Birmingham-based foundry's technology. Belliss & Morcom produced a range of paraffin-engine-driven dynamos to many jute factories including Calcutta's Cheviot Mills.

End of the old order

World War I signalled the abrupt end of the old order and ushered in change on a radical scale. Although Indian mines dug record amounts of coal, Indian industry braced itself for the new order and began courting electrical power. The jute industry, although not in the forefront of this transition, nevertheless began to phase out many of its obsolete steam engines. The new technology was fraught with strong reservation and the cost was 'prohibitive'.

Electricity from turbines made its small mark – perhaps somewhat grudgingly – when the Gondalpara Jute Mill ordered from British Thomson-Houston a turbo-alternator in 1919. Similarly, General Electric Company, from its installed a huge synchronous motor in Calcutta's Bansberia Jute Mill, plus all other electrical plant in that same year. Later, General Electric Company increased its supply to the mill with additional induction motors, making it one of the most modern jute mills in India. The mill relied on new English Electric steam turbines installed in modern power plants for Calcutta Electric Supply Company to supply its current. From 1920 Metropolitan-Vickers, of Trafford Park supplied numerous small turbo-alternators to a number of jute mills, as well as synchronous drives fed from the new power plants, also commissioned by Calcutta Electric Supply.

By 1870, Bengal and Dundee were synonymous with jute, and Bolton's connection with Bombay's cotton industry was legendary. Both industries employed thousands of workers. India's rapid emergence as an industrial economy was assured and the textile industry clamoured for the latest technology; the advent of electricity over the next two decades created 'new and better conditions' and workers flooded into the cities.

Chapter 17

SUGAR, TEA AND COFFEE INDUSTRIES

*If the English working class enjoy rotting their tea with sugar
or acquiring a taste for tea and coffee, then taxed it shall be.*
ENGLISH PARLIAMENT DECREE, *c.*1700

Coffee is Satan's drink.
POPE CLEMENT VII (1478–1534)

The sugar industry

Sugar cane has been cultivated in India throughout the centuries. It had always been an important crop, from which two sweetening agents, gur and khandsari, were made. During the formation of the EIC from around 1640 to 1750, India was an exporter of khandsari. A few modern refineries began to be set up on an experimental basis from the 1870s but the industry grew slowly. This lack of progress can be attributed to the huge volume of cheap sugar beet arriving from the Caribbean and Central and South America. India could not serve Europe with this commodity at a time when emphasis was on constructing railways and harbours, as well as building the textile, jute and extraction industries.

Sugar was grown for many years near the coast in western India, which had the required rainfall. Another area that benefited from a favourable climate was Hyderabad, under the guidance of the Nizam himself. However, poor roads failed to spread the cultivated crop to other parts of India. The absence of any highway in the accepted sense meant that local farmers grew cash crops as they saw fit, with opium well ahead of sugar and other commodities. It was the free, uncontrolled market in operation until the middle 19th century.

From the 1760s onwards, with EIC commerce spreading its wings, sugar, of varying degrees of refinement, was made in almost every district of

Bengal and Bihar where cane was raised. Superior sugar was produced at Rangpur, Birbhum, Radhanagar, Bengal and various districts of Patna. Not unnaturally, the transition to mechanisation penetrated those districts along with the spread of canals.

Early sugar mills

The family sugar mill before the arrival of the British was basic but functional and had served local communities well over the centuries. When EIC farmers extended their influence, changes in agriculture were made with the knowledge that mechanised sugar mills could process sugar 'by the ton rather than by the bag'.

From the 1830s the Bombay government took positive steps to promote the cultivation of various crops. Restrictive laws discouraged opium, which had been grown in Ahmedabad, Kaira and Khandesh. Strong complaints about the trade were raised in the British Parliament. EIC directors, having made huge fortunes from the opium crop, especially from exports to China, gradually got the message. Two agricultural stations were established by the government – one in the Kaira district in 1837 and the other in Poona in 1841 – which were instrumental in extending the cultivation of sugar cane, along with potatoes, rice and wheat.

Mauritius sugar cane was then introduced by the government in several districts and was, from all accounts, successful. This Mauritius sugar cane imported by the EIC was necessary, as native cane grown chiefly in the Telegu zamindaris was of very poor quality.

Sugar became 'an accepted cash crop of significance' in the 1850s. Cultivated acreage increased as the numbers of masonry wells for irrigation increased, and local prosperity rose as families could buy smallholdings, provided the moneylenders were kept at bay.

Despite the importation of mechanised mills, many local farmers still relied upon the bullock and the wooden wheel to squeeze out the juice. The animal and the wheel, along with some of the land, were loaned by private lenders at extortionate rates of interest that reduced many families to beggary despite their hard work. Many could not pay and fled to other states.

Sugar imports to India were causing concern to the authorities towards the end of the 19th century. In 1896, 137000 tons were imported, rising to 203000 tons in 1899. A report on the industry assessed that 'of India's land mass amounting to about 200 million acres, only some three million acres were under cane cultivation. Allowing for 1 ton of cane per acre to be grown, India could be self-sufficient if a concerted approach to remedy this problem was applied'. However, complete mills were by then arriving with modern machinery, the trickle of machinery developing by 1900 into a flood before the outbreak of World War I. A *Blue Book* on the sugar industry was issued, documenting its progress. During the years from 1897 to 1898, 96 mills were in production but only 13 were of any significance in sugar refining. Three of those mills were in Madras, with the first plant in production in 1888.

In 1894 India's sugar industry took a turn for the better. Three large new sugar plants were under construction in Bengal, the Bombay Presidency and Cawnpore. The engines arrived from Fawcett, Preston – 'Fossetts' – of Liverpool, with all ancillary items such as boilers and evaporators supplied from Glasgow.

Sugar industry development after 1900

To encourage further investment in India's fledgling sugar industry, import duties were imposed by the central government. This was very much to India's economic advantage, as comparable-sized mills in Central America were employing over 1000 people engaged not only in cutting and hauling the cane to the factory, but also in processing it and exporting the finished product on narrow-gauge railways. The influence of Manchester was on the wane.

The number of mills was reported as having increased from 27 to 150 between 1929/30 and 1936/37. In 1832, an assessment was ranking the Indian sugar industry third among all organised industries in terms of total capital invested. Between those years, the average acreage had increased by 59%, with many modern mills installed alongside rivers, mainly in Bengal and Bihar.

The modern sugar industry in India developed as a result of the Sugar Industry Protection Act of April 1932, which imposed large duties on imported sugar, mainly from Malaya and Australia, as well as on molasses. The tariffs were 31% *ad valorem* on molasses and Rs.9 1 anna per cwt on sugar itself. Previously, Indian producers of refined sugars had competed fairly unsuccessfully against more efficiently produced imports, although local industry continued to be sustained, producing khand, jaggery, gur and non-crystalline sugar.

One concern that supplied numerous tower cranes to the sugar industry was John M. Henderson, of Aberdeen. With most sugar mills isolated from distribution supplies, the factories were obliged to raise their own steam to drive dynamos and generators. A Henderson 5-ton fixed electric tower crane installation was used for lifting cane from barges into the Pamba River Sugar Mill. A Belliss & Morcom steam-engine-driven alternator supplied power and the same manufacturer's machinery was installed at Sitapur, Oudh, where the district had a large sugar industry and later constructed three 'model mills'. A sugar mill and rum distillery were constructed at Shahjahanpur, in what is now known as the Rosa Sugar factory.

By 1914 there was a glut of sugar worldwide, but the price failed to drop because sugar was in only a few hands. Even so, more mills were constructed, mainly in India as the Caribbean industry was saturated, with over 2200 Glasgow engines working in Cuba alone. India was keen to grab a slice of the market and after World War I British sugar equipment engineers set up many centres, mainly in the northern part of the country. Fossetts was one foundry that enjoyed a good working relationship with India's sugar producers.

Immediately after November 1918, Fossetts shipped no fewer than nine complete sugar factories to India, with several of the company's engineers dispatched on the same machinery-hauling vessels to supervise erection. These factories, which cost around £35,000 each and were capable of crushing up to 600 tons of cane every 24 hours, were complete to the last detail. Each factory consisted of about 100 major items, ranging from 10-ton gear wheels to small strips of lagging. They were all steam driven, with horizontal engines. The new and improved Fawcett-patent (Fossett) cane knives shredded the cane before its entry into the rollers. The Liverpool factory night shift operated for 11 months to help complete these orders as a strict penalty clause for late delivery was then in force.

A direct competitor to Fossetts was Geo Forrester, also from Liverpool, but in a smaller league than its neighbour. Even so, the firm is documented as having supplied plants to Bengal and Bihar before 1900, possibly capable of crushing around 200 tons per day.

After Manchester, Glasgow was possibly Britain's greatest city for heavy engineering products. However, Manchester did not produce complete sugar mills from one manufacturer but did furnish ancillary plant. By the time India embraced sugar production on a grand scale with Glasgow-furnished machinery, she could check the rise of sugar imports.

With Glasgow-based Messrs P.W. McOnie, established in 1840, also shipping complete mills to India from around 1885, competition was intense, with all companies producing excellent cast-iron engines, boilers and evaporators from 1845. During the period from 1837 until 1848, they turned out some 50 engines and 40 mills between them. A further 820 steam engines, 1650 sugar mills, 1200 boilers and 117 waterwheels, as well as 169 evaporating pans, were exported from 1851 until 1876. By 1900, there were nearly 1800 complete sugar mills in Cuba alone, and around 130 similar plants crushing cane in Puerto Rico. It was now India's turn to take a large slice of the market.

In 1885 McOnie works number 1524 – a set of rollers and evaporators – was installed in the Madras Presidency. It was India's first large sugar-crushing plant. Works number 1656 in the same year also went to Madras. A complete plant, including engines and three rollers, was installed in the same presidency in 1893. The firm was unsuccessful in bidding for the Cawnpore Sugar Works in 1899, but was successful in supplying a steam engine connected to a dynamo from Crompton for the same factory.

Between 1901 and 1924, 13 Glasgow contracts were furnished to the expanding Indian sugar industry, with a huge Mirrlees engine comprising cylinders 26 in. × 66 in. to the Phorbhanga Mills at Lohat. Mirrlees all but developed the Amritsar sugar industry with two huge mills in 1924. Although the combine provided small steam, and later diesel, engines for driving 'Dinky-toy dynamos' for lighting, fans and office duties, Glasgow could not compete with the ubiquitous Birmingham foundry of Belliss & Morcom, which virtually dominated the Indian sugar factories' demand for small, highly efficient steam engines, mainly for lighting and pumping duties. Most of the dynamos and, later, alternators were from Crompton, Dick Kerr, General Electric Company, Phoenix, Scott Mountain and British Thomson-Houston.

From 1946 to 1965, Mirrlees supplied three huge mills to Bihar, similar to many of the plants delivered from 1900. The R. Laidlaw foundry of Glasgow furnished most centrifugal machinery, being a specialist in this technology.

Preserved sugar mill industry engines

Unlike the jute, textile or cotton-spinning plants, sugar mills have managed to retain many vintage machines in service from the Edwardian era. The oldest, located at Barrah Chalkis, Bihar – where steam locomotives were reported in use into the 21st century – had three Harvey steam engines from 1906 in seasonal commission. The Cawnpore Sugar Works at Marhowrah, also in Bihar, retains two Harvey Engineering engines installed in 1920 and 1924. A water injection engine from Blairs of Glasgow, 1904, in the same mill continues to function.

Other sugar mills throughout Bihar use a host of Mirrlees engines from the late 1920s and early 1930s. The Central Provinces, with ten vintage sugar plants from 1930, such as Balrampur Chini Mills, installed 1933/34, see no reason to phase out the steam engines installed and placed into service when the complex was first commissioned. At Prattapur Sugar Mill, two Harvey engines installed in 1923 continue to perform as originally designed.

The tea industry

Tea was introduced into England from China sometime in the middle of the 17th century, possibly in a ship belonging to the EIC. Throughout the Celestial Kingdom it was revered for its medicinal effects. King Louis XIV of France (1638–1715) drank tea to 'cure his vertigo'. Only in 1657 is the first account of its sale in England recorded. Together with the fragrant leaf came respect for the drink and the ceremonial way in which it was prepared and served. This ceremony may have originated in China and then passed on to Japan, where (green) tea-drinking ceremonies are held even today.

Tea took over from gin and was pivotal in the history of Britain in the late 18th and early 19th centuries, until the introduction of coffee into Europe partially knocked tea off its once unassailable pedestal. However, tea and opium were inextricably interlinked and again it is to China that British merchants – including the EIC – looked for profit and power in the exploitation of both commodities.

The first traders to capitalise on China's weakness for opium were, from 1700, the Portuguese in Macau, with business accelerating to such a degree that in 1781 Warren Hastings felt tempted to dispatch a cargo of opium to China. In 1819 an opium mart opened in Bombay; the returning vessels from China hauled tea. One of the oldest tea companies in business today is Twining, which can trace its roots back to 1705.

At the time when tea was introduced to India, it was believed to be therapeutic. After all, reasoned those in the know, why did so many Chinese live to be octogenarians? Was it not because of the huge quantities of tea that they drank? In England people accorded it time and space, and this alone must have had the effect of producing a sense of wellbeing.

Assam and Darjeeling tea-growing areas

Tea consumption increased dramatically during the early 19th century. Fashion and reduced costs built a market that suppliers were finding hard to meet. To break the Chinese monopoly, tea traders looked to India to fill the gap. As tea consumption increased from about 1820, EIC traders looked for new sources of supply.

The first experiments with Chinese tea were conducted in Assam where climatic conditions, with heavy rainfall, were ideal. Initially it was a failure, although the same seeds subsequently grew well in Darjeeling and northern India. Looking farther afield, in 1820 English botanists led by General Robert Bruce (c.1785-c.1850) stumbled across the single-stem *Camellia sinensis* bush in the Sandiya district of Upper Assam. Elated, the team sent leaf samples to London for analysis as well as to Calcutta for botanical evaluation. The samples were immediately recognised as tea – a plant previously unknown in India – and from that recognition the India tea industry was born.

The locally grown 'weed' was found to be genetically similar to the Chinese tea plant and the two were initially nurtured together. In the early 1840s around 42 000 saplings were transported to Assam, Darjeeling, southern India – not successfully – and some other hill pockets in the north bordering the Himalayas. Although many of the plants died in transport, enough survived to begin production. But it was a Dr Campbell, posted to Darjeeling as the town's civil surgeon after it became a health resort for the British in 1837, who is credited as the pioneer of tea cultivation in this area.

After tea samplings took root in Dr Campbell's backyard, the government laid out tea nurseries in the area during 1847. Five years later, enterprising Scotsmen planted the first commercial tea gardens, growing in number to 39 within two decades. Plantation labourers were imported from Bihar State and Nepal. Strangely, Governor-General Lord Bentinck only announced the discovery of tea officially in a speech he gave in 1844, calling for the development of the industry that by then was well under way.

The first shipment of Indian tea reached the newly created London market in 1838. In that same year Assam tea seeds were successfully planted in Ceylon. During those early days, Indian tea growers and their British managers were mere beginners dabbling in tea production – but they were quick learners. Eventually they got it right and Indian tea became a great success, as it is today.

Two factors contributed to its popularity. There was no duty on Indian tea as there was on Chinese tea, and anybody could ship it to Britain, as the EIC then no longer had the monopoly on trade to India. P&O and BISNC shipping lines were fast competing as the principal cargo services from England to Calcutta and Bombay and vice versa, with other companies providing regular coastal tramp services. Crates of tea were noted as deck cargoes on the return sailings to London. Darjeeling tea was once termed the 'Champagne of the world's tea industry'. This accolade was not misplaced.

Tea in Travancore

Power generation came to a remote part of north Travancore because of the establishment of the tea industry. The steady increase in the yield of the leaf came about from experiments in the 1860s and 1870s, in which bushes were planted in the Kanan Devan Hills, which led to the formation of a company that took its name from the area. By 1901 three organised factories at Sevenmally, Nallatanni and Periavurray were in full seasonal production.

Nilgiri

Nilgiri is situated in the hilly Western Ghats. Tea bushes were first planted in 1835 in the Ketti Valley, Ooty, on an experimental basis. Prior to the planting of tea, a lake was constructed between 1823 and 1825 by John Sullivan, possibly the only European in the district. The lake was 1.5 miles long by 150 yards wide. A small hydraulic power plant was constructed after 1900. Today, Nilgiri provides some 25% of India's output of 750 million kg of tea and 3.5% of total world consumption.

Finlay & Company's tea interests

The rapid development of cotton and jute mills, augmented by shipping, failed to limit Finlay & Company's commercial interests. 'India is ripe for any development an industrialist cares to undertake. All categories of good, reliable labour are there for recruitment. Forget Africa; she is synonymous with becoming a white-man's grave,' stated *The Times* in 1870. Tea was now a commodity in great demand and Finlay expanded to embrace the production of this vital crop. The firm initially set up numerous gardens in Assam and Darjeeling. The notion that tea garden staff need not be specially selected and trained nearly saw the demise of its fledgling interests in that industry.

Finlay did not have things all its own way. The rise of Sir Thomas Johnstone Lipton (1850–1931), a Glasgow grocer, began to be felt when he opened his first teashop in 1876. After purchasing extensive tea, coffee and cocoa plantations in Ceylon to supply his retail outlets, he directed his interests to getting huge amounts of tea from newly acquired estates in northern India.

Gilkes Hydraulic Turbines of Kendal, England

Tea brought hydropower to Darjeeling in its wake. The first hydroelectric plant was installed there in 1885, with machinery not from Gunther Bros, of Oldham, as has been sometimes suggested, but by Gilkes, of Kendal. It had first exported hydraulic turbines to India in January 1869, with a single guide blade unit fed from a low fall of a mere 8 ft. Further units were dispatched to India, until an order was received from the Darjeeling Tea Company in 1883 for a turbine fed from a 70 ft fall of water. It is possible that this turbine drove a dynamo and can, therefore, lay claim to being the first non-municipal electric power plant in Assam.

'Darjeeling tea plantations go to pot'

A *Daily Telegraph* half-page feature article on 18 October 2003, claimed: 'Darjeeling tea plantations go to pot.' It stated: 'Innumerable tea estates, ranging from several hundred to several thousand acres, are available to-day for a token Rs.1 (about 1.4p) each. Mounting liabilities make them an unattractive proposition, forcing owners to suffer recurring losses before abandoning them.' Where, in the once majestic Darjeeling Planters Club, Mallory and Irvine stayed shortly before embarking on their ill-fated 1924 Everest Expedition, there are now peeling walls, and dust covers the regal library.

The majority of Darjeeling's 78 tea gardens sold their 2002 harvest for about half of what it cost them to produce it. Where 2.2 lb of tea cost around 95p to grow, the consumer pays just 60p to 65p to buy it in India. Those estates cover 40 000 acres and once employed 90 000 people. In the neigh-bouring Dooars and Terai plains, where a substantial portion of India's annual 1.75 billion lb of tea is produced, another 20 estates have been aban-doned. There is no alternative work for the unemployed. Yet, the legacy of the tea industry introduced by the British in the 18th century has estab-lished India as the world's largest tea producer.

Coffee history

For well over a century after its introduction, coffee had a low rating in India, restricted in cultivation and consumption to the Malnad farmers, who grew the crop for subsistence and personal consumption. EIC farmers and agronomists came across this crop after about 1750, and one unnamed English farmer is credited with spreading the coffee plant beyond the hills of Chandragiri.

The renowned trading firm of Parry & Company, founded by Thomas Parry in Madras in 1788, was established for free trading – free of the in-fluence of the EIC – initially selling superior-quality two-year-old Madeira wines. In 1805 the firm built a tanning factory in Madras and can lay claim to founding the first industry in the city. Parry's vision was for the expan-sion of commodities, with tea plantations gaining momentum. Ideally based in southern India, he looked at the potential of coffee, saw a market for the beverage and encouraged further planting. Parry was fortunate in possessing an enterprising manager, J.H. Jolly, who petitioned the Mysore Kingdom for a lease of 40 acres of prime agricultural land to cultivate coffee for export. The petition was duly approved, and it proved to be a turning point for the coffee industry in India.

Jolly's enterprise and exploitation of the drink stimulated other British planters to seek their fortunes in this crop. From about 1850 coffee was cultivated on a grand scale. Over the next 50 years smallholdings coalesced into larger ones that created huge coffee estates, almost all situated in the Coorg district of what is now Karnataka.

The British planters realised that coffee was a variable crop by nature and soon came to accept that markets for this delicacy were volatile. Only the courageous and resourceful would survive to reap its benefits. By about 1880 the landscape in and around the coffee-growing areas was trans-formed, and expatriate planters noted the community changing. Small steam engines had found an additional market for their use.

Just as the tea growers depended on the Calcutta market, coffee estate owners needed the benefits of coastal agents who arranged freight for their produce and guaranteed its safety during transportation. Managing agents also established coffee-curing works, whose subordinates organised seasonal manpower for this labour-intensive industry.

The industry was cruising along nicely without too many problems, part mechanised – with Glasgow and Aberdeen foundries, which had previously supplied the sugar industry, tailoring their engineering to coffee planters' requirements – until 1930, when the winds of global depression swept across India's shore to bite the commodity market. The demand was certainly there – but the money wasn't. For the first time, an industry that had consistently forged ahead on its own efforts was forced to go cap in hand to the government for help. This led to the setting up of the Coffee Cess Committee, which funded activities to promote coffee consumption throughout India. At that time exports had virtually dried up. This board, created in 1936, altered India's landscape for many decades.

Today Tata Coffee has breathed new life into the industry. However, Indian coffee cannot hold a candle to its rival domestic beverage, tea. The country's exports of coffee are merely a trickle compared with those of Latin America and East Africa. Europe today relies mainly on Brazil and Central America for its coffee.

Chapter 18

EARLY AIR SERVICES

Four days to London from Calcutta, don't be daft.
LETTER TO THE *TIMES OF INDIA*

There is still reasonable doubt as to when the first aircraft arrived in India, whether crated or under its own power. What is fact is the date when air transport in India was born. On 18 February 1911, Henry Piquet, flying a Humber bi-plane, carried the first airmail from Allahabad to Naini Junction, some 6 miles away. Little appears to have developed in the way of air transport until 1914, when two aircraft arrived in boxes during World War I, with the sole objective of bombing directly, or directing the fire of British warships upon, the German cruiser *Konigsberg*, which was humiliating the British Admiralty in the East.

The first aircraft were unsophisticated and totally unsuited to tropical conditions, being merely embryonic 'flying kites' designed for the European war theatre and 'held together with glue and tape'. Two new Sopwith-type 807 seaplanes, built at Kingston-upon-Thames, arrived in India in 1915 assembled and test flown, causing some consternation among the locals. The aircraft were reported to be German and about to bomb the city. Most people had never seen an aircraft before and panic broke out. Frantic citizens mobbed the railway station for immediate evacuation. Filled with fuel and bombs, the planes set off to destroy the *Konigsberg*. They had neither firepower nor bombs capable of destroying the 4000-ton cruiser, which was finally disabled by conventional shellfire.

In 1919, when Britain was slowing emerging from World War I, Winston Churchill (1874–1965), who was determined to keep the British Empire intact at all costs, commented on the planned service of Imperial Airways – formed properly in 1924 – on the Cairo–Karachi sector as 'the important link that buckles the Empire together'. Two operational survey flights were carried out in 1925 between Cairo and Karachi, and on Boxing Day 1926 a DH66 Hercules of Imperial Airways left Croydon Airport for India. The Secretary of State for Air, Sir Samuel Hoare, and Lady Hoare, were on board for the full journey. Sir Samuel was determined to 'put all the emphasis on the reliability of air travel'.

Regular passenger-carrying flights between Cairo and Karachi started in April 1927. A subsidy agreement had been negotiated between Imperial Airways and the Indian government, providing for an annual payment of £93,000 at the rate of £1,200 for each Cairo–Basra flight and £900 for the Basra–Karachi sector.

Ground facilities had been laid down as a result of the earlier RAF services and the Imperial Airways surveys of the previous year. In 1921, the RAF had sent out two convoys from Amman and Baghdad to mark out on the ground with a plough towed by a tractor a visible route guide that could be followed across the desert from the air. The furrow still existed until the war and Imperial Airways supplemented the facilities by constructing petrol dumps at some of the landing grounds along the route. These were secured and locked, with a key aboard each aircraft. So that the key could not be forgotten, it acted as a double lock on the aircraft cabin door.

Wandering desert Arabs exhibited great curiosity about these fuel dumps. Their interest in getting at the precious liquid, so it was said, was in order that they could give it to their horses, and perhaps camels, to drink. It was believed that each animal would then sprout wings and carry its favoured rider with all the ease and comfort of Imperial Airways. The showplace of the desert was Rutbah Wells, midway between Amman and Baghdad. A Beau Geste-style fort was constructed where passengers and crew could stop overnight, safe from marauders.

However, the route to India was not secure, with German interests well entrenched with the Persian government. Persia revoked its permission to overfly its territory, which included nearly everything beyond Basra. Severe diplomatic pressure was applied by Imperial Airways to secure permission to fly through Persian territory. The first service from Cairo to Karachi was inaugurated in April 1929.

In August that year, when it became possible to fly from England to India in a mere seven days for £130, Imperial Airways was 'literally put on the map'. Finally, it had a long-range route that operated regularly, and this was the backbone on which could be hung other limbs or routes – eastward on to Australia, and southward from Cairo to central and southern Africa.

The journey may have been relatively swift but it was not easy. Passengers from Croydon flew in an Argosy aircraft to Basle, where they would transfer to a train for travel to Genoa. This was because the Italians refused permission for aircraft to enter their country from France, and the Swiss/Italian Alps were too high to be considered safe to fly over. From Genoa, a Calcutta flying boat flew, with a number of stops, to Alexandria, where there was a transfer to the DH66 that would fly across the desert and over the Gulf to India.

Major Brackley and Captain A.S. Wilcockson, later to achieve fame for his pioneering work on transatlantic services in the latter part of the 1930s, flew the first sector of the first UK–India service.

The first direct flights to India

Back in its London headquarters, Imperial Airways was planning to make travel far easier for the frustrated passenger forced to undertake part of the journey by train. Longer-range aircraft that eliminated many of the irritating refuelling stops would soon find favour with its customers.

The first change came in 1929 when, exasperated by Italy's refusal to offer terms for flying over its territory, Imperial Airways negotiated and opened an all-flying route through Germany, Austria and Hungary and down to Salonica, in Greece, by Argosy aircraft, then onward by flying boat to Alexandria. Regrettably, the Central European winter was not kind to air travel in those days and the service was discontinued after just two flights. It was resumed the following April. At the far end of the route the Karachi service was extended through Jodhpur to Delhi. That operation was under charter to the Indian government.

The second change was the ordering of a new fleet of comfortable, longer-range aircraft. The first of the new fleet, rolled out of its hanger in November 1930, was the Handley Page HP42 – the famous *Hannibal*.

In 1933, London–Karachi, Karachi–Singapore, Amsterdam–Batavia via Karachi, and Paris–Saigon with two stops in India were established on a twice-weekly basis. Between 1933 and 1938, passenger numbers rose from 155 000 to 2.1 million, and mail carried from 10.5 tons to 244.6 tons.

Domestic services

The first domestic service – between Bombay and Karachi – was instituted during Sir George Lloyd's governorship of Bombay (1918–1923), but proved unsuccessful for two reasons: fear of flying and a fast, reliable train service. However, those with India's future transport needs in mind saw the plane and international commerce as intertwined. In 1923 the governor suggested a scheme for training young Indians in England, and extending Imperial Airways' Croydon–Karachi service to New Delhi in 1929.

The new service was directly under the control of the Indian Postal Department. Subsequently, a Karachi–Calcutta service was inaugurated, but it had to be abandoned in 1931 owing to financial stringency. In 1933 the issue was revived with the formation of a number of private Indian companies. By 1 January 1934, 4780 miles of air service in India had been established, including Karachi–Bombay–Madras, Calcutta–Rangoon, and Calcutta–Madras. However, the railway companies had nothing to fear 'as those in the air accounted for merely the loss of a day's tea service in Nagpur Railway Station', according to an official from the Bengal Nagpur Railway. If other feeder services are taken into consideration and added, the total mileage operated in that year amounted to 5180.

In 1932 a ten-year agreement was entered into between the Government of India and Tata for the operation of a weekly airmail service between Karachi and Madras via Bombay. This service connected with the Imperial Airways international flight from Karachi to London. The domestic portion covered a distance of 1320 miles and was operated with two De Havilland Puss Moth aircraft each capable of carrying 350lb of mail. The cruising speed was a mere 105 mph. A third machine of the same make but of the Fox Moth type was added to the fleet in 1934. Provision was still not made for passengers.

The Delhi Flying Club operated a mail service between Karachi and Delhi, covering the 609 miles distance in slightly less than 6.5 hours. This service also connected up with the Imperial Airways flight to London. In 1934 the London service showed only a small increase in airmail carried but passenger intake and revenue was up by approximately 50% over 1933.

Chapter 19

ESTABLISHING AN ADMINISTRATIVE INFRASTRUCTURE

And that England has taken on India is without doubt the greatest luck
for India; also the blossoming of that good fortune is now just in its
beginnings. In another one hundred years a new world power may
have grown in India on this basis.
WILHELM HÜBBE-SCHLEIDEN, GERMAN THEORIST, 1898

The Indian subcontinent is a landmass nearly the size of Europe, and the period of British involvement approached 350 years. At the British Empire's apogee, there were around 400 districts throughout India, with a district officer presiding over each. Fewer than 1500 British officials governed the whole area. Today, in Delhi, that number of civil servants occupies just two buildings.

Most civil servants left the shores of Britain with a sincere belief that their efforts were ultimately to benefit the indigenous people. Britain, having then seen off the Portuguese and French, proceeded to mop up a collection of scattered 'states' of small and large competing kingdoms, later uniting the area, through the English language, transport and communications, into one great nation. Before the transfer of power in 1947 a Parliament was established, with a recognised national government freely elected through the democratic vote. Dedicated civil servants administered the whole structure that continues even today. No other world power has left a colonised state with such dignity.

There were devoted men who, from the middle of the 19th century, enforced a period of sustained peace on their host nation. They mapped the fields and made lists of every man's rights, while simultaneously starting the task of building roads, bridges and railways and harnessing the rivers for irrigation. An integrated infrastructure was their goal.

The civil servants of the EIC soon began to learn that they must be diplomats, administrators, traders and soldiers. Once settled, they transformed themselves into a robust body of men 'minutely just, inflexibly upright', believing in the right to rule millions of subjects after commanding victorious armies of peace at the gates of hostile capitals, according to *The Times* newspaper in London.

The need for an integrated infrastructure, rather than state development on an ad hoc basis, became paramount after the 1857 Mutiny. The Mutiny was a wake-up call to the Government of India, which was until then managed and underwritten by the EIC.

After the Mutiny, the British Parliament, as well as the Indian people themselves, demanded more reforms and a dedicated civil service. The once routine greed and irregularities of the EIC's legacy were apparent soon after the Company lost its power to the British Parliament, 'with the dirty washing now hung out to dry'. The unfair trade and commerce practices came to a halt. However, to the EIC's credit, railways, roads, telegraph, canals and the English language had all but unified the collection of motley, feuding states into one country, which was still controlled, if not governed outright, from Calcutta. The EIC must also be credited with a list of civil and social reforms including the eradication of thuggee, ensuring safe travelling for all; the banning of sati (suttee), preventing the burning of widows on their husbands' funeral pyres; and making female infanticide unlawful.

Two important acts, one relating to the economic and the other directly concerned with the moral welfare of the people (especially the poor), were passed in Governor-General Lord Lansdowne's time. The first was the Factory Act of 1891, which amended and amplified the Factory Act of 1881. Women's daily hours of labour were limited to 11. The minimum age at which children could be employed was raised from 7 to 9 years and they were classified as children until they were 14 rather than 12 years old; children were to be employed for a maximum of 7 hours daily, and that in daylight hours. Many British police and supervisors were employed solely to implement those acts 'with force if necessary'. All workers in factory labour, whatever their age or sex, were to have a weekly holiday.

These hours appear hard today but they were, in fact, better than the vile and cruel working conditions in the Lancashire and Yorkshire mills and foundries in Britain that were powering the wheel of India's transition into an industrial society.

Lansdowne also reinforced the crime of sati, which overruled Queen Victoria's proclamation of 1858 that all religious scruples of the Indian people should be respected.

A decade after the Mutiny, in 1868/69, the country was divided into nine territories – Lower Provinces, North-West Provinces, Oudh, Central Provinces, Punjab, Mysore, Bihar, Madras, Bombay and Sind. Burma was also a province for some time, but considering India alone, the population was assessed at 159 million for the 1802 629 square miles that the country comprised at the height of British rule. In 1869, 4283 miles of railway were in service, enabling the census takers easy entry to all major cities. A road network was under way, providing additional access into most major towns to lighten the compilers' burdens. When news of a dedicated policy to build up the whole of India's infrastructure was reported in Britain's daily press and engineering journals, it conformed to most people's image of Britain's Empire.

The first real civil service

From 1858, the British government took control of India and established an Indian Civil Service (ICS), often referred to as 'the steel frame' of the British Raj. Among the reforms introduced was a complete reorganisation of the ad hoc administrative system left by the EIC. A Secretary of State, aided by a council, began to control Indian affairs from London. A viceroy implemented London's policies from Calcutta. These took virtually immediate effect as the undersea telegraph link, subject to no interference from foreign prying eyes, was in force and 'rapidly overloaded'. The army was reorganised and the ratio of British to Indian soldiers was reduced.

Career civil servants were recruited by a very competitive and tough examination held in London for graduates, usually achievers from Oxford and Cambridge with an additional couple of years of training in law, language and Indian history.

The ICS was responsible under the viceroy for civil duties in India, dispensing justice and grappling with an infinity of local crises ranging from petty law and order matters to full-blown epidemics and famines. The ICS was by any measure the most efficient bureaucracy in world history. As Kipling said, that a single British civil servant was really able to run the lives of about 3 million Indians spread over the vast area of a whole district was only possible because the master himself often worked like a slave.

One of the most extraordinary statistics of the Raj era was the compact size of the ICS: a mere 1000 competent and dedicated officers successfully managing a population of almost 500 million people of diverse caste, culture, language and religion, spread over 1802 629 square miles, right up to Indian Independence in 1947. It was under Lord Mayo that the first census of India was undertaken during the 1860s; he also organised a statistical survey of the country.

Special departments were created, such as the Indian Forest Service, the Indian Political Service and the Police Service, and there were also departments with responsibility for transport, canals, land reclamation, archaeology, ordinance land survey, mapping, etc, with the top echelons recruited from the old EIC. The Indian Police Force in its early days included many army officers, but from 1893 onwards recruited its upper division by an annual examination held in London.

Calcutta Municipality – as opposed to Bengal as a whole – was allocated £282,500 in 1868. Most funding was apportioned to canals, tramways, roads, parks, public buildings, gas lighting and 'training locals to become honest administers of public money'. It was also the first time rubbish collection featured in Calcutta.

A Public Service Commission was established to co-ordinate most states' activities in 1926, resulting in a Federal Public Service Commission in 1935. By then, India fully benefited from an 'acceptable' police force, tax standards not manipulated at the whim of some local bureaucrat, free parks, museums and art galleries, cheap transport throughout the subcontinent, and a generally tolerant society despite warning clouds of war from Hitler. The last UK appointments into the ICS were made in 1942.

The North-West was divided into 43 sub-districts, run by four commissioners. Its 13 033 square miles of land were valued at £1255,259. Public works expenditure for the period being discussed was £226,125, of which over 40% went on roads and public buildings. Approval was given to construct a canal to water all territory lying between the Gogra and Ganges rivers, with water fed from the Sardah River. The canal was completed eight years later, to the overall benefit of many scattered villages in that area.

The Central Province, comprising 112 121 square miles – of which 82 860 square miles was under British rule – contained 17 divisions with £545,000 allocated for civil, and some military, works. It was first placed into a civil service administration in 1861. Here irrigation from reservoirs was considered more suitable than that from other sources. One exception was the Godavari Navigation Works, ably superintended by Arthur Cotton. Machinery was brought in to remove centuries-old rocks that had frustrated navigation throughout the ages. When completed some eight years later, it was not only inland navigation that was achieved but also the cultivation of cotton.

Judiciary

One of the most valuable legacies the British left behind were the administration, education and judicial systems. The British impact on the administrative life of India was enormous. The pre-existing condition of arbitrary rule enforced by officials – from the lowliest of local office to the more elite – and headed by Nawabs and Rajas was replaced by the rule of law. The great writ of habeas corpus, the most powerful bulwark of British liberty, became available to every inhabitant of India. A somewhat amusing but instructive episode needs to be recalled to memory.

After its victory in the battle of Buxar in 1764, the EIC was granted the diwani (fiscal administration) of Bengal, Bihar and Orissa with the authority to collect revenue from farmers and enforce a levy against defaulters by arresting them and placing them under detention. A group of barristers, who had arrived from England, moved for a writ of habeas corpus, which was issued by the newly established Supreme Court in Calcutta. When the officers of the court sought to execute the writ they were themselves arrested by officers of the EIC. This created a most chaotic situation and had to be resolved by amending the law to prevent the court from exercising any jurisdiction in matters of revenue in the future. But what is instructive is that in issuing a writ the court rejected the defence that they were acting under the orders of the EIC. The judges concluded: 'you might as well tell us that you are acting under orders of the King of Fairies'.

The dispensation that no person could be arrested or detained without the written order of a duly empowered local executive or judicial authority – even if the Governor-General had desired the arrest or detention – was great relief to the suffering populace. It is little wonder that the general populace extended its allegiance to the new and foreign power. This new system rested upon the significant principle of equality of all in the eyes of the law. This was a novel feature to a caste-ridden society and brought enlightenment to what had been a 'system' of widespread oppression and humiliation.

In 1764 Governor Clive obtained the rights of a diwani granting him control of the civil administration and taxation for the EIC from an impotent and needy Emperor Shah Alam II. Shah Alam II having suffered defeat

Calcutta High Court, c.1870 (Courtesy of the British Library)

by the Afghan and Persian kings was left without a kingdom, subjects and a treasury. He lived off the contribution which the EIC made in lieu of the diwani – an amount of 26 lakhs rupees a year, a shameful pittance.

Amongst the great reformers during the EIC's rule, who won affection for the British, was Lord William Bentinck, who became the Governor-General in 1828 effecting financial and judicial reforms, suppression of the slave trade and in particular thuggee (thugs) and sati. After the demise of EIC rule in 1858, the organisation of the ICS – which worked according to the codified rules and with efficiency and impartiality – was a major facet of British administration in India. The English officers of the ICS worked as collectors, magistrates and judges, maintaining the unprecedented high standards of the rule of law.

The British further established a codification of law. The Code of Criminal Procedure laid down in clear and precise terms, the law applicable to all citizens, irrespective of caste, creed or religion. The British also set up a network and hierarchy of courts, civil and criminal, for the trial of petty and heinous crimes, all with the right to appeal to the high courts, and even to the Privy Council in London.

The Indian High Court's Act of 1861 reorganised the then prevalent judicial system by abolishing the supreme courts at Fort William, Madras and Bombay, and also the Sadar Adalats in the Presidency Towns. The high courts were established having civil, criminal, admiralty, vice-admiralty, testamentary, intestate, and matrimonial jurisdiction, as well as original and appellate jurisdiction.

The justice system eschewed the outdated and inadequate features of the prevailing Sharia system. British law proved to be in harmony with ancient Indian values and the secular ethos of the future. More than a thousand courts of all sizes and types were established nationwide for dispensing justice to the common people. In small towns a district collector often worked as a second-class magistrate from a makeshift tent, dispensing justice and attending to local disputes.

The dominant Mughal power that had earlier established its sovereignty over a pliant populace had imposed on it the Sharia, an importation from distant Arabia. Islamic jurists had already divided the Sharia into four schools of law, and the most retrograde was imposed on the population of Hindustan. Under the prevailing law a Muslim woman had no escape from a tyrannical husband. While a husband could divorce his wife without judicial intervention by just pronouncing the word *Talaq* three times, the wife had no escape from the matrimonial prison. Every wife wishing to obtain her liberty had to denounce Islam and take advantage of the Islamic rule under which apostasy of a spouse annulled the marriage. This continued until Muslim society realised that a change of law was necessary. In a public lecture delivered in Lahore in 1924 Dr Mohammad Iqbal expressed concern about such conversions – which were becoming more frequent, allegedly under the encouragement of Christian missionaries. Dr Iqbal advocated that Muslim women must not be compelled to abandon Islam in order to free herself of a bad husband. Nothing happened until 1939 when

J.J. Cotton, collector and magistrate, sitting outside his tent, 1900 (Courtesy of the British Library)

the Indian Legislature passed the Dissolution of Muslim Marriages Act. It repealed the rule of annulment by apostasy but conferred upon a Muslim woman the right to obtain divorce from the courts – even from non-Muslim judges – on grounds including the impotence of the husband, cruelty or failure to provide maintenance.

The British brought in a civilized system of rules of evidence. A code drafted by the great jurist Sir James Stephen became law in 1872. It abolished the ugly distinction between the value attached to the testimony of a female and that of a male. The ancient Sharia rule that adultery could be proved only by the evidence of four eyewitnesses was repealed. Without a single protest, the Muslim populace accepted uniform justice and equity. Sharia law was itself a travesty of justice that Indians of all races and religions had for centuries been subjected to – a system alien to them, and at the same time neither rational nor equitable.

Today in India, criminal law is wholly secular, as are the laws of contracts and torts, mercantile law, and laws regarding the transfer of property; these are all mostly adapted from the British legal system. Religious law is limited to the fields of marriage and succession, and here too it is modified by a secular legislature. Today's Indian system is almost entirely based on British law and judiciary, remaining conducive to globalisation and welcoming to foreign investment.

Police

During the Mughal Empire, village Panchayates kept a check on crime and disorder. The urban centres had their own 'police forces' under the Kotwali system, which functioned until the late 18th century. The EIC did not tamper with the status quo until Lord Cornwallis introduced a new Police Act in 1792. Indigenous village policemen were appointed in Calcutta, Bombay and Madras in 1814. After Charles Napier conquered Sind in 1843, a separate police organisation using his own officers was created in the province. EIC officials in Calcutta initiated a police force after trials in London, and in 1861 the Police Act came into force. Individual states were given full autonomy to run their own units. Each reported to a newly appointed District Superintendent.

The Governor of Madras appointed a Torture Commission in 1854 to eliminate a practice that had existed for centuries, and the practice was soon eradicated. After 1857 the government reorganised the whole criminal

Four officers of the Punjab Police, c.1860s (Courtesy of the British Library)

Police officers and men, Gujranwala, Punjab, 1869 (Courtesy of the British Library)

justice system and in 1860 brought in the Indian Penal Code. State police forces came into existence, and criticisms levelled against local police for bribery and corruption were dealt with firmly by imported British.

The Indian Police (Superior) Service in its earlier days included many European officers from the Indian Army. It was reorganised in 1893, when most policemen up to the rank of sergeant were locals; a few rose to District Superintendent level. In 1905 a further reorganisation was effected and the rank of Deputy Superintendent was created within the subordinate services. Between 1924 and 1941 the force was sometimes known as the Indian Imperial Police.

One crusading official was Sir William Henry Sleeman (1788–1856), who upon getting the go-ahead from Governor-General Bentinck, launched an operation against the thuggees with an unprecedented efficiency that eliminated gang rule during his 20-year tenure in Jabalpur.

In 1881 a fund was established to provide benefits for the widows and children of the ICS, and especially those of police force members. The Indian Order of Merit – awarded to both the police and the military – was created in 1902. Its origin goes back to the EIC: a similar award was established for its troops in 1837, the oldest gallantry award in the whole of the British Empire. Among those who earned this distinguished award, the Sikhs have the highest number of decorations. A distinguished service medal was inaugurated in 1907 in both the police and military forces.

Taxation

Taxation in India goes back about 2500 years to the days of Kautilya, when land revenue was fixed at 16% of the produce grown. Import duties were imposed along with tolls, and ferry charges were levied. All types of liquor were subject to 5% tax; tax evaders were fined 600 panas. There is some wisdom in the Mughal idea that the administrative efforts required to collect taxes from the peasants, plus the expense of paying officials to gather this money and bring the funds to the hierarchy, made the endeavour madness itself!

In Bengal a Board of Revenue was established for the collection of taxes. The first district appointment was at Jagir, on the outskirts of Madras, in 1796. Governor-General Wellesley then ordered the government in Madras to adopt the Bengal system for tax collection, and this did not go down well with settlers. One commented caustically: 'How could any sensible man establish the practice of farming when tax collectors would screw what they can from the peasants?' EIC directors cautioned the Government of Madras to tread slowly with this issue, and the advice was acted upon.

In small stations around the country, the district would be administered by a judge/tax collector. This official served as a magistrate and also trained the senior and junior indigenous staff in clerical and other miscellaneous duties. The engineer and policeman were yet to come, and meanwhile this one tax collector performed their functions himself. Such people attempted to serve the locals well – not surprisingly as many of the English were married into the community and wished to gain support from those they governed.

For the printing needs of taxation, new steam-driven presses were imported 'by the dozen'. Walmsley's, of Bury, were the principal suppliers. One firm that supplied in excess of 12 small printing presses 'expressly for the tax-collecting industry' was Furnival with its 'Express Platen' model.

James Wilson, who became India's first Finance Minister, created the Income Tax Act of 1860, modelled on the English statute. This was deemed necessary since suppression of the Mutiny entailed heavy expenditure, which added to the public debt. In the year before the Mutiny, Rs.17 crores was budgeted for the military. This rose to Rs.32 crores during and in the year after the Mutiny, largely because of the expense of recruiting more European soldiers and officers into the army.

Army

If the civil service was the right hand of the Governor-General, the army was his left. Like the civil administration, each presidency army was at first independent. In the early days, a company of Europeans, a body of topasses and a number of undisciplined peons sufficed. Their chief business was to grace processions in the EIC's gardens, to fire salutes whenever possible and to keep order in the settlement. The real beginning of the company's armies came during the Anglo-French wars, when Stringer Lawrence (1697–1775) embodied the Madras Europeans Regiment and raised a number of Indian companies. From that time the armies of the three presidencies developed independently. The Regulating Acts of 1773 and 1783 gave the Governor-General overall control, but the armies remained separate until the Mutiny. As the Bengal Presidency expanded, its army grew with it and came in time to overshadow the others by reason of both its numbers and the greater wealth of fighting material at its disposal.

The British fought two Sikh wars in 1845 and 1848, with a loss of over 10000 Sikhs, nearly 3000 British and over 20 000 soldiers of the native Indian army, far higher casualties than any other war in the subcontinent. The experience taught the British administration that this martial group of people were better off under British leadership than as an enemy. Once the Punjab was annexed and Sikh belligerence brought under control, the British took many Sikhs into the regular army. A short time later these fighting men proved their worth in the Afghan wars and in World War I

7th Bombay Lancers officers and non-commissioned officers seated, c.1887 (Courtesy of the British Library)

8th Bombay Lancers: infantry on duty at time of Bombay plague, 1896–7
(Courtesy of the British Library)

and World War II: Sikhs received more Victoria Crosses and Indian Order of Merits than any other Indian community. In the British–Afghan wars, they earned about 80% of all medals awarded for gallantry.

While Lord Kitchener was the Commander-in-Chief, the native regiments were re-armed; better Enfield rifles and cannon were supplied to the artillery, and the whole transport service was re-organised. In 1901 the Imperial Cadet Corps was founded, consisting initially of young men of princely and noble families before those from other classes entered the service. Disciplined military training was provided to the rank and file of the native army, where Indians of various cultures and languages, castes and regions, were recruited to work together in greater harmony. It was in the army cantonments that the common Hindustani language evolved.

Soldiers of the 4th, 8th and 10th Indian Divisions give the victory salute on their return to India after serving with PAIFORCE (Persia and Iraq Force), February 1946 (Courtesy of the Council of the National Army Museum, London)

Soldiers of the 25th Indian Division searching Japanese troops after their surrender in Kuala Lumpur, Malaya, 1945 (Courtesy of the Council of the National Army Museum, London)

The services of the Indian army were at this time employed for wider duties than the protection of India itself. During the five decades prior to World War I in 1914, the well-trained, disciplined and loyal Indian army were used in more than ten Imperial campaigns from China to Abyssinia. Indians were employed against the Boxer insurgents in China (then under British hegemony) and against the Mullah in Somaliland, while in South Africa troops from India helped to hold Ladysmith and to save Natal. In all these wars, including the two world wars, Indian soldiers fought well and made great sacrifices, which unfortunately remain under-recognised.

The British left India with the legacy of having created a world-class, formidable and unified army, from the same culturally and linguistically diverse forces that were defeated in almost all of the battles with the EIC, with the notable

A Sikh soldier receives a garland of flowers from a nurse, 1946 (Courtesy of the Council of the National Army Museum, London)

exception of the brave Maratha assault, defeating the British in 1774 with the use of rockets – and the first recorded use of kilometre-range rockets in combat. The high standards of training and discipline painstakingly introduced in the Indian Army ranks remain sustained in today's India thanks to the 200-year ethos and culture inculcated by the special training centres. The elite Indian Military Academy in Dehradun was established in 1933 based on Britain's Sandhurst Academy. The year 2009 marked the 250th anniversary of the founding of the Madras Regimental Centre, raised by Robert Clive on 4 December 1758. Only a few decades later the Madras Native Infantry under the command of Major-General Wellesley (Duke of Wellington) spearheaded the defeat of Tipu Sultan.

Banking

The concept of modern banking in India can be traced back to 1773, when Warren Hastings submitted to the EIC's Board of Revenue a 'Plan' for a General Bank in Bengal and Bihar. Hastings' General Bank, set up that year, functioned as a treasury for revenue collections, and as a repository for remittances from merchants to the aurungs – the company's depots for manufactured goods. The bank had offices at Calcutta and Mushidabad, with 14 branches and a few sub-agencies elsewhere. Two independent bankers were appointed – one in each of these towns. Both were particularly noteworthy. Hastings' bank, however, was short-lived. Despite a handsome profit, it closed on 15 February 1775.

Modern banking as we know it started in India at the beginning of the 19th century with the establishment of the Bank of Calcutta in 1806, renamed as the Bank of Bengal three years later. Bankers from Scotland, whose predecessors had founded the Bank of England in 1694, managed the new bank. Their practices and policies became ingrained in the embryonic Indian banking system, with basic accounting and systems then being overseen by EIC directors.

In 1840 the Bank of Bombay was established, followed by the Bank of Madras in 1843, and the Punjab National Bank in 1895. In 1861 the Paper Currency Act was passed, which largely relegated bartering to the most isolated communities. The Bank of India was founded by a group of prominent, mainly Parsi, businessmen in Bombay in 1861, at a time when huge steam-driven textile mills 'could not be installed fast enough to meet demand'. By 1913 there were 41 Indian banks, but in 1921 the banks of

Bengal, Bombay and Madras were amalgamated to form the Imperial Bank of India.

In April 1935, in Bank Street, Bombay, a large brass plaque announced the 'Reserve Bank of India'. It became famous for being managed by a Scotsman, W.T. McCallum, with a staff of 180. It took over all functions from the Imperial Bank of India. After Independence, the State Bank of India was established in July 1955.

Legacy of secular democratic rule

Whatever shortfalls British rule implanted in India, the administration deserves maximum credit for stamping out many thoroughly evil aspects of religious dictates, principally that of sati. Infanticide, temple prostitution and enforced purdah or seclusion from public society were also assessed as moral evils and the British made them punishable by law. The Governor of India was doggedly determined to crush these practices and protect Indian women from outright religious fanaticism.

India's female society has much to be grateful to the British for. Augmented by Christian missionaries, the concept of elevating womanhood into Indian society was seized upon after 1830. The first schools for girls were commenced from 1830 in Calcutta; the governor demanded that all education be free at source. In 1849, Lord Dalhousie upheld the Bethune School from his private purse. Medical development started and the first woman doctor arrived in Bengal in 1874, much to the annoyance of some religious leaders.

By 1941 Indians outnumbered the British in the ICS. As the time neared for the handover of power, the apparatus of civil administration was self-sufficient, fully functional and run by highly trained civil servants. There is no doubt that the British saw it as their responsibility to ensure the ICS and its prolific Public Works Department (PWD) endured to serve an independent India. This British colonial legacy was radically different from that of Spain, Portugal or France. The administration of the Spanish and French colonies was highly centralised and controlled entirely by Europeans. When the French and Spanish withdrew from their colonies they left in their wake emptied administrative structures and power vacuums that resulted in coups d'état, corruption and civil wars. When the British handed over power to independent India, they did so to highly qualified Indian civil servants in a fully functional secular democracy.

Chapter 20

EDUCATION AND HEALTH:
ENGINEERING AND MEDICAL COLLEGES

It is my wish that there may be spread over the land a network of schools and colleges, from which will go forth ... citizens, able to hold their own in industries and agriculture, and all the vocations in life ... It is through education that my wish will be fulfilled, and the cause of education in India will ever be very close to my heart.
KING GEORGE V, ADDRESS TO CALCUTTA UNIVERSITY, 1912

By the mid-19th century, a rising and increasingly powerful and influential Indian mercantile and business class was agitating for modern European subjects in the sciences, especially in engineering and medicine. Colonial rule, too, recognised that India needed an educated workforce in the engineering and medical disciplines to allow India to progress, but the school and college system was mainly funded by private money and a combination of British and Indian, principally Parsi, philanthropy. Demand was further driven by the expansive programme of public works in the huge irrigation and infrastructural projects that saw the nationwide construction of canals, roads, railways, bridges and public utilities. India's youth travelled great distances to learn a useful trade in an economy still desperate for skilled artisans.

In 1854 the EIC issued a dispatch for a modern state education system in India; the following decades would see important strides in government support of an egalitarian state education provision. The English language proliferated and became the principal medium for training in the sciences; this legacy endures today. A single language of education allowed a cohesive higher education system, with independent learning institutions across the Indian subcontinent facilitated and united by the strong shared bond of a common language of science.

Engineering colleges

George Resto Jervis opened an engineering college in 1834 in Poona with the local Marathi language as the medium of instruction. He named it Guneet-Shilpa Kala Vidyalaya. Later it became the Poona (Pune) Engineering College. By 1892 four official engineering schools had been established in India. Private companies, including the foundries of Burn, Jessop, Richardson Cruddas, Garden Reach Shipyard and the emerging electrical enterprises built many others. The four engineering colleges were Roorkee in the North-West Province; Poona College of Science, Bombay; Seebpoor, Bengal; and the Madras Engineering College & Surveying School. From 1887, 40 engineers graduated and many more gained junior qualifications. Steam-engine theory and practice was a principal subject in all syllabuses.

The oldest of the four learning centres was the College of Engineering in Madras. Founded in 1803, during the early days of canal construction, the college was dominated by civil and steam engineering courses until 1859. Then, telegraph theory and practice were introduced. With the construction of a fine university in the city, the college was affiliated to the new centre of education in 1877. The older portion of this handsome building was originally the palace of the Nawab of Carnatic at Chepak, and was ideally positioned on Madras's south beach. It was then known as the Kalsamahal, or domed palace. Future additions neatly blended into the original design. Modelled on the Indo-Saracenic style of architecture, the sea face of the college was over 300 ft long, and the building was described as 'the most commodious building of its class in India' by an English traveller.

The Roorkee College was established in 1847 under the auspices of the Hon. James Thomason (1801–1853), Lieutenant Governor of the North-West Provinces. The college was subsequently renamed the Thomason Civil Engineering College of Roorkee in 1854. It was created to provide theoretical and practical instruction to Europeans and natives alike, and excelled in its purpose.

The phenomenal increase in India's public works programmes was all but outstripping the education facilities available. In 1870 the decision was taken to establish a college at Coopers Hill, in Surrey, England, and it was opened on 5 August 1872. The course lasted three years and cost £50 per term, which included board, lodgings and laundry. Queen Victoria bestowed the title 'The Royal Indian Engineering College' on the establishment on 4 January 1875. The emphasis on practical training was

Hooghly College, Calcutta, c.1851 (Courtesy of the British Library)

accentuated in 1877 when a fourth year was added to the course. That same year saw the foundation of Honorary Fellowships at Coopers Hill. In due course, the initials 'FCH' became a coveted distinction won by some 75 of the alumni. The college tutored not only Indians but Egyptians and others. The college was closed on 26 July 1906, when the final prizes were presented. It had lasted for 53 years.

By 1947, with the British having established many colleges of high rank such as that in Poona, well over 250 000 students were placed into engineering courses.

Hospitals and the nursing services

The period from 800 BC to AD 1000 may be considered as the Golden Age of Indian medicine. During this time Indians are also believed to have pioneered human dissection, which gave them a better understanding of anatomy.

Western medicine was introduced in 1510, with the construction of the Royal Hospital in Goa. In 1703 an elementary course in medicine was organised in the same hospital. Before that, in 1664, the EIC had built a military hospital in Madras, which catered for local requirements. In 1750 the same military hospital was opened to civilians at no charge. The first hospital to open in Bombay, in 1676, was 'lavish for the times', according to a contemporary. A group of hospitals was established in 1843 from a combination of EIC and Parsi patronage, with a medical college responsible for introducing to western India orthodox medical practice using approved drugs. Named Grant Medical College after Sir Robert Grant (1779–1838), then Governor of Bombay – who adopted a benign attitude towards his charges – it opened in 1837. (Some five years earlier medical schools had been established in Calcutta and Madras.) While missionaries were instrumental in the college's administration and application of medicine – all imported from England – local women were quickly trained as nurses 'and more than earned their keep'.

The EIC opened the Native Hospital in 1793, near Fort William, for its employees. In 1829 a surgeon arrived in Moulmein from England, on the seagoing steamer *Irrawaddy*, to introduce vaccination against smallpox in both Bengal and Burma. Charitable dispensaries were built, mainly by missionaries in the villages, and some form of hospital constructed from 1830 in the larger towns. Modern English and Continental European methods of curative and preventative medicines were introduced throughout the country.

The Public Works Department created by Hastings added medical facilities to its list of civil engineering departments. Clinics, again using dedicated missionaries, had the edge in relieving the suffering of the poor and infirm from the first quarter of the 19th century. The British Army – later the Corps of Engineers – established a medical unit in 1810 that catered for all classes. Throughout the height of Hinduism and Mughal rule, 'not one reasonably equipped establishment dedicated to relieving the suffering of the poor for its day was created', observed a Dr Owen, who had arrived in Calcutta in about 1840. He went on to state that 'Only the arrival of British expertise with surgical instruments accompanying their cannon and steam engine baggage, was responsible for laying down some form of organised hospital system that would doctor the afflicted and impecunious without charge at the source of the treatment'. It was a form of free healthcare that perhaps anticipated the National Health Service laid down a century later in Britain.

The Madras Medical School was created in 1835, with Calcutta and Bombay following. A Dr Mortimer, resident in the Madras Medical School, taught native apprentices and pupils the function and repair of muscles and bones from pasteboard models. In 1910 Simla boasted 'the best hospital in India for treating tuberculosis', while a Government of India Malaria

Bombay Public Works Department, c.1870s (Courtesy of the British Library)

Prevention Hospital was created in 1912. Major General Sir Leonard Rogers (1868–1963) founded the Calcutta School of Hygiene & Tropical Medicine in 1919.

The nursing profession proper was brought to India some time in February 1888 when ten nursing sisters arrived from England. Earlier, in 1872, training classes for 'women attending the sick' were held in Delhi and later in Madras, in 1897. The first Indian nurse, Bai Kashibai Ganpat, of Thane, was training in Bombay in 1897. The first nursing school was set up by the British and established at Cama Hospital, Bombay, in 1886.

It was missionaries, however, who were responsible for attending the sick and creating hospitals. In Bangalore, in 1854, a group known as the Good Shepherd Sisters devoted most of their time to attending the afflicted. Their attitude to the less fortunate was of such renown that the Maharaja of Mysore donated a 20-acre site in 1884 for the construction of a hospital.

Many dedicated single nurses arrived from Britain carrying with them a philanthropic attitude to 'serve the Empire and the poor'. One such nurse who carved an honourable name for herself was Lillias Anna Hamilton (1858–1925), who practised in Calcutta.

In 1926, with hospitals spread throughout the country, a prestigious establishment with imperial connections was built in Bombay. Doctors who had all qualified under British training staffed the newly founded King Edward VII Memorial Hospital.

Perhaps the most famous of the early 20th-century hospitals is that at Vellore, some 88 miles from Madras. Ida Scudder, an American schoolgirl,

New General Hospital, Patna, 1913 (Courtesy of the British Library)

was visiting her parents in India in about 1894 and was asked to assist in three young women in childbirth. Being ignorant of such practices she refused, and to her horror all three women died. This prompted her to study medicine in America. On returning to India she started a clinic at Vellore in 1900, a school for pharmacists in 1903, a school for nurses in 1909, and finally a medical school for women in 1918. Today, the hospital contains 1500 beds.

The earliest records of institutions for tending the mentally ill can be traced back to the 15th century in what became the Central Provinces. But the term 'mental hospital' or asylum was wholly British, and in India set up by the EIC to cater mainly for European soldiers. Lord Cornwallis – Governor-General of India from 1786 to 1793 – had established the first mental hospital in Calcutta in 1787, attended to by a surgeon called Kenderline. In South India a mental hospital was opened at Kilpauk, near Madras, in 1784. The Government Act 36 in 1858 announced guidelines for the creation of asylums and admission procedures. New asylums were built in Patna, Dacca, Calcutta, Berhampur, Cuttack, Waltair, Trichinopoly, Poona, Ahmedabad, Hyderabad Sind, Banares and Agra. Today, some of those late 19th-century buildings still serve modern-day India.

Foundations of a modern education system

The British laid the foundations of a modern education system. By 1904 there were 88 technical schools serving over 5000 students; by 1919 the number of technical schools and pupils had more than doubled. In addition, by 1904 there were over 5500 secondary schools, with an estimated 558 000 students. That same year an official resolution was passed to increase expenditure in education, based on the principles of egalitarian and free education at source. That education should be unequivocally egalitarian and available regardless of caste or gender was explicit in official policy, yet the practicalities of providing free primary and secondary education were problematic, principally because of funding. After 1904, total expenditure in education nearly doubled, greatly spurred on by Lord Curzon's government who introduced significant educational reform. Primary education was also given renewed attention and recognised as lacking. The education of girls was also widely advocated and a significant concern of the Government of India. Official figures put State spending at 44% but more was needed. In conclusion to the 1904 resolution on education provision in India, the Government of India appealed to India's philanthropists:

> Such in broad outline are the present outlook and general policy for the near future of the government of India. The Governor General in council trusts that the growing section of the Indian public which is interested in education will join in establishing, under the guidance and with the help of Government, those quickening systems of education on which the best minds in India are now convening and on which the prospects of the rising generation depend. He appeals with confidence to wealthy citizens throughout India to give of their abundance to the cause of education … and the provision for research of every kind. There is … a noble opportunity for the exercise on modern lines of that charity and benevolence for which India has been renowned from ancient times.

Chapter 21

Indian Heritage and Culture: Conservation, Restoration and Appreciation

There is no country the antiquities and arts and monuments of which are more precious than those of India.

LORD NATHANIEL CURZON

One of the many paradoxes of the British Raj was their attitude to forests, hunting and wildlife in the subcontinent. Typical of all human endeavours, there were those who exploited the natural landscape and those who implemented pioneering conservational and scientific feats. The great Indian forests were an important resource for the EIC and Crown rule and their yields were exploited for shipbuilding, fuel, construction and later the building of railway lines, for which vast numbers of wooden sleepers were required.

As early as 1786 Colonel Robert Kyd, who had served in the Bengal Engineers before rising to Military Secretary to the Government of Bengal, proposed the creation of the Calcutta Botanic Garden to the EIC Court of Directors. He appealed to the EIC's commercial interests stating that the Botanic Garden would allow 'extension of the national commerce and riches'. Kyd understood the need to press the commercial benefits to the Company. At the time, India was draining British coffers. The EIC was quick to see the benefits of India developing as a supplier of raw materials such as cotton, spices, tea, sandalwood and teak in order to rebalance the trade deficit. Kyd's own motivations, however, were driven by his shock at the devastation of the 1770 famine. A prodigious botanist, his private studies into drought-resistant crops motivated his proposal to the EIC and he made clear that the purpose of the Garden was 'not for the purpose of collecting rare plants as thing of mere curiosity or ... for the gratification of luxury, but for establishing a stock for disseminating such articles as may prove beneficial to the inhabitants'.

Opened on the banks of the Hooghly in 1787, the Calcutta Botanic Garden also helped to supply the EIC with a more sustainable supply of teak for its shipbuilding interests. Kyd's successor at the Botanic Garden, William Roxburgh, the 'father of Indian botany', would later put much energy into persuading the EIC of jute's potential as a viable commodity.

It was recognised that forests had to be conserved in order to be sustainable. The Bombay Forest Conservancy was founded as early as 1847. The Governor-General Lord Dalhousie issued a Forest Charter in 1855, and in 1864 the Imperial Forestry Department was founded. This became one of the most significant forestry services in the world, greatly influencing the foundation of state forestry departments in many other countries of the British Empire. In Britain itself, the Forestry Commission was only founded in 1919. A training school for foresters was also founded in Dehra Dun.

Attitudes towards forests were closely bound with hunting and wildlife conservation. The British adopted the concept of the great ceremonial hunt from the Mughals. Using elephants and many auxiliary helpers, the spectacle was regarded as an important display of state power. Hunting was an activity enjoyed by the elite of British officialdom, as well as by the military and forest officers. The shooting of tigers was seen as a symbolic protection of the Indian rural population, while the hunting of wild elephants and pigs was regarded as a significant aspect in the management of agricultural production.

However, by the late 19th century it was becoming apparent to the British that excessive hunting with modern, highly accurate firearms was beginning to put some animal populations at risk. Early preservation policies were introduced with 'closed seasons' implemented in order to leave stocks for hunting. Preservation soon turned to conservation whereby hunting was entirely banned in certain areas.

At the same time, many natural history societies were founded, first in Bombay in the 1890s and later in South India and elsewhere. These were sometimes allied to the natural history collections of museums and were important pressure groups in influencing official policies in conservation and appreciation. Reserves and national parks emerged from these policies and the work of pressure groups. Independent India inherited important means for the study of natural history, for the development of its magnificent museums and the emergence of its world-famous national parks, and significant contributions were made to the natural sciences, to global scientific exchanges, as well as to the revenue-earning tourist sector of the Indian economy.

Wildlife conservation and protection

As early as 1870 wild elephants had received a degree of state protection. In 1905 the Kaziranga Forest in Assam became India's first national park, where the one-horned rhinoceros, an endangered species, came under the protection of law and government. Full credit must be extended to the Viceroy's wife, Lady Mary Curzon, who had visited the area in 1904. Lady Curzon had no truck with the 'sport' of killing wild animals, and after finding only the hoof marks of a rhino, after repeated trips, persuaded her husband to protect the animal. In 1905 Lord Curzon set aside more than 57 000 acres of Kaziranga as a reserved forest. The forest was formally closed to shooting in 1908. Although at 170 square miles it is far from being the largest of the Indian national parks, it is one of the most celebrated in the world for its astonishing biodiversity and its range of landscapes.

The Kaziranga initiative motivated others to view India's rich diversity of animal life in a similar way. Famous British hunters such as Jim Corbett and Colonel Richard Burton (both born in India) began to argue for con-servationist policies in north and south India respectively, and reserves

were created. One of these became the vast Jim Corbett National Park in Uttarakhand, originally established in 1936. More legislation followed in the early 20th century, including the Wild Birds and Animals Protection Act in 1912 and the Bengal Rhinoceros Preservation Act in 1932.

Lord and Lady Curzon, 1899 (Courtesy of the British Library)

Restoration and heritage

Credit for the early large-scale and serious study of archaeological and historical studies in India must be given to Sir William Jones, an extraordinarily accomplished man who founded the Asiatic Society in Calcutta in 1784. Jones was an avid Indologist and his studies in Sanskrit led him to the conclusion that Sanskrit stood as one of the major root languages of the world. In 1833 another exceptionally distinguished scholar, James Prinsep, became secretary of the Asiatic Society. Also devoted to the study of antiquities of India, Prinsep deciphered the Brahmi and Kharoshthi scripts between 1834 and 1837, re-opening the gates to the rich ancient Indian history and culture which had fallen into oblivion.

In 1848 an assistant of Prinsep, Alexander Cunningham of the Bengal Engineers, first put in motion the plan for an Indian Archaeological Survey. Eventually Cunningham's efforts paid off and the first official Archaeological Survey was sanctioned in December 1861. The Archaeological Survey of India maintained many buildings under protection orders that received full approval from the respective viceroys.

Lord George Curzon (1859–1925), Viceroy of India from 1898 to 1905, was strongly associated with the rescuing of several long-neglected historic monuments, including the Taj Mahal, and the Archaeological Survey gathered renewed momentum under Curzon's viceroyship. In 1902 Curzon appointed the 26-year-old archaeologist John Marshall who, inspired by earlier though inconclusive excavations of the Harappa site, determined to organise a serious excavation of the area. Hampered by the outbreak of World War I, work eventually began in 1920. The years 1921 to 1925 saw the discovery of the great Indus Civilization, and so it goes that Marshall 'left India two thousand years older than he had found it'.

The British showed great sensitivity and refinement of taste in their appreciation of Indian art, architecture and heritage – irrespective of Hindu or Muslim origin. The preservation, restoration and conservation of monuments and buildings across the subcontinent received tremendous impetus during Lord Curzon's tenure as Viceroy. He introduced the Ancient Monuments Preservation Act of 1904 to prevent the misuse and neglect of historic monuments. He also issued orders for the restoration and beautification of the great heritage sites scattered across the entire subcontinent. Today, the Archaeological Survey of India has declared 3598 monuments to be of national importance, of which 16 are UNESCO World

Victoria Terminus railway station, Bombay (Courtesy of the British Library)

Heritage sites. India is also the legatee of outstanding monuments of the colonial era. Bombay's Victoria Terminus, built in 1888, deserves its status as a UNESCO World Heritage site, and the famous Gateway to India, which commemorates the landing of King George V and Queen Mary in 1911, remains a major sightseeing destination and landmark.

Taj Mahal, Agra

Agra became the scene of one of the first and certainly the best known of the great works of conservation and extensive restoration, with the Taj Mahal restored to its former glamour and seduction. Dusty wastelands in the city were also converted into green parks, and gardens and numerous neglected and tumbled-down ruins restored to their original form. This colonial contribution was enormously helpful in introducing a new culture of appreciation and conservation to the Indians for their priceless and ancient heritage of art and architecture.

Museums and galleries

The culture of museums and art galleries was unknown in India before the Raj period. The first museum in India was established by the Asiatic Society in 1814. Today, the society – with its headquarters in Kolkata – contains over 20000 volumes, including 8000 rare Sanskrit, Arabic, Persian and

Hindi manuscripts. Its sculpture collection goes back to 250 BC, and a 12th-century image of Brahma is the centrepiece of the exhibits. Between the late 19th and early 20th centuries, the principal city of each province was provided with museums. The National Museum was set up during British rule and opened in 1949 in New Delhi.

The traditional museums later gave rise to the establishment of specialist museums with a comprehensive collection of exhibits from 19th- and 20th-century Indian industrial history that map the country's rich industrial heritage – from the casting of metals to electric locomotives and Rolls-Royce jet engines – from Mughal times to Independence, during which time all invaders, in some shape or form, played their part and left their legacy. Many waterworks with 150 years' service, such as the Victoria Jubilee Waterworks at Rajkot, retain their original sluice gates and the magnificent headworks of Sir Arthur Cotton's Godavari Delta Irrigation (1852) is virtually as he left it.

Printing and newspapers

Before the arrival of EIC merchants, India had inherited some form of printing from China, via Nepal. It was printing in the loosest sense. During the next 50 years the EIC hauled into Calcutta printing presses of an embryonic design that were used chiefly to print its own notices. The establishment of the Asiatic Society and its extensive researches warranted permanent recognition of its findings rather than handwritten in ledger form. Printing presses were purchased in Manchester, and Daniel Stuart in 1785 placed these presses into service for the printing of the *First Asiatic Miscellany*. The presses must have been successful, for a second volume of the same journal was printed the following year.

Over the next decades larger and more efficient presses arrived until in 1830 steam engines were employed to drive newspaper machinery. One steam-driven press was exported to Goa in 1821. In about 1905 Walmsley & Company was chosen to build the largest mill paper in India, complete with all machinery and chemicals to produce a range of quality paper, mainly for government use. The specification for the contract placed by Punjab Pulp & Paper Mills was for a plant capable of sustaining a yearly output of 7500 tons. The renowned German foundry and engineering firm of MAN competed with many UK printing machinery suppliers for various lucrative contracts. In around 1908, MAN exported a huge steam-driven printing press to Bombay that soon found service supplying daily newspaper editions.

In 1776 the first attempt at the publication of newspapers in India was made, unsuccessfully, by the Englishman William Bolts in Calcutta. Four years later, James Augustus Hicky, also from England, started the *Bengal Gazette*. He immediately lost money and took advertising to make ends meet. Five years later, the *Madras Courier* made its debut, published by Londoner Richard Johnson 'with official support'. A Mr Boyd edited the paper. The *Bombay Herald* made its entry in 1789. By 1800, there were around 40 newspapers 'all in English and for the English'.

The *Bombay Times* came into existence in 1838. The *Bombay Telegraph & Courier* quickly followed in 1847, with a new title, *Bombay Standard*, appearing in 1858. All three papers merged in 1861 to form the *Times of India*. By 1885, the *Times of India,* printed in Bombay, was the most popular newspaper in India. In 1860 editor Charles Lawson published the first newspaper in Cochin, entitled *Western Star. The Bengalee* – strangely titled, for it was printed in English – was launched in 1907.

The first non-English title was an Armenian monthly published in Madras in 1794. Vernacular newspapers spread quickly, appearing in Calcutta around 1820, in Bombay (in Gujarati) in 1822 and in Ahmedabad in 1849. Orissa came into the newspaper age in 1872, following an embryonic magazine in 1866. A Persian language newspaper was printed on steam-driven machinery in Calcutta in 1893, and simultaneously printed in Tehran. Newspapers came out in Telugu, the language of Hyderabad and the Central Provinces, from about 1908. The widespread adoption of newspapers also gave rise to further education and the establishment of colleges. In Calcutta a printing machine imported by James Wilkins in 1778 stimulated a growing demand for books in both English and local languages. British philanthropists helped in the founding of the Hindu College, Calcutta, in 1816; Elphinstone Institution, Bombay, 1827; Delhi College, 1827; and the Madras University High School, 1841. Each is believed to have had its own printing press.

Libraries

The first printed book in Bengal, *Bengali Grammar,* written by Nathaniel Brassey Halhead, was distributed in 1778. Four years later, the first library of books in British India was established by the Serampore Mission. Another library, the first to promote secular knowledge in the arts and sciences – with much space devoted to steam-engine theory and practice now that Britain had embraced the Industrial Revolution – was established by Fort William College in Calcutta in 1801. By 1805, the prodigious Asiatic Society had built its own library.

The Calcutta Public Library was the first major library in India. It was private and not supported by any government institution. It ran on a proprietary basis: each person subscribing Rs.300 – in one payment or three instalments – to use its facilities was to be considered a proprietor. The then Governor-General, Lord Metcalfe, transferred 4675 volumes from the library of Fort William College to the Calcutta Public Library. Naturally enough, Shakespeare and other English literature and history were well represented, along with some novels, including the then-scandalous *Tom Jones* by Henry Fielding. By 1850 the Calcutta Public Library held pride of place in India's capital. Indian and foreign books, especially from Britain, were bought for the library although many were donated and came out of trunks on P&O and British India Steam Navigation steamers. The library was so well run that it earned a global reputation for diversity and efficiency. Its standards were extremely high, which was rare even in Europe at that time.

The Imperial Library was formed in 1891 by combining a number of secretariat libraries under its umbrella. Of these the most important and interesting were the library of the Home Department, which contained many books once belonging to the library of the East India College, Fort William, and the library of the East India Board in London. Lord Curzon conceived the idea of opening libraries for public use on a wide scale. By the end of the 19th century he noticed that libraries were under-utilised for the want of facilities or restrictions. He therefore decided to amalgamate a number of Secretariat libraries – used mainly by the literate and 'upper class'. The combined library was called the Imperial Library, being formally opened to the general public on 30 January 1903. The first dedicated librarian appointed to this now huge library was John Macfarlane, formerly the Assistant Librarian of London's British Museum. This new library was stocked with a huge number of technical books – especially on railways and early electrical engineering – and this fine model for India was soon emulated in other major cities.

The Bombay and Madras libraries acquired huge collections and were popular with India's growing student population and with young qualified engineers branching out in their careers. The Punjab, too, was not slow to grasp the benefits of libraries, forming one of the earliest dedicated library associations in India. In 1916 a Dr A.C. Woolner was brought over from England and enrolled with the title Honorary University Librarian of the Punjab University. In Madras the first Library of Science was established in 1929 and staffed by senior British engineers and, in 1931, Madras also created the first of many travelling libraries with books in English and local languages.

CINEMAS

INDIA'S FIRST EXPOSURE TO MOTION PICTURES began in 1896 when the French Lumière Brothers' Cinématographe unveiled six short films at the Watson Hotel – now the Esplanade – in Bombay. The first cinema opened in 1899. The first motion picture, *The Wrestlers,* produced by a Marathi Indian, H. Bhatavdekar, was screened in 1899. It was shot in two scenes, each lasting three minutes and exhibited under Edison's projecting kinetoscope. Short narrative silent films continued to be imported to India. Some of the most famous films included *Life of Christ* (1901), *Aladdin and the Wonderful Lamp* (1902), *Ali Baba and the Forty Thieves* (1903) and *Napoleon Bonaparte* (1904).

In 1907 Jamshedji Madan opened the Elphinstone Picture Place in Calcutta. His early films focused on topical and historic subjects such as the *Great Bengal Partition Movement and Procession* (1905), *Delhi Durbar and Coronation* (1911) and *Cotton Fire at Bombay* (1912).

In 1912 the silent film *Pundalik,* a joint British–Indian collaboration, was released. Another Marathi pioneer and great entrepreneur, Dadasaheb Phalke, who has most deservedly earned the title 'the father of Indian cinema', made the first entirely Indian-produced feature film *Raja Harish Chandra* in 1913, establishing the foundations of Bollywood. In 1914 Phalke showed three of his films in London. In that year the Coronation Cinema, Bombay, released his film with English and Hindi subtitles. In

Dadasaheb Phalke

1917 Bengal established its own film industry through Madan's Elphinstone Bioscope Company, while Madras produced its first silent picture in 1919.

The silent era of motion movies continued from 1897 to 1930, with the release of around 1200 films, of which very few films print are available now. Between 1913 and 1929 Phalke alone had produced a record number of 95 feature films and 26 short films, perhaps the world record achieved by any producer in those years. Phalke was among the world's greatest producers of the time and has perhaps not received the level of national recognition that he deserves. He was a great friend of the legendary director-producer Prithviraj Kapoor.

The first Indian 'talkie' *Alam Ara* produced by A. Irani of the Imperial Company was released on 14 March 1931 at the Majestic Cinema in Bombay. That same year saw films with sound in Bengal and South India. Soon after, Bombay became the hub of film production in India. Moti Gidwani is credited with India's first colour film, *Kisan Kanya*, in 1937, followed by hits including *Khazanchi* in 1941, which raised Lahore's film industry to national prominence.

The 1930s and 1940s witnessed the rise of great film personalities, such as V. Shantaram, Prithviraj Kapoor, Debaki Bose, Sohrab Modi, S.S. Vasan, Nitin Bose, Ashok Kumar, Nargis, Raj Kapoor, Dev Anand, Dilip Kumar and others. Their contributions helped Indian cinema grow further. By this time, aside from Bombay, the Indian film industry shaped up well in several talented regions of South India. These were tumultuous times: India was buffeted by the Great Depression, World War II, the India independence movement and the violence of Partition. Most Bollywood films were unabashedly escapist, but there were also a number of filmmakers who, due to modest film censorship regulations, felt enough freedom to tackle tough social and national issues, including the struggle for Indian independence, as a backdrop for their plots.

After Independence the Indian film industry continued to keep pace. Prithviraj and Raj Kapoor were the first father and son superstars. This legendary family has continued its line of major film stars with Shami Shashi and Rishi Kapoor in the 1970s, followed by the grandchildren Karishma, Kareena and Ranbir Kapoor, who also rose to superstar status. In the year 2015 India is home to a galaxy of cinema royalty including Salman Khan, Shah Rukh Khan, Aamir Khan, Akshay Kumar, Katrina Kaif, Kareena Kapoor, Ranbir Kapoor and others besides the legendary Amitabh Bachchan, who has enjoyed success for over four decades.

Chapter 22

DIASPORA:
MIGRATION AND OPPORTUNITY

The sun never sets on the Indian diaspora
from Fiji to Canada around the world.
DR. L.M. SINGHVI,
FORMER HIGH COMMISSIONER OF INDIA IN THE UK

At the time of Independence, India benefited from the inheritance of some distant territories, including the strategic Andaman Islands, over 800 miles away, annexed to the subcontinent by the ever expanding and ambitious EIC. The 18th- and 19th-century pioneering adventures and the enterprise of the world's first multinational corporation, the EIC, provided significant collateral benefits for India in the 20th and 21st centuries. As a result an Indian diaspora in excess of 250 million people emerged across the world. This huge movement of native Indians happened largely as a result of the late 19th- and early 20th-century migration of contract labour designed for settling workers several thousands of miles away in colonies such as Fiji.

Additionally, in the same period, many more Indian workers migrated to several of the newly emerging island nations about 8000 miles away in the Caribbean and some in the nearby islands in the Indian Ocean, such as Mauritius and the Seychelles. The remarkable globalisation effect of the EIC's expansion of commercial interests – despite the many criticisms and abuses – would change the destiny of many Indians, their families and their successors who desired to migrate to the British-held South Africa and British East Africa, in Kenya, Uganda and Tanzania. Today, the second largest Indian population outside of India is in South Africa, home to over 1.3 million citizens of Indian origin. It is only exceeded by the 1.5 million UK citizens of Indian origin living in Britain, all of whom settled voluntarily.

From the early 20th century Indians realised the scope and opportunities for migrating to Britain and all its colonies, including some small and lesser-known places such as Gibraltar and Malta. Soon after, Indians also saw the opportunity of moving to the prosperous predominantly white British commonwealth of Canada, Australia and New Zealand. By the mid-1920s Indians were voluntarily trickling into the US, and later settling in far greater numbers after the end of World War II. The gradually increasingly strong position of the Indian diaspora in all of these countries is now history.

Today, the Indian diaspora is the focus of much attention in policy and developmental discourse. Globalisation and the communication revolution are allowing the diaspora to reconnect and contribute to a modern India. In recent years the Indian government has been increasingly vocal in its recognition of the hugely valuable asset of the Indian diaspora, who are contributing to the continued making of India in all fields, including the IT revolution, the financial and investment sectors, healthcare and international diplomacy. The presence of this prolific and accomplished diaspora is one of the most overarching factors in bilateral relations. Prime Minister Narendra Modi attributed the Indian diaspora as India's 'capital and [its] strength', appealing to non-resident Indians (NRIs) and persons of Indian origin (PIOs) to help transform India, garnering further recognition and respect across the world for their homeland.

A uniquely Indian history of migration

There are an estimated 20–25 million persons of Indian origin living outside of India, Pakistan and Bangladesh. The figures vary depending on whether the statistics include non-resident Indians (NRIs) and often omit those who settled in Sri Lanka, Nepal and Myanmar. Exceeded only by China, India has the second largest diaspora in the world spread across every major region in the world. Its value is immense. From its diaspora, India is the recipient of over US$70 billion per year, which makes it the beneficiary of the largest remittance in the world, accounting for 4% of its GDP. Beyond the financial considerations, the opportunities for international trade, development and diplomacy are as prodigious.

The origins of the Indian diaspora, for the most part, are tied to British rule in India, from the expanded opportunities in mercantilism in the early days of the EIC to the later mass migration of indentured Indian workers to far-flung British colonies in the late 19th century and early 20th century. Colonialism also provided opportunities for Indian clerks and soldiers to administer territories overseas in service to the Empire. The study itself of

South Asia migrants started with the British colonial government. Clerks would systematically observe, count and detail the number and makeup of the Indian migrants, their religious backgrounds, working conditions etc. These reports are still the main sources of South Asian migration history.

In addition to the merchants, civil servants and indentured labourers, more than two million Indian soldiers served and fought on behalf of the British Empire and its interests on foreign soil. For many of those serving overseas, their experiences in the British Army were hugely transformative, and many developed a deeper understanding of their place in the world: both in terms of limitations and possibilities. This sense of existentialism and agency is characteristic of the South Asian identity, and served the Indian diaspora well as first wave migrants and their successors seized new opportunities, adapted, organised and, uniquely, went on to play fundamental roles in the independence movements in both India and later in their adoptive homelands – independence movements that, too, were unique and defined by, for the most part, peaceful handovers of power.

Trade migration

Though often overlooked in the history of the Indian diaspora, Indian trade migration continued under British colonial rule and comprised a significant sector of the Indian diaspora. In his research of the Indian mercantile sphere, Claude Markovits calculated that an estimated 1–1.5 million merchant migrants left India between 1840 and 1930. Though this was predominately characteristic of the 'circular' and temporary migration of the pre-colonial era, many traders did settle overseas, particularly in Zanzibar, South Africa and British East Africa. Whilst European colonialism opened up trade routes, tensions over land rights and economic conflicts of interests pervaded these new multi-ethnic societies. Added to the tensions were the racial prejudices and injustices that pervaded the political and social landscape.

Indian merchants settled in many countries alongside indentured labourers. For example, in East Africa, non-indentured Indians, particularly Gujarati merchants, became shopkeepers, settling in the new towns that sprang up as a result of the new railways that the indentured labourers were building. Indians also migrated as clerks and teachers in service to colonial governments and the British Empire overseas. Trade and commerce would also became a viable vocation for many of the enterprising contract migrant labourers and their families who had left India in search of opportunity under indentured labour contracts.

Indian labour migration – the free and the unfree
Early slave diaspora

A less well-known but significant origin of the Indian diaspora is the convict diaspora, as well as the Indian slave trade, which was utilised extensively by the French and Dutch. The expansion of European colonies and interests in the 17th and 18th centuries saw the mass migration of many thousands of South Asian slaves. The Dutch Indian Ocean slave trade channelled thousands of Indian slaves to Dutch territories including the Cape in South Africa and Ceylon (Sri Lanka). South African archives reveal that 63 000 Indian slaves were imported to the Cape between 1652 and 1808. The French also transported thousands of slaves to their territories including the islands of Mauritius and Réunion. Accurate statistics and information about the fates of theses slaves are difficult to determine, but there is clear evidence that they contributed to an Indian diaspora, particularly in Mauritius and Réunion.

So endemic was the institution of localised and unregulated slavery that, as researcher Marina Carter highlighted, '*sepoys* or *lascars* might all too easily find themselves sold as slaves once they strayed beyond the relative comfort zone of an EIC ship, or barracks.' Slavery in the subcontinent had been an age-old institution. In 1843 the British illegalised slavery throughout the Empire, providing freedom and legal status and recognition to an estimated 10 million Indians held in bondage in the subcontinent.

Convict diaspora

During the late 18th century and early 19th century, an estimated 80 000 Indian convicts were transported to the newly acquired European colonies spread across the Indian Ocean. Detailing his observations in Mauritius as part of his voyage around the world, Charles Darwin wrote in 1837: 'These convicts are generally quiet and well conducted; from their outward conduct, their cleanliness, and faithful observance of their strange religious enactments, it was impossible to look at these men with the same eyes as our wreched [*sic.*] convicts in New South Wales.'

Indian convicts worked side by side with both slaves and early indentured labourers, and intermingled freely with the early indentured Indian labourers, identifying themselves as part of an Indian community. Upon release, many established themselves as part of this burgeoning Indian community in Mauritius where they stayed on as free labour. These convicts recognised opportunity and many were literate, evident from the 'prodigious' letter writing to family back in India. Such mobility, though arduous, is typical of the transience and complexity of the new landscapes the resilient Indian diaspora navigated and shaped.

Indentured and assisted labour

Migration during the period of British colonial rule is chiefly identified with the large-scale exportation of Indian indentured labour to the British colonies, in particular to the sugar plantations of the Caribbean and the Pacific. After the abolition of slavery in Britain in 1834, a labour deficit existed. Indentured labour provided a solution to the sustained demand for plentiful, reliable and cheap labour. Many agreed to indentured contracts – commonly lasting for a period of five years – to escape the widespread poverty in India, either travelling alone or taking their families with them.

Such indentured apprenticeships were neither new nor exclusive to Indian labourers. As Niall Ferguson explained: 'Between a half and two-thirds of all Europeans who migrated to North America between 1650 and 1780 did so under contracts of indentured servitude.' Many Chinese migrants were also later employed under indentured contracts. This system of temporary servitude alleviated the labour shortage in the colonies. For the Indian workers it presented a means for affording the otherwise prohibitive cost of the voyage overseas.

In 1834 an unregulated system of emigration of indentured Indian labourers began with the export of contracted Indian labourers to Mauritius. After 1842, immigration under indentured contracts became more systematic and documented. A Protector of Immigrants was appointed in Mauritius and agents in India had to be licensed following widespread claims of unscrupulous and dishonest practices. The fixed-term contracts (usually five years) were written in both English and the vernacular, including Hindi, Urdu and Bangla, and employers were obligated to provide fixed wages and basic amenities, including access to medical facilities.

An act in 1856 granted the Governor-General of India powers to prohibit the provision of indentured labour to any British colony where 'there was reason to believe that proper precautions were not taken for the protection of emigrants immediately upon their arrival in such a colony, or during the residence therein, for their safe return to India, or to provide a return passage at or about the time at which they were entitled to it'.

More than one million Indian labourers were employed under the reformed indenture system, principally to work on sugar plantations. The chief importers of Indian indentured labour were Fiji, South Africa, Mauritius, Malaysia and the Caribbean states. Most indentured labourers came from the north of India and embarked from the licensed 'depots' in Calcutta and Madras. By the turn of the 20th century, increasingly the diaspora were gaining more ground in their adoptive homelands and demanding better conditions and rights to citizenship.

During the same period, another assisted migration system came into operation, incorporating a system of contractors or recruiters in India and overseers at the migrant workers' destinations. These overseers were also of service to the migrant workers in their new homelands. Having amassed substantial wealth through their trade in migrant labour, the overseers had the opportunity to purchase land and also act as moneylenders. These rights allowed the migrant workers themselves to access the funds necessary to purchase land in their new homelands.

This new system had far-reaching consequences for the Indian diasporic communities. To purchase land, even modest smallholdings, represented status and stability. It meant workers were able to acquire tangible capital after all their hard work and travails. By 1940, the Indian labour diaspora in Malaysia owned approximately 39% of the plantations in form of small holdings. By the end of the 19th century the recruiter–overseer system overtook indentured migration even in the more distant colonies of Fiji, Malaya and Trinidad, resulting in a source of credit for labourers to obtain leases on smallholdings or own land.

The experience and outcome of the migrants who left India in search of opportunity vary considerably from country to country, depending on their terms of employment, their freedoms and rights, and how inclusive the migrants' host country was. For some, particularly the trade migrants, opportunities were plentiful and they prospered. Yet even they faced hostility and adversity when their gains provoked envy and prejudice. For others it was a life sentence and an enduring struggle for the most basic of rights. Many faced segregation and prejudice. Yet, although the perception of the duped 'coolie' migrant has remained prevalent, it denies the diversity, determination, adaptability and the significant progress both the free and the indentured migrants made in a remarkably short space of time. Indentured

Indian labourers voluntarily chose short-term hardships with the vision of forging a better life for the future. Most apparently viewed the transition as temporary, though few returned to India. Whether this was due to the prohibitive cost of the return voyage, the dangers of the crossing, a reluctance to uproot and start over, or a determined decision to stay in their adoptive homeland is not always obvious. Most likely the reasons were manifold. But with courage and determination the Indian diaspora adapted and endured. Though by no way exhaustive, the following few countries exemplify both the differences and the shared experiences of the colonial Indian diaspora.

Mauritius

In Mauritius the effect of labour immigration was the creation of a 'plural' society from the numerous Indian convicts, indentured labourers, African slaves and French settlers. There was no indigenous society as such to speak of and no determined policy of racial segregation. However, the situation in Mauritius was very difficult for most Indians. Mauritius was first settled by the Dutch in 1598, but later abandoned in 1710. In 1715 it was occupied by the French and came under the administration of the French East India Company before being transferred to the French Crown in 1767. It was conquered by the British in 1810 during the Anglo-French wars. From 1810 to 1903 Mauritius and the Seychelles were administered as a single British colony. The plantation owners, predominantly of French descent, represented an unyielding elite. Under the indenture system, Indian migrant labourers were employed to work on the sugar plantations and often suffered draconian abuses.

Today, the Indian diaspora or persons of Indian origin (PIOs) form 70% of the Mauritian population and are a major socio-political force. It was the son of an indentured labourer that led Mauritius to independence from Britain in 1968. Born on 18 September 1900 at Belle Rive, Mauritius, Seewoosagur Ramgoolam was deeply influenced by the independence movement in India. He won a scholarship and excelled in his studies. At his college he came under the tutelage of British tutors who made a lasting impression on the young Ramgoolam. He was impressed by British culture and manners, and he became a devoted lover of the English language and literature, as well as French literature. In 1921, Ramgoolam set sail for London where he graduated from University College London. Politicised and determined, he rose through the ranks to lead the Mauritian Labour Party to victory. This would become a unique trait of the Indian diaspora: to lead their adoptive homelands to peaceful liberation in the same manner of non-violence as achieved in their country of origin.

Fiji

The experience of the Fijian Indian diaspora is profound. Fiji was the last importer of indentured labour. In 1874 it became a British colony. European planters had settled on Fiji from the 1860s seeing the opportunity for cotton cultivation after the devastation of the industry in America during the Civil War. Local Fijians did not want to leave their ancestral lands to work on plantations and so began an extensive recruitment of Indian indentured labour. The first sailing ship to transport indentured labourers, the *Leonides*, arrived in Fiji in 1879 with 463 indentured labourers. The 1600-ton vessel belonged to the Nourse shipping line. The founder, James Nourse, built up a fleet of sailing vessels for the transport of contract labour from India to the West Indies and Fiji. In 1916 the practice of indentured labour migration ended. Over 60 000 indentured labourers had arrived in Fiji.

The enduring Indian diaspora responded to the adversities by ensuring their children had access to professions that did not limit them to the land. Indo-Fijians, typical of the Indian diaspora, embraced education. A number of the descendents of the indentured labourers were also being sent abroad to study, and a gradual urbanisation of settlers occurred as they left the plantations after their contracts were up. Most indentured labourers did not return to India. For some it was a life sentence, for others it was a hardship to be endured for no more than ten years. However, the experience for many of the first-generation of Indian indentured labourers was also one of unification – a leveller – with their fellow Indians. The new working conditions, though difficult, were based on merit and not caste. Caste segregation could not be maintained in these close quarters and camaraderie was needed. The disparity in gender ratios – with more significantly more male labourers than female, particularly in the early wave of immigration – resulted in cross-caste marriages which would have been unthinkable in India. Yet religion and culture were strong impulses, and traditions an important connection to their homeland and sense of identity.

Punitive taxation burdens hit the Indo-Fijians hard and prejudices endured. Land-owning prohibitions and the suppression of Indo-Fijian political leaders, alongside continued social prejudices led to the migration of a significant number of Indians to Australia, New Zealand and Canada. Yet, those who remained built a distinctive community and culture. Hindi and English became the scholastic languages. By the 1950s Indo-Fijians were embracing radio and cinema in a big way, and were avid consumers of Bollywood and Hindi cinema. In testimony to the importance the community placed on education, literacy and expression, the 1950s also saw an 'explosion of Hindi newspapers in Fiji'. The diaspora were politicised and determined. Today there are approximately 313 000 Fijian citizens of Indian origin comprising 44% of the electorate. These Indian Fijians make a significant impact on the political and social directive of the country.

South Africa

On 16 November 1860, around 340 Indian indentured labourers travelling on board the *Truro* arrived in Durban, in the province of Natal, destined for the sugar and cotton plantations. Ten days later, the *Belvedere* arrived with 305 more indentured labourers. Six years later, the importation of indentured labourers was suspended due to breaches in contract and ill treatment. In 1874 Natal sent a plea for urgently needed labour. The Government of India acquiesced on the strict proviso that contracts for the labourers would be honoured and conditions be improved. One of the terms was that Indians on completion of ten-year contracts would be allowed to buy land in Natal.

In addition to the wave of indentured immigrants, free traders, principally from Gujarat, began to arrive in South Africa in the late 1870s. The future seemed relatively optimistic for the Indian settlers. Their rights appeared to be protected and they were considered 'in all respects, free men'. Fifty expired-contract Indians were listed as rate-payers and voters on the electoral register. By the 1880s the Indian diaspora in the South African provinces of Natal and Transvaal had grown to a population of over 20 000. Such was the success of the traders and business migrants, and the new ability of expired-contract labourers to purchase land, that the political tide changed and the Indian population began to face determined opposition from the European settlers and South African policymakers. Indians' movements were restricted by a nine o'clock curfew and the introduction of a £3 tax hit the indentured labourers particularly hard, forcing many to stay in perpetual indentured labour.

In other diasporic communities, it was the levelling experience and mutual cooperation among Indians from all backgrounds, castes and religions that helped to strengthen the diasporic communities in the their new homelands – a sense of being 'Indian'. In the 1890s Mohandas Gandhi was working in South Africa and took on the struggle for Indian workers' rights in

South Africa. He appealed to the free migrants and the indentured that their fates were intertwined and their strength was in their unity. In 1894 Gandhi founded the Natal National Congress and went on to start up the periodical the *Indian Opinion*. Moderate in its criticisms, the newspaper highlighted the hardships of the indentured labourers. Its editor Henry Polak travelled to India to raise funds for the newspaper and spread awareness of the indentured labourers' plight.

In 1911 the Government of India prohibited the provision of any more indentured labour to South Africa. Since 1860, over 150 000 indentured labourers had arrived in Natal. An estimated 25% of indentured male labourers chose to return to India at the end of their contracts, but the majority chose to stay. In 1913 the Viceroy of India, Lord Hardinge, spoke out against the mistreatment of Indians by the South African authorities. A year later Gandhi achieved victory in securing the abolition of the £3 tax, and secured the rights of Indian traditional marriages to be legally recognised in South Africa. His mission in South Africa completed, he left for England a month later. It was during his years in South Africa that Gandhi formulated his core ideology and strategy for India's independence. On his return to India in 1915, after his sojourn in England, he received a hero's welcome.

In the 1960s, after a long struggle, Indians were formally recognised as a part of the South African community. Today the South African Indian diaspora numbers approximately 1.2 million. Their contribution to the anti-apartheid struggle was recognised by President Nelson Mandela who appointed a number of Indians to prominent positions. Many have excelled in their professions in the fields of law, medicine and academia, and make a valuable contribution to the country's economy.

Independence

In the struggle for their respective independence and recognition of their citizenship, India and its diaspora were uniquely tied. Indians both at home and overseas were struggling towards freedom and a national identity. In India the early nationalist goal was towards home rule and dominion status, while for the Indian diaspora it was for the rights of citizenship in the countries in which they had settled. Gandhi's struggles in South Africa had gained widespread attention in India, and both the Government of India and the India Office in London began to take a direct involvement in the checking of colonial applications for indentured labour. Lord Curzon, then

Viceroy of India, regarded indentured labour as 'the slavery of the day' and refused to yield to the pressure of plantation owners who wanted to renege on their contractual obligations to provide indentured Indians their return passages. Curzon's attitude was clear and the Government of India commissioned C.F. Andrews and W.W. Pearson – close friends of both Gandhi and Rabrindranath Tagore – to report on the conditions of indentured Indian labourers in Fiji, Kenya and British Guiana. The findings of the Andrews and Pearson report contributed to the official abolition of the indenture system by the British government in 1917.

'A national resource'
– the making of a modern, global India

After World War II, Indian emigration was characterised by the 'brain drain' – the migration of highly educated professionals, especially doctors, lawyers and educators, to the UK, the US and Canada. In the 1970s a new wave of migrants travelled to the Middle East, attracted by the new opportunities in the construction industries. More recently there has been an exodus of IT professionals to the US in particular. In 2006 remittance from its diaspora was estimated at US$22 billion. In less than a decade that figure is now estimated at over US$70 billion. India, too, is making a massive commitment in its recognition of its diaspora. A report by the Indian High Level Commission stated that: 'Since India achieved Independence, overseas Indians have been returning to seek their roots and explore new avenues and sectors for mutual beneficial interaction from investment to the transfer of economic skills and technology, to outright philanthropy and charitable work. This trend has become more marked in the last decade, as the Indian economy has opened up, giving rise to a new range of opportunities for emerging generations.' In a reciprocal gesture of unity, Prime Minister Narendra Modi announced in November 2014 that India was offering Fiji a line of credit and development assistance totalling US$80 million in recognition of the 'timeless link' between the two nations. Home Minister Rajnath Singh, too, has made it clear that it is not just for financial return that India wants to forge closer ties with its diaspora but recognised the multiple ways that the Indian diaspora can contribute to the 'transformation' of India in the 21st century 'irrespective of the country they are residing in.'

In the same year, the 1.5 million-strong British-Indian diaspora was recognised at the first UK Regional Pravasi Bharatiya Divas (Overseas Indians

Day) by the then Deputy Prime Minister Nick Clegg as 'an integral part of British life, contributing to every aspect of our society and helping to strengthen ties between Britain and India.' UK companies have an estimated US$85 billion stake in India – more than any other country. Yet, in recent changes to visa regulations, which saw the easing of the application process for tourists and business travellers to India, there was one glaring absence in the list of the 43 recipient countries of the simpler system: Britain. As a reporter for *The Times* put it: 'It looked like a snub. It certainly felt like one.'

In an article in the *Asian Age* published on 24 June 2014, Mohan Guruswamy, the writer and head of the Centre of Policy Alternatives, New Delhi, an independent and privately funded think-tank, raised the problem of historic bias: 'It is difficult to be entirely objective when writing history... As a young student ... in recently independent India, the first history lessons ... [were] about the British. We were taught that the rule was a most benign and beneficial period for Indians... reforms like the abolition of sati and the building of great canal systems and railways happened during this period. The unification of India into one great political entity also happened in this period... But in 1957, when the centennial celebrations of the First Indian War of Independence [the Mutiny] happened, I discovered that what my history textbook would have me believe was wrong.'

As Guruswamy elucidates, historical revisionism was legitimate but now there is a danger that historical opinion of the British legacy in India has swung out of balance, and again the history books are in need of revision: 'Quite clearly if Indian society has to be inclusive, all its various peoples must share a common perspective of the past. This is not so at present, to my mind at least the history textbooks need to be rewritten.'

Conclusion

Though perhaps not 'fashionable', many British-Indians are proud of both their country of origin and their adoptive homeland, recognising all aspects of colonial rule, from the obvious subjugation to the massive opportunity and uplift that colonialism brought. By the 20th century, India was the beneficiary of an extensive physical infrastructure at the cutting edge of modernity and a sophisticated network of civil, legal and political institutions to underpin the largest democracy in the world. Today, the legacy of a global Indian diaspora may well be the most enduring legacy of colonialism yet in the story of the making of India.

Appendix A
Milestones in the Making of India

1498   Vasco da Gama's Portuguese fleet lands at Malabar Coast (Kerala)

1600   EIC established on 31 December

1612   EIC establishes trading house in Surat

1618   EIC negotiates first trade agreement with Mughal Empire

1695   EIC Court of Directors left reeling from the first parliamentary investigation into charges of corruption

1739   The Persian King Nadir Shah plunders Delhi in the most savage invasion in Indian history. Over 20 000 soldiers are slaughtered in only two hours and many more enslaved as caravan after caravan emptied Delhi of its people and treasures, which included the Koh-i-noor diamond (later retrieved 74 years later in 1813 by the formidable Sikh kingdom under Ranjit Singh)

1748   Wadia begins construction of the first dry-dock facilities at Bombay to EIC designs

1750   EIC military hospital in Madras opened to the public to provide free healthcare

1757   Battle of Plassey in Bengal consolidates EIC rule in India and is a critical turning point in pushing the French out of India

1761   The Afghan King Abdali plunders Delhi, Lahore, Agra and the north-west region for the third time in a series of devastating Afghan raids, emptying Delhi of every conceivable treasure that had escaped the previous Persian invaders. The Afghans outdid the Persians by taking away even the inhabitants' kitchen utensils, furniture and clothing. Among the cargo were Delhi's young women and slaves

1764   EIC victory at the battle of Buxar against the combined French and native forces is a major defeat against France's claim in India

1764   EIC is granted the rights of the diwani – fiscal administration – from Shah Alam II, entirely weakened and left without a kingdom, subjects and a treasury after the Afghan and Persian invasions

1771   Colaba lighthouse built in Bombay

1774   Coal discovered in Bengal by the EIC

1778   Printing press established in Bengal

1779	Scottish economist Adam Smith publishes *An Inquiry into the Nature and Causes of the Wealth of Nations*
1784	Asiatic Society founded by Sir William Jones
1784	EIC share prices drop in London for the first time in their history due to famine in eastern India
1788	The historic seven-year impeachment trial of Warren Hastings begins
1789	A Mr Burn arrives from England and starts an iron foundry in Calcutta
1792	First Police Act introduced to establish a recognised paid police force
1799	Jessop & Company establishes a foundry in Calcutta
1880	College of Fort William founded
1880	The Great Trigonometrical Survey of India established
1801	First metallised road in India
1801	Construction of Cochrane's Canal (later part of the Buckingham and East Coast Canal) in the Madras Presidency commences
1803	EIC set up the Kidderpore Docks, later bought in 1807 by the Anglo-Indian master shipbuilders James and Robert Kyd
1803	College of Civil Engineering founded in Madras
1803	Work commences on huge dockyard in Bombay
1808	First iron lighthouse established at the entrance to the Hooghly
1813	Trade monopoly of the EIC abolished
1814	First public museum in India established
1815	Iron bridge constructed in Lucknow
1816	India's first coal mined in Burdwan, Bengal
1816	Hindu College in Calcutta founded
1817	Restoration of the Western and Eastern Jumna Canals begins
1820	First steam-operated textile mill in Calcutta (though later folded)
1825	PS *Enterprise*, 464 tons, is the first steam vessel to reach Calcutta from London (funded by Anglo-Indian joint capital)
1827	Elphinstone College, Bombay and Delhi College founded
1829	Lord Bentinck bans age-old ritual of sati – immolation of widows
1830	Military road to Darjeeling opened
1831/2	Presidency of Madras conceives the idea of India's first railway
1832	India's first medical schools established in Madras and Calcutta
1836	Construction of the Grand Trunk Road, Calcutta–Lahore, begins
1837	Grant Medical College opens in Bombay with EIC and Parsi joint patronage

1841	Archaeological Survey of India established to protect and restore Indian monuments and heritage
1847	Roorkee College established
1851	Telegraph connection between Calcutta and Agra established
1852	First (EIC) postage stamps issued
1852	Sir Arthur Cotton's Godavari Anicut completed, irrigating over 700 000 acres
1853	Inaugural passenger train in service (Bombay–Thana)
1854	Ganges Canal completed at a cost of £3 million, transforming the landscape and agrarian economy and producing enough additional grain to feed 1.5 million people
1854	India's first cotton mill, The Bombay Spinning Mill, is founded
1856	8749 miles of hardcore roads completed
1857	The great Indian Army Mutiny
1858	On 1 September the British government takes full formal control of India from the EIC and enacts reforms
1858	Richardson & Cruddas establishes a major foundry and bridge-building yard at Bombay at Byculla ironworks
1861	37 000 miles of metalled roads completed
1861	First railway opened in the Punjab
1862	Rolling stock manufacture begins in Jamalpur, Bengal
1862	Total of 2495 928 tons of hardware imported for railway and bridge construction within ten years on 3012 ships
1865	Calcutta–Bombay railway opened
1865	First bridge across the Jumna opened
1866	Reliable telegraph service connected London with India
1867	A record 5000 miles of railway completed in 14 years
1867	Steam-road locomotive road arrives in the Punjab
1868	J.N. Tata, the pioneering entrepreneur, lays the foundation of the Tata Industry Group
1869	Nearly 1.5 million acres of land irrigated in the North-West Provinces
1869	Suez Canal opened – within one year over 200 ships pass through to India via the Mediterranean
1870	Public Works Department (PWD) greatly expands with 363 Royal Engineers and 545 senior engineers
1871	Imperial government conducts first census in India
1874	J.N. Tata opens textile mill

1874   First bridge across the Hooghly in Calcutta
1875   Bombay Stock Exchange established
1876   Prongs Reef Lighthouse, Bombay, enters service
1877   Empress Bridge completed, spanning 4500 ft across the river Sutlej in the Punjab
1877   Tata's Empress Cotton Mill opens in Nagpur
1879   Electricity arrives in Karachi
1879   First telephone in service
1884   First mental health hospitals opened in Madras and Calcutta
1886   India's first nursing school set up in Bombay
1887   Darjeeling electricity supply established for public service
1887   Dufferin Bridge, Benares, constructed
1887   Jubilee Bridge completed, allowing new rail service from Calcutta to Darjeeling
1887   New Kidderpore Docks commissioned
1888   Punjab Sher Shah Bridge opened
1888   The landmark Victoria Terminus station in Bombay is completed
1889   Lansdowne Bridge in the Punjab opened
1890   Engineering schools established in Roorkee, Puna, Madras and Seebpoor
1894   Ten oil wells drilled in Assam (all dry)
1894   Crude oil extraction from Digboi oilfield
1896   Indian Agricultural Research Institute founded at Pusa in Bihar
1897   20 577 miles of all-terrain railway completed
1897   44 648 miles of telegraph in service
1897   Aluminium industry commenced
1900   Crompton builds electrical factory in Calcutta
1901   Palta Waterworks in Calcutta delivers 6 million gallons daily
1901   70 000 miles of first-class metalled roads and 200 000 miles of smaller compacted roads
1902   First line for electric tram opens in Calcutta
1902   Nagpur textile industry introduces diesel-engine power
1903   J.N. Tata establishes India's first landmark luxury hotel, Taj Mahal, in Bombay
1906   Munaar Valley Electrical Power Scheme in Travancore commissioned
1907   Tata Iron & Steel Company officially incorporated
1908/9 Monazite deposits discovered in Travancore

1910   Tata sets up first of the three major hydroelectric supply companies. Three major dams are built, Lonavla, Walwhan and Shirawta, with first high-voltage transmission supplying electricity to Bombay

1910   Hospital for tuberculosis founded in Simla

1911   Indian Institute of Science in Bangalore opens – its founder, J.N. Tata, did not live to see its opening

1911   Jamalpur railway workshop employs 11 000 workers

1911   King George V and Queen Mary land in India and lay foundation stone for grandiose New Delhi

1912   Bombay–Delhi rail journey covered in 28 hours

1912   Tata Enterprises is first to introduce eight-hour working day and pioneers the culture of social benefits for workers in India

1912   Allahabad Agricultural Institute founded

1913   First 100 000-volt scheme commenced to supply Bombay

1913   Bollywood's first silent feature film *Raja Harish Chandra* released by D. Phalke

1914   Outbreak of World War I

1915   Hardinge Bridge railway crossing at Sara (over the Lower Ganges) opened

1918   First medical school for women in Velore, near Madras, opens

1919   Government of India provides limited self-rule for Indians

1919   Calcutta Medical School of Hygiene and Tropical Medicine founded

1919   Amritsar Massacre by Brigadier Dyer. The atrocity, carried out by a lone racist, marks the darkest moment in British rule in India and is heavily condemned in Parliament amidst public outrage in Britain

1922   Railway mileage 37 266 completed

1925   State takes over the EIR, EBR and GIPR

1927   Benares Hindu University launches mining courses

1928   Magnificent parliament building completed on time

1931   India becomes a Dominion within the British Commonwealth

1931–4 Ajmer Railway Workshops build their largest steam locomotive, a YD Class 2-8-2 weighing 98.5 tons, at a cost of Rs.75,000

1932   Tata Enterprises starts India's first air postal service

1934   Cauvery-Mettur Dam, Madras Presidency, completed. It was then the largest dam in India and the sixth-largest in the world

1935   Imperial Bank of India, renamed as Reserve Bank, established in
        Bombay
1935   Government of India Act provides for elected provincial
        parliaments and Federal Congress
1939   Tata establishes India's first heavy chemical industry
1939   Outbreak of World War II
1941   Tata builds India's first cancer hospital
1941   Construction of the Howrah Bridge, Calcutta, begins
1943   Calcutta cantilever bridge completed (1500 ft and 28 000 tons of
        steel)
1945   Tata becomes the first Indian company to manufacture
        locomotives
1946   One year before Independence, India already possessed 42 railway
        systems and some 250 000 students established on engineering
        courses, with roughly the same number of law graduates, doctors
        and nurses, and thousands of hospitals
1947   The year of the transfer of power and the birth of the world's
        largest democracy, sustained by a very wide range of massive civil
        infrastructure, including the all-important Indian Civil Service
        (ICS), judiciary, free press, educational institutions, museums,
        libraries, universities, hospitals and health centres, sports facilities,
        and a cohesive, well-trained and professional police and military.
        All comprehensively and meticulously underpinned by an equally
        important physical infrastructure of colossal magnitude, providing
        45 000 miles of railways with 136 000 bridges and over 200 000
        miles of roadways, communications, post and telegraph, mining,
        harbours and canals. New cities and towns had been built, tea
        and coffee estates planted, and state-of-the-art irrigation and
        agriculture systems implemented. Such innovation placed India
        much ahead of all countries between Japan and Europe, including
        Korea, Taiwan, Singapore, Hong Kong and China

Appendix B
Biographies: British Engineers in India

Many hundreds of British Victorian engineers devoted much of their lives to the making of modern India, and space does not permit us to list them all. But below are just a few of the many unsung heroes of that time who can rightly claim to have been instrumental in laying the foundations of the most challenging and vast infrastructural undertaking in 19th- and 20th-century India.

To compile a gazetteer of all the British engineers who advanced their careers in imperial India would doubtless occupy several volumes. In recent years, the renowned Institution of Civil Engineering (ICE) in London has embarked on compiling a historical record covering every known civil engineer member since the founding of the institution in 1818.

In respect to this appendix, some of those who served in providing India with its all-important infrastructure through the establishment and proliferation of railways, roads, bridges, canals, trams, docks, lighthouses and harbours, power generation, as well as the post and telegraph systems and various public works departments, are acknowledged in brief paragraphs. Britain exported her best engineers, machinery, brains and technology to her Indian Empire. Their phenomenal achievements during the 19th and 20th centuries, until the transfer of power in 1947, speak for themselves. This very brief listing is compiled in alphabetical order, rather than chronologically, as all engineers mentioned deserve equal merit.

JAMES JOHN BERKELEY (1819–1862) was educated at King's College, London, before serving newly formed English railway companies from 1842 to 1849. Berkeley was recommended to lay out the first railway system in Bombay, constructing the first 33 miles 'on an experimental basis'. Later, he spent four years surveying the Bhore Ghat incline for the Great Indian Peninsula Railway as part of the planned 1237 miles of the network. He extended lines to Nagpur providing an outlet for that area's cotton industry.

MAJOR-GENERAL SIR JAMES BROWNE (1839–1896) was commissioned into the Bengal Engineers in 1857, where he distinguished himself as soldier, military engineer and political officer, before being transferred to the Punjab frontier. While building the Kandahar Railway to the Afghan border, he mastered Pushtu and Persian and was to play an intelligence role in the various Afghan Wars. Browne was instrumental in surveying the East Coast Railway from Calcutta to Madras, including the impressive Kistna River crossing (12 × 300 ft spans). In the Punjab, Browne completed the survey in 1874 for bridging the Indus River and three years later he was appointed by Lord Lytton to survey the most suitable route from Sukkur to Quetta. Subsequently, he became the *de facto* ruler of Baluchistan.

GEORGE BRUNTON (1823–1900) was aged just 15 when joined his uncle, Robert Brunton, at the Indian Iron & Steel Company's works at Porto Novo. After graduating as manager, he transferred the works to Beypore, remaining there until its closure. He invented a cotton press, embodying a valuable improvement called the 'extractor', which expedited greatly the process of compression, and was adopted by the Bombay textile industry. His inventive capacity diversified into the development of a hydraulic valve (*c*.1880) that was successfully applied to steam machinery used for irrigating vast tracts of rice land in southern India, replacing the traditional – and inadequate – water wheels.

WILLIAM ALEXANDER BRUNTON (1840–1881) started engineering overseas at an early age, joining his father in 1855 to build the Reukioi Hospital in Turkey. Aged 17, he was appointed assistant engineer on the Scinde Railway, where his father was chief engineer. Having proved himself, he was put in charge of building a stone viaduct comprising 32 × 45 ft spans across the River Bahrun. In 1868 Brunton became district engineer for the Oudh & Rohilkund Railway, where he remained until fever compelled him to return to England in 1870. He never returned to India, dying 11 years later, aged just 41.

HENRY ROBERT PASLEY CARTER (1833–1901), having served his apprenticeship on Irish railways, went to India in 1858 to join the engineering staff of the Madras Railway. He was involved in the construction of a portion of the Bangalore branch that traverses the Saidanur Pass, a valuable experience that enabled him, in 1874, to restore the bridge across the Gudiyatam River, which had been damaged by abnormal flooding. Most of his 36 years in India were spent serving the Madras Railway, but he was forced to return to England for approximately two-and-a-half years during that time to recuperate from sickness.

GENERAL FRANCIS RAWDON CHESNEY (1779–1872) had exploration and adventure in his blood. After visiting Continental Europe for two years, he travelled to Constantinople and on to Asia Minor, with his mind set on establishing direct steam communication with India. He surveyed the Euphrates and Tigris rivers, traversed the Syrian Desert, and then crossed the Persian Gulf to Bushire, before exploring the Karoon River. His account of this journey was published in the *Survey of the Euphrates & Tigris Rivers* (1830). The British government provided £20,000 for this survey. Chesney was the first man to sail down the Euphrates in a steamboat, and again surveyed both the Tigris and Euphrates routes for a rail project, which was subsequently abandoned. The general, whose portrait by an unknown artist hangs in the National Portrait Gallery in London, had previously surveyed the Suez Canal (1829), proving that Napoleon's expedition to assess building the waterway was incorrect in so far that the water levels did not vary by the calculated 36 ft. Ferdinand de Lesseps rightly described Chesney as 'the father of the Suez Canal'.

GENERAL SIR ARTHUR COTTON (1803–1899) obtained a cadetship at the age of 15 for India and trained at a military academy at Addiscombe, near Croydon. A year later he rose to the rank of second lieutenant and, in May 1821, he embarked for Madras, before joining an expedition that took part in the First Burmese War.

In 1836 Cotton devised a scheme for controlling the Cauvery River, saving its priceless water from running to waste. This achievement preceded a brilliant career in civil and water engineering that had a major beneficial impact on India. The Rajahmundry District was known for succumbing to the vagaries of monsoons, responsible for causing frequent famines. Cotton was given a free rein to harness the waters of the Godavari River, with completion of the Godavari Anicut (dam) in March 1851. Locks and canals were constructed with such success that the government undertook a similar venture for an anicut across the river Kistna. Cotton, the acknowledged expert of his day for irrigation and flood control, was also instrumental in a similar scheme in Orissa. He later returned to Rajahmundry, where he successfully controlled the Godavari to irrigate some 720 000 acres, via 500 miles of inland canals to the port of Kakinada. In total, Cotton spent 40 years in India and his dedication to control the ravages of nature cannot be underestimated.

His name will live on in the civil works that have survived for posterity. Statues were erected to his memory in both Rajahmundry and Hyderabad, where his is one of 32 erected along a 2 km stretch of road on the embankment holding the waters of Hussain Sagar Lake. Without Cotton's efforts, the map covering the districts of East and West Godavari would be very different today, with habitation all but denuded.

GEORGE HARDINGE (1831–1879) was an articled pupil to Sampson Lloyd (founder of Lloyds Bank) of Lloyds, Fosters & Co, where he had a rigorous training in mining and bridge building before entering the service of the Bombay, Baroda & Central India Railway in 1858. His first three years were spent advancing branch lines from towns such as Meagama (to Baroda), for example, and at one time had more than 40 miles of line and numerous viaducts under his charge. All work was undertaken without contractors. During one survey he narrowly escaped capture by Tantai Topee and his army of mutineers, fleeing for his life.

He returned to England, albeit briefly, before immersing himself from 1863 in developing the Indian Tramways Company, Madras, for the construction of the first 20 miles between Arconum and Conjeveram. On completion, he joined the Madras Railway Company as senior engineer, where his initial duties were to construct the first 150 miles on line to Raichur. From around 1873, he undertook a survey of the 64 miles between Puttamby and Cochin, before being selected to construct the new Madras Central Station. This was an important project, which he also completed without outside contractors.

Hardinge later built the goods station in Madras along with the first locomotive service shop at Perambore. In 1878, he was appointed resident engineer at Bangalore, but the hot season took a heavy toll on his health and he died of an abscess of the liver in Madras the following year.

HENRY WALTER HUDSON (1841–1879) is virtually unknown today, yet his dedication to serve India should not be forgotten. As an apprentice to the sugar machinery manufacturer Buchanan, of Liverpool, he later felt that exposure to railway engineering was more to his liking and served the London, Dover & Chatham, and Great Northern Railway lines in the UK before accepting an engagement as district engineer on the South Indian Railway. He was placed in charge of construction of the Madurai and

Chingleput branch lines. In 1875 the Cochin government appointed Hudson as chief engineer for the construction of roads, railways, canals, bridges and public buildings, as well as the reclamation of land – a post he held for 21 years. Later, his dedication to irrigation works brought immense benefits to the locals and stimulated much prosperity in the state. Regrettably, Hudson's constitution was impaired by attacks of malaria and he died at sea in 1879 en route back to England.

HENRY BURDON HUTCHINGS (1854–1880) was educated at Winchester College and the Royal Indian Engineering College at Cooper's Hill. He decided to make his career in India and, in 1875, undertook his first appointment on irrigation works in the Tinnevelly District. In 1876 he was transferred to the Nellore District in charge of construction for a section of the Buckingham Canal, designed to alleviate famine, with between 7000 and 8000 workers under his command. Two years later he undertook the appointment of assistant engineer in Madurai for civil works, but failing health in September 1879 prompted Hutchings to travel to New South Wales, Australia, where he died.

LIEUTENANT COLONEL JOHN PITT KENNEDY (1796–1879) began his career with the Royal Military Academy, passing out with distinction to take a position with the Corps of Royal Engineers. In 1819 he served on civil works in Malta and Corfu before being introduced to the Acting Resident at the Court of the Guicowar of Baroda, who, with a Colonel French, planned to construct the first lines for the Bombay, Baroda & Central India Railway. The aim was to open the most effectual line from Bombay to meet the railways in progress from Delhi and Calcutta, thus creating an integrated network.

Pitt was in joint charge of the first 308 miles from Bombay to Ahmedabad, which involved huge bridging across wide rivers and sea inlets. He was a strong advocate of broad gauge, but was occasionally overruled when metre-gauge workings ran in parallel. He devoted virtually his entire working career to that one railway company, which allowed him to write many pamphlets on Indian subjects, ranging from engineering to arts and culture. He resigned his post on 20 June 1879 and died eight days later.

JOHN PITT KENNEDY (1824–1897), nephew of the above, began his career as resident engineer on the Great Southern & Western Railway of Ireland, before being promoted to take charge of constructing the Derry &

Coleraine Railway, also in Ireland. He then joined his uncle on the Bombay, Baroda & Central India Railway in 1853 as managing agent and district engineer for a three-year period before returning to England. The lure of India must have held sway, for Kennedy returned in 1864 to serve the railway firm once again as its consulting engineer until 1882 when the network was considerably expanded with lines extending to Delhi. He later teamed up with Sir Alexander Rendel (see below), whose plans for India added not only a considerable expansion of the railway network but also docks and harbour facilities.

PHILIP GLYNN MESSENT (1862–1925), as a young engineer in Britain, superintended the erection of a wrought-iron lighthouse, built on piles on a groyne at the entrance of the river Tyne in Newcastle, England. In September 1884 he was appointed Specialist Engineer to the Bombay Port Trust where he was put in charge of the completion of a concrete-block quay wall at Modi Bunder as well as the removal, by divers, of several reefs of rock in the harbour. He next was appointed Resident Engineer on the Prince's Dock extension works which commenced in early 1885. The works comprised a dock of 24 acres in water area, with an 80-ft sea entrance complete with gates. A 64-ft communication passage connected the newly built Victoria Dock with the Prince's Dock to form an integrated dock system, closed by a caisson. The docks' facilities included sheds, hydraulic-engine cranes, gate machines, capstan and cargo cranes. Messent was also in charge of the removal of rock, by means of blasting carried out by divers, to deepen the channel to the dock.

GRANVILLE MILLS (1858–1915) was perhaps the most eccentric of all Queen Victoria's brilliant railway engineers who served the Raj. Having graduated from the Royal Indian Engineering College, Cooper's Hill, he joined his elder brother in India after completing his mechanical/civil engineering training with the Great Western Railway. In 1884 Mills served the fledgling Noakhali-Bengal Railway (Calcutta) before accepting a position as assistant engineer with the newly established Assam Bengal Railway. He was in his element during the early surveying days, planning routes, railway stations and engine workshops. In 1895 he was offered a senior position with the East Bengal Railway that considerably broadened his outlook.

Back in Calcutta Mills did a stint with the Calcutta Public Works Department at a time when electricity generation and tram routes were being constructed. Perhaps bored with city life, Mills returned to Assam where further routes and the flourishing tea and coal industries demanded more railways. Shortly after assuming these duties, he was tempted to accept a superintendent engineering position in Burma, where lines were being projected to Mandalay. But restlessness set in and an opportunity to shine for the Great Indian Peninsula Railway in the bridging of the Godavari River at Basa encouraged him to accept the appointment.

Mills, along with his wife, were distinguished painters and he could never resist any opportunity to haul his easel, chalks and paint with his bridge-building tools. One can only speculate at the reaction from locals when tigers briefly interrupted the construction work. Mills, indifferent to the danger, would portray the scene on canvas. His paintings were of such a high standard, and life-like, that he was to achieve a measure of fame in England when a selection of his pictures was reproduced in London's *Illustrated Graphic*.

SIR GUILFORD LINDSEY MOLESWORTH KCIE (1828–1925) was born into affluence, with his education planned at King's School, Canterbury and Manchester Grammar School, which he left, aged 16, to enter the Civil Engineering College at Putney. A career in railway engineering was ingrained in his character with several appointments before the outbreak of the Crimean War in 1854, when his services were urgently required for the construction of a munitions works in Woolwich. He left England to join the Ceylon Railway Company and on completion of the Colombo–Kandy line, joined the Indian State Railway. Although he reached the compulsory age of retirement in 1883, he was persuaded to remain in India and was involved in the construction of some 3500 miles of new permanent track. In recognition of his services, he was made a Knight Commander of the Indian Empire in 1888. His legacy survives today with the Attock Bridge across the Indus completed in 1883.

WILLIAM POLE (1814–1900) was articled at the age of 15 as an engineer to the Horseley Company in Tipton (then making steam engines for India), before joining a London gasworks as manager. A specialist in Cornish engines, he was appointed in 1844 as the first professor of engineering at Elphinstone College, Bombay. His mainly Parsi and Brahmin students were instructed in surveying, levelling and measurement, which was put to good use when surveying the Great Indian Peninsula Railway in 1846. Regrettably, bad health in 1847 (believed to be malaria) forced Pole to leave India for good.

HENRY PRINCE (*c*.1835–1906) received a scientific training at King's College, London. In 1858 he obtained an appointment in the Public Works Department of India, based at the Calcutta Canal Division, dealing with the construction of iron bridges and laying out the new town of Muttra. Prince was put in charge of the Iron Bridge Yard, Calcutta, to fabricate bridges, roofs and sluice gates solely for local use. After the yard closed in 1863 he was offered the unusual post as engineer in charge of the penal settlement at Port Blair, Andaman Nicobar Islands. When he arrived he was appalled at the conditions – especially as the inmates were suffering from disease caused by the inadequate sanitary conditions. Prince immediately set about improvements whereby every prisoner was properly housed. Transferred to Rangoon, he took charge of the town and port and was later appointed engineer-in-chief for the Rangoon and Prome Railway. In 1872 Prince went back to India, taking temporary charge of the Roorkee Workshops. He enjoyed a period of semi-retirement but perhaps boredom set in and from about 1906 he acted as superintendent engineer for the Rohilkund-Kumaon Railway before finally returning to England to spend his final days in London.

CALLCOTT REILLY (1829–1900) began his career by running away to sea, visiting America and the East Indies before being articled to a Chester millwright. He then joined the steam-engine foundry of Knight & Woods of Bolton, before selecting the training of Indian students to advance his future. In 1871 Reilly was appointed to the important professorship of Engineering Construction in the Royal Indian Engineering College at Cooper's Hill, where he remained until 1897. Ironically, he never visited India.

SIR ALEXANDER MEADOWS RENDEL KCIE (1829–1918) began his career with the London Dock Company before accepting an appointment as consulting engineer to the East India Railway in 1857. He served the organisation with merit before being promoted to chief consulting engineer to the Secretary of State for India. Among his responsibilities were many thousands of miles of railway construction including the Empress, Upper Soane, Alexandra and Lansdowne bridges and the prestigious Hardinge Bridge at Sara, East Bengal. An indefatigable benefactor to India, he kept a tight rein on budgets, while ensuring that no standards were compromised that would have involved injury to the indigenous workers 'who placed so much faith in British engineers for their safety'.

FREDERICK WILLIAM STEVENS (1847–1900), articled in 1862, was attached to the India Public Works Department in 1867. Following a year's service in Poona, he joined the office of the Architect to the Government of India. In 1877 he was loaned to the Great Indian Peninsula Railway for the design of the Victoria Terminus, probably the second most highly photographed building in the country after the Taj Mahal. He subsequently designed the Municipal Corporation Building, the Royal Alfred Sailors' Home, the Post Office Mews (Apollo Bunder), the head office of the Bombay Baroda & Central India Railway at Churchgate, and the Oriental Life Assurance offices at the Floral Fountain. He died of malaria and is buried in Bombay's Sewri Cemetery.

SIR FREDERICK ROBERT UPCOTT KCVO, CSI (1847–1918) travelled to India on the steamer *Stanley* in 1865 to survey and construct the Indus Valley Railway. He was partly responsible for the building of the Victoria Bridge over the Jhelum River and the construction of the Sind–Sagar Railway. Later, Upcott accepted the position of consulting engineer (and later director-general) for railways in Madras. In 1901 he was appointed governor-general of Indian Railways. For five years he dedicated his efforts to providing schools for the children of the mainly indigenous railwaymen. His services were called upon to accept the prestigious title of chairman of the East India and Assam Bengal Railway Companies. He completed his career in 1913 as an appointed member of the Royal Commission of Railways.

CHARLES WOOD (1834–1901) was apprenticed to Ransomes & May of Ipswich, before being dispatched to India by the firm in 1853 to teach employees of the Madras Railway. There he made chairs for his client before erecting machinery for the foundry of the East India Iron Company at Porto Novo. Later, Wood was sent to Beypur to take charge of the ironworks and blast furnaces for the same company. Still with the Ipswich firm, he was transferred to St Petersburg, Russia, but on his return to England, and with India very much in mind, he invented a wages-calculating machine for rupees that was shown at the Great Exhibition of 1862. In 1878 his foundry experience was put to good use in the experimental production of steel sleepers 'for hot countries such as India'.

Bibliography

The following sources were referenced extensively.
India Office Select Materials – The British Library
Minutes of the Courts of Directors and Proprietors of the East India Company
Minutes and Proceedings of the ICE (Institution of Civil Engineers)
House of Commons Parliamentary Papers
Minutes and memoranda of the Committees and Offices of the East India Company
General Correspondence of the East India Company

Chapter 1

Baden-Powell, B.H., *Land-Systems of British India* (Oxford: The Clarendon Press, 1892).

Bowen, H.V., *Revenue and Reform: the Indian Problem in British Politics, 1757–1773* (Cambridge: Cambridge University Press, 1991).

Bowen, H.V., *The Business of Empire: the East India Company and Imperial Britain, 1756–1833* (Cambridge: Cambridge University Press, 2008).

Dasgupta, Swapan, 'History is ignored' in *Asian Age*, 12 December 2011.

Datta, Kalikinkar, *Shah Alam II and the East India Company* (Calcutta: World Press, 1965).

Ferguson, Niall, *Empire: How Britain Made the Modern World* (London: Penguin Books, 2004).

Fernandes, Naresh, *Bombay Then, Mumbai Now*, (New Delhi: Lustre Press, 2009).

Hobson, John M., *The Eurocentric Conception of World Politics: Western International Theory, 1760–2010* (Cambridge: Cambridge University Press, 2012).

House of Commons, Parliamentary Papers, Vol. 43, paper no. 109.

Kumar, Dharma and Desai, Meghnad (eds), *The Cambridge Economic History of India, Volume 2 c.1757–1970* (Cambridge: Cambridge University Press, 1983).

Lambert, A., 'On shipbuilding in Bengal' in John Phipps (Com.) A Collection of Papers Relative To Shipbuilding In India (Calcutta: 1848).

Markovits, Claude (ed.), *A History of Modern India, 1480–1950* (London: Anthem Press, 2004).

Mehrotra, S.R., *The Emergence of the Indian National Congress* (Delhi: Vikas Publications, 1971).

Nechtman, T.W., *Nabobs: Empire and Identity in Eighteenth-Century Britain* (Cambridge: Cambridge University Press, 2010).

Raghuvanshi, V.P.S., *Indian Society in the Eighteenth Century* (New Delhi: Associated Publishing House, 1969).

Ray, I., *Bengal Industries and the British Industrial Revolution 1757-1857* (New York: Routledge, 2011).

Roy, Tirthankar, *The East India Company: The World's Most Powerful Corporation (The Story of Indian Business)* (New Delhi: Allen Lane, Penguin Books India, 2012), pp. 139–141.

Sarkar, J.N., *Private Traders in Medieval India: British and Indian* (Calcutta: Naya Prokash, 1991).

Singh, J., *Jinnah: India–Partition–Independence* (Oxford: Oxford University Press, 2009).

Sutherland, Lucy S., *The East India Company in Eighteenth-Century Politics* (Oxford: Oxford University Press, 1952).

Chapter 2

'Account of Bombay and Surat in the East Indies', *The London Magazine*, 28 (1759).

Annals of Lloyd's Register (In-House Publication, 1934).

Birchwood, G., Introduction to: *The Register of Letters of the Governor and Company of Merchants In London Trading Into the East Indies, 1600–1619* (London: Quaritch, 1893).

Bowen H.V., *Elites, Enterprise, and the Making of the British Overseas Empire, 1688–1775* (London: Macmillan, 1996).

Bowen, H.V., Lincoln, Margarette and Rigby, Nigel (eds), *The Worlds of the East India Company* (Suffolk: Boydell & Brewer, 2002).

Bowen, H.V., *Revenue and Reform: The Indian Problem in British Politics, 1757–1773* (Cambridge: Cambridge University Press, 1991).

Bowen, H.V., *The Business of Empire: The East India Company and Imperial Britain, 1756–1833* (Cambridge: Cambridge University Press, 2008).

Bulley, A., *The Bombay Country Ships 1790–1833* (Richmond, Surrey: Curzon Press, 2000).

Chaudhuri, K.N., *The Trading World of Asia and the English East India Company, 1660-1760* (Cambridge: Cambridge University Press, 1978).

Chaudhuri, K.N., *The English East India Company: The Study of an Early Joint-Stock Company 1600–1640, Volume 4* (London: Taylor & Francis, 1999).

Danvers F.C. and Foster, Sir William, *Letters Received by the East India Company from its Servants in the East* 6 Volumes (London: Marston, 1896–1902).

Farrington, Anthony, *Trading Places: The East India Company and Asia 1600–1834* (London: British Library, 2002).

Fawcett, Sir Charles, *The English Factories in India*, 4 Volumes (Oxford: Oxford New Series, 1955).

Gardner, Brian, *The East India Company* (London: Rupert Hart-Davis, 1971).

Hunter, Sir William Wilson, *History of India, Volume VII: From the First European Settlements to the Founding of the English East India Company* (New York: Cosimo Books, 2008). (Originally published in 1907.)

Keay, John, *The Honourable Company: A History of the English East India Company* (London: Harper Collins, 1993).

Kumar, Dharma and Desai, Meghnad (eds), *The Cambridge Economic History of India, Volume 2 c.1757–1970* (Cambridge: Cambridge University Press, 1983).

Kyd, James, Esq., 'On Indian Timber and Ship Building', John Phipps (Com.) A Collection of Papers Relative To Shipbuilding In India (Calcutta: 1848).

Lawrence, James, *Raj: The Making and Unmaking of British India* (London: Little, Brown & Co., 1997).

Lubbock, Basil, *The Blackwall Frigates* (Glasgow: Brown, Son & Ferguson, 1927).

Markovits, Claude (ed.), *A History of Modern India, 1480–1950* (London: Anthem Press, 2004).

Mottram, R.H., Traders' Dream: *The Romance of the East India Company* (London: D. Appleton-Century Co., 1939).

Philips C.H., *The East India Company 1784–1834*, 2nd edition (Manchester: Manchester University Press, 1961).

Rajagopalachari, C., 'Essential to retain English language', *Deccan Chronicle*, 2014 (Reprint of article '50 years ago').

Rao, Jaithirath, 'Requiem for the Raj', *The Indian Express*, 21 August 2007.

Robins, Nick, *The Corporation That Changed the World: How the East India Company Shaped the Modern Multinational* (London: Pluto Press, 2006).

Roy, Tirthankar., *India in the World Economy: From Antiquity to the Present* (Cambridge: Cambridge University Press, 2012).

Skempton, A.W., *A Biographical Dictionary of Civil Engineers in Great Britain and Ireland: 1500–1830* (London: Thomas Telford, 2002).

Staples A.C., 'India Maritime Transport in 1840', *Indian Economic and Social History Review*, 7 (1970).

The Engineer, March 1857.

Wadia R.A., *The Bombay Dockyard and the Wadia Master Builders* (Bombay: Ruttonjee Ardeshir, 1957).

Wild, Antony, *The East India Company: Trade and Conquest from 1600* (London: Harper Collins, 1999).

Chapter 3

Brock, W.R., *Britain and the Dominions* (Cambridge: Cambridge University Press, 1951).

Chaudhuri, K.N., *The Trading World of Asia and the English East India Company, 1660–1760* (Cambridge: Cambridge University Press, 1978).

East India Company, *Fort William India House correspondence and other contemporary papers relating thereto* (Delhi, National Archives of India, 1971).

Engineering, 22, (1877), 45.

Farrington, A., *Catalogue of East India Company Ships' Journals and Logs 1600–1834* (London: British Library, 1999).

Fletcher, R.A., *Steam-Ships: The Story of Their Development to the Present Day* (London: Sidgwick & Jackson, 1910).

Headrick, Daniel R. *Power over Peoples: Technology, Environments, and Western Imperialism, 1400 to the Present* (Princeton: Princeton University Press, 2012).

Hoskins, H.L., *British Routes to India* (London: Frank Cass & Co., 1966).

Lesseps, Ferdinand Marie, *The Suez Canal: Letters and Documents Descriptive of Its Rise and Progress in 1854–1856* (Cambridge: Cambridge University Press, 2011). (First published in 1876.)

Lubbock, Basil, *The Blackwall Frigates* (Glasgow: Brown, Son & Ferguson, 1927).

Onley, James, *The Arabian Frontier of the British Raj: Merchants, Rulers, and the British in the Nineteenth-Century Gulf* (Oxford: Oxford University Press, 2007).

Ovington, John, *A Voyage to Surat in the Year 1689* (ed. by H.G. Rawlinson; London, 1929).

Philips C.H., *The East India Company 1784–1834*, 2nd edition (Manchester: Manchester University Press, 1961).

Prakash, Om, *European Commercial Enterprise in Pre-Colonial India* (Cambridge: Cambridge University Press, 1998).

Scammell, G.V. *The World Encompassed: The First European Maritime Empires, c.800–1650,* (London: Routledge, 1981).

Symson, W., *A New Voyage to the East-Indies* (2nd edn, London, 1732), p. 212.

Who Was Who 1897–1916 (London: Adam & Charles Black Ltd., 1920).

Wilson, J.H., *Facts Connected with the Origin and Progress of Steam Communication between India and England* (London: Johnson, 1850).

Chapter 4

'An improved steam train for navigating shallow rivers', *The Civil Engineer & Architects Journal,* 12 (1849).

Bernstein P.H.T., *Steamboats on the Ganges* (New Delhi: Government of India 1960).

Bolton, A.J., 'Progress of Inland Steam-Navigation in North-East India from 1832', *Minutes of the Proceedings of the ICE,* 88 (1890) 330–42.

Calcutta Englishman, August 1861.

'Communications in India', *Engineering* (Nov 1866).

Haw, Duncan, *British India S.N. Co* (Hereford: TCL Publications, 1991).

'Indian River Steamers', *Minutes of the Proceedings of the Institution of Civil Engineers,* 119 (1894).

Kennedy, John. *The History of Steam Navigation* (Liverpool: Charles Birchall, 1903).

Kumar, Dharma and Desai, Meghnad (eds), *The Cambridge Economic History of India, Volume 2 c.1757–1970* (Cambridge: Cambridge University Press, 1983).

Lesseps, Ferdinand Marie, *The Suez Canal: Letters and Documents Descriptive of Its Rise and Progress in 1854–1856* (Cambridge: Cambridge University Press, 2011). (First published in 1876.)

Munro, J. Forbes, 'East India Merchants, 1823–61', in *Maritime Enterprise and Empire: Sir William Mackinnon and His Business* (Suffolk: Boydell Press, 2003).

Philips (ed.), C.H., *The Correspondence of Lord William Cavendish Bentinck, Governor-General of India, 1828–1835,* 2 Vols. (Oxford: Oxford University Press, 1977).

Pittman, Susan, 'The Fire King of Greenwich', *Bygone Kent,* 2 (1981), 130–6 (Merryweather's fire appliance business).

Rennell James, 'Account of the Ganges and Burrampooter Rivers', Read at the Royal Society, 25 January 1780 (London, 1781 et seq.).

Report From the Select Committee On Steam-Communication With India: Together With the Minutes of Evidence, Appendix and Index 1837. Ordered By the House of Commons.

Skempton, A.W., *A Biographical Dictionary of Civil Engineers in Great Britain and Ireland: 1500–1830* (London: Thomas Telford, 2002).

Staples A.C., 'India Maritime Transport in 1840', *Indian Economic and Social History Review,* 7 (1970).

'Steam Fire Engine for India', *The Engineer* (Dec 1882), 615.

'Steam Trains on Indian Rivers', *The Engineer* (Aug 1861).

'The Indus General Steam Navigation Company's Steamer "Tezpore"', *Engineering* (April 1879), 276.

'The P. and O. Twin-Screw Mail Steamer "Mooltan"', *Engineering* (March 1906), 304.

Who Was Who 1897–1916 (London: Adam & Charles Black Ltd., 1920).

Wilson, J.H., *On Steam Communication Between Bombay and Suez, With an Account of the Hugh Lindsay's Four Voyages* (Bombay: Government Gazette Press, 1833).

Chapter 5

Carrington, R.C., *List of Lighthouses and Light Vessels in British India* (Calcutta:
Madras Survey Department, 1879).

The Engineer, 16 August 1901.

Chapter 6

Arnold, David, *Science, Technology & Medicine in Colonial India* (Cambridge:
Cambridge University Press, 2000).

'Bombay Waterworks', *The Engineer* (Nov 1856), 636.

Brown, Joyce M., 'Contributions of the British to Irrigation Engineering in Upper
India in the 19th Century', *The Newcomen Society Transactions*, 55 (1983).

Buckley R.B., *The Irrigation Works of India and their Financial Results* (London, 1880).

Captain Chambers' *Report On Irrigation From the Taptee River*, Issue 61 of Selections
From the Records of the Bombay Government, 1861.

Cautley, P.T., *Report on the Ganges Canal Works*, 3 Volumes (London, 1860).

Clibborn, J., *Papers Relating to the Construction of Wells for Irrigation* (Roorkee, 1883).

Colvin J., 'On the Restoration of the Ancient Canals in the Delhi Territory', *Journal of
the Asiatic Society*, 15 (1833).

Crofton, J., *Report on the Ganges Canal, with Estimates and Plans*, Volume 1 (Calcutta,
1865).

Deakin, A., *Irrigated India; an Australian view of India and Ceylon, their irrigation and
agriculture* (London: Thacker & Co.,1893).

Dutt, Romesh Chunder, *The Economic History of India in the Victorian Age: From the
Accession of Queen Victoria in 1837 to the Commencement of the Twentieth Century*,
Trübner's Oriental Series (London: Routledge, 1950).

Engineering (April 1867).

Kuriyan, 'Irrigation in India', *Madras University Journal*, 15 (1943).

Maine H.S., Minute, 30 September 1863, India Public Works Department – Irrigation
Proceedings, April 1864.

Medley, J.G., 'Head Works–Ganges Canal', *Professional Papers On Indian Engineering*,
3 (1865).

Nicolls, 'Agricultural Engineering', *Engineering*, 46 (1888).

Preston S., 'Recent Irrigation in the Punjab', *Minutes of Proceedings of the Institute of
Civil Engineers*, 153 (1906).

Report on the Famine of 1860–1 in the North-Western Provinces of India, XL, 1862.

'Settlement Report of the District of Muzaffarnagar 1866' in Cadell, A., *Muzaffarnagar
SR* (1882).

Stone I. 'Canal Irrigation and Agrarian Change', in K.N. Chaudhuri and C.J. Dewey
(eds.), *Economy and Society: Essays in Indian Economics and Social History* (Delhi,
1979).

'The Bombay Waterworks', *The Mechanics' Magazine* (Feb 1859), 108.

The Calcutta Engineer's Journal, 1864.

The Times, London, 26 October 1865.

The Times, London, 11 November 1865.

Who Was Who 1897–1916 (London: Adam & Charles Black Ltd., 1920).

Chapter 7

'Colonial Connections: Royal Engineers and Building Technology Transfer in the Nineteenth Century', *Construction History* 12 (1996).

Corfield, Justin and Morson, Ian (eds), *British Sea-Captain Alexander Hamilton's A New Account of the East Indies (17th–18th Century)* (Lewiston, NY; Lampeter, 2001).

Cotton, Arthur, T., *Public Works in India: Their Importance; with Suggestion for their Extension and Improvement* (London: 1854).

Dutt, Romesh Chunder, *The Economic History of India in the Victorian Age: From the Accession of Queen Victoria in 1837 to the Commencement of the Twentieth Century*, Trübner's Oriental Series (London: Routledge, 1950).

Goodwyn, H., 'The Taper Chain Tension Bridge at Ballee Khal, near Calcutta, in its Renewed Form after Failure in June 1845', *Papers on Subjects Concerned with the Duties of the Corps of Royal Engineers*, 9 (1847).

'Indian Government Steam Train Engine, Ravee', *The Engineer* (Oct 1871), 287.

Johnson, J & Randell, W., *Colonel Crompton and the Evolution of the Electrical Industry*, (London: Longman Green, 1948).

Lane, Michael R., *The Story of the Steam Plough Works: Fowlers of Leeds* (London: Northgate Publishing Co., 1980).

MacLeod, R. and Kumar, D., (eds.) *Technology and the Raj: Western Technology and Technical Transfers to India, 1700-1947* (New Delhi: Sage Publications, 1995).

Mechanics' Magazine, (Oct 1844), 258–61.

Minutes of the Proceedings of Civil Engineers, 1 (1837–1841).

Nolan, E.H., *The Illustrated History of the British Empire in India and the East, From the Earliest Times to the Suppression of the Sepoy Mutiny In 1859* (London: J.S. Virtue, 1860).

Parliamentary Papers. 1863.

Philips (ed.), C.H., *The Correspondence of Lord William Cavendish Bentinck, Governor-General of India, 1828–1835*, 2 Vols. (Oxford: Oxford University Press, 1977).

Sarkar, K.M., *The Grand Trunk Road in the Punjab: 1849–1886* (Lahore: *Punjab* Government Record Office Publications, 1926).

'Steam Road Roller for Bombay', *The Engineer* (Nov 1867), 387.

'Suspension Bridge over the Ballee Khal', *Mechanics' Magazine*, 41 (1844).

Who Was Who 1897–1916 (London: Adam & Charles Black Ltd., 1920).

Chapter 8

Adams, J.M., 'Development of the Anglo-Indian Telegraph', *Engineering Science and Education Journal* 6 (1997), 140–8.

'Indian Railways and Telegraphs', *Engineering* (July 1897).

'Indian Telegraph Lines', *The Engineer* (March 1871), 202.

Kerr, Ian, J., *Building the Railways of the Raj, 1850-1900* (Delhi, 1995).

Luke, P.V., 'Early history of the telegraph in India', *Journal of the Institution of Electrical Engineers* 20 (1891).

MacLeod, R. and Kumar, D., (eds.) *Technology and the Raj: Western Technology and Technical Transfers to India, 1700-1947* (New Delhi: Sage Publications, 1995).

Sandes, E.W.C., *The Military Engineer in India*, 2 Volumes (Chatham, 1935).

'Telegraph between England and India', *The Times*, 17 March 1860.

The Engineer, 15 (1863).

'The telegraph cable to India', *Illustrated London News* (July 1865).
'The Telegraph to India', *The Illustrated London News* (Sept 1863), 280.

Chapter 9

Ashton, T.S., *The Industrial Revolution, 1760–1830* (London: Oxford University Press, 1948).
'Bombay, Baroda & Central India Railway', *The Railway Gazette* (Dec 1929), 9.
Bose, D.M. (ed.), *A Concise History of Science in India* (New Delhi: Indian National Science Academy, 1971).
Calcutta Englishman, July 1865.
'Construction along the Foot of the Himalayas', *The Railway Gazette* (July 1950), 8.
Davidson, E., *The Railways of India: With an Account of Their Rise, Progress, and Construction* (London: E. & F.N. Spom, 1868).
Delhi Gazette, 1847.
Derbyshire, Ian, 'The Building of India's Railway: The Application of Western Technology in the Colonial Periphery 1850–1920' in Roy Mcleod and Deepak Kumar (Eds), *Technology and the Raj: Western Technology and Technical Transfers to India, 1700–1947* (New Delhi: Sage Publications, 1995).
Hurd, J. II., 'Railways and the Expansion of Markets in India, 1861–1921', *Explorations in Economic History*, 12 (1975).
ICE Minutes of the Proceedings, Volume 29, Issue 1870. in *Artha-Vijnana*, XVII, 3 September 1975.
Indian Railway Fan Club (IRFC). Accessed 01 November 2014. www.irfca.org
James, J.G., *Overseas Railways and the Spread of Iron Bridges c.1850–1870* (Strawberry Hill: J.G. James, 1987).
Kerr, Ian J., *Engines of Change: The Railroads that Made India* (Westport: Praeger, 2007).
Kumar, Deepak, *Science and the Raj: 1857–1905* (Oxford: Oxford University Press, 1995).
Kumar, Dharma and Desai, Meghnad (eds), *The Cambridge Economic History of India, Volume 2 c.1757–1970* (Cambridge: Cambridge University Press, 1983). 'Railways' chapter.
'Large Metre-Gauge Locomotives for India', *The Railway Gazette* (Jan 1945), 62–3.
Lehmann, Frederick, 'Great Britain and the Supply of Railway Locomotives to India: A Case Study of "Economic Imperialism"', *Indian Economic and Social History Review* (Oct 1965).
Lewis, C.B., *Engineer's Journal and Railway, Public Works, Mining Gazette, of India and the Colonies*, 2 (1859).
Lowe, James W., *British Steam Locomotive Builders* (Barnsley: Pen & Sword, 2014).
MacLeod, R. and Kumar, D., (eds.) *Technology and the Raj: Western Technology and Technical Transfers to India, 1700–1947* (New Delhi: Sage Publications, 1995).
Macpherson, W.J., 'Investment in Indian Railways 1845–1875', *Economic History Review*, 8 (1975).
Morris, M.D. and Dudley, C. B., 'Selected Railway Statistics for the Indian Subcontinent 1853–1946/7',
OIOC Record Series L/PWD/3/56–66 'Railway Letters and Enclosures From Bengal and India, 1858–1867'.
Report from the Select Committee on East India Railway Communications 1884.

Report From the Select Committee On Steam-Communication With India: Together With the Minutes of Evidence, Appendix and Index 1837. Ordered By the House of Commons.

Report of the Administration and Working of Indian Railways (London: HMSO, 1903).

Sahni, J.N., *Indian Railways: One Hundred Years, 1853 to 1953* (New Delhi: Government of India, 1953).

Sanyal R.N., *Development of Indian Railways* (Calcutta: University of Calcutta, 1930).

Sargeaunt, Lt.-Cl. R.A., *Administration Report on the Railways in India for 1890–91*. House of Commons Parliamentary Papers. 1891.

Singh, K., *A Complete Story of the Assam Rail Link Project* (Assam: Ministry of Railways, 1951).

Tann, J. and Aitken, J., 'The Diffusion of the Stationary Steam Engine from Britain to India, 1790–1930', *Indian Economic and Social History Review*, 29 (1988), 211–32.

Thorner, D., 'Great Britain and the Development of India's Railways', *Journal of Economic History*, 11 (1951).

Chapter 10

Davidson, E., *The Railways of India: With an Account of Their Rise, Progress, and Construction* (London: E. & F.N. Spom, 1868).

'Heavy Superheated Consolidations for India', *The Railway Gazette* (April 1911), 420.

'Overseas Railway Affairs', *The Railway Gazette* (June 1838), 1156.

'Rolling Stock for Light Railways', *Engineering* (Nov 1929), 723.

'Rolling Stock in India', *The Railway Engineer* (Dec 1898), 351.

Chapter 11

Barton, E.G., 'Pontoon Bridges for Road Traffic Over Rivers in the Darbhangah District, Bengal', *Minutes of the Proceedings, ICE*, 169 (1907), 292–6.

'Bridge At Bassein, Bombay Presidency', in *Engineering*, 7 (1869), 211–12.

English, Peter, 'A Concise Early History of River and Rail Transport in Bengal', *Trans. Newcomen Soc.*, 149 (1991), 13–202.

English, Peter, 'Iron Bridges for the Raj', *Foundry Trade Journal* (March 1993), 116–18.

Gales, R.R., 'The Hardinge Bridge across the Ganges at Sara 1912–1915', *Proceedings of the Institution of Civil Engineers*, 205 (1918), 62–71.

Hart, J., 'Dharwar Bridges', *Professional Papers on Indian Engineering*, 5 (1868).

Hume, John and Moss, Michael, 'Bridge Building Achievements of P. & W. MacLellan & Co., (1850–1914)', *Trans. Newcomen Soc.*, 72 (2000) 179–202.

Kumar, J., *Select Documents on India Trade and Industry* (New Delhi: Janaki Prakashan, 1981)

Mechanics' Magazine (Jan–June 1857).

Medley, J.G., 'Head Works–Ganges Canal', *Professional Papers On Indian Engineering*, 2 (1865).

Percy, S., 'The Sagar Iron Suspension-Bridge', *Iron: An Illustrated Weekly Journal For Iron and Steel*, 25 (1836).

Talbot, Frederick A., *The Railway Conquest of the World* (Philadelphia: Lippincott, 1911).

Thomas H.P. and Meares, J.W., 'The Uhl River Hydro-Electric Project', *Journal of the ICE*, 16 (1941), 461–3.

Chapter 12

Balfour, Edward, *On the Iron Ores, the Manufacture of Iron and Steel, and the Coals of Madras Presidency* (Madras, 1855).

Bhattacharya S., 'Iron-Smelters and the Indigenous Iron and Steel Industry of India', in Sinha S. (ed.), *Aspects of Indian Culture and Society* (Calcutta: Indian Anthropological Society, 1972).

'Combined Oil Engine and Dynamo for the Calcutta Mint', *The Engineer* (Sept 1911), 267.

Engineering, 16 August 1867.

Heatly S.G.T., 'Contribution towards a history of the development of mineral resources of India', *Journal of Asiatic Society of Bengal*, 12 (1843).

Johnson W.A., *The Steel Industry of India* (Cambridge, Mass.: Harvard University Press, 1966).

Kumar, Dharma and Desai, Meghnad (eds), *The Cambridge Economic History of India, Volume 2 c.1757–1970* (Cambridge: Cambridge University Press, 1983). 'Western India' chapter.

Oldham T., 'Preliminary notes on coal and iron at Talcher', *Memoirs of the Geological Survey of India* (1856).

Chapter 13

Administration report on the railways in India for 1894-95. By Lieutenant-Colonel T. Gracey, R.E., officiating Director-General of railways.

Engineer (October 1873).

Engineer (November 1873).

Kumar, Dharma and Desai, Meghnad (eds), *The Cambridge Economic History of India, Volume 2 c.1757–1970* (Cambridge: Cambridge University Press, 1983).

MacLeod, R. and Kumar, D., (eds.) *Technology and the Raj: Western Technology and Technical Transfers to India, 1700–1947* (New Delhi: Sage Publications, 1995).

Smith, David, *Report of the Sigrowlee and Kurhurbaree Coal Fields* (1857).

The Engineer (September 1895).

'The Warora Colliery, Central India', *The Engineer* (Oct 1877), 294–5.

Chapter 14

Armytage, W.H.G., *A Social History of Engineering* (London: Faber & Faber, 1961).

Barlow, G.J. and Meares, J.W., *Preliminary Report on the Water Power Resources of India* (Calcutta, 1919).

'Calcutta Electric Supply – Multi-polar Generators', *The Engineer* (Aug 1902), 120.

Dasgupta, Arunabha, *Colonel Crompton's India: A Story of Progress Through Invention and Discovery* (Archive Publishers, 1998).

Dunsheath, P., *A History of Electrical Engineering* (London: Faber & Faber, 1957).

Johnson, J & Randell, W., *Colonel Crompton and the Evolution of the Electrical Industry*, (London: Longman Green, 1948).

MacLeod, R. and Kumar, D., (eds.) *Technology and the Raj: Western Technology and Technical Transfers to India, 1700–1947* (New Delhi: Sage Publications, 1995).

Meares, J.W., *Electrical Engineering in India: A Practical Treatise for Civil, Mechanical, and Electrical Engineers* (Calcutta: Thacker, Spink & Co, 1914).

Narayan, S., *Hydro-Electric Installations of India* (Y.T. Mangaokar, 1922).

'The Pykara Hydro-Electric Scheme', *Engineering* (Jan 1934), 107.
Who Was Who 1897–1916 (London: Adam & Charles Black Ltd., 1920).

Chapter 15

Bond, Winston A., 'Madras Trams – Export Nightmare', *Modern Tramway* (1973), 417.
'Bus services in Calcutta', *Modern Tramway* (May 1978), 151.
'Cawnpore Electric Tramways', *The Light Railway and Tramway Journal* (March 1908), 137–41.
'Centre Entrance Cars of the Delhi Tramways', *The Light Railway and Tramway Journal*, (Dec 1923) 327.
'Delhi Electric Tramways', *The Light Railway and Tramway Journal* (Sept 1908), 168.
'Guy Trolleybuses for Delhi', Transport World, Sept 1934.
Mackay, John Charles, *Light Railways for the United Kingdom, India, and the Colonies* (Cornell: Cornell University Library, 1896).
Wiseman, R.J.S., 'The Tramways of Bombay', *Tramway Review*, 157 (1994), 184–91.

Chapter 16

Chaudhuri K.N., 'The Structure of the Indian Textile Industry in the Seventeenth and Eighteenth Centuries', *Indian Economic and Social History Review*, 11 (1974).
Desai M., 'Demand for Cotton Textiles in Nineteenth-century India', *Indian Economic and Social History Review*, 8 (1971).
Dodwell H., 'Madras Weavers Under the Company', *Proceedings of the Indian Historical Research Commission* (1922).
Guha, A., 'Raw Cotton of Western India: Output, Transport, and Marketing 1750–1850', *Indian Economic and Social History Review*, 9 (1972).
Harnetty P., *Imperialism and Free Trade: Lancashire and India in the Mid-nineteenth Century* (Manchester: Manchester University Press, 1972).
Kumar, J., *Select Documents On India Trade and Industry* (New Delhi: 1981).
Mehta, M.M., *Structure of Indian Industries* (Bombay: Popular Book Depot, 1955).
Mehta S.D., *The Indian Cotton Textile Industry, An Economic Analysis* (Bombay: The Textile Association, 1953).
Parse, A.S., *The Cotton Industry of India: The Report of the Journey to India* (Manchester: International Federation of Master Cotton Spinners, 1930).
Piramal, G. and Herdeck, M., *India's Industrialists, Vol. 1* (Washington: Three Continents Press, 1986).
Rutnagur S.M., *Bombay Industries: The Cotton Mills* (Bombay: Indian Textile Journal, 1927).
Tripathi, D., *The Oxford History of Indian Business* (New Delhi: Oxford University Press, 2004).
Wallace D.R., *The Romance of Jute: A Short History of the Calcutta Jute Mill Industry, 1855–1927*, 2nd edition (London, 1928).

Chapter 17

Clarence-Smith, William G. (eds), *The Global Coffee Economy in Africa, Asia and Latin America, 1500–1989* (Cambridge: Cambridge University Press, 2003).
'Darjeeling tea plantations go to pot', *The Daily Telegraph*, 18 October 2003, pp. 12–13.

Kumar, Dharma and Desai, Meghnad (eds), *The Cambridge Economic History of India, Volume 2 c.1757–1970* (Cambridge: Cambridge University Press, 1983).

Chapter 19

Checkland, Sydney, *British Public Policy 1776–1939: An Economic, Social and Political Perspective* (Cambridge: Cambridge University Press, 1983).

Edney, Matthew H., *Mapping An Empire: The Geographical Construction of British India* (Chicago: University of Chicago Press, 1997.)

Ganguly, D.C. (eds.), *Select Documents of the British Period of India History* (Calcutta: The Victoria Memorial, 1958).

Martin, R. Montgomery, *The History of the Indian Empire*, 3 Volumes (London: The London Printing & Publishing Co., 1858).

Metcalf, Thomas R., *Ideologies of the Raj* (Cambridge: Cambridge University Press, 1995).

Moir, Martin. *A General Guide to the India Office Records* (London: British Library, 1988).

Philips, C.H., *The East India Company, 1784–1834* (Manchester, England: Manchester University Press, 1961).

Priolkar, A.K., *The Printing Press In India: Its Beginnings and Early Development* (Mumbai: Marathi Samshodhana Mandala, 1958).

Roberts, P.E., *History of British India: Under the Company and the Crown*, comp. T.G.P. Spear (Oxford: Oxford University Press, 1952).

Thorner A. 'Secular Trend of the Indian Economy', *Economic Weekly*, 14 (1962).

Chapter 20

Chamberlain, W.I.. 'Recent Developments in the State Educational System of India', *The Journal of Race Development*, 9 (1919), 298–313.

Chapter 21

Roberts, P.E., *History of British India: Under the Company and the Crown,* compl. T.G.P. Spear (Oxford: Oxford University Press, 1952).

Chapter 22

'Modi announces $80 million for Fiji', *Asian Age*, 20 November 2014.

Carter, Marina, 'Colonial Diaspora' In: K. Kesavapany, A Mani and P. Ramasamy (eds), *Rising India and Indian Communities in East Asia* (Singapore: institute of Southeast Asian Studies, 2008).

Guruswamy, Mohan, 'A Historic Bias' in *Asian Age*, 24 June 2014.

Kumar, P.P., *Indian Diaspora: Soio-Cultural and Religious Worlds* (The Netherlands: Brill, 2015).

Markovits, Claude, *The Global World of the Indian Merchants 1750–1947: Traders of Sind from Bukhara to Panama* (Cambridge: Cambridge University Press, 2005).

Oonk, Gijsbert (ed.), *Global Indian Diasporas: Exploring Trajectories of Migration and Theory* (Amsterdam: Amsterdam University Press, 2007).

Sharma, J.C., 'Indians Around the World' In: *Indian Foreign Policy: Challenges & Opportunities* (Foreign Service Institute, 2007).

Acknowledgements

Many people have provided me with invaluable help and encouragement over the years of work on this project, which has been my passion for several decades. I am immensely grateful to you all.

Special thanks go to the late Peter English, a civil engineer retired from British Rail, for his invaluable assistance in helping me to bring to light the extraordinary engineering endeavours of those fine 19th- and 20th-century engineers. Peter spent week after week collecting volumes of hitherto untold information from the archives of many different libraries. Most of the infrastructural information was obtained from the collections in the basements of the Institution of Civil Engineers (ICE) in Westminster. My thanks also to authors and journalists Bob Whittington from London and B N Uniyal, former Chief Editor from Delhi, who undertook the task of editing the original manuscript down to manageable proportions from the enormous quantity of valuable information Peter and I had uncovered, and finally made me focus on getting this great story into print. I reserve great appreciation for the British Library and above all the Institution of Civil Engineers (ICE) for their support during the painstaking research process. Janice Murray, Director General of The National Army Museum in London also provided valuable assistance in sourcing hitherto unpublished photographs documenting the courageous Indian contribution to the British armed forces in the two world wars. I thank Field Marshal Sir John Chapple for some valuable information provided for the chapter on the British Indian Army, and Mrs Didy Grahame of VC and GC Association for her information on the Victoria Cross and other medals.

I am also grateful to the historian Professor John MacKenzie and Jonathan Aitken for their expert advice and guidance. My thanks also to Dr Paul Flather of Mansfield College, Oxford, Mike Toynbee from London and the senior journalist and editor Anil Dharker, Director and Founder of Bombay International Literary Festival for their critical input and help with some historical detail. Special thanks also to Dr Aroon Tikekar, former Editor at Express Group, Bombay and past President of the Asiatic Society, Bombay for his large and valuable information from archives of the Asiatic Society and libraries and A.B. Damania for his valuable paper on crop improvement in the British Raj. I am most grateful to Linsey Hague, my editor, who picked up the reins after the untimely death of Peter English, for the enormous support she provided in assimilating my additions and further refining, editing and compiling the manuscript with great care, competence and speed.

I am also indebted to Prof. Ram Jethmalani, MP and Former Cabinet Minister of Law and Chairman of Bar Association of India, not only for his invaluable guidance on the introduction of British judiciary in Sharia India but also for taking the time for his critical reading of the manuscript and to provide his wonderful Foreword to my book.

My special thanks to Robert Taylor, Senior Vice President of Vitabiotics, London for his invaluable efforts in steering the book to publication. And thank you to my publisher, Bloomsbury, for taking on this project and turning my dream into reality.

I owe my sons Ajit and Tej a special debt of gratitude: Ajit, Professor of Medicine at Imperial College London, for his invaluable intellect, contributions and the fine tuning of my thoughts and Tej for his continual support for the project and for the inspired design of the cover of this book, which uncovered yet another personal story of the British engineers in India.

And, finally my sincere thanks to my wife, Rohini, for her patience and understanding as I worked on this story.

Kartar Lalvani

Index